OXFORD STUDIES IN MODERN EUROPEAN CULTURE

GENERAL EDITORS

Elizabeth Fallaize, Robin Fiddian and Katrin Kohl

Oxford Studies in Modern European Culture is a new series conceived as a response to the changing modes of study of European literature and culture in many universities. Designed to combine focus with breadth, each title in the series will present a range of texts or films in dialogue with their historical and cultural contexts—not simply as a reflection of history but engaged in a mediation with history, conceived in broad terms as cultural, social and political history. Flexible, interdisciplinary approaches are encouraged together with the use of texts outside the traditional canon alongside more familiar works. In order to make the volumes accessible not only to students of modern languages but also to those studying the history or politics of modern Europe, all quotations are offered in both the original language and in English.

HEIMAT

A German Dream

Regional Loyalties and National Identity
in German Culture 1890–1990

Elizabeth Boa and **Rachel Palfreyman**

OXFORD
UNIVERSITY PRESS

Great Clarendon Street, Oxford OX2 6DP
Oxford University Press is a department of the University of Oxford.
It furthers the University's objective of excellence in research, scholarship,
and education by publishing worldwide in

Oxford New York

Athens Auckland Bangkok Bogotá Buenos Aires Calcutta
Cape Town Chennai Dar es Salaam Delhi Florence Hong Kong Istanbul
Karachi Kuala Lumpur Madrid Melbourne Mexico City Mumbai
Nairobi Paris São Paulo Shanghai Singapore Taipei Tokyo Toronto Warsaw

and associated companies in Berlin Ibadan

Oxford is a registered trade mark of Oxford University Press
in the UK and certain other countries

Published in the United States
by Oxford University Press Inc., New York

First published 2000

British Library Cataloguing in Publication Data

Data available

Library of Congress Cataloging in Publication Data
ISBN 0–19–815922–6
ISBN 0–19–815923–4 (Pbk.)

1 3 5 7 9 10 8 6 4 2

Typeset by Graphicraft Limited, Hong Kong
Printed in Great Britain
on acid-free paper by
Biddles Ltd,
Guildford and King's Lynn

Acknowledgements

Elizabeth Boa would like to thank the British Academy for generous support enabling two periods of research in Germany. Thanks are due too to the University of Nottingham for research funding and leave. Many thanks also to Barbara and Hans Jürgen Heinrich for thoughts on Heimat and for the introduction to the pleasures of Hubert von Goisern and the Alpinkatzen.

Rachel Palfreyman is grateful to the British Academy for a three-year studentship during which she completed a PhD on Edgar Reitz's *Heimat* and undertook much of the research which has contributed to this study.

Both authors would like to thank Dr Karl Ditt of the Westfälisches Institut für Regionalgeschichte for his kind help with bibliography.

The authors are grateful for permisssion to reproduce the following paintings:

to the Bayerische Staatsgemäldesammlungen, Neue Pinakothek, Munich for *In der Bauernstube* by Wilhelm Leibl (Inv.Nr. 7803) and *Leibl und Sperl auf der Jagd* (Inv.Nr. 8724) by Johannes Sperl and Wilhelm Leibl;

to the Städtische Galerie im Lenbachhaus, Munich for *Eisenbahn bei Murnau* (Inv.Nr. GMS 49) by Wassily Kandinsky;

to the Nolde-Stiftung Seebüll for *Schwüler Abend* by Emil Nolde.

The authors wish to thank Edgar Reitz Filmproduktion GmbH for permission to reproduce three stills from the film *Heimat*.

Every effort was made to obtain permission for all other illustrative material.

Contents

List of Illustrations

Introduction **Mapping the Terrain**

Phases in the Discourse of Heimat

This study concerns a multifaceted tradition of cultural reflection and political aspiration which through many transformations has informed debate on German identity for at least a century. The core meaning of the word 'Heimat', its denotation, is 'home' in the sense of a place rather than a dwelling, but as the many combinations such as *Heimatstadt* (home town), *Heimatland* (native land), *Heimaterde* (native soil), *Heimatliebe* (patriotism, whether local or national), *Heimatrecht* (right of domicile), *Heimatvertriebene* (refugees driven out from a homeland), *Heimatforschung* (local history), *Heimatkunde* (local geography, history, and natural history) suggest, it bears many connotations, drawing together associations which no single English word could convey. Hence we have chosen to use the German word, and to do so without italics to avoid confusion with *Heimat* as a title. Hidden within the difficulty of translation lies the sediment of the troubled history of the German-speaking lands. The transition from the particularist patchwork of states to the Prussian-dominated, unified Germany of 1871 was marked by tensions between regional and national identity which were intensified by the extreme rapidity of industrialization and urbanization. In the period from the 1840s to 1900 Germany overtook Britain to become the second biggest industrial power after the USA and her population was changing from being predominantly rural to becoming urban. In 1871 two-thirds of the German population still lived in parishes of under 2,000 inhabitants whereas by 1910 around half lived in towns of over 5,000 inhabitants and over a fifth in towns of more than 100,000, the number of such large towns having increased from eight to almost fifty by 1910. Mobility was increasing rapidly so that by 1907 48 per cent of the population lived outside their place of birth and in many regions the countryside was becoming urbanized as villages and towns became ever more interlinked by new means of local transport which enabled the growth of shopping and commuting.[1] Fastest growing of all was Berlin, which came to symbolize the new modern

---

[1] On demographic change see Thomas Nipperdey, *Deutsche Geschichte 1866–1918*, vol. i. *Arbeitswelt und Bürgergeist* (Munich: Beck, 1993), ch. 1.

Germany. The population of Berlin doubled between 1815 to 1850 to 400,000, reaching 1 million by 1877, 2 million by 1910, and by 1920 Greater Berlin was a metropolis of almost 4 million. At the height of this process the term *Heimatkunst* (Heimat art) began to be used in the 1890s to both advocate and categorize literature and other art forms dealing with provincial or rural life. Some of the main essayists propagating *Heimatkunst* will be discussed in the next chapter.

Heimat literature was one aspect of a great variety of activities and institutions—in part reactionary, in part practically reformist, in part idealistically utopian—which have sometimes been drawn together under the umbrella title of the 'Heimatbewegung' or Heimat movement and which can be seen as responses to Germany's rapid modernization. By no means ideologically homogeneous, the Heimat movement embraced activities stretching from environmental planning and countryside protection (*Heimatschutz*), though local history societies, museums documenting local customs and costumes, tourist guidebooks, geography textbooks and syllabuses for primary schoolchildren, to local rambling and sports clubs and folk festivals and touched too on such developments as the German garden city movement and even city allotments. Much of this activity was comparable to what would now be called *Bürgerinitiativen* or citizens' initiatives to sustain the quality of life in a locality and like such present-day activism was politically diverse. Key oppositions in the discourse of Heimat set country against city, province against metropolis, tradition against modernity, nature against artificiality, organic culture against civilization, fixed, familiar, rooted identity against cosmopolitanism, hybridity, alien otherness, or the faceless mass. Such oppositions might remain antagonistic as in the polemics of the reactionary or pessimistic critics of modern civilization, some of whom will be discussed in the next chapter. Or they might, as in much popular literature, be sentimentally reconciled or just evaded, leaving the economic practices of capitalism and class injustice untouched, in accordance, as Marx had argued, with the function of ideology as an opium of the people designed to inhibit political consciousness. The work of the popular Bavarian author Ludwig Ganghofer (1855–1920) exemplifies this trend. Or they might form part of a difficult negotiation as individuals struggled to find a stable ground from which to cope with rapid change, to forge a liveable identity, and 'to express a sense of national as well as local belonging and to celebrate, however, superficially, a community of common purpose', as Celia Applegate puts it in her history of the Heimat movement in the Palatinate.[2] Heimat

---

[2] *A Nation of Provincials: The German Idea of Heimat* (Berkeley and Los Angeles: University of California Press, 1990), 17.

literature before the First World War evinces all these tendencies, sometimes in ambiguous combination in the same text as in some of Clara Viebig's work, hence the choice of Viebig to represent this period. Examples of her work will be discussed along with the theorists of *Heimatkunst* in Chapter 1. Heimat literature is a strong tradition not only in Germany but also in Austria and German-speaking Switzerland, overlapping especially with the long-standing genre of the *Dorfgeschichte* or village tale, but since one short study could not cover such a vast and heterogeneous field, we shall concentrate here on Germany with Bavaria to provide an Alpine note.[3]

During the First World War the *Heimatfront* or home front became a further connotation as Heimat, increasingly emptied of specific regional associations, was co-opted in the service of the nation and gendered as a place of security associated with the mother and the sweetheart back at home in contrast to the Fatherland for which men fight and die in foreign fields. No longer antagonistically set over against each other, Fatherland and maternal Heimat increasingly coalesced in the myth of nation and were both set in opposition to the foreign foe or the enemy within. In retrospect, even the trenches of the western front might be transmuted into a kind of Heimat. Writing in 1937, Herbert Freudenthal defines Heimat in an extended sense as the product of communal endeavour:

> **Das schönste und stolzeste Beispiel dafür ist die 'Schützengrabenheimat' des Großen Krieges, jene feldgraue Welt von Kampfstellungen, Unterständen, Drahtverhauen, Waldlagern auf erstrittenem und verteidigtem Boden, in der sich als Einsatz und Opferdienst der Kamaradschaft für die höchste Verpflichtung des Mannes ein deutsches Schicksal vollzog.[4]**

In *Mythologies* (1957) Roland Barthes describes the process of mythmaking as the draining of meaning from a figure in one discourse to leave an almost empty signifier in a second-order mythic discourse, but the draining is also the flowing over of residual meaning from the first sphere to enrich the myth. The draining away of concrete regional meaning from the concept of Heimat as it was appropriated in nationalist ideology in the

---

[3] On the continuing theme of Heimat in Austrian literature since 1945 see Karl K. Pohlheim, *Wesen und Wandel der Heimatliteratur am Beispiel der österreichischen Literatur seit 1945* (Bern: Peter Lang, 1989); also W. G. Sebald's fascinating essays, *Die unheimliche Heimat: Essays zur österreichischen Literatur* (Frankfurt am Main: Fischer, 1995).

[4] 'The finest and proudest example of this is the "trench Heimat" of the Great War, that field grey world of battle positions, dugouts, wire entanglements, forest encampments on land to be fought over and defended, in which a German fate unfolded in the shape of comradeship, dedication, and sacrifice in the service of man's highest duty.' *Was ist Heimat? Rede zum 'Tage der Verpflichtung' am 4. Oktober 1937* (Langensalza: Verlag Julius Beltz, 1937), 9.

Fig. 1. Oskar Martin-Amorbach, *Der Sämann* (The Sower, 1937)

1920s exemplifies such a process: Heimat, already tinged with myth in its local sense, becomes 'a formless, unstable, nebulous condensation', to use Barthes's terms,[5] signified by a few mythic figures such as the *Scholle* or clod of earth or the peasant, not actual peasants but a vacuously ideal peasant spirit of the German race. The peasant symbolized 'den wahren deutschen Menschen; denn dieser ist immer Bauer gewesen. Damit ist

---

[5] *Mythologies*, selected and trans. from the French by Annette Lavers (London: Picador, 1973), 119.

schon gesagt, Bauerntum sei eine innere Haltung, nicht ein Erwerbszweig'
as the ethnographer Hanns Fischer, writing in 1936, put it.[6] In the iconography of the Third Reich, the peasant is heightened to represent the
German spirit, as in the painting *Der Sämann* (*The Sower*) by Oskar
Martin-Amorbach, shown at the Great German Art Exhibition of 1937,
which shows a giant figure casting seed, the rainbow behind him signalling his mythic status. Thus whereas at the turn of the century Heimat
discourse conveyed a tension between regional and national identity,
throughout the 1920s and then under the Third Reich Heimat was ever
more identified with nationhood: 'Damit gewinnt der Heimatbegriff
seine nationalsozialistische Vertiefung . . . Das Volk liegt nicht außerhalb
der Heimat, sondern in ihr und die Heimat im Volk.'[7] In the identification
of Heimat with the German people, Heimat was changed from a conservative value into a dynamic token of expansionist ambitions or a reactionary expression of German identity under threat. Was German identity
to be defined with reference to linguistic, cultural, ethnic, or political categories? Many ethnic Germans did not speak German; many whose native
language was German or who felt themselves to be culturally German
were not German citizens. Territorially, the smaller Germany of Bismark's
Reich, further diminished in the Weimar Republic, failed to satisfy pan-
German ambition for a greater Germany. This lack of match between
the political, cultural, or linguistic categories defining national identity
aroused resentment intensified by defeat in the First World War, by the
provisions of the Treaty of Versailles, and by the French invasion in 1922
of much of the Rhineland including the Ruhr region, Germany's industrial
heartland. (Only in 1930 did France finally withdraw completely.) The
border regions of East Prussia or Schleswig-Holstein or the Sudetenland
were perceived as under threat of such rape by the foreigner or of internal
dispersal of identity in ethnically mixed populations. The loss of African
colonies stipulated in the Treaty of Versailles left the Germans in the eyes
of some as a people lacking space, as the title of Hans Grimm's novel *Volk
ohne Raum* of 1926 put it. In this novel Heimat was extended to incorpor-
ate colonial territory, for in the propaganda of the times the labour of
German colonists, whether modern-day settlers in Africa or medieval
Teutonic Knights moving eastwards through Prussia and along the Baltic,

---

[6] 'the true German, for he has always been a peasant. To be a peasant is an inner disposition, not
a mode of employment.' Hanns Fischer, *Aberglaube oder Volksweisheit: Der wahre Sinn der
Bauernbräuche* (Leipzig, 1936), cited in Wolfgang Emmerich, *Germanistische Volkstumsideologie:
Genese und Kritik der Volksforschung im Dritten Reich* (Tübingen: Tübinger Vereinigung für
Volkskunde, 1968), 171.

[7] 'Thus the concept of Heimat gains its National Socialist depth . . . The people do not exist outside
Heimat, but within it, and Heimat within the people.' Freudenthal, *Was ist Heimat?*, 13.

fructified the land and made it German, whereas alien invasion of German territory was rape.

One of the leading theoreticians of Heimat in the 1920s, Eduard Spranger, makes the distinction between milieu or environment as the surroundings into which any human individual is born and Heimat which is the outcome of a process of growing together with the land: 'Zur Heimat wird diese gegebene Geburtsstätte erst dann, wenn man sich in sie hineingelebt hat.'[8] It follows, so Spranger argues, that human beings can make somewhere other than their birthplace into Heimat through the investment of physical labour and a concomitant spiritual attachment. Spranger's basic thought, that Heimat is not a place in itself, but a mentality or subjective state of mind arising from a relationship between human beings and places, could serve also as a socialist definition of Heimat; the framework of Brecht's play *Der kaukasische Kreidekreis* conveys a very similar message—the land should go to those whose labour makes it bloom. It could, however, also serve as an imperialist definition, justifying the colonialist's appropriation of land. What would turn it into a National Socialist concept of Heimat is the addition of racist or *völkisch* thinking which Spranger duly provided in an appendix dating from 1938 added to his essay, originally of 1926, the two sections then published together in 1943 in the middle of the war. Together the two essays chart the corruption of an intellect and of ethnography or *Volkskunde* as an academic subject. In the appendix Spranger adds the collective concept of the *Volk* to his original definition which had been couched in individual psychological terms. Admittedly, given the European history of the mixing of peoples there is, so Spranger suggests, no racial purity left: what defines a people is language, as Fichte had argued, and *Gemüt*, that indefinable cast of mind and character which is the product of shared cultural history over the centuries. So far, so seemingly free of racist thinking. But central to the ethos of the *Volk*, so Spranger suggests, are Germanic manhood ('Mannestum') in its peasant, warrior, craftsman, and merchant avatars and Germanic womanhood ('Frauentum'); in contrast to the avatars of manhood, woman rules in one sphere only, the household. Central to the preservation of that ethos is the ordering of sexual relations: 'Hier handelt es sich um Werte, die mit dem Blut und Erbgut in Verbindung stehen.'[9] Such ordering demands purity or hygiene—Spranger here uses the technical terms of racist thinking—and so, by implication, the Nuremberg laws are after all justified, despite the initial rejection of a racial definition of the *Volk*.

---

[8] 'The place of birth only turns into Heimat when one has lived one's way into it.' *Der Bildungswert der Heimatkunde* (Leipzig: Phillip Reclam jun., 1943), 12.

[9] 'This is a question of values related to blood and biological inheritance.' Ibid., 58.

Heimat discourse is not intrinsically racist. Even terms such as *Scholle*, signifying the native heath to which man is supposedly attached, could be used to propagate an ideal balance between local loyalties, national citizenship, and cosmopolitan openness. Moreover in a mobile age local loyalties may attach to a first childhood Heimat or a second or third Heimat as an adult. Thus in a pamphlet of 1918, *Heimat! Grundsätzliches zur Gemeinschaft von Scholle und Mensch*, which from its title and date could lead one now to expect the worst, Paul Krische allows for modern mobility, pleads against xenophobia, and writes enthusiastically of the exceptionally intense fabric of Jewish family life as the expression of Heimat consciousness of a people bereft of the original community of man and soil.[10] Yet it is easy to see how this liberal vision could harden into the anti-Semitic doctrine of the rootless Jew. Anti-Semitism served at once to sustain German identity by providing the antagonistic figure of the alien, non-German other, but also to fuel anxiety of dilution of identity through infiltration: if the eastern Jew in caricature represented a radically different, alien being, almost more laden with hatred was the stereotype of the assimilated western Jew who was identified with international capitalism and portrayed as a mimic who could never become a true German but who, without roots in a Heimat or a national identity of his own, might infiltrate and undermine German identity. These two figures fulfilled different roles in the reactionary version of Heimat discourse in that Jews could be portrayed both as an archaically demonic threat *and* as the very acme of a rootlessly cosmopolitan modernity which threatened to destroy traditional communal values. In Veit Harlan's film *Jud Süß* (1940), the main hate figure is less the exotically garbed alien Jew of the ghetto than the urbanely elegant financial wizard Süß Oppenheimer who mixes with court society, got up like a German nobleman. Thus as resentment, fear, and expansionist ambitions added poison to the identity crises of the peoples identifying as German—an ill-defined category which could include or exclude ethnic Germans living beyond the extended borders of the Reich and various linguistic or other minorities within the Reich—the myth of Heimat, emptied of concrete meaning, fed into racist *Blut und Boden* ideology propagated by Richard Walther Darré in his tracts *Das Bauerntum als Lebensquell der nordischen Rasse* (1929) and *Neuadel aus Blut und Boden* (1930).[11] Such ideas found climactic expression in the ritualistic assertion of *völkisch* unity under the Führer combined with rootedness in *Gau* or

---

[10] Paul Krische, *Heimat! Grundsätzliches zur Gemeinschaft von Scholle und Mensch* (Berlin: Gebrüder Paetel, 1918).

[11] *The Peasantry as the Vital Source of the Nordic Race* and *A New Aristocracy of Blood and Soil*.

province as shown in Leni Riefenstahl's film of the Nuremberg rallies, *Der Triumph des Willens* (1935).

By contrast with the nationalist and National Socialist appropriation of Heimat as an empty signifier, some writers of the 1920s continued to concentrate on the idea of a specific region rather than the nation as Heimat, but with a highly critical inflection in showing how provincial obstinacy and resistance to centralizing policies could shade into a fascist mentality and how local culture might be infected by nationalist resentments. Marieluise Fleißer's plays of the late 1920s, set in Bavaria in her native town of Ingolstadt, and her novel *Mehlreisende Frieda Geyer* (1931), republished after the war as *Eine Zierde für den Verein* (1968), stand on a margin between a critical Heimat literature which still sets regional values against the centralizing tendencies of an aggressive nationalism and an anti-Heimat invective which undermines the whole mode. When the National Socialists came to power Fleißer, whose work had been briefly taken up by Bertolt Brecht, received an official ban from all forms of literary production, though she continued to live in Ingolstadt. Fleißer's play *Pioniere in Ingolstadt* will be examined in Chapter 2. Ödön von Horváth, by contrast, who had lived for many years in Murnau in Bavaria, emigrated first to Austria and then Paris. Horváth revived the tradition of the south German and Austrian *Volksstück* (folk play) in a new realistic form where dialect functions as a radical marker of social identity, and he can be said to have initiated a new phase in the development of this genre in Austria as well as Germany. All his plays were censored by the National Socialists, but were revived in the 1960s and 1970s at the same time as the rediscovery of Fleißer and are now sufficiently canonical to figure on the school syllabus. Another author whose work can be categorized as critical Heimat literature is the Bavarian novelist and short story writer Oscar Maria Graf. The work of these authors forms an important antecedent of later Bavarian writers such as Martin Sperr, Franz Xaver Kroetz, and Herbert Achternbusch. While left-wing writers generally treat the Heimat theme with critical scepticism, a quite straightforward anti-fascist appropriation of Heimat is the 'Börgermoor Song', written in a concentration camp by the miner Johann Esser, with a refrain by the left-wing theatre director Wolfgang Langhoff and music by Rudi Goguel. The 'Börgermoor Song' conveys the longing for return to their Heimat of convicts, shut up in barracks at night and labouring by day to make the moorland arable. Verses 2 and 3 run:

> Morgens ziehen die Kolonnen
> In das Moor zur Arbeit hin.
> Graben bei dem Brand der Sonnen
> Doch zur Heimat steht der Sinn.

Heimwärts, heimwärts jeder sehnet
Zu den Eltern, Weib und Kind.
Manche Brust ein Seufzer dehnet,
Weil wir hier gefangen sind.[12]

Rather different from critical Heimat literature is retreat into the province first as an escape from the traumas of the First World War and the perceived chaos of the Weimar Republic and then as a mode of inner emigration from the Third Reich. Exemplary of this tendency is the work of Ernst Wiechert (1887–1950). Wiechert was the son of a forest warden in Masuria in East Prussia, a thinly populated region of lakes, marshland, and forests. The motif of the forest, so prominent in many of Wiechert's novels and stories, marks their marginality to the Heimat mode, for the forest signifies a more total rejection of civilization, a deeper regression from an unbearable world than do villages and ploughed fields: 'Wälder sind dunkel und schweigsam. Wälder fliegen nicht und singen nicht. Aber es gibt den großen Bogen der Jahreszeiten über ihnen. . . . Aber dann mußte ich ein Kind der Städte werden. . . . Ich trug das Kreuz wie jedermann. Es war mir nichts erspart. Sie verschütteten mich, aber das Gras bebte über mir.'[13] Wiechert's first novel, *Die Flucht*, was written before the First World War though it was not published till 1916. It follows the flight of its hero from city life back to the Masurian Heimat where he tries to become a peasant, but there is no escape from the corrosion of a decadent civilization which, etched in his psyche, finds expression in his sexual thraldom to a degenerate urban woman rather than to the dignified and morally upright village maidservant whose love for him he only notices when it is too late. The novel closes as he is about to shoot himself. Wiechert's work suggests a continuity of reaction against the modern world, which was but intensified by the horror of the First World War, the perceived chaos of the 1920s, and the philistine brutality of the Third Reich, all these seen as part of an overarching catastrophe engulfing modern civilization. Such a vision has much in common with the reactionary cultural pessimism (it too often figured through degenerate neurasthenic women in contrast to healthy Germanic womanhood) which fed into

[12] 'Every morning the columns march out to work on the moors. They dig in the heat of the sun, but their thoughts turn to home. Homewards, homewards, goes their longing, to parents wife and child. Many a breast heaves a sigh because we are prisoners here.' Cited in J. M. Ritchie, *German Literature under National Socialism* (London: Croom Helm, 1983), 148–9.

[13] 'Forests are dark and silent. Forests do not fly or sing. Yet the great arc of the seasons curves above them. . . . But then I had to become a child of the cities. . . . I bore the cross as everyone did. I was spared nothing. They buried me, but the grass shook above me.' From an article of 1932, cited in Ulrike Haß, *Militante Pastorale: Zur Literatur der anti-modernen Bewegungen im frühen 20. Jahrhundert* (Munich: Wilhelm Fink, 1993), 56. Haß tracks the leitmotif of the forest to which wounded warriors retreat in novels of the Weimar period.

National Socialist ideology, but with the crucial difference that Wiechert eventually saw the Third Reich as a symptom of, not a cure for, the disease, though he continued to write and publish. The success of Wiechert's best-known work, his novel *Das einfache Leben* (1939), which within two years had sold over a quarter of a million copies, exemplifies the dubious adaptability of the Heimat theme which could appeal both to followers *and* opponents of the Nazi regime, hence its inclusion in Chapter 2 as a text for analysis. Wiechert's novel will be considered as a response, written on the very eve of the Second World War, to the effects of the First World War on a whole generation.

If the literature of inner emigration from National Socialism often expressed a morally or religiously fuelled, quietist spirit of opposition, the same cannot be said of the escapist mode of the Heimat film through which a demoralized people found comfort in the 1950s. This will be one of the topics treated in Chapter 3. The astonishing success of the Heimat film—in the 1950s and early 1960s some three hundred Heimat films were produced—can be put down to two broad reasons. The first is flight from the past and from the bitter questions of guilt and responsibility for the Third Reich: as *Vergangenheitsflucht* (flight from the past) 1950s Heimat films are an important foil against which to measure the bitter literature of *Vergangenheitsbewältigung* (facing up to the past) by writers like Heinrich Böll or Günter Grass whose rage was levelled not just against the crimes of the past but the escapist mentality of a broad swathe of the German public. The second reason is that such films were not all just a meaningless flight into fantasy, but offered a masked solution to conflicts which could not be confronted directly. After the Second World War, Germany's total defeat meant that officially the National Socialist image of the Heimat and of a heroic German *Volk* rooted in German soil and through whom peasant blood flowed was utterly invalidated. Yet the Heimat films of the 1950s represent a remarkable continuity of a genre that seemed to survive every twist and turn of history. Antecedents include the genre of the mountain film produced in the 1920s and 1930s by directors like Arnold Fanck, Luis Trenker, and Leni Riefenstahl.[14] These films exploited the sheer excitement of a new medium to capture the grandeur and dangers of climbing in the high Alps. The later 1950s films scarcely ever rival the aesthetic achievement of these earlier films; for that one must look to the critical Heimat films of Werner Herzog, one of the leading directors in the New German Cinema which emerged a decade after the high-point of the 1950s Heimat film. A number of the 1950s films were remakes of films

[14] See Christian Rapp, *Höhenrausch: Der deutsche Bergfilm* (Vienna: Sonderzahl Verlagsgesellschaft, 1997), esp. ch. 10.

made during the Third Reich and indeed a number of the prominent directors of Heimat films such as Hans Deppe, Paul May, or Rolf Hansen had trained at the UFA studios (Universum Film AG) in the 1930s and 1940s. Many of the new Heimat films were formulaic in the extreme: the world depicted offered no questioning of social relations or political tendencies, but an entirely unproblematic view of life in 'Agfa-colored images' with a suitably sentimental soundtrack and an obligatory happy ending.[15] But feature films do need a plot, so something has to disturb the idyllic peace of sand dunes, purple moorland, or Alpine meadows and many films reverted to the Heimat literature of the turn of the century for plots offering the satisfactions of conflict followed by restoration of peace and reconciliation, but reconciliation of the social conflicts dating from another, often pre-modern era and often in the mode of Oedipal family melodrama. In this the German Heimat film of the 1950s served a similar function to American westerns urging farmers and cowmen to be friends which flourished during the McCarthy era when the Cold War was at its warmest, the nuclear arms race was under way, and Coca Cola was conquering the world. The immense popularity of the Heimat genre can be attributed, then, partly to escapism, partly to nostalgia in a period of deprivation followed by intense and hectic economic activity, partly to the desire for social cohesion as a salve for the traumas of war, and partly to a thirst for easy reconciliation instead of recognition of crimes which could neither be forgiven nor forgotten. Close to the surface was also the theme of the lost Heimat following the division of Germany and the loss of lands in the East. Heimat films satisfied the perceived need of refugees and exiles to identify with a positive image of West Germany or Austria. The end of the war and its aftermath saw a huge movement of peoples across Europe including forced repatriations eastwards to the Soviet bloc. To the German refugees who fled westwards before the advancing Soviet forces was added the expulsion, agreed at the Potsdam Conference, of over seven million Germans from Poland, Hungary, and Czechoslovakia, of whom the Federal Republic absorbed the largest proportion. The division of Germany and the loss of territories led to bitter debates between left and right in which right-wing, revanchist forces and refugee associations appealed to the lost Heimat in the East. Heimat films offered balm but in sustaining the myth of Heimat also stoked resentment.

Although by the early 1960s the formulaic Heimat film was running out of steam in a saturated market which was in any case dominated by Hollywood, the full reaction only set in towards the end of the decade as a

---

[15] Anton Kaes, *From Hitler to Heimat: The Return of History as Film* (Cambridge, Mass.: Harvard University Press, 1989), 15.

disillusioning anti-Heimat rhetoric emerged in the theatre and in the New German Cinema at a time which saw also the growth of student protest as the younger, post-war generation sought a reckoning with their elders. The directors of the New German Cinema, though not a unified group or school, were nevertheless united in their contempt for what they called first 'Papas Kino' and later 'Opas Kino'. As part of an attempt to evaluate national identity in the light of the Holocaust and the social conditions of the Federal Republic, they inverted the mode to make anti-Heimat films in which the Heimat is figured as repressive and xenophobic. Much of this work is set in south Germany and Austria, following on from the critical Heimat tradition of Fleißer, Oscar Maria Graf, and Ödön von Horváth. A central implication of anti-Heimat films is that rural communities operate a structure designed for the oppression and marginalization of 'outsiders': in Peter Fleischmann's *Jagdszenen aus Niederbayern* (1968), for example, the other is a homosexual, in Fassbinder's *Katzelmacher* (1969) a *Gastarbeiter* or foreign worker. By showing how the difference of such outsiders is used by the community to stabilize its own system, these works implicitly link the anti-Semitic Nazi past to the continuing dangers of racism and xenophobia in the present. The New German Cinema broached Heimat themes in a variety of idioms. Volker Schlöndorff's *Der plötzliche Reichtum der armen Leute von Kombach* (1970), is an example of a historical film which deploys Heimat discourse. Based on a historical case of the early 1820s, the film tells the fairy tale in documentary style, with a voice-over narration (spoken by Margarethe von Trotta, author of the screenplay) and monochrome filmstock. Rural life is emphatically represented as harsh and unjust. But the characters are not shown as ignorant stereotypes nor is the rural Heimat represented as irretrievably violent and repressive. In an attack on the oppression of the poor comparable to Georg's Büchner's *Woyzeck*, the film unmasks the role of the institutions of church and school in inculcating the ideological message of submission so that the peasants come to sustain their own subjection through having internalized the oppressive mechanisms. But the final outcome does not entirely undo the utopian moment of resistence in the film's earlier sequences. Equally critical if less bleakly naturalist in effect are the films of Herbert Achternbusch whose experimental style and montage of different genres and dialects offer a less claustrophobic image of Heimat and leave space for resistance. Some of the directors of the New German Cinema, for example Achternbusch and Fassbinder, were also writers and many films drew on literary models: *Jagdszenen aus Niederbayern* was based on the play by Martin Sperr, premièred in 1966 and the first of his Bavarian trilogy; Fassbinder's *Wildwechsel* (first shown on television in 1973) was based on a play of 1968 by Franz Xaver Kroetz.

Kroetz is a central figure in this widespread move to reject traditional Heimat forms as uncritical and politically reactionary. The anti-Heimat rhetoric of his early plays is designed to shock spectators with the brutality of the rural life, the cruelty of dysfunctional families, and the scapegoating of the disabled or of outsiders. But in line with his joining of the German Communist Party in 1972 Kroetz's work increasingly took on a critical, activist tendency designed to alert the public to the destructive environmental effects of industrial pollution on a Heimat worth fighting for. Fassbinder's film version of *Wildwechsel* and some examples of Kroetz's work as well as Sperr's *Jagdszenen aus Niederbayern* will be discussed in Chapter 3 which will track a dialectical movement as the sentimental Heimat film drew forth a disillusioning response, but eventually also a move towards a recuperation of Heimat values.

The shift in Kroetz's work is a symptom of the growing currency from the late 1960s on of Heimat, no longer as a mode of trivial entertainment, nor simply as an ideology to be attacked, but as a token in serious literature and political debate. Our study concentrates mainly on developments in West Germany, but one chapter is devoted to East German films which much earlier than in the West can be seen as appropriating Heimat discourse to serious purposes in films of contemporary life. From the mid-1950s, such films present Heimat both as a remembered past of the older anti-fascist generation driven from their Heimat and as a project for the future: to make of the GDR a society in which the new generation might feel at home. Like much of the critical Heimat literature in West Germany, the East German films often centre on broken families and inter-generational conflict arising from Germany's troubled past. But whereas the main representatives of the older generation in the East German films are shown as anti-facists who suffered persecution or exile during the Third Reich and have to explain to the younger generation what they have lived through, the older generation in West German critical Heimat literature are generally shown as hiding or repressing a guilty past which they fail to explain to the younger generation. Thus in West Germany the issue of different modes of guilt and responsibility during the Third Reich was posed through an interrogation of the discourse of Heimat, as for example in Siegfried Lenz's *Deutschstunde* (1968), which will be discussed at length in Chapter 5, and a decade later in his novel *Heimatmuseum* (1978), which was filmed for television in 1987, a couple of years before Michael Verhoeven's film *Das schreckliche Mädchen* of 1989 which satirizes the Heimat mode in a bitter yet comic reckoning with the Nazi past. Along with *Deutschstunde* and *Das schreckliche Mädchen*, Chapter 5 will also discuss the work of the Expressionist painter Emil Nolde, on whom the main character of *Deutschstunde* is based. His paintings reveal an ambiguous blend of Heimat art and modernism which failed to find favour with the National Socialists despite Nolde's own political commitment to National Socialism.

Deutschstunde appeared at a high point of political activism in West Germany in the late 1960s. The 1970s, by contrast, have been seen as marking a shift in mood, the so-called *Tendenzwende*, away from left-wing political analysis of class oppression towards apolitical subjectivism but also towards a critique of rationalism and technology heralding the rise of green politics. The work of some film-makers reflects aspects of this shift. Werner Herzog's *Herz aus Glas* of 1976, for example, might be seen as a return to the anti-urban and anti-modern Heimat tradition and to the filmic mode of the mountain film, such as Leni Riefenstahl's *Das blaue Licht* (1932) or Luis Trenker's *Der verlorene Sohn* (1934). John Sandford sees this as the least successful of Herzog's films, but does praise the compelling intensity of its landscape shots.[16] Nature mysticism had been a feature of *Blut und Boden* ideology, but the effect of texts is highly context-dependent. Man dwarfed by, at one with, or heroically rising above natural forces has been a pervasive theme since the invention of the sublime in the eighteenth century up to the American western, and the encounter with nature in sublime or terrible mode is a commonplace in Heimat literature and art. Herzog's documentary film *Die große Ekstase des Bildschnitzers Steiner* (1974) celebrates both the craft of woodcarving, which continues in the Alpine region as an unbroken tradition flowing from the south German baroque and had for that reason long been a popular motif in Heimat literature and film, and ski jumping as a modern variation of the striving for mastery over nature. The camera tracks the soaring airborne passage across the landscape and the fall to earth of the ski jumper as twentieth-century Icarus. The aesthetic is comparable both to Leni Riefenstahl's nature photography and to the brilliant capturing of sporting achievement in her Olympic film, but the political context is different. Herzog's documentary appeared at the time of the *Tendenzwende*, but in retrospect, this was also the time of a colour-shift from red to green which would culminate with the founding of the Greens as a federal party in 1980.[17] Seen in that light, Herzog's celebration of the ecstatic ski jumper is questionable, not as a nationalistic revival of neo-Nazi *Blut und Boden*—the film documents a competition held in Palnica in Yugoslavia and the hero is Swiss—but as boosting the very sport which creates the mass tourism so threatening to the fragile mountain ecology which the film also celebrates in marvellous images.

[16] *The New German Cinema* (London: Eyre Methuen, 1981), 57.
[17] See Andrei S. Markovits and Philip S. Gorski, *The German Left: Red, Green and Beyond* (London: Polity Press, 1993).

A film-maker very much in the ambit of radical green politics is Herbert Achternbusch, the Bavarian writer and film-maker who provided the screenplay for Herzog's *Herz aus Glas*.[18] Achternbusch's work is harshly critical of the German past and of continuing xenophobia and prejudice, even if his use of Bavarian dialect sometimes gives expression to a strong local identity with fleeting moments of mystical or utopian vision. Achternbusch's love-hate relationship with Catholic Bavaria precipitated a spectacular case of state interference in the arts when his film *Das Gespenst* of 1983, in which Achternbusch himself played a latter-day Christ descending from the Cross, was accused of blasphemy and the payment of a grant he had been awarded under the state system of film subsidy was for a while held up. Achternbusch has continued as one of the most radical critics in films such as *Wanderkrebs* (1984), a bitter and surreal lament for the despoliation of nature which shows the Bavarian Forest transmuted into a nightmare army of plastic trees. Achternbusch's main theme is Bavaria as the place of the destruction of Heimat, as many of his titles with their sardonic allusions to folksy tourist images suggest, films such as *Das Andechser Gefühl* (1974—Andechs has a famously intoxicating monastery-brewed beer), *Bierkampf* (1977—set in the Munich Oktoberfest), *Die Föhnforscher* (1985—this tells of an atomic weapon supposedly hidden in the tower of a baroque church in Herrsching; the Föhn is the Alpine wind which produces headaches and brilliant blue skies, the perfect backdrop for baroque onion domes and atomic power stations), or the blackly comic farce *I Know the Way to the Hofbrauhaus* (1991).

The work of Herzog and Achternbusch, being only marginal to the Heimat mode with its central focus on family relations, will not be further explored here. Absolutely central, by contrast, is Edgar Reitz's episodic film, or *Filmroman*, *Heimat*, as a family saga which documents in panoramic detail the social life of a village from the end of the First World War to 1982. *Heimat* was shown in 1984 by ARD to huge popular success and much critical controversy which took on an international dimension following the screening of *Heimat* on television and in cinemas in Britain, America, and elsewhere. *Heimat* will be the topic of Chapter 6. In the same year *Herbstmilch: Lebenserinnerungen einer Bäuerin* by Anna Wimschneider came out; an immediate success, it was filmed in 1988 with Josef Vilsmaier as director.[19] In 1984 too Kroetz was working on *Bauern Sterben*, an experimental play on the destructive effects worldwide of

---

[18] Johannes G. Pankau, 'Figurationen des Bayerischen: Sperr, Fassbinder, Achternbusch', in Helfried W. Seliger (ed.), *Der Begriff 'Heimat' in der deutschen Gegenwartsliteratur* (Munich: iudicium verlag, 1987), 133–47.

[19] *Autumn Milk: Memoirs of a Peasant Woman.* Anna Wimschneider, *Herbstmilch: Lebenserinnerungen einer Bäuerin* (Munich: Piper, 1984).

modernization on the rural Heimat whether in Germany or India; *Bauern Sterben* was then premièred in Munich in 1985, the same year as Horst Bienek, himself the author of a notable sequence of novels in the critical Heimat mode, edited a volume of essays, prompted by Reitz's film and with contributions from several authors: *Heimat: Neue Erkundigungen eines alten Themas*.[20] Also in 1985 the film *Heidenlöcher*, directed by Wolfram Paulus, drew on the Heimat mode to explore the Nazi past in a film which set local patriotic values against nationalist aggression and power politics. Heimat was clearly 'in' in the mid-1980s and can be seen in retrospect as a symptom of the great sea changes bringing the end of the Cold War and German reunification. A text heralding the new positive evaluation of Heimat in the 1980s was Martin Walser's *Seelenarbeit* (1979) which treats the theme of the lost Heimat in divided Germany before any obvious signs of the cataclysmic change that would happen in 1989. In the mid-1980s Martin Walser was a leading voice in debate among intellectuals who began to query whether Germany's division into two political states should continue indefinitely. This aspect of *Seelenarbeit* explains its inclusion as a text for discussion in the last chapter. In the GDR, a renewed interest in Prussian history and culture ambiguously signalled not only the aspiration to construct a legitimate past as basis for a present national identity specific to the GDR, but also the appeal to a cultural heritage shared by all Germans which arguably merely intensified the growing crisis of legitimacy. For the Rhineland as much as Prussia belonged to the German Heimat as the East German author Monika Maron, herself of mixed German-Polish-Jewish origin, wryly noted in a speech delivered in Munich in 1989, just as the crisis was breaking which, so suddenly and unexpectedly, yet in retrospect so long in the making, precipitated the demise of the GDR.[21] Since unification of the two Germanies, the discourse of Heimat, more laden than ever with intertextual and historical baggage, has continued to serve as a prism of cultural reflection on a whole range of issues: Kroetz's *Bauerntheater* (1991) and Reitz's *Die Zweite Heimat* (1992), ostensibly very different, do have in common a turn towards reflection on the position of the alienated intellectual or artist vis-à-vis Heimat which has been a recurrent sub-theme of the mode since the turn of the century; Hans-Ulrich Treichel's *Heimatkunde oder Alles ist heiter und edel* (1996) continues the anti-Heimat mode, albeit in a mood of lightly satirical whimsy rather than the drastic naturalism of the late 1960s. In post-*Wende* Germany, which has seen the emergence of the

---

[20] *Heimat: Neue Erkundigungen eines alten Themas* (Munich: Hanser Verlag, 1985).
[21] Hans-Jürgen Wischnewski, Peter-Jürgen Boock, Wolf Graf von Baudissin, Monikà Maron, Richard Löwenthal, Peter Slotedjik, *Reden über das eigene Land: Deutschland 7* (Munich: C. Bertelsmann, 1989), 67–86. Maron's speech was one of a series given in the Kammerspiele theatre in Munich.

so-called New Right and re-emergence of old racist xenophobia, perhaps the most interesting new development in the protean Heimat mode is the multicultural theme, which the last chapter will touch on, of the lost, or hybrid, or plural Heimat in the work of German-Turkish authors such as Renan Demirkan or Emine Sevgi Özdamar.

Political Implications of Heimat in Recent German Historiography

Three factors may be adduced to account for the increasing currency throughout the 1970s and intensifying in the 1980s of Heimat as a focus of debate. The first is the reconsideration of German national identity which accompanied the growing distance from the Nazi past. The second factor, which also impinged on the question of identity, was change in German–German relations with first the relative success of the *Ostpolitik* pursued by Willi Brandt and Helmut Schmidt in negotiation with Erich Honecker in normalizing relations between the two Germanies, and then the signs of the end of the Cold War and, if still below the horizon, of the East–West divide. The third factor is a shift in political fashion after the late 1960s from class politics to environmentalism with the rise of the ecological movement and of green politics.

To look first at the issue of national identity, in retrospect it seems evident that the flurry of work on the theme of Heimat in the mid-1980s was an outcome of the same historical conjuncture which gave rise to the so-called *Historikerstreit*, or historians' quarrel, conducted in the press and other media in 1986 and 1987 and which brought to a head longer-standing differences of view among German historians. The integration of the Federal Republic as the leading economic power in the European Union and the key partner in dialogue with her neighbours constituted a process of normalization which in the eyes of some should at long last allow the Federal Republic to take her place as one nation among others rather than remaining a special case. Other voices, by contrast, argued that as long as Germans still resisted acknowledgement of the full atrocity of the Holocaust, no proper accounting of what the Third Reich meant and what it still means for Germans as a national community persisting through time could take place. The theoretical issue of how, and indeed whether, history should form the medium for national self-consciousness lay at the heart of the quarrel. While leftist sceptics might question the whole concept of national identity, they also rejected the view, so memorably put by Margaret Thatcher, that there is no such thing as society. Arguably, then, as long as the nation state remains a political institution through which social relations are ordered and negotiated, some form of national self-awareness is needed if citizens are to participate in a democratic politics and, in the German case, to take active responsibility for the Nazi past in ways which would shape future policy of the nation; even the aspiration to transcend nationalism in a commitment to transnational democratic values, as advocated by one of the main combatants in the *Historiker-streit*, the social scientist Jürgen Habermas, rests on an interpretation of national histories. Given that historiography is an important source of collective self-awareness of a community, then different historical narratives will tend to promote different senses of identity. As Charles S. Maier puts it: 'Historians in Germany have long understood that they legitimized national identity. They have conceded less frequently that they legitimize differing sorts of national identity.'[22] Apart from the philosophical question of whether history should serve to underpin a usable sense of national identity or to dissolve national identity as a dangerous illusion, the more concrete point at issue was whether the Holocaust should be regarded as a genocide unparalleled in history or whether it could be compared with other genocides in the twentieth century and earlier. Thus conservative and revisionist historians argued that as long as the Holocaust was viewed as a horror without parallel, proper historical analysis was inhibited, hence a revision of German historiography was needed to locate the roots of the Holocaust in European and world history since the Enlightenment. This is a thesis worth arguing over, but one of the leading revisionists, Ernst Nolte, argued more dubiously that both communism and fascism, to which latter National Socialism might be subsumed, were pathological symptoms of the malaise of post-Enlightenment civilization and, most dubiously of all, that German history was shaped primarily not by internal factors but by her geographic position in Central Europe which put her at the mercy of external pressures: 'Auschwitz is not the consequence primarily of inherited anti-Semitism and was in essence not merely a "genocide", rather it was a matter of a reaction born of fear of the destructive processes of the Russian Revolution.'[23] By such sleight of hand the Nazi perpetrator was

---

[22] *The Unmasterable Past: History, Holocaust, and German National Identity* (Cambridge, Mass.: Harvard University Press, 1988), 4.

[23] 'Zwischen Geschichtslegende und Revisionismus? Das Dritte Reich im Blickwinkel des Jahres 1980', in Rudolf Augstein et al., *'Historikerstreit': Die Dokumentation der Kontroverse um die Einzigartigkeit der nationalsozialistischen Judenvernichtung* (Munich and Zurich: Piper, 1987), 32; originally *Frankfurter Allgemeine Zeitung*, 24 July 1980; on geographical fatalism see also Mark Bassin, 'Geopolitics in the *Historikerstreit*: The Strange Return of the *Mittellage*', in Jost Hermand and Jamés Steakley (eds.), *'Heimat', Nation, and Fatherland: The German Sense of Belonging* (New York: Peter Lang, 1996), 187–228.

transformed into the deluded victim of Bolshevik excesses. Habermas and a number of left-wing historians insisted by contrast on the primacy of internal social and political explanation and on the singularity of the Holocaust. They condemned revisionism as designed not only to play down German responsibility for the Nazi regime, but also as the expression of right-wing irrationalism which they saw as a threat to democratic politics. A paradox of the whole dispute is that those most sceptical of the concept of national identity argued for the explanatory primacy of German internal politics and hence the continuing need for Germans to confront a national past, whereas those most concerned to underpin a robust sense of German identity underplayed German responsibility for the Third Reich.

Where does the discourse of Heimat belong in this bitter battlefield? One aspect of Nolte's thesis, namely that National Socialism and the Holocaust were a pathological response to the increasing emancipation and abstraction of modern society which left people bereft of identity and community grounded in traditional beliefs and values, has obvious affinities with the cultural pessimism of the more reactionary proponents of Heimat at the turn of the century who were hostile to modernization and to liberal democracy as its political expression. But it also has affinities with left-wing cultural criticism of alienation under capitalism, with neo-Marxist critique of the oppressive instrumental reason at the heart of the enlightenment project, and with postmodern critique of the impact on traditional cultures wrought by Western cultural imperialism. As Detlev Peukert has argued, anti-modern sentiment does not necessarily entail anti-democratic politics though historically they have often gone together; hysterical cultural pessimism and perceptive cultural criticism are not always sharply distinct, and utopias of the right and left may overlap.[24] This is especially so in literature and film, which, in contrast to political philosophy or to historiography, tend to raise rather than answer questions, hence the value of Heimat literature and film as a field of study impinging on some of the most profound and difficult issues of our time. As to the question of uniqueness or comparability, this applies above all to the Holocaust, but also to cultural analysis. In approaching the texts to be studied here the aim will be to explore *both* how they belong in a culture which led on to and followed after the Third Reich as a defining moment unique to German history *and* how they belong within and contribute to cultural debate and reflection on change which are by no means unique to Germany.

---

[24] *The Weimar Republic: The Crisis of Classical Modernity,* trans. Richard Deveson (Harmondsworth: Penguin, 1991), esp. ch. 9.

One way in which Germany at the time of the *Historikerstreit* remained unnormalized was, of course, the division between East and West Germany, literally enforced and symbolically expressed in the wall dividing Berlin. The *Ostpolitik*, in the West historically the policy of the SPD (Sozialdemokratische Partei Deutschlands (Social Democratic Party of Germany)), aimed at normalization of the division and found broad pragmatic acceptance among mainstream politicians across the political spectrum and on both sides of the East–West divide with the difference, however, that whereas the GDR formally dropped any aspiration towards a unified Germany, the FRG retained the claim to represent the German people, a position also inherent in the nationality law of the FRG, dating back to 1913, which enshrined the right to citizenship on ethnic grounds not only of Germans in the GDR but of ethnic Germans in enclaves throughout Eastern Europe. At the opposite extreme from a normalization which would permanently establish the FRG and the GDR as separate states was the right-wing, revanchist refusal not just to accept the division of Germany but also the loss of former German territories to the Soviet Union, Poland, and Czechoslovakia. While mainstream politicians made no territorial claims, some border questions remained to be finally settled and flared up from time to time, signalling that normalization was not yet achieved. Moreover, the widespread pragmatic acceptance of two Germanies and of the national boundaries of post-war Europe did not translate fully into popular identification with the FRG and still less with the GDR. A troubled yet potent sense not of East or West but of unqualified *German* identity remained. Indeed, there has been a stronger posthumous nostalgia for an East German Heimat than there was national identification with the East German state when it still existed. As that example suggests, the discourse of Heimat and the appeal to regional culture and loyalties can function in many different ways in relation to nationalism, whether as a source of communal identity more concrete and less dangerous than nation, or as a way of revaluing the nation as a heterogeneous cultural realm rather than an economic or military power, or as the place, whether region or nation, to which exiles looks back with longing or bitterness, or as the emotional fuel firing revanchist resentments and latter-day nationalistic xenophobia. The rhetorical value of Heimat in opposition to, tension with, or as a variously defining quality of, nationhood will be one main strand of enquiry in this study.

The last of the three factors accounting for the wide currency of Heimat in the 1970s and 1980s is the rise of environmental politics which has an oblique bearing on some of the issues underlying the *Historikerstreit* such as the disputed evaluation of modern civilization and the diagnosis of fascism as a pathological response to the modernizing process. Germany has a particularly strong tradition of environmentalism dating back to the nineteenth century and stretching from practical activities, through philosophical reflection, to quasi-religious metaphysics with antecedents in the Romantic *Naturschwärmerei* (enthusiasm for nature) and earlier still in the eighteenth-century cult of nature. In the period after 1945, this tradition, or at least the phase from the 1890s on, was interpreted largely as an antecedent of National Socialism, notably by Klaus Bergmann in an influential study of 1970, but through the prism of today's environmental thinking has been subject if not to total re-evaluation, then at least to more differentiated analysis.[25] A case in point illustrating the disturbing double face of environmentalism is Ernst Haeckel (1834–1919), the man who coined the term 'ecology' to designate that aspect of biology concerned with the interaction of organisms with their environment. An atheistic materialist and influential mediator of Darwin, Haeckel developed a virtual alternative to religion in his 'monistic' philosophy: underlying the many species and indeed all inorganic nature too was one vitalistic substance; hence man was not, as Christianity proposed, set in dominion over nature but was an animal among others; as our brothers, animals should never be mistreated; nor were men set in dominion over women, man and woman are different but complementary and sexual love is a great good. The affinity between this view and today's animal rights movement or a mythologically coloured cult of Gaia in green New Age thinking is clear. Yet Haeckel supported Germany's imperialist ambitions and shared the endemic racism of his time and the vulgar sub-Darwinian view of Africans as closer to man's primate ancestors than the white races. Or there is the case of the campaigning organization founded in 1904, the Bund Heimatschutz (Union for Heimat Protection), which aimed to foster 'an harmonious civilization, one that combines the use of the earth with a respect for it', as the first chairman, Paul Schulze-Naumburg later put it in 1917.[26] The term *Heimatschutz* was first used in an article of 1897 by Ernst Rudorff and designated various activities rather like the programme of the National Trust in Britain which was founded around the same time, in 1894. The Bund Heimatschutz had twenty-five regional associations whose largely middle-class membership pursued policies to preserve the built and natural environment and like much of today's conservation, local effort was perceived also as part

[25] Klaus Bergmann, *Agrarromantik und Großstadtfeindlichkeit* (Meisenheim am Glan: Anton Hain, 1970); for more positive evaluations of the Heimat movement see Applegate, *A Nation of Provincials* (1990) and William H. Rollins, *A Greener Vision of Home: Cultural Politics and Environmental Reform in the German Heimatschutz Movement 1904–1918* (Ann Arbor: University of Michigan Press, 1997).

[26] Cited in William Rollins, 'The Early Heimatschutz Movement', in Hermand and Steakley (eds.), *'Heimat', Nation, and Fatherland*, 87–112 (91).

of a national crusade which was later appropriated by the National Socialists. Indeed as early as 1930, Schulze-Naumburg became a principal spokesman of the Nazi Kampfbund für deutsche Kultur (Militant League for German Culture).[27] On the other hand, the Nazi policy of *Gleichschaltung* (bringing into line) destroyed local associational life and with it the essence of a movement of conservative hue which had little in common with the radical modernizing policies in transport and communications of a regime which went on to wreak such terrible material damage in exploiting scientific warfare. Environmentalism in our time has, of course, taken on an international aspect. But the electronic revolution, globalization, and supranational European institutions have if anything strengthened the idea of regionalism; Europe of the regions competes with *Europe des patries* and the global village has become a literal, if still utopian, possibility in an age when the modem could link village to village with no need for routing through a metropolis. The postmodern Heimat seems likely to continue as a focus of debate, as, for example, in Gertrud Leutenegger's novel *Kontinent* (1985) which juxtaposes the damaging effects on a Swiss village and the Alpine ecology wrought by industry and agribusiness with urban tensions in modernizing China, showing also, however, the oppressive nature of traditional patriarchy and the potential for fascist and xenophobic populism in societies under stress, whether in Switzerland or in China.

Paralleling the discontinuous political history of Germany, then, four key phases in the discourse of Heimat may be distinguished: first, Heimat as a response to modernity and its discontents and to regional tensions in the new Reich in the period between 1871 and the First World War; second, the 1920s and 1930s when the Heimat mode divided into right-wing and National Socialist ideology, critical opposition on the left, and inner resistance to the Third Reich; third, a dialectic in the post-war decades between the escapist Heimat films of the 1950s and right-wing claims to the lost lands in the East to which the anti-Heimat theatre and film in the 1960s and 1970s and some aspects of the literature of *Vergangenheitsbewältigung* were a response, filmic representations of Berlin suburbs in GDR film as an urban Heimat adding an interesting twist; fourth, the increasing exploration of German identity and of regional culture beyond the divisions of the Cold War paralleled by the rise of environmentalist politics. The theme of Heimat in literature and film has been a significant point of reference in recent and still continuing

---

[27] See Matthew Jefferies, 'Heimatschutz in Wilhelmine Germany', in Colin Riordan (ed.), *Green Thought in German Culture: Historical and Contemporary Perspectives* (Cardiff: University of Wales Press, 1997), 42–54.

debates on historiographic representation of German history and looks likely to continue in a postmodern and multicultural mode. The aim here cannot be exhaustive cover of such a massive and complex tradition. Rather, we hope to illuminate particular examples of the mode in film and literature and by discussing these in their immediate context and within the larger tradition to sketch methods and a field which readers can further explore in studying other individual texts.

Socio-Psychic Connotations and Aesthetic Contours

The sheer persistence of the concept of Heimat through the twists and turns of German history suggests that it may connote a deep-seated psychological need, which may even be intrinsic to identity formation, but which is mediated differently through changing history and in different cultural contexts.[28] The term has many different usages in the fields of law, politics, the natural sciences, anthropology, sociology, psychology, philosophy, religion, and literature as well as in political discourse.[29] These discourses feed on, yet also aim to stabilize within their own specialist boundaries, the wealth of meaning in the everyday usage of a term which is hard to pin down.

The spatio-temporal Heimat

Built into most usages, however, is the notion of a linking or connecting of the self with something larger through a process of identification signified by a spatial metaphor. Heimat is, then, a physical place, or social space, or bounded medium of some kind which provides a sense of security and belonging. As a surrounding medium, Heimat protects the self by stimulating identification whether with family, locality, nation, folk or race, native dialect or tongue, or whatever else may fill the empty signifier to fuel a process of definition or of buttressing which feeds and sustains a sense of identity. Heimat is an intrinsically conservative value connoting originary or primary factors in identity, or at least it expresses the longing, perhaps illusory, for such an absolute foundation or unchanging essence. Even when Heimat is an achievement to be won through effort such as

[28] See Ina-Maria Greverus, *Auf der Suche nach Heimat* (Munich: Beck, 1979) on the psychological value of Heimat.
[29] See Andrea Bastian, *Der Heimat-Begriff: Eine begriffsgeschichtliche Untersuchung in verschiedenen Funktionsbereichen der deutschen Sprache* (Tübingen: Niemeyer, 1995).

the colonist's labour which transmutes stange land into homeland, the land takes on the metaphorical maternal value of the encompassing medium and foundation of identity. But since identity denotes continuation through time, time and change are built into the spatial metaphor of Heimat: time is the ever-present enemy of Heimat which is only ever overcome in the heavenly home of paradise or the Garden of Eden. The inexorable passage of time brings distance from the imagined Heimat of childhood, hence the yearning nostalgia and sense of loss which the idea of Heimat so often evokes. Heimat literature and film often convey a tension between a physical landscape suggesting timeless nature and the signs of time and change, like the telegraph wires cutting across the rolling high plateau of the Hunsrück in Edgar's Reitz's *Heimat*. Or there is the domestic interior juxtaposing a deal table which could belong in a museum with a radio set or television. A cityscape too can create such a tension: some of the most critical East German films such as *Berlin Ecke Schönhauser* or *Berlin um die Ecke* set a contrast between old Berlin tenements evocative of an imagined proletarian solidarity of yesteryear and modern department stores in West Berlin or the soulless new high-rise flats in the East signifying fear of failure to create a socialist Heimat. Even the face of an old woman near death may in close-up become a kind of landscape evoking the remembered image of a young mother—Maria in Reitz's *Heimat* presents such a changing aspect. Such interplay of space/place and time is a key structural facet of Heimat literature and film.

Heimat as Image

In Reitz's *Heimat*, each episode begins with a flurry of photographs which preserve the unchanging image of moments and faces even as the paper fades and curls with age and the faces of those still alive have wrinkled. The motif of photography signals the phenomenological aspect of Heimat as image. Nothing is intrinsically the Heimat: only when a piece of countryside becomes a landscape, when it is *perceived* as an image, does it turn into Heimat. In his study of the *Heimatschutz* movement at the turn of the century William Rollins emphasizes the strongly aesthetic aspect: 'Through pictures and photographs and rhetoric the Heimatschützer pressed their fellow Germans to . . . confront the consequences of tailoring land to the requirements of capitalist-mechanist "rationality".'[30] Photographs served not merely to show the idyllic landscape in tourist

---

[30]   *Greener Vision of Home*, 266.

guidebooks but could also document in polemical pamphlets the ravages destroying it. Citing Prussia's Disfigurement Law of 1907 and many local guidelines protecting neighbourhood aesthetics, Rollins argues that the *Heimatschutz* movement fed into a progressive tradition of city planning and municipal socialism. At the same time, however, the visual rhetoric of images is under constant threat of descent into kitsch: when trees trans-mogrify into 'the German forest' they signify Heimat. 'Der Wald ist die Urheimat des Deutschtums', so one study proclaims in text juxtaposed with a photographed woodland scene on the facing page labelled 'Im Schwarzwald' but which could as well have been taken in Sherwood Forest.[31] When the camera angle creates a framed image for a postcard, the country cottage becomes Heimat kitsch. Country people do not live in the Heimat, only when they pose to be seen do they enter the realm of Heimat, like the Scottish Highlander in a kilt playing his bagpipes where the tourist buses stop or the Bavarian village maiden in the poster, her bosom bursting from her bodice as the Alps rear up behind her. If time is the enemy of Heimat, corroding its promise of unchanging idyll, time can also be the astringent acid which saves the Heimat from its sentimental tendency. Kitsch results from the exclusion of too much harsh reality. The best Heimat literature and films are those works which allow time in, whether to undo the illusion or at least to allow for change, a step which is in any case necessary to bring action into the static Heimat which has great potential for tedium. Occasionally, Heimat can switch from a back-ward-looking nostalgia to become a dynamic utopia of a left tradition conveying a future we must work towards: 'etwas, das allen in die Kindheit scheint und worin noch niemand war: Heimat', as Ernst Bloch put it in the frequently cited last sentence of *Das Prinzip Hoffnung* (1954–7).[32] The playing-off of different perspectives can also serve to relativize the imagin-ary Heimat by uncovering changing economic or class relations or the high tuberculosis rate among the inhabitants of country cottages. Thus at the turn of the century, even though Heimat and the Naturalist movement were supposed to be ideologically antithetical, Heimat and Naturalism often mix ambiguously in an interplay of utopian ideal and harsh reality. In his novel *Deutschstunde*, Siegfried Lenz sets the Expressionist land-scapes of Emil Nolde, thinly disguised in the novel as Max Ludwig Nansen, against the kitsch Heimat films of the 1930s. Such play of perspectives often takes the form of the arrival of an outsider or the departure and return of an insider-become-outsider who wants to come back. In such

[31] 'The forest is the original German Heimat'. Konrad Guenther, *Die Heimatlehre: Vom Deutschtum und seiner Natur* (Leipzig: R. Voigtländer Verlag, 1932), 8–9.
[32] 'something that appears to everyone in childhood and where no one has ever been: Heimat'. *Das Prinzip Hoffnung* (Frankfurt am Main: Suhrkamp, 1977), 1628.

eyes, a place takes on the promise of Heimat to be granted or withheld, but may also pose the threat of suffocation, as K. perhaps feels at the end of *Das Schloß* (1922; pub. 1926), Kafka's grim anti-Heimat novel, when as a stranger seeking entry he finds an interim place in the village in a darkly oppressive maid's room. Michael Haneke has recently made a bleak film of *Das Schloß* (1997) in the critical Heimat idiom. In analysing Heimat art, then, visual images and metaphorically laden locations are a leading factor, but so too in the more interesting texts is the focus or perspective through which the Heimat effect is produced.

The Maternal Heimat as Threshold between Nature and Culture

Strangers or returnees tend to be male, whereas the nostalgic Heimat of childhood is generally associated with the mother and in metaphorical extension with the maternal earth. Elisabeth Bütfering has suggested that Heimat discourse is patriarchal.[33] In her view, Heimat is based on an economy of inheritance along the male line: men inherit a family home, a trade, and 'acquire' a wife and children. Women, by contrast, do not own the Heimat but embody it: they are part of the package of hearth and home as the inner world at the heart of Heimat. Maternal health or sickness may symbolize the health and sickness of the Heimat, decadence or poverty often being signified in the figure of a sickly mother. Women *are* the Heimat for men, but only as long as they fill their place in the patriarchal order over which men preside. The marriage bed is the route to full integration into the Heimat, but a too sexually powerful woman will turn into the snake in paradise. Heimat connotes womb-like security and warmth. But Heimat may become claustrophobic so that sons long to cut the umbilical cord and escape to the wider world of the fatherland. Or nature can turn into an overwhelming power as Mother Earth takes on the lineaments of the phallic mother, to use the terminology of psychoanalysis. Gisela Ecker has detected a pervasively Oedipal structure in much Heimat writing and film.[34] In the tradition associated with the French psychoanalyst Lacan, Heimat constitutes a paradigm example of the so-called Imaginary, the phase of blissful attachment to the Mother preceding the painful process of identity formation through separation and differentiation which comes with the entry into language and into the Symbolic order of the Father. Just as the Imaginary is illusory, for the post-partum

---

[33] 'Frauenheimat Männerwelt: Die Heimatlosigkeit ist weiblich', in *Heimat: Analysen, Themen, Persepktiven*, vol. 294/I (Bonn: Bundeszentrale für politische Bildung, 1990), 416–36.

[34] '"Heimat": Das Elend der unterschlagenen Differenz', in Gisela Ecker (ed.), *Kein Land in Sicht: Heimat—weiblich?* (Munich: Wilhelm Fink, 1997), 7–31.

infant already belongs in a social world, so Heimat is never purely natural. It is the threshold between nature and culture. The infant passes from the maternal womb into the domestic world over which the mother presides and where the little animal is socialized and acquires a mother tongue or *Muttersprache*. Accordingly, the mother figure has a double aspect, each of these aspects in turn being doubled. As nature from which man came and to which he must return Mother Earth is life-giving yet death-dealing, so that the longing to return to the Heimat can take on a regressive and deadly aspect. (In *Doktor Faustus*, Thomas Mann's novel of 1947 reckoning with the Third Reich, the hero Leverkühn regresses to just such a maternal realm in the countryside in a radical inner emigration into madness and then death.) The domestic mother likewise protects and loves, yet the very weight of her love weighs down on and may imprison her children. The turn of the century and the 1970s up to the mid-1980s, twin peaks in the range of Heimat literature, are also the crest of two waves of feminist agitation. An important differentiating factor between Heimat kitsch and Heimat literature and film of substance is the degree to which the patriarchal discourse is shaken and unsettled, or even overthrown.

Self and Other

Heimat belongs to an antithetical mode of thinking in terms of identity and difference, of belonging and exclusion, which operates in two ways. Heimat may work to integrate differences and resolve conflict, for example between the sexes or between generations, whether by a conservative re-establishment of patriarchal order or by a liberal loosening: many Heimat plots follow such a structure of reconciliation of difference between men and women, social classes, or between strangers and locals. One frequent plot in Heimat films finds reconciliation within the Heimat of aristocrats and peasants; another allows townies and villagers to resolve their hostilities; or in the 1950s comic Berliners and Bavarians reach a truce. (For a horrible example combining these motifs see Harald Reinl's *Die Prinzessin von St Wolfgang* of 1957.) Such plots express the ideal of folk unity (*Volkstum*) transcending feudal divisions or else the division of the German people during the Cold War (but bracket out foreign workers, for example, who do not get to marry princesses). Heimat must always be ultimately bounded and defined through visible or hidden exclusion of the radically different and alien. The stranger may become one of us, but the boundary remains to exclude the alien. Norman Tebbit's cricket law offers a simple example: a member of the West Indian community in England can become one of 'us' if he supports the 'home' team, but to do so entails crossing sides and expunging his difference, for the 'home' team only exists to play against 'them', the West Indian 'away' team. In the terminology of deconstruction, Heimat as Self/Same depends on a balancing notion of the Other or the Exotic, in German *Fremde* (strangeness) or *Ferne* (distance).[35] Who must be excluded and who can be integrated are as crucial to the definition of a community as who is from the start included: a place is as much defined by its others as by the self. For Jacques Derrida, all names or headings—'Heimat' would be an example—'designate at once a limit, a negative limit and a chance, . . . which is the opening of its identity to the future'.[36] Heimat thus contains within itself its negative and other. The chance or opportunity is the potential to go beyond delimited identity in an opening to the other. The opening remains always potential not actual, for the integration of the other expunges difference and so the boundary simply recedes: the other is always necessary to define what we who belong are not, as Tebbit's law demonstrates. Thus in a picture book of 1938, *Deutschland: Ein Buch der Heimat*, the author asserts that Faust-like 'der Deutsche drängt nach Weite' ('the German yearns for faraway places') only to conclude a few lines down that *Heimweh*, homesickness, is the German malady: distance is but a mirror in which the soul may the more strongly perceive its intimate bond with Heimat.[37] In this way, binary systems such as home and away or self/same and other set up contradictions within each pole. Take, for example, the opposition of Inside–Outside: Heimat as the desirable security, warmth, and inclusion (Inside) does not always hold true, for Heimat as the excluder of others and a kind of fortress which admits no one, works in an inverted way as well—it stops people from leaving (going Outside) and so produces the tension between *Heimweh* (homesickness) and *Fernweh* (wanderlust and the longing for distant places). Heimat as kitsch pays little heed to this 'other' side of the in-side: the Heimat community welcomes suitable outsiders into a cotton-wool cocoon, passing over other Others in silence. Heimat as racist Nazi propaganda, by contrast, highlights the dangers of infiltration by the loathsome outsider disguised as one of us. But even during the Third Reich, more differentiated pieces convey the dual nature of the Heimat. The hated 'Other' whom the insiders may seek to expel can turn into an erotic, desired 'Other'. In one episode of *Heimat* Edgar Reitz shows his characters' *Fernweh*, their attraction to the distant and exotic, as they watch Detlef Sierck's film *La*

---

[35] Hans-Georg Pott (ed.), *Literatur und Provinz: Das Konzept 'Heimat' in der neueren Literatur* (Paderborn: Schoningh, 1986), 8.

[36] *The Other Heading*, trans. Pascale-Anne Brault and Michael B. Naas (Bloomington, Ind.: Indiana University Press, 1992), 35.

[37] Werner Beumelburg, *Deutschland: Ein Buch der Heimat* (Berlin: Paul Franke Verlag, 1938), 6.

Habanera (1937) and then come home and imitate the lead actress Zarah Leander. In the film Leander embodies the Heimat woman seduced by a dark stranger, but she also dresses up to perform as an exotic Carmen seductively singing her habanera. Such a composite figure of Heimat and its Other combined in one image as object of the spectator's desiring gaze catches the Janus-faced aspect in Heimat of *Heimweh* and *Fernweh*. Likewise America or the threatening metropolis of Berlin can be both the source of anxiety and contempt, and a promised land and symbol of a utopian freedom. The representation of those who belong or are welcomed into the Heimat and of the others who leave or are excluded is a crucial distinguishing aspect dividing the mode into subcategories of different political tendency.

The first part of this introduction sketched phases in the discourse of Heimat as a mode of reflection and commentary on the discontinuous history of Germany in the twentieth century and as an intervention in the cultural construction, occasionally also deconstruction, of national identity as mediated through region and locality. The selection of literary texts and films to be discussed in detail is designed to exemplify these phases, but also to pursue a whole variety of themes such as environmentalism or the class politics as well as gender and ethnic codes through which national and regional identity is mediated. Each of the chapters concentrates on a key theme. Thus Chapter 1 focuses on tradition and change in the emergent world power of the new German Reich. Chapter 2, dealing with the period between the two world wars, centres on men returning from or preparing for war. Chapter 3 centres on the family as the key institution through which a shattered, post-war society sought restoration of social order. Chapter 4 and Chapter 5 both take the family theme further to look at the inter-generational tensions between young Germans and their parents in East German film, then under the long shadow of the Nazi past in West German literature and film. Such themes all reappear in Chapter 6 in considering Edgar Reitz's film epic *Heimat*. The last chapter broaches two main topics, unification of the two Germanies and Heimat in a multicultural society. In addition to locating individual texts within German history and in the history of the Heimat mode, the discussions will centre on the specifically literary and filmic qualities of the texts to show how time structure, narrative perspectives and plots, characterization, metaphorical subtexts, and, above all in this mode, locations and visual images work together to produce an often ambiguous rhetoric of identity and difference.

1 Heimat at the Turn of the Century
The Heimat Art Movement and
Clara Viebig's Eifel Fictions

'Los von Berlin?' The Heimat Art Movement

The foundation of the German Reich in 1871 was in large measure the outcome of a drive towards a market unfettered by internal customs boundaries. The consequent economic growth had its impact also on publishing and the press as did the growth of Berlin and other big cities in producing a rapidly expanding reading public and so stimulating the circulation of ideas. New journals, newspapers, and publishing houses sprang up to become the arena for the battle over the values which should prevail in the new German Reich. As Steven Nyole Fuller puts it:

> Through feuilleton articles, book reviews, and literary criticism, journals and newspapers sold a particular world view, and with it a particular canon of literature. At the same time, both literature and the critic came to exist within a hierarchy of publishers, who imposed their own demands and conditions of production upon those texts. The literary critic existed within the context of a literary institution that manufactured a product marketed towards a specific consumer. The character of the reading public in the 1880s and 90s was predominantly middle-class, conservative and nationalistic.[1]

Heimat discourse catered for that conservative public and could shade into a more radically reactionary mode. A polemic favoured on the centre-right of the urban intelligentsia around the turn of the century when the Heimat novel too reached a mass readership, Heimat discourse was a product of a new chattering class of journalists and sub-Nietzschean cultural critics. This was an age of literary manifestos setting battle-lines between opposing camps, although in practice the divisions were not always clear-cut. The term in currency was *Heimatkunst*, literally Heimat art, and was used indifferently of the visual arts and literature. The proponents of Heimat art defined their aims in opposition to the Naturalist movement. Heimat art was to celebrate the life of ordinary German people in rural or provincial communities, to show forth the links between the landscape and human beings, and so to celebrate the sturdy

---

[1] *The Nazis' Literary Grandfather: Adolf Bartels and Cultural Extremism, 1871–1945* (New York: Peter Lang, Steven Nyole Fuller, 1996), 52.

Fig. 2. Wilhelm Leibl: *In der Bauernstube* (*In the Farm Kitchen*, 1890), Inv.Nr. 7803

German spirit of survival rooted in provincial loyalties and expressed in the daily struggle with the elements. Such is the spirit informing the work of painters like Wilhelm Leibl (1844–1900) in his genre studies of Bavarian peasants or his landscapes. Heimat art was thus to be the very antithesis of Naturalism, the foreign import from France which propagated a destructive scientific ideology and depicted the degenerate products of the urban lower depths. As will be seen in the example of Clara Viebig, however, the boundary between Naturalism and Heimat literature was by no means clear-cut. The literary texts often proved more complex and less ideologically shrill than the journalistic polemics. Moreover, both Naturalism and Heimat literature aspired to convey the everyday life of ordinary people in realistic detail and to locate individuals in a milieu, as did also realist painters such as Leibl who evokes a whole mode of life in each precise detail. The anti-urban bias of Heimat literature marked much Naturalist literature too and though some Heimat novels were idyllic in mood, many deployed Naturalist techniques to paint a picture of harsh conditions and

Fig. 3. Wilhelm Leibl and Johannes Sperl, *Leibl und Sperl auf der Jagd* (*Leibl and Sperl Out Hunting, c.*1890), Inv.Nr. 8724, Bayerische Staatsgemäldesammlungen, Neue Pinakothek, Munich

rural poverty, which in its very grimness, however, heightened the heroic stature of the men and women who battled to survive. A key feature distinguishing the Heimat mode from the often fatalistic pessimism of Naturalist art is precisely the tendency to celebrate heroic triumph over adversity, a tendency exemplified in the eponymous hero of Gustav Frenssen's novel of rural life in Schleswig-Holstein, *Jörn Uhl* (1901), one of the best-sellers of the Heimat art movement.

It may be misleading, however, to speak of a movement given that the proponents of Heimat were so geographically scattered. Moreover, though many lived in cities, they polemicized against the very institutions such as the literary café where urban intellectuals congregated to form movements and plan manifestos. But for a brief span of three or four years beginning in 1900 a focus was provided by the journal *Heimat: Blätter für Literatur und Volkstum* (even harder to translate than Heimat, *Volkstum* denotes the collective character of a nation defined in populist or folk terms).[2] Published in Berlin, the journal sold well especially in Schleswig-

[2] On Heimat journals see Karlheinz Rossbacher, *Heimatbewegung und Heimatroman: Zu einer Literatursoziologie der Jahrhundertwende* (Stuttgart: Ernst Klett, 1975), 16–19. This remains the fullest study of Heimat literature at the turn of the century.

Holstein and north Germany generally, and several articles were also issued as pamphlets achieving sales in the thousands. That many proponents of Heimat art originated from border areas explains their acute need to assert the Germanness of a regional identity. This was certainly true of Friedrich Lienhard (1865–1929), the first editor of *Heimat*, who came from Alsace. Using the forename Fritz, the more folksy version of Friedrich, Lienhard was a romantic idealist who provided one of the main slogans of the movement in a programmatic article of 1902, 'Los von Berlin?', attacking the decadence of city life, its hectic pace, and, as he saw it, the soulless rationalism of Berlin intellectuals with their pursuit of fashionable trends and lack of the larger vision.[3] His own stories, poems, and memoirs, set in Alsace or in Thuringia—Lienhard eventually moved to Weimar—seek a return to the purity of nature and assert spiritual oneness with the peasants back in the hills of home: 'Bei uns daheim in den Bergen, Ihr Herr'n, da weht eine andre Luft'.[4] The lines echo a poem by Robert Burns, one of Lienhard's heroes: 'My heart is in the Highlands, my heart is not here'. Characteristically, in both poems the mountain Heimat is somewhere where the poet is not: Heimat art gives voice to the yearnings of urban intellectuals whether in the metropolis or in provincial centres like Munich and Weimar, or indeed Edinburgh. (The so-called kaleyard tradition in Scotland can fairly be called Heimat literature.) The title of Lienhard's article, 'Los von Berlin?' had a question mark, for as he confessed, he was at that time himself living in Berlin. His call is less for a flight from the city than for a new high idealism, for healthy wholeness rather than alienation and the negative spirit of critique. Lienhard withdrew from *Heimat* after only a few numbers because of doubts at the narrowly reactionary tone of some contributors and in 1901 published a volume of essays, *Neue Ideale*, setting out his programme. Two of the essays, 'Persönlichkeit und Volkstum', and 'Heimatkunst', sketch his conception of a new literature which should express individual greatness of character rooted in an organic culture arising from the people. Lienhard is here drawing on a tradition stretching back to Herder and the pre-Romantic *Sturm und Drang* movement of the 1770s. In vaguely enthusiastic tones Lienhard denies that Heimat art is a turn backwards against the modern world, rather it represents expansion and completion: 'wir wünschen ganze Menschen mit einer ganzen und weiten Gedanken-, Gemüts- und Charakterwelt, mit modernster und doch volkstümlicher

---

[3] 'Away from Berlin?' 'Los von Berlin? Ein Schlußwort', *Deutsche Heimat* 5/1(1901/2), 504–8; abbreviated in Jürgen Schütte and Peter Sprengel (eds.), *Die Berliner Moderne 1885–1914* (Stuttgart: Reclam, 1987), 220–4. *Heimat* changed title to *Deutsche Heimat* in 1901.

[4] 'Back at home in our hills, gentlemen, a different wind blows'. Friedrich Lienhard, *Thüringer Tagebuch, Helden, Wasgaufahrten* (Berlin: Josef Singer, n.d.), 62.

Bildung . . . wir wünschen Stadt und Land'.[5] Further essays discuss the Oberammergau passion play, the movement for an autonomous Alsatian culture, Robert Burns and Rudyard Kipling, folk festivals and countryside theatres to house regional art like that of the great creative men of the past who were 'eng mit ihrer Scholle verwachsen', closely linked to the earth of their region and to their 'Stammeseigentümlichkeit', their ethnic or clan character, yet who also breathed a universal spirit; Storm, Mörike, Keller, Meyer, and Wagner are the examples cited. Lienhard would later distance himself from the extreme reactionary and racist views of Adolf Bartels, his collaborator in 1900. But the vague idealistic longings and the attacks on cultural degeneracy, on scientific reason, on proletarian or female emancipation, on the unleashed eroticism in the cities were the kind of anti-modern reaction fuelled by religiose hopes of a new beginning and by *völkisch* sentiment which later proved fertile ground for the blandishments of the National Socialists. Yet the longings for wholeness and community were also shared by many who rejected National Socialism and had their counterpart in other countries in which fascism never triumphed.

Closely associated with Lienhard at this time was Adolf Bartels (1862–1945). Bartels began his journalistic career with articles for *Der Kunstwart*, a journal edited by the influential conservative publicist Ferdinand Avenarius (1856–1923). By the turn of the century this journal had become a leading force in shaping a conservative aesthetic canon and an ideal of German style through book reviews, essays, reproductions of paintings by artists such as Dürer, Rembrandt, and Holbein, and in advocating German music. One contributor in the 1890s was Paul Schulze-Naumburg, then active in the German Arts and Crafts Movement and who would become first chairman of the Bund Heimatschutz (League for Heimat Protection) in 1904, but who during the Weimar Republic became a leading spokesman of the rabidly anti-Semitic Kampfbund für deutsche Kultur (Militant League for German Culture). The conservative aesthetic of the German style need not, however, be condemned root and branch because of later developments and indeed faced by the rise of National Socialism some came to review earlier positions critically even as the vaguely racist thinking of others in the conservative camp hardened into programmatic anti-Semitism in the 1920s. But no hindsight is needed in the case of Bartels who from early on was overtly anti-Semitic. Bartels launched an aggressively nationalist polemic in articles and reviews for *Heimat* and his essay of 1900 on 'Heimatkunst' was also distributed as a

---

[5] 'we want whole human beings inhabiting a whole and wide-reaching world of thought, spirit, and character, with at once modern yet traditional culture rooted in the people . . . we want town and country'. *Neue Ideale* (Leipzig and Berlin: Georg Heinrich Meyer Heimatverlag, 1901), 198.

pamphlet. For Bartels, *Deutschtum*, Germanness, meant vigorous health and ethical and ethnic superiority in contrast to what he called 'modernitis', the disease of alien decadence infiltrating Germany from the old enemy France and infecting cities such as Paris or Berlin.[6] The opposition of alien sickness and Germanic health would remain up to the Third Reich a key metaphor in racist discourse. Besides journalism, Bartels became known as a pugnacious historian of German literature. The rise of historical linguistics and literary history, the two sides of academic German studies, created an arena in which language and literature became tokens in a battle over German identity. The battle was by no means limited to the academy, however. Bartels was not a university man and like many of the prophets of Heimat shared Nietzsche's loathing of the small-minded tribe of professors. The first of Bartels's many contributions to literary history appeared in 1901 and was an immediate *succès de scandale*. Bartels can fairly be claimed to have originated racist literary history in Germany, his vulgar anti-Semitism proving too much to stomach for conservatives such as Avenarius and eventually also Lienhard. Initially contenting himself with blanket attacks on *Judentum* (meaning either Jewishness or Jewry) as a sickness infecting German culture, by the 1920s Bartels took to annotating individual authors cited in the ever longer and more vapid versions of his literary history as Jews, or as married to Jews, as in the case of Clara Viebig. Although Bartels was never a member of the Nazi Party, he had become by the 1920s an institution in himself as the anti-Semitic guardian of German cultural purity. His four-volume historical Heimat novel *Die Dithmarscher* (1898), celebrating the victory in the seventeenth century of a peasant army over the Danish forces of Duke Friedrich of Schleswig-Holstein, was set in Dithmarschen, a region in west Schleswig-Holstein with a particularly strong Heimat tradition, being home also to Gustav Frenssen (1863–1945), author of *Jörn Uhl* (1901). Jealousy of Frenssen's success perhaps explains Bartels's denigration of Frenssen's 'fürchterliches "Getue" ' (terrible fuss) over his characters, which in Bartels's view was alien both to the true Dithmarschen spirit and to Heimat art.[7] There is, then, a choice as to who the Heimat prophet mentioned in Siegfried Lenz's *Deutschstunde* (1968), discussed in Chapter 4, might in reality have been. Julius Langbehn, to be discussed below, is yet another candidate.

Both Bartels and Lienhard saw Heimat art as an intermediate stage leading to an authentic German High Culture which would overcome the

---

[6] See Fuller, *Nazis' Literary Grandfather*, 62 on the pervasive metaphors of sickness and health.

[7] Adolf Bartels, *Geschichte der deutschen Literatur*, 13th and 14th impression (Braunschweig, Berlin, Hamburg: Georg Westermann, 1934), 616.

vulgarity of the current literary market dominated by foreign influences and would revive the spirit of great German literature and art of the past. But authors interested in sales did not necessarily share this pursuit of a high cultural aim and tended to write mainly lowbrow, popular fiction. The novels of Ludwig Ganghofer (1855–1920), who was a prominent Heimat writer, exemplify the trivial end of the scale. His novels showed detailed knowledge of Alpine landscapes and customs, but were extremely sentimental. They tended to blur social reality and present class divisions as a fixed reality which could not be changed. Although no single work by Ganghofer could compete with Frenssen's *Jörn Uhl*, overall sales of his works with their trivial humour and undemanding linguistic style reached millions. He was a prolific writer, producing eighteen novels (such as *Edelweisskönig*, 1886; *Der Klosterjäger*, 1892; *Der laufende Berg*, 1897; *Das Schweigen im Walde*, 1899; *Gewitter im Mai*, 1904) as well as plays, novellas, and poems. Many of his novels were later made into films and Alpine landscapes were to remain perhaps *the* most popular Heimat setting, although many of the leading figures associated with Heimat art came from the Protestant North. The Protestant Lienhard, however, forged a link from the North-German Heimat movement through his contributions to the Munich journal *Hochland* (*Highland*) edited by Karl Muth, which first appeared in 1903 and became a leading Catholic organ propagating the Heimat ideal in south Germany. As Karlheinz Rossbacher notes, the title in itself indicated the aspiration towards the cultural high ground from whence to pit a healthy, German, and Christian folk-spirit against the sickly decadence of the cities of the plain dominated by social democracy and the rootless spirit of Jewish intellectualism.[8]

Muth was a great admirer of another key figure linking North and South, Julius Langbehn (1851–1907). The *éminence grise* of the whole Heimat art movement, Langbehn was yet another prophet from Schleswig-Holstein, but who converted to Catholicism at the end of the 1890s and moved to south Germany where he died in 1907 in Rosenheim in Bavaria. Langbehn's polemical essay *Rembrandt als Erzieher* (1890), published anonymously as 'von einem Deutschen' ('by a German'), explains the importance of the visual arts as a point of reference in Heimat discourse around 1900, for it celebrates Rembrandt as the presiding genius of the Low German cultural realm which, so Langbehn argues, has displaced south Germany which had been the centre of German cultural gravity in the Middle Ages. The return to the north is a return of the German spirit to its origins in Schleswig-Holstein, so Langbehn asserts, as the land from which the Germanic tribes first spread out through Europe down to

[8]   Rossbacher, *Heimatbewegung und Heimatroman*, 18.

Lombardy and Venice and westwards round and across the North Sea to the Low Countries and Britain: for Langbehn Shakespeare is more quintessentially German than the classicizing Goethe. The Germans spread east too, of course, where in Prussia the continuing failure of oil and vinegar to blend comes out in the contrasting types of the tall, blond Junker and the short, dark Wends and other Slavic peoples who now, according to Langbehn, overwhelmingly formed the urban masses in Berlin. Langbehn inhabits the pervasively racist discourse of the age and links characterological qualities to physiognomic signifiers of racial identity. Thus Langbehn contrasts the tall, thin Prussian guards officer who clings tenaciously to his inherited values with the mobile, dark-haired, Slavic type who tends to progressive politics or to nihilism. Observing the population of Venice, he contrasts the Italianized Germanic type with the Italianized Slavic type, the former broad-browed, with squat profile and straight hair growth, the latter with narrow visage and hooked profile. The double inheritance lends the Venetians their elascticity, so Langbehn claims, resulting in a politics which mixes Low German tenacity with Slavic mobility.[9] But unlike Bartels, for example, he was not anti-Semitic, one of his great heroes being Rembrandt's younger contemporary, the philosopher Spinoza, who was of Jewish decent. Indeed Rembrandt's liking of his Jewish fellow citizens is for Langbehn a sign of his nobility, just as a noble aristocracy of spirit inheres in the ancient people of the Jews. Langbehn's horror is reserved for the decadent falling away from type ('Entartung') whether of Jews or Italians or Germans, in the mobile modern world which mixes blood to produce 'mulattos' and 'mulatto art', such as the modern fashion for chinoiserie. Following the right-wing theologian and essayist Paul de Lagarde (1827–91), who remained influential into the 1930s and who, in contrast to Langbehn, was rabidly anti-Semitic, Langbehn sets out a pyramidic structure of identity based in humanity, rising through nationality, tribe, and family, and culminating in individuality which, he says, is closer to heaven than the base. Thus Langbehn values strong individuality over common humanity and the man over the human being. The pyramidic logic implies that mixing at any of the levels would result in adulteration and loss of identity, just as at the base a mixing of the human with the animal would engender a hybrid monster. In the field of gender, female emancipation was producing the virilized woman, the monstrous *Mann-Weib*. The level of the family might seem to be an exception to the rule forbidding mixing, but anxiety over the infiltration of the patriciate and aristocracy or of the cultivated middle

---

[9] Julius Langbehn, *Rembrandt als Erzieher. Von einem Deutschen*, 4th edn. (Leipzig: C. L. Hirschfeld, 1890), 127–9.

class or *Bildungsbürgertum* by vulgar upstarts marrying in was endemic at a time of a perceived shift from a society differentiated by fixed rank (*Ständegesellschaft*) to a mobile class society (*Klassengesellschaft*) in which money bought social advancement. As the pervasive trope of monsters and metamorphosis suggests, the fear of loss of identity in the mixing of types was a widespread feature of modernism in contrast to postmodern discourse which values the pleasures of hybridity and cultural mixing. Where modernist literature conjured up the monsters with fascinated horror, Heimat literature offered the antidote of womanly women and manly men. Within nation and tribe, Langbehn sets the basis for strong individual characters in an inverted triangle with the peasant as the fundamental German type dividing then into the warrior and the artist (a contemporary avatar of the medieval priestly caste).[10] In Heimat literature too, the peasant-artist (Ganghofer's *Der Herrgottschnitzer von Ammergau*, for example) or the peasant-warrior (Wiechert's *Das einfache Leben*, to be discussed in the next chapter) appear as types. But the tensions between cultivating the soil or the mind, a leading theme in Frenssen's *Jörn Uhl* or Viebig's *Das Kreuz im Venn*, show that hybrid mixing has infected even Langbehn's triangle and the anxieties over loss of identity infiltrate the most remote rural settings.

Rembrandt als Erzieher apes Nietzsche's aphoristic manner and loose association of topics, but where Nietzsche at his best writes with brilliantly allusive concision, Langbehn's style echoes his name in its long-windedness. In Langbehn's polemics, the visual chiaroscuro of Rembrandt's canvases is translated into a shady irrationalism which substitutes cloudily resonant assertion for reasoned argument. Even so, Langbehn's tract does circle round one unifying theme: the pursuit of stable identity under the perceived threat of the modern urban mass. Its success surely came from its mix of folk psychology, cultural theory, and an aesthetic programme, the three elements combining to form a symbolic universe of signs imbued with vaguely expansive meaning. The signs, which might include bodily or facial features, clothes, landscapes, details of domestic interiors, architecture, painting, become the interchangeable signifiers of a trans-historical Germanic essence. Langbehn expatiates polemically on values which the visual signs signify, but for his anxious conservative readership as for the intellectuals and artists he attracted, the signs could serve in themselves without need of spelling out. They become mythic and feed into the mythopoeic Heimat mode. Meaningfulness, but without too much definition, offered a salve to the anxieties in

---

[10] On the cult of archaic types of the peasant, the priest, the warrior, see Ulrike Haß, *Militante Pastorale: Zur Literatur der anti-modernen Bewegungen im frühen 20. Jahrhundert* (Munich: Wilhelm Fink, 1993).

an age of rapid change which was perceived to threaten traditional beliefs, values, rights and privileges, and ultimately identity. Fears induced by the flight from the land, which was producing the urban proletariat and social democracy, could be assuaged by a cult of the earth-rooted peasant signified in handcrafted clogs or hand-woven linen, in the traditional peasant costumes or *Tracht* which Langbehn celebrates, or in the long lankiness of the Junker aristocrat-peasant. Such a response offered a way of bypassing the bitter antagonisms of class warfare, it hovered ambiguously between a socialistic sympathy with the people and reactionary rejection of the modern world. Fear of the masses was assuaged by identification with the *Volk*. Awkward questions about the distribution of power and wealth were deflected into an aesthetic doctrine of the simple life signified in handicrafts such as the delicacy of hand-made lace as against the coarse machine-made product. Among Langbehn's admirers were the artists' colony of Worpswede who practised arts and crafts and the poet Rainer Maria Rilke (1875–1926).[11] Quite in the Langbehn spirit if infinitely better written is Rilke's touching poem 'Die Spitze' (1906), about the long-dead, blind lacemaker who put her eyes into the patterns in the lace:

> Menschlichkeit: Namen schwankender Besitze,
> noch unbestätigter Bestand von Glück:
> Ist das unmenschlich, daß zu dieser Spitze,
> zu diesem kleinen dichten Spitzenstück
> zwei Augen wurden?—Willst du sie zurück?
>
> Du Langvergangene und schließlich Blinde,
> ist deine Seligkeit in diesem Ding,
> zu welcher hin, wie zwischen Stamm und Rinde,
> dein großes Fühlen, kleinverwandelt, ging?
>
> Durch einen Riß im Schicksal, eine Lücke
> entzogst du deine Seele deiner Zeit;
> und sie ist so in diesem lichten Stücke,
> daß es mich lächeln macht vor Nützlichkeit.[12]

[11] On Heimat motifs in Rilke's work see Ulrich Fülleborn, ' "... die sich gebar im Verlust". Heimat in Rilkes Dichtung', in Rüdiger Görner (ed.), Heimat im Wort: Die Problematik eines Begriffs im 19. Und 20. Jahrhundert (Munich: iudicium verlag, 1992), 90–105.

[12] 'Die Spitze' I, Neue Gedichte, in Rainer Maria Rilke, Sämtliche Werke, Werkausgabe vol. ii, produced by the Rilke-Archive in collaboration with Ruth Sieber-Rilke, ed. Zinn (Frankfurt am Main: Insel Verlag, 1955), 518. 'Humanness: name for wavering possession, | still undetermined term for happiness: | is it inhuman that there went to fashion | this piece of lace's fine enwovenness | two eyes?—Do you regret their absentness? || You long-departed and at last benighted, | is all your bliss within this thing, where went, | as between trunk and bark, your lofty-flighted | feeling in magical diminishment? || Through some small chink in destiny, some gaping, | you drew your soul from temporality; | and it's so present in this airy shaping, | I have to smile at the expediency.' 'The Lace' I, in Rilke, Selected Works, ii. Poetry, trans. J. B. Leishman (London: The Hogarth Press, 1980), 167.

Through his recognition, the poet restores the lacemaker's alienated eye-sight, so giving meaning to the life of a simple woman but also himself drawing strength from that life. Rilke's poem celebrates a craft associated with the Low Countries and resonates with many paintings in the Dutch School so admired by Langbehn. But its opening line invokes the com-mon humanity which for Langbehn was but the lowest common denom-inator. For Rilke is not a German nationalist and rather consciously played the role of the wandering poet of modernity. But such a projection of rootlessness draws with it its antipode of a lost Heimat as the foil against which to define the modern experience. Thus in Rilke's Paris novel, *Die Aufzeichnungen des Malte Laurids Brigge* (1910), there is more vitality in the death struggles of the larger-than-life grandfather back in his rural world than in the death-in-life existence of the faceless denizens of the metropolis. In 'The Lace' the poet of modernity draws upon a popular craft and a simple woman, these in turn evocative of the high cultural tradition of Flemish and Dutch painting, to transmute a fragment of lace into a signifier of a realm of meaning and of identity beyond the ravages of time. To see that such transmutation of tradition into modernism is strikingly evident also in the visual arts one need only compare the work of a painter such as Leibl with the Alpine landscapes, or genre interiors, or stylized peasant motifs in the work of Wassily Kandinsky (1866–1944) and Gabriele Münter (1877–1962). Likewise, the old German or Dutch manner appears in the early work of Max Liebermann (1847–1935), before he fully developed his own Impressionist idiom and emerged as a leading figure in the Berlin Secession at the turn of the century.

Langbehn's aesthetic philosophy appealed to a wide range of artists and writers, then, who were by no means all in the right-wing camp. Yet a cultural definition of Germanness, which in embracing Rembrandt or Shakespeare might seem remote from power politics, could also fuel resentment at the mismatch between an indefinitely extensive tribal and cultural German realm and the actual body politic. Moreover, that Langbehn's cult of character rooted in soil was also explicitly a cult of manhood meant that his ideas could be appropriated to lend an aesthetic lustre to militaristic nationalism. 'Das Männliche ist der höchste Ausdruck des Menschlichen.' ('Manhood is the highest expression of humanity.')[13] Langbehn deploys the widespread metaphoric gendering of art—male artists combine within themselves feminine sensitivity with masculine creativity. Women, by contrast, embody the Heimat. They may excel in performance art such as dancing or in handicrafts: women make the

---

[13] Julius Langbehn, *Rembrandt als Erzieher*, 281.

babies or the bread, at most the lace. But men paint the pictures and write the poems. Freud too allocated to women the handicraft of weaving, a division of labour which persists into Edgar Reitz's *Heimat*, though Reitz would make amends to women artists in his second film sequence, *Die Zweite Heimat*. In contrast to the *Jugendstil* fashion of the 1890s with its fluidly metamorphozing, epicene figures, Langbehn's tract lent hard definition to Germanic manhood by locating it within a cosmos of mythic signs and essences. 'All that is solid melts into air' is the phrase from *The Communist Manifesto* which Marshall Berman took as title for his study of the experience of modernity.[14] As a bulwark against what the authors of the *Manifesto* call 'the everlasting uncertainty and agitation of the bourgeois epoch', Langbehn seeks to re-establish 'the fixed, fast-frozen relationships' of an imagined past by appeal to a conservative bourgeois aesthetic. Langbehn's aesthetics and the discourse of Heimat before the First World War belong together, then, in the same ambit. But turning now to the example of Clara Viebig's work, it remains to be seen whether the signs still convey the same message or become more melting and uncertain in a literary context.

Clara Viebig (1860–1952)

Clara Viebig, born a decade before the unification of Germany, lived to see the division of Germany following the Second World War. Like Ganghofer, Viebig was a prolific best-seller who, from the late 1890s to the end of the Weimar Republic, published her stories and novels in episode in a great variety of outlets before they appeared in book form, averaging a novel or anthology per annum over some thirty years. In the first decade of the century she was consistently among the top three best-selling German authors and up to the mid-1920s her work was published and reprinted in impressions of between 20,000 to 60,000 copies. Paralleling the rise of cinema and before the advent of television, Viebig's work exemplifies the modern phenomenon of mass distribution of culture across different levels of society. The press outlets for her stories and serializations signal her borderline status between literary ambition and popular entertainment, stretching as they do from intellectual and artistic journals such as *Die Deutsche Rundschau, Die Jugend, Simplizissimus*, or *Die Freie Volksbühne*; newspapers and political publications such as the *Frankfurter*

---

[14] Marshall Berman, *All that is Solid Melts into Air: The Experience of Modernity* (New York: Simon and Schuster, 1982).

Zeitung or the social democratic organ *Vorwärts*; magazines of some intellectual pretension such as *Westermanns illustrierte deutsche Monatshefte* or the *Berliner Illustrierte Zeitung*; to the popular family magazine, *Die Gartenlaube*, proverbial for propagation of escapist fantasy and the ostensibly apolitical, conformist ideology of the petit bourgeois *Spießer*.[15] Viebig's marriage in 1895 to the publisher Theodor Cohn ensured the publication of her work which was then so successful that she became one of the few authors who, quite apart from her husband's support, earned more than enough royalties to live on, until the Second World War when royalty payments ceased for a while and she lost much of her property. Her first book publication, the anthology of short stories *Kinder der Eifel* (1897), established Viebig's reputation as a regional writer, confirmed by the serialization in 1899 of her novel *Das Weiberdorf* in the *Frankfurter Zeitung*, published in book form a year later. *Das Weiberdorf* also marked her breakthrough as a best-seller in a *succès de scandale*, for just as Thomas Mann's *Buddenbrooks* (1901) attracted the hostility of the good citizens of Lübeck who recognized themselves in caricature in his novel, so Viebig's drastic Zolaesque picture of village women, driven by sexual and economic hunger because the men are all off in the towns working in factories, and her picture of a hypocritical and ineffective Catholic clergy, immediately drew bitter protests which forced a change of place name in mid-serialization from the real Eifel village of Eisenschmitt to an invented Eisendorf and finally to a thinly disguised Eifelschmitt when the novel appeared in book form. Far from being a pastoral idyll, *Das Weiberdorf* centres on social trends of the time when more than two-thirds of women in employment still worked in agriculture or domestic service and when the phenomenon of male labour commuting between villages and industrial cities was on the increase. *Das Weiberdorf* is a striking novel well worth study, in which the peculiar German mode of poetic realism is stretched to breaking point to become poetic Naturalism.[16] This is the closest Viebig ever came to a modernist aesthetic, for the incongruous stylistic juxtapositions mutually estrange the scientistic milieu study *and* the poetic vision of nature, so partially unmasking Naturalist fatalism *and* Heimat sentimentality as rhetorically driven discourses open to question. *Das Kreuz im Venn* (1908), the main text to be considered here because of the greater range of issues it addresses, is also critical of many aspects of provincial life, but shifts somewhat from the Naturalist idiom

---

[15] On Viebig's life, her place in the literary market, and the scandal over *Das Weiberdorf* see Barbara Krauß-Thiem, *Naturalismus und Heimatkunst bei Clara Viebig* (Frankfurt am Main: Peter Lang, 1991), 111–28.

[16] Gerhard Hauptmann's play *Hanneles Himmelfahrt* (1893) is a comparable experiment. See Krauß-Thiem, *Naturalismus und Heimatkunst* on the mix of Naturalism and Heimat in Viebig's work.

towards a less radical, realist mode and leaves the town and the village of Heckenbroich decently anonymous but for the regionally typical suffix '-broich'. Whereas *Das Weiberdorf* is almost an anti-Heimat novel, *Das Kreuz im Venn* belongs squarely in the Heimat mode.

In addition to novels of provincial life Viebig also wrote Berlin novels, such as *Das tägliche Brod* (1900) and its sequel *Eine Handvoll Erde* (1915) which deal with the alienation from her rural roots of a young woman who moves to the city to earn a living as maidservant.[17] Born and brought up in Düsseldorf at a time when the city was growing rapidly as an industrial and cultural centre, Viebig moved in 1883 with her widowed mother to Berlin where she lived for the rest of her long life, with the exception of a brief visit to Brazil to see her son who had emigrated in 1934 and the years between 1941 and 1946 when she moved to a small town in Silesia from which she was expelled at the end of the war along with the German population, returning to West Berlin where she died in 1952. Viebig is thus a writer whose stories and novels of rural life construct a milieu remote from her own metropolitan existence, though she was familiar with the villages and towns of the Eifel region from her childhood on. With the growing political polarization of cultural life in the 1920s Viebig became increasingly isolated. Having little in common with the radical writers of the Expressionist generation or with the left, though she had a friendship of many years with Käthe Kollwitz whose work had some affinity with her own, Viebig's conservative aesthetic and her rural themes might seem to place her more in the ambit of the regressively escapist *Blut und Boden* cult of a mythical peasantry which flourished during the Third Reich. Moreover, after the emigration of her son in 1934 and the death of her Jewish husband in 1936, Viebig, who was related to Hermann Göring, was not persecuted. Her work continued to be reissued if less regularly than hitherto, she was celebrated in the press as a Heimat writer on the occasion of her eightieth birthday in 1940, and her penultimate novel *Insel der Hoffnung* (1933), which deals with German–Polish tensions, is imbued with German nationalist feeling.[18] On the other hand, her particular ambiguous combination of Heimat motifs with naturalism or critical realism is different from the racist and ahistorical abstraction of *Blut und Boden* literature while her correspondence conveys Viebig's distance from National Socialism. To what extent, however, some features of her early successes might have affinities with *völkisch* ideology will be an

---

[17] For a highly critical discussion of *Das Weiberdorf* and *Eine Handvoll Erde* see Gisela Ecker, 'Wo alle einmal waren und manche immer bleiben wollen: zum Beispiel Viebig, Beig und Walser', in Ecker (ed.), *Kein Land in Sicht: Heimat—Weiblich?* (Munich: Wilhelm Fink, 1997), 129–42.

[18] On *Blut und Boden* writing see Uwe-K. Ketelsen, *Völkisch-nationale und nationalsozialistische Literatur in Deutschland 1890–1945* (Stuttgart: Metzlar, 1976), 72–8.

issue in now looking at her work in more detail while at the same time trying to avoid the reductive backward vision which looks only for symptoms, as if the Third Reich were the inevitable final phase of a cultural disease. Viebig's erstwhile enormous popularity and the difficulty of placing her work unambiguously make her an excellent case study to explore the problems of evaluating how far German culture differs from or parallels responses to modernization and social change in industrializing societies generally and to find perspectives which might link the popular literature of the beginning of the century to our own time without expunging the intervening terrible history.

Kinder der Eifel (1897): 'Simson und Delila'

Heimat marks the threshold between nature and culture. The physical place of childhood in the life of an individual, Heimat is also a social space in which the little animal is socialized to join humankind. In the period of Viebig's first successes, Heimat also connoted the rural or provincial roots from which urban industrial society was moving in a trajectory away from nature towards ever-greater civilization or, alternatively, alienation. Heimat is not only a geographical place or a social space, then, it is also imbued with time, whether the cyclic time of day and night and the seasons, the personal time of an individual's life phases, or epochal time shaped by historical change. The physical structuring of Heimat as liminal between the natural and the human environment, the ordering of the social space as an arena of power relations and conflicts played out through inherited and changing traditions and belief systems, and tensions between different modes of time measurement, whether cyclic and so essentially unchanging or epochal and historically changing, offer in combination a complex of factors through which to analyse Viebig's texts.[19] 'Simson und Delila', the first story in Viebig's *Kinder der Eifel* collection, may serve as a first example.[20]

'Simson und Delila' tells the story of Hubert, the son of the forest warden Willem Pantenburg. Against his will Hubert is apprenticed by his father to a shopkeeper in the town of Wittlach on the Mosel despite his mother's pleading on his behalf that he be allowed to take up forestry work. Hubert runs away to hide in the old ruined abbey of Himmerod, deep in the forest, but is persuaded to return to the fold by his mother,

[19] For a subtle, extended study of formal and aesthetic approaches to writing with provincial settings, see Norbert Mecklenburg, *Erzählte Provinz: Regionalismus und Moderne im Roman* (Königstein: Athenäum, 1981).
[20] 'Simson und Delila', in *Kinder der Eifel: Erzählungen* (Rustatt: Moewig bei Ullstein, 1994), 7–80.

only to be sent away to the town. Three years later, while on military service in Trier and having just received a letter from his mortally ill mother, he meets up again with his childhood companion, Susanna Endenich, nicknamed Suß, the daughter of a poor broom-maker who supplements his living by poaching and is thus the enemy of Hubert's gamekeeping father. Suß and Hubert go dancing and, like Don José in 'Carmen', Hubert, under the spell of Suß, misses the hour of return to the barracks and is in consequence refused permission to return home to see his dying mother. Three months later, after his mother's death and his father's indecently hasty remarriage to the very widow with property to whom he had been trying to marry off his son, Hubert returns home and, denied his inheritance from his mother, shoots and injures his father and runs away to hide in the ruined abbey where he is betrayed by Suß for the reward money of 300 marks.

Heimat in this story is divided between Hubert's childhood home and the surrounding woodland, this double realm in turn contrasted with the towns of Wittlach and Trier which, still within the region, scarcely mark a real break from the Heimat. Far from being a place of idyllic harmony the patriarchal household is riven by Oedipal conflict. In a Grand Guignol plot with fairy-tale undertones, the ogre-like father intervenes to divide mother and son, banishing the son, symbolically murdering the mother, and marrying the son's fiancée so turning her into a wicked stepmother. (The alternative plan to marry off the son to a wealthy older woman would have been another, if less total, assertion of the father's exclusive sexual and economic rights, comparable to plots about arranged marriages of young women to old men who may sometimes be their surrogate father or guardian.) Given the mother's failure to withstand the father's power, Heimat cannot be this terrible domestic scene but recedes to a secret woodland place of childhood games with Suß, the ruined abbey of Himmerod where Hubert twice hides, like an animal in its lair, first to escape being sent off to the town and then following the attack on his father.

Our first sight of the ruined abbey in the forest comes when Suß, hopping through the undergrowth like a little kobold, leads Hubert's mother there to bring her son back home before he is sent off to Wittlach. Its great ruined portal standing free in radiant moonlight amidst the surrounding canopy of trees has a stern grandeur softened by the dew-bespangled willow twigs growing through the crumbling masonry like tresses of hair. The abbey points back to an earlier age of faith from which the materialistic present has fallen away and evokes a utopian harmony of culture and nature and of masculine grandeur and feminine grace. But the woodland in Viebig's story is, like the domestic household, a disputed territory. The

German word 'Forst' is a false friend, for it does not designate 'forest', the English term for wooded wilderness, but rather woodland managed for timber and game. 'Wald' is the word for the measureless forest where panic may strike, though like 'forest', 'Wald' may also be an idyllic place of sylvan beauty or a utopian realm of human regeneration, like Shakespeare's Forest of Arden. Hubert's prosperous father, the 'Förster', is there to ensure that the writ of law runs to secure ownership and economic exploitation of the woodland. Suß and her poor poacher father, by contrast, are lawbreakers, the father transgressing against property rights, the wild, nut-brown daughter with her tangled tresses against the denatured and artificial feminine norms of respectable society. Sylvan lawbreakers traditionally oppose unjust laws which serve the rich and powerful and like Robin Hood they may even establish an alternative utopian order. Like Annette von Droste-Hülshoff's *Die Judenbuche* (1842), Viebig's story is implicitly critical of strict woodland enclosure, harshly enforced by Hubert's father, and of the consequent loss of traditional rights of foraging and wood-gathering so damaging to someone like Suß's broom-maker father. Thus, just as the childhood home is the arena of a deadly battle between patriarchal power and maternal love, so the economic value of the woodland Heimat, policed by the father, conflicts with its imaginary value, embodied in Suß and symbolized in the abbey. Heimat here connotes the blissful dream of emotional and erotic fulfilment in which oneness with the mother will transmute into union with the desired other. As children Hubert and Suß had dreamed of a greenwood life in the abbey and in many passages Suß appears to Hubert as the very spirit of the Eifel hills and woodlands of his youth. But the dream proves deceptive: as the mother, however reluctantly, had colluded with the father in drawing her son back out of his lair to send him away, so in the end Suß colludes with the law for the sake of the blood money, an outcome anticipated in descriptions associating her with a snake, a creature at home in a paradise from which she will help to expel her lover, so destroying the Edenic dream.

An outcome anticipated of course also in the title, 'Simson und Delila'. The enmities here are not tribal as in the biblical tale, however, but economic. The loss of customary rights of foraging and wood-gathering signals the capitalization of the rural economy which contributed to the pauperization exemplified in the Endenich household and to consequent flight from the land. There are other tiny signs of change: the birds which gather in autumn, as they always have, traverse, as they always have, vast tracts stretching far beyond the Eifel, but they now gather on telegraph wires which link distant places and so open up the Heimat (in a painting of 1909 by Kandinsky, *Eisenbahn bei Murnau*, telegraph wires and the rail-

Fig. 4. Wassily Kandinsky, *Eisenbahn bei Murnau* (*Railway near Murnau*, 1909), Inv.Nr. GMS 49, Städtische Galerie im Lenbachhaus, Munich

way drive through the pre-Alpine landscape and telegraph wires will be a leitmotiv signifying modernization in Reitz's Heimat film, set just across the Mosel from Viebig's Eifel in the Hunsrück); conversely the building of new, straighter, faster roads can consign villages, through which the mail coach once travelled, to a backwater, so increasing isolation and poverty. But the dream of Heimat is destroyed here less by modern civilization or urban encroachment than by gender and generational conflict shown as intrinsic to the traditional patriarchal family. Viebig's story is as much about Heimat as an imaginary dream of escape as it is about a real place. The story shows not a flight from the land to the city, but a doomed flight from the modern world into fantasy. By implication, Hubert's *Heimweh*, his longing to escape from life's prosaic trials into a maternal or erotically infused Heimat (the musical equivalent would be Debussy's *L'Après-Midi d'un faune*), represents an infantile failure of masculinity which helps to motivate Suß's contempt and final betrayal. (The man's dream of Woman, his failure to break the attachment to the feminine, unmans Samson before ever Delilah gets round to cutting his hair.) Yet Hubert's *Fernweh*, his dream of escape to the prairie-lands or virgin forests of America, is an equally regressive fantasy of true manhood which the American western

would play through in endless variations. (More realistically, in Gustav
Frenssen's *Jörn Uhl* (1901), the biggest selling Heimat novel of all, the
redundant farm servant Fiete Krey goes off to America as a settler to found
a new Heimat but returns to Germany many years later a failure, at home
neither in the Old World nor the New World.) Instead of going off to be
a settler, Viebig's Hubert creeps back into his woodland lair, succumbing
to a crisis comparable to the afflictions besetting heroes from Mann's
Hanno Buddenbrook, fleeing like a nymph from life's rough embrace
(*Buddenbrooks*, 1900), or Kafka's Gregor Samsa, creeping under his sofa
instead of going off to America ('Die Verwandlung', 1912) to Grass's
Mahlke in his underwater mousehole ('Katz und Maus', 1961). The
achievement of Manhood is a struggle made the more painful by the
failure of young women such as Suß, an ancestress of Grete Samsa or
Tulla Pokriefke, to play the supportive maternal role. (Of course if they did
take on a maternal role, they would immediately turn into a threatening
emotional entanglement.)

Rather than propagating a reactionary ideal, the plot of 'Simson und
Delila' undoes the dream. Yet the sometimes overwritten nature descriptions arguably reinscribe the idiom of the Heimat idyll, drawing the reader
into just the dreams of natural harmony which the plot undoes.[21] And if
Heimat is unmasked as illusion, there is no pointer to a way forwards to
combat rural poverty or the patriarchal tyranny which Oedipal father–son
conflict merely confirms. From a feminist angle too, the animalesque
images of Suß with her strong white teeth (another of these peripatetic
signifiers which also wander through the work of Thomas Mann, Kafka,
and Grass), her wind-blown hair, and snake-like wriggling through the
undergrowth evoke the stereotypes of woman as nature or the femme
fatale rather than awakening the reader to thoughts of the franchise campaign. It must be said too that if *Kinder der Eifel* opens with a deconstruction of Heimat in 'Simson und Delila', the dream is reassembled in the
closing story, 'Margrets Wallfahrt', where the heroine returns safely from
her pilgrimage, *virgo intacta* and hand in hand with a local boy-protector,
to the cottage where her mother waits, crossing the yard with its well and
the ruined goat stall transmuted by silver moonlight from signifiers of
poverty into markers of an idyllic homecoming. Such a homecoming
offers the illusion which Kafka undoes in his little sketch 'Heimkehr'
(1920), where an anonymous prodigal son traverses the farmyard, past
puddles and broken bits of farm machinery, towards an uncrossable
threshold back into an irrevocably lost Heimat. By contrast with innocent
Margret, Suß/Delila, the femme fatale with a head for figures, does have

---

[21] See Krauß-Thiem, *Naturalismus und Heimatkunst*, 149 n. 15 on this point.

some radical potential and Viebig would treat the pilgrimage theme very differently in her later novel, *Das Kreuz im Venn*.

Das Kreuz im Venn (1907)[22]

The stories in *Kinder der Eifel* deal with many issues, such as religious faith and superstition, female sexuality and moral convention, or who gets included or excluded from the Heimat (the disabled or mentally retarded are included and lovingly cared for by their impoverished families till their longed-for death; the dowry-less, pregnant farm servant or the anonymous draggle of Slovakian 'gypsies' are excluded), and deploy symbolically laden motifs such as the abbey in depicting landscapes, interiors, and figures. (The ruined castle in Reitz's *Heimat* gestures towards such symbols of a bygone order.) The weaving together in *Das Kreuz im Venn* of many such themes and symbols loses the stark concentration of some of the shorter texts, but represents a gain in complexity. It is less radical in its use of dialect, making it more accessible than, for example, *Das Weiberdorf*. On the other hand, the juxtaposing of several motifs, turned by repetition into leitmotivs, resists easy interpretation or the stark either/or judgements which some of the stories provoke: the meaning of the eponymous cross on a rock overlooking the Venn high moorland remains opaquely mysterious to the end. This multifaceted picture of life in an Eifel village and nearby small town leaves much for the reader to think about concerning rural tradition and modern progress. Seen through the green filter of environmental debate in our day, the novel takes on new life and is well worth study while also raising issues about the particular history of Germany.

Das Kreuz im Venn covers roughly a year and is set in an early twentieth-century present. Written in a loose sequence of episodes, the narration is multi-perspectival, being focused through several characters and sometimes through the impersonal narrator whose comments are, however, often an ironic refraction of communal attitudes and prejudice. The technique could be seen to accord with Zola's definition of the Naturalist work of art as a corner of nature seen through a temperament, or rather, like the constantly shifting focus of Thomas Mann's ironic narrator in *Buddenbrooks*, through several temperaments, though Viebig's narrator does at times offer authoritative commentary as Mann's does not.[23] The

---

[22] *Das Kreuz im Venn: Roman aus der Eifel* (Briedel/Mosel: Rhein-Mosel Verlag, 1997).

[23] On Zola's famous formula see Lilian R. Furst and Peter N. Skrine, *Naturalism* (London: Methuen, 1976), 31.

focus often shifts within a single chapter as episodes start up in mid-chapter, intertwining with other strands and ending before the chapter does or spilling over into the next. Rather than centring on one individual, this technique conveys the sense of a community and of life's mingled ups and downs, though key characters shown in depth and extended episodes do emerge to stand out against a chorus of minor figures and and a backdrop of shorter incidents. Such techniques, comparable to the episodic structure of Reitz's *Heimat*, are even closer than the film to the modern soap opera in being designed to sustain interest across chapter breaks.

Topography is a key organizing factor. Heimat is here a complex network of physically, economically, and metaphorically connected places imbued with material and imaginary values. The heart of the network, the North Eifel village of Heckenbroich with its straggle of smallholdings, each house surrounded by high, dense, 100-year-old hedges and by paddock land, is linked by a narrow road through woodland to the nearby small town down below in the valley. The village stands on high ground on the edge between wooded hillsides and the bare high moorland of the Venn. The moorland stretches to the Belgian border, but in some key passages is also figured as a boundless space which in springtime assumes the aspect of a pastoral Eden but which in the winter can become a deadly, featureless wilderness. The hedges of Heckenbroich which shield the cottages against the winds sweeping across the moor also shut out strangers, but the village cannot survive without the umbilical connection to the town (anonymous, but easily identifiable as Monschau) where the village girls work in the local cloth factory and where many of the men catch the train at the beginning of the week to go to work in factories in Düren or across the Belgian border in Verviers. (In contrast to agribusiness, part-time working of smallholdings supplemented by industrial wages remains still today a typical pattern in many regions of Germany.) The railway also connects the town with the regional capital, Aachen, seat of the Landtag from which modernizing policies to improve the rural environment and stimulate economic development issue. At the end, the mayor of Heckenbroich, Bärtes (Bartholomäus) Leykuhlen, grown in stature to become almost a folk-hero, is nonetheless about to leave the village to take up a seat in the Reichstag in Berlin as a member of the conservative Zentrum party. Like the Belgian border, the unseen metropolis signifies somewhere else that is not the Heimat. But nor is Berlin shown as antithetical to the village; it represents rather a national arena where the mayor will fight for local interests. This quite complex political and economic geography conveys a relationship of tension but not enmity between village and metropolis, between farming and industry, and between province and nation. It offers a fictional solution to the tensions in the German Reich between nationhood and older loyalties, for besides the politico-economic links to Aachen and Berlin, the village is also connected through religious faith and folk tradition to an extended cultural region: in a key episode, plumb in the middle of the novel, the village girl, Bäreb (Barbara) Huesgen, and her disabled brother, Dores, go on pilgrimage to a German equivalent of Lourdes, the festival of St Willibrord in Echternach, just south of Bittburg at the edge of the South Eifel. The two travel there by the regional railway system, a criss-crossing network of branch lines providing the material infrastructure which serves to turn local religious tradition into the modern phenomenon of a mass folk festival as thousands converge on the small town. The Oberammergau Passion Play is the most famous German example of such an event, which even in the late nineteenth century already drew an international public and today attracts visitors who jet in from all over the world to a peasant performance in a mountain village. In 1900, on the very threshold of the new century, Friedrich Lienhard celebrated the Passion Play as 'ein Sommerfestspiel in deutscher Landschaft' ('a summer festival in the German landscape'), contrasting a winter urban Shakespearean theatre of great individuals with the Festspiel mode as an old yet new form of communal expression which Wagner had dreamt of. Lienhard goes on to greet Adolf Bartels's call for Dionysian festivals.[24] The feast of St Willibrord is just such a Dionysian ritual as the pilgrims leap and jump along the long route through the streets to St Willibrord's well to pray for a cure for all manner of illnesses: Bäreb leaps on past the kindly fat man she had met on the train as he lies dying of a heart attack and, in a heightened state of ecstatic distance from everyday life, she loses her virginity in the perfumed night-time town park. Thus Viebig transmutes a Christian feast into a festival of life and death with pagan undertones.

The Heimat is linked or extended to other places, then, by outward movement as villagers and local townsfolk go to work in factories or sit in legislatures (mainly men) or go on pilgrimage (a girl and a mentally retarded child) so merging into a wider folk culture. But movement is two-way as outsiders enter the Heimat and are either integrated, or remain on the fringes, or else are excluded as permanent strangers. Social integration, marginality, or exclusion are conveyed topographically. For example, a regiment of soldiers is stationed in barracks located on the edge of the moorland, marginal both to the village and the town. Even in peacetime, the military, which draws together young men at their most

---

[24] Friedrich Lienhard, 'Oberammergau', in *Neue Ideale* (Leipzig and Berlin: Georg Heinrich Meyer, 1901), 139–53 (152). Anti-Semitic Bartels would not have been disturbed by the demonizing of the Jews as the murderers of Christ which was only recently cut from the Passion Play.

sexually active time of life and removes them from the constraints of their own Heimat, will impact on any community where soldiers are stationed. (This was true also of students until women were admitted to the universities.) Twice over the military disrupts Heimat in removing or introducing young men, so tending to turn young women into the embodiment of the lost Heimat which has been left behind or of the threatened Heimat which might be violated, but they serve also as the channel through which strangers might find a legitimate way in. The figures Viebig develops, two young officers, are further up the social scale than the military engineers in Marieluise Fleißer's play *Pioniere in Ingolstadt* (1929). (Fleißer's work, to which we shall return, provides a key link between earlier Heimat literature and critical or anti-Heimat literature after the Second World War.) They are also less sexually predatory than Fleißer's sappers: one of them is more the seduced than the seducer of the merry widow Helene, the sexy landlady of The White Swan (small-town hostelries, like metropolitan hotels and village inns, are always the scene of key encounters), and leaves the village physically and morally damaged; the other, penniless but aristocratic, is moved more by financial than sexual lust for the local factory owner's daughter and is safely integrated, economically and sexually, through marriage to a good dowry.

The thick hedges of Heckenbroich preserve the village maidens from the soldiers whose activities are concentrated in the town. More threatening is a penal colony of convicts, sentenced to hard labour to make the moorland arable. Their draughty, damp, barn-like dormitory is located well outside both town and village and stands out like a sore thumb, visible for miles around on the high Venn. This ugly eyesore competes with the cross as an antithetical symbol which signals the Heimat as the site of a battle between tradition and modernity. The convicts remain permanent strangers under the vigilant guard of their overseer, Simon Bräuer, himself something of an exile who longs for his wife and child back in Siegburg: what is Heimat for the locals may be a place of loneliness and exile for the stranger. At first, the convicts appear through the focus of the townsfolk as a demonized collective of dark, subhuman figures to be visited for a day out like a human zoo. But later the focus changes to a more differentiated, inward perspective centred on the most sinister of the convicts, the rapist nicknamed Rotfuchs (Redfox), a man driven by murderous sexual instinct whose brutish closeness to nature is signalled in his name. Rotfuchs is a supreme test for the integrative values of Heimat: is he to remain excluded as a monster or can nature at its most fallen be recuperated, man at his most degenerate or primitive be rehumanized or civilized? (The degenerate and the primitive mix ambiguously in Rotfuchs as in much modernist literature.) Viebig does redeem her monster through the instrument of a child, Kathrinchen Huesgen, but only at the cost of his death when Rotfuchs runs away less from the colony than from his urge to rape the little girl, only to perish like a wounded animal in the moorland wilderness. The little cowherd Kathrinchen and Rotfuchs together stretch the idea of nature to its idyllic and destructive extremes. Rotfuchs belongs in the rogues' gallery of those rapacious monsters who form a leitmotiv of modernist literature and film from the drunken incestuous father in Hauptmann's *Vor Sonnenaufgang* (1889), through Jack the Ripper in Wedekind's *Die Büchse der Pandora* (1892/94) and the eponymous hero of Brecht's *Baal* (1918), to the child-killer in Lang's *M* (1931) or Musil's Moosbrugger (a name which would suit the Venn landscape) in *Der Mann ohne Eigenschaften* (begun in 1924 though some material dates back to 1911). In our day too, paedophilia has become a hot issue testing the limits of liberal society and so-called community values, and dividing those who attack an overdue concern with male perpetrators to the neglect of female or child victims from those who are wary of the punitive demonization of sex criminals. Viebig's lucid rather than lurid presentation of Rotfuchs and Kathrinchen, however stereotyped the figures, does raise interesting issues and casts an oblique light on the more complex texts of high modernism. The overseer Bräuer, the animalesque prisoners, and the destabilizing effect of visitors to the colony would also make an interesting comparison with Kafka's story 'In der Strafkolonie' (1914).

If the soldiers are in part integrated whereas the convicts remain excluded, the most marginal figure is Josef Schmölder, the bachelor brother of the local factory owner. Rather like the younger brother Christian in Thomas Mann's *Buddenbrooks*, Josef is a bit of an outsider and eccentric who has travelled the world and on his return does not feel at home in his brother's household. But rather than going off on his travels again, he determines instead to traverse the Heimat to the very threshold with nature by living in an old hunting lodge up on the moor, taking Bäreb Huesgen with him as housekeeper, however, for it is inconceivable that a middle-class man in his forties, however close to nature, could cook or keep house for himself, as the narrator makes plain with a deal of subterranean irony. The experiment, which proves a failure, has two facets: one is the attempt at immersion in the natural environment, the other is the temptation of sexual union between the alienated intellectual and the village maiden, the two facets coming together grotesquely when increasing sexual tension indoors finds a musical accompaniment outdoors from the roaring stags in rut roaming round the lodge. But the erotic mood is brutally dispersed when brother Heinrich arrives at the start of the hunting season and shoots the stags. Immersion in nature almost proves deadly when Josef gets lost and wanders for hours in circles through the snowy waste in a scene anticipatory of the climactic chapter of Thomas Mann's *Der Zauberberg* (*The Magic Mountain*, 1924) where Hans Castorp too ventures further up the mountain than ever before, away from human habitation towards the last frontier, for human beings can only finally merge with nature in the dissolution of death, the consummation tubercular Rotfuchs does achieve. If Josef cannot cross the threshold to nature except at the cost of his life, he recognizes too that he cannot find a way back into Heimat through Bäreb who may live in the village but is no longer a village maiden, having a personal and sexual history unknown to him. The narrator too is rather discreet and the reader never learns why the ecstatic consummation Bäreb experienced at Echternach had no lasting consequences: Bäreb comes back, neither pregnant nor with a lover, to a rather low-key continuation of life as before (as Hans Castorp did after his moment of illumination). The episode of the bachelor and the village maiden would make an interesting comparison also with Kafka's last novel, *Das Schloß*. In their different ways, soldiers, bachelors, and rapists are difficult to integrate in the Heimat. These are all male types. The only problematic female is the sexy landlady, Helene, who risks going too far or getting too old. (By contrast, Sudermann's play *Heimat* of 1893 centres on an excluded woman artiste who returns from America and is finally reintegrated.) In contrast to male outsiders, the Heimat is largely figured through young women and little girls, for although Viebig's plot has lots of acid, sentimental images aplenty add sugar, especially the many glimpses of Kathrinchen in headscarf and sprigged skirts herding cattle in springtime or peeping out from behind the great hedge round the Huesgen cottage. Kathrinchen's mother is more in the Naturalist mode, left ailing by too many births and ground down by poverty.

Girls may embody Heimat as idyll, but Heimat in the heroic mode of spiritual leadership is conveyed through the mayor, Bärtes Leykuhlen. Leykuhlen defends traditional values and religious faith against the proponents of progress and science: von Mühlenbrink, the local representative on the Landtag, and the vet Dreiborn. The theme of tradition versus progress is argued out in an extended episode when drought and the fear of typhus strike the village and the mayor's earlier decision to spend money from a sale of common land on building a fine new church, the 'cathedral of the Venn', instead of investing in a piped water system, comes under criticism. Leykuhlen's great project is a motif which gestures towards various movements of the time for the preservation of monuments and conservation of landscapes through promotion of traditional or vernacular building styles. These are tendencies which later intensified in the struggle for dominance in the 1920s between Bauhaus modernism and the proponents of a conservative aesthetic, just as today too architecture remains an arena of shifting battle lines between traditionalism, modernism, and the parodic citation of tradition in the postmodern mode.[25] Urban neo-Gothic monuments in Germany's cities symbolized a continuity of cultural identity stretching back to the Middle Ages with an even stronger nationalist implication than English neo-Gothic, for the Gothic was popularly conceived of as the German style. Cologne Cathedral, begun in the Middle Ages, was completed only in 1880. Leykuhlen's cathedral of the Venn is a rural competitor, a grandiloquent assertion of local pride in German identity. Leykuhlen has chosen to express the spirit of his community rather than investing in physical hygiene. The modernizing bureaucrats come to test the village wells, several of which are ordered to be closed, but as the drought continues the people use the forbidden wells. In the end it turns out, however, that the typhus came not from the well-water which was good, but from drinking stagnant water up on the moor. Further negative aspects of modernity are the exhaust fumes of the growing number of motor cars racing through the village en route from Belgium to the Rhineland or the demand that the villagers should cut down the ancient hedges to open up their cottages to light and air (and to bureaucratic control). The hedges, in a vernacular style responding to the local climate and environment, complement the new church: hedges and church together express German Heimat. On the other hand, the sharp-tempered vet's efforts to introduce modern hygiene and scientific method in coping with a breeched birth (to judge from the English radio Heimat soap, The Archers, a continuing battle still today) are implicitly upheld just as the villagers' superstition and readiness to seek scapegoats are criticized. In his negative evaluation of the novel, Karlheinz Rossbacher suggests that the enlightened, liberal vet is presented as a ludicrous figure and that Viebig's title says it all: 'The cross on the Venn means in the novel both cross *and* Venn, religion and land-scape, earth-determined and a numinous, religiose orientated feeling for Heimat.'[26] But the author need not so simply be identified with her characters and the characters are more complex than Rossbacher allows. Nor is the calculus of plus and minus in judging new developments so straightforward: the cloth factory brings much-needed income, so help-ing to stem the haemorrhage of population into the cities (a point Edgar Reitz too makes through the optics factory in his Hunsrück village), but working conditions are exploitative and the cheap method of deriving cloth from rags presents health hazards; likewise Kathrinchen's summer

---

[25] On the significance of architecture and contesting versions of national identity see Rudy Koshar, 'The Antinomies of *Heimat*: Homeland, History, Nazism', in Jost Hermand and James Steakley (eds.), '*Heimat', Nation, Fatherland: The German Sense of Belonging* (New York: Peter Lang, 1996), 113–37.

[26] Rossbacher, *Heimatbewegung und Heimatroman*, 242.

work herding on the moor brings needed income and is arguably healthier than factory work, but it interrupts her schooling. (Child labour remains still today a difficult economic and cultural problem to solve.) Emotionally, the novel is weighted towards tradition if only because none of the modernizers is shown from within, whereas the mayor's agonizing through the long, hot summer confirms the moral integrity of his choice of priorities while making clear the undoubted value of piped water which he fully recognizes. Bäreb's pilgrimage too finds justification, albeit with grimly Kleistian irony, in that her mother's recovery from lingering depression is helped not only by her simple faith but by the death of much-loved yet burdensome Dores, the disabled child whom the pilgrimage was supposed to cure. Whether the closing distanced vision, focalized through Josef, of the terrible toll of sweated labour exacted by the Heimat from its inhabitants, the harsh exploitation of the convicts, the oppressive weight of tradition weighing down even a good man like Leykuhlen, effectively counterbalances the emotional pull is liable to differ from reader to reader. But it does avoid ideological closure and opens up the values of Heimat to debate.

If *Das Kreuz im Venn* can be accused of reactionary escapism, it is less through the plot or any anticipation of *Blut und Boden* than through such images as Kathrinchen herding cattle in the flowering moorland of high summer or being helped with her tangled knitting wool by Rotfuchs, which are a literary equivalent of sentimental genre painting—or of the photographs the tourists take at the feast of St Willibrord with their Kodak cameras, for Viebig does make clear that the picturesque Heimat is an outsider's perspective; the narrow alleys, little stairways, and grey slate roofs of the town which the tourists exclaim over (and still do today for Monschau is extremely picturesque) seem narrow and dark to the local Leykuhlen just as behind the image the little village girl presents to tourists passing through in their motor cars is Kathrinchen's poverty-driven labour which robs her of education. And yet Kathrinchen is pretty and sings her songs happily and is not just a victim, whether of environment or a sex murderer as she would become in a Naturalist novel. Thus Viebig highlights critically yet at the same time exploits the sentimental appeal of Heimat. Can the novel be accused of standing in a *völkisch* tradition on which National Socialist ideology would feed? Together Leykuhlen's anguished passion through the long drought as the villagers turn against him and the communal celebration when he is in the end justified lend him the aspect of a folk hero of the sort celebrated in the visual arts during the Third Reich while Hitler would draw upon comparable images of a Christlike leader suffering for his benighted people. The festival in Echternach too with its undertones of Dionysian merging of individuals into an ecstatic collective could seem to presage theatrical political rallies whipping up mass hysteria. But the open ending is demythologizing as Leykuhlen goes off to his prosaic work as a democratic representative and the novel has no trace of the exclusionary racist doctrine which is arguably the defining characteristic of National Socialism. The grim closing account of Rotfuchs's burial lacks the heroics accompanying the death of a Germanic Siegfried and the last image of the cross overlooking the black earth does not celebrate the German ploughed furrow, the *Scholle*, but conveys instead the costs of Heimat and its potentially oppressive narrowness.

2 A Land Fit for Heroes?
Ernst Wiechert's *Das einfache Leben* and
Marieluise Fließer's *Pioniere in Ingolstadt*

The First World War marked a huge watershed, both material and mental, as the great adventure, on which so many had euphorically embarked, turned into an orgy of senseless violence. Hopes nurtured by the more romantic enthusiasts that the cleansing flames of war would sweep aside the base materialism of a decadent modern age were dashed as trench warfare turned out to be a peculiarly modern affair of incompetent bureaucracy presiding over organized mass slaughter. In the German case, around two million men died in the war. A further eleven million who served in the armed forces survived, many of them, however, wounded or permanently maimed. Yet at the end of the war in the winter of 1918/19, the vast edifice of the German military forces unravelled with astonishing speed as over six million soldiers demobilized themselves and returned home within a period of some four months. But the very speed with which the army disintegrated left a vacuum. Faced with a collapse of discipline as the navy mutinied and the regular army melted away, the government turned to the Freikorps, paramilitary groups of right-wing mercenaries, for help in putting down revolutionary uprisings in Berlin and Munich in 1919, an action with fatal long-term effects in cementing the enmity between the social democrats and the communists and so setting the seeds for the later failure to form a united front against the National Socialists. The train of violence can seem in retrospect to have a fatal inevitability. As well as brutally putting down their fellow Germans, the Freikorps were used against Polish irregulars in the troubles accompanying the implementation of the Treaty of Versailles which provided for border changes and the loss of one seventh of former German territory with 6.5 million inhabitants, around half of whom were German-speaking and of whom some 700,000 came to Germany as refugees. Right-wing violence continued with assassinations of politicians such as the Jewish industrialist and statesman Walter Rathenau (1867–1922), with attempted coups such as the failed right-wing Kapp putsch of 1920 or Hitler's first attempt to seize power in the Munich putsch of November 1923, and with paramilitary acts of sabotage following the French occupation of the Ruhr in January 1923. After an all-too-short period of relative stability in the mid-1920s, mass unemployment along with increasingly violent confrontations and street battles between paramilitary formations across the whole political spectrum, right and left, fascist and anti-fascist, heralded the end of a republican order which could seem to have been doomed from the start by a militaristic culture of violence from which National Socialism sprang.

The militarization on an unparalleled scale of the male population during the war, the loss of so many lives with defeat as the only outcome, and the violence of the immediate post-war crisis and the early Weimar years left a bitter legacy of readiness to turn to military measures to answer political needs. But was this the readiness of a whole generation of men as has sometimes been fatalistically argued? What were the generation of men returning home from the front looking for? Did the failure of revolution in 1919, born of and destroyed by violence, already foreshadow the violent triumph of the fascist right? Or was the democratic constitution of the Weimar Republic a compromise which with more luck and political wisdom might well have survived? Richard Bessel has queried the theory of a monolithic 'front generation' of men psychologically crippled by war and prone to violence, arguing that the vast majority of German soldiers and sailors wanted nothing more than to return home and noting that the biggest recruiting ground for the Nazi Party was not those who had served, but those who were children at the time of the war.[1] Yet though many were left with a horror of violence and a profound sense of the absurdity of war, Bessel suggests nonetheless that Weimar politics were stamped by an extraordinary respect for, and even glorification of, things military. Nor is it surprising that the First World War cast a shadow across German culture and the arts during the 1920s and 1930s: how to make sense of the war, how to integrate the legacy of war and defeat in the post-war world, the meaning or meaninglessness of the war for those who survived, how to come to terms with death on such a scale? These were tormenting questions from which there was no easy escape. The great inflation of 1921–3 added to a widespread sense of confusion and fear which in some provoked violence but in many a great longing for security and stability. Yet the very desire for stability may have contributed to the catastrophic failure to cope with the huge changes affecting German society and hence also to the ultimate failure of the Weimar Republic. It is not just violence which is dangerous. The dangerous longing for stability could turn into a crippling inertia which found expression in illusory dreams of an idealized Heimat. Such dreams blocked the capacity to deal rationally with messy realities.

The discourse of Heimat as it functions in two very different texts may serve to exemplify the working through of the tormenting questions left

---

[1] Richard Bessel, *Germany after the First World War* (Oxford: Clarendon, 1995), esp. ch. 9.

by the war and the radically different answers which flowed from different political perspectives. How to find some meaning in the great defeat; how could the experience of the war and the knowledge of mass death be integrated in the continuing life to be led of those who had returned; could the concept of martial honour still have meaning and by what values should those who had served now live; what kind of Heimat should the returning soldier seek to build? These are the questions which Ernst Wiechert addresses in his novel of 1939, *Das einfache Leben*. As the title of her play, *Pioniere in Ingolstadt*, suggests, Marieluise Fleißer is concerned with military mores and the effects on the provincial Heimat when a sapper regiment is stationed in the town of Ingolstadt. Much shorter than Wiechert's novel, Fleißer's play too addresses, but in a highly subversive way, the value set on things military which was so marked a feature of Weimar culture. In contrast to Wiechert's novel which centres on male comradeship, women play a central role in Fleißer's text. One of the goods which it was hoped might follow the great evil of the war was the emancipation of women. Under the Weimar constitution the franchise was extended to women on a par with men and the 90 per cent turnout among women in the first elections of January 1919 as well as the forty-nine women elected to the National Assembly heralded a new age.[2] In the field of employment too things were changing. Although many of the jobs which women had taken on during the war reverted to men—a priority which most women too accepted so that by the mid-1920s the figure of 35.6 per cent of women in employment scarcely differed from the 34.9 it had been in 1907—the structure of female employment was changing with three times as many women in white-collar jobs as in 1907. Higher education had been opened to women in 1908, so that Marieluise Fleißer was able to study drama at the University of Munich, and under the Weimar constitution many formal barriers to women in the professions were dismantled in line with the constitutional commitment to sexual equality, though quotas still limited the numbers of women students and the growing economic crisis in the later 1920s strengthened the calls for women to return to their true place in the home. Thus pressure grew to roll back a key facet of the modern world as it was represented in the culture of the Weimar Republic, namely the perceived gender revolution personified in the figure of New Woman. By day the New Woman appeared as a bob-haired, short-skirted, athletic, young office worker who earned her own wage by her skills on the typewriter; by night she went out to cafés and danced the charleston, but could modulate into the vamp whose active sexuality threatened the

---

[2] On the position of women under the Weimar Republic and the Third Reich see Ute Frevert, *Women in German History: From Bourgeois Emancipation to Sexual Liberation* (Oxford: Berg, 1989), pts III and IV.

submissive love which, along with motherhood, was the essence of true womanhood. The New Woman is an urban creature significant by her absence from *Pioniere in Ingolstadt*, though whether she could exist in the provincial Heimat is the central theme of Fleißer's novel *Mehlreisende Frieda Geyer* of 1931. Fleißer's play and her novel form a critical foil both to the Heimat mode and to the urban myth of the New Woman who was largely a construct of male writers intrigued by or frightened of social change. The novel is if anything more centrally within the Heimat mode than the play, but since the play had such an influence on the revival of the Heimat mode in the 1960s and 1970s it will be our main text here. Fleißer's play dates from a decade earlier than Wiechert's novel, but it makes sense here to look first at *Das einfache Leben* because in offering an elaborate formulation and ambiguous defence of a martial ethos it illuminates the culture which was the context for the scandal provoked by Fleißer's devastating demythologization of military honour when *Pioniere in Ingolstadt* was produced in Berlin in 1929.

Ernst Wiechert: *Das einfache Leben* (1939)

Ernst Wiechert (1887–1950), the son of a forest warden in Masuria in East Prussia, studied at the University of Königsberg, taking the state examinations to become a teacher before serving as an officer in the First World War. After the war he resumed his career as a teacher first in Königsberg, then from 1930 in Berlin, resigning from his post in 1933 to devote himself full time to writing, helped by the gift of a piece of land from the Hitler regime. By that time Wiechert was widely recognized and was classed along with the right-wing cultural critics and nationalist-conservative authors who became associated in the early 1930s with the journal *Die Neue Literatur* edited by Will Vespers. These were the kind of established authors, critical of modern decadence and resentful of what they perceived as the dominance of the Berlin cultural scene by a left-wing clique, whom the Nazis hoped to win over to the cause. Wiechert proved unexpectedly resistant, however, and by 1936 came under attack by the Nazi newspaper, the *Völkische Beobachter*, for lack of positive spirit and failure to be properly anti-Semitic. Such attacks were prompted less by his writing than by public gestures such as his address on the topic of the writer and youth to students in Munich in 1935, in which he appealed for moral integrity and independence and which, to add insult to injury, was then published in the Moscow émigré journal *Das Wort*. A reading in 1937 in Cologne, interrupted by the Gestapo, from a text with a coded appeal for justice, his protest at the arrest of the Protestant theologian Martin Niemöller in 1937, and his public opposition to the *Anschluß*, the annexation of Austria confirmed by a plebiscite in March of 1938, finally prompted Wiechert's arrest by the Gestapo in May 1938. He was imprisoned first in Munich, then transferred to Buchenwald where he remained for four months. Despite such public acts of opposition, Wiechert was not prevented from publishing and on his release from Buchenwald *Das einfache Leben* came out in 1939. The novel was criticized in the Nazi press as an expression of individual defeatism, but enjoyed great success with the reading public. In 1939, Wiechert also wrote an account of his time in Buchenwald, *Der Totenwald*, which he buried in his garden, publishing it only in 1946. After 1945, Wiechert was for a few years one of the most widely read German authors, his reception being helped by his record of public resistance, but since then his stock has fallen somewhat, though recently there has been renewed interest. Yet if one aim of cultural study is historical understanding which avoids oversimplification, then the immediate public appeal of Wiechert's rather ambiguous novel—by 1941 it had already sold over a quarter of a million copies—as well as his record of initial closeness but subsequent opposition to National Socialism make his work worth studying. The following analysis will consider first the broad historical meaning of Heimat in Wiechert's novel within the context of Germany's defeat in the First World War, then look at the physical, economic, and ecological features of the experimental utopia which the hero sets out to construct as well as at the class and gender relations it entails, and will finally examine affinities between Wiechert's utopia and the reactionary ideologies of the *Männerbund* (male bond) and *Blut und Boden* (blood and soil).

Das einfache Leben, criticized by the Nazis for defeatism, is a utopian novel in the tradition of the so-called *Robinsonade* novels of the eighteenth and nineteenth century modelled on Daniel Defoe's *The Life and Strange Adventures of Robinson Crusoe* (1719).[3] Metaphorically, Wiechert's hero is a Robinson Crusoe who seeks to create a new existence on a remote island where he can be self-sufficient and lead the good life. Quite literally too, naval captain Thomas von Orla, like Crusoe, just escapes drowning when he is thrown overboard by mutineers at the end of the war in the midst of the great shipwreck of German national ambition. Orla survives and lives for five years in Berlin with his wife Gloria and his son Joachim, but is then suddenly gripped by the desire to go away and start a new life. His decision signifies that there can be no going back to things as

---

[3]   *Das einfache Leben: Roman* (Berlin: Ullstein, 1998). Page numbers in brackets following quotations and references refer to this edn.

they were before the war; a new way of life is needed if the war experience is to be integrated by the survivors. Wiechert's handling of the Heimat mode is in keeping with this theme. Orla comes originally from the Mark Brandenburg, the region around Berlin, but he does not return to his childhood Heimat which would signify the desire to return to things as they had been. In the grip not of *Heimweh* (homesickness) but of the opposite longing of *Fernweh*, he sets off to faraway East Prussia (where of course Wiechert came from), travelling a night and half a day in the train and then cycling for a further ten days before he comes upon an island in a remote lake surrounded by forest. Here he will embark on the experiment of making a new Heimat where he can lead the eponymous simple life. Determining there and then to live out his life and die in this quiet place, he takes over a fishing tenancy belonging to the elderly General von Platen who also owns the island and lives in a nearby country house with his granddaughter Marianne. The novel goes on to cover a period of some seven years, ending around the time when the Weimar Republic was drawing to a close, though no dates are mentioned. Nothing much happens: occasional visits from his son, one visit from his wife who comes to the island to die, friendship with a tiny handful of people in the locality, a fire in which a local woman dies, the cycle of the seasons. The most significant events are the arrival of Orla's Man Friday, able seaman Bilderman who had saved Orla's life when he was thrown overboard and who stays on to serve his master, and Orla's later decision not to marry the much younger Marianne von Platen despite their mutual love. *Das einfache Leben* belongs in a German tradition of long novels—*Der Nachsommer* (1857) by the Austrian novelist Adalbert Stifter is the crowning masterpiece—in which nothing much happens, or rather in which things such as marriages emphatically do *not* happen. Such parsimony of action is in itself the aesthetic reflex of an ideological position of disengagement from political activism. That the novel nonetheless remains readable testifies to the moral urgency of its response to Germany's troubled history which is conveyed in an intricate web of metaphor and through the interplay of the genres of Heimat and the *Robinsonade*.

Before Orla ever sets off, it is established that as a mariner he is more at home on the oceans of the world with their scattered continents and islands than he is in Berlin. The opening two paragraphs of the novel describe the exotic masks lining the walls of his study and the large globe which stands between his bookshelves. When Orla gazes down at the gently whirring, revolving globe, it is the metropolis of Berlin which becomes 'abseitig' (p. 360), that is remote or esoteric, the distant noise of city traffic sounding like breaking waves on some remote shore. Then again at the close of the chapter he sees the turning globe as 'die alte

Heimat' (p. 384), whereas here he is on a strange star. As the globe slows down, he sees Europe, then Berlin as a little dark circle amidst water and forests which stretch away eastwards across ever emptier space towards the mutilated border of the Reich (p. 385). He will go eastwards. Thus the first chapter establishes Orla's sense of alienation in post-war Berlin. It establishes too a metaphorical equivalence between going east to settle on an island in a lake in East Prussia and travelling the globe and being at home in the wide world: the simple life goes along with a universal spirit which knows no xenophobia and is familiar with the artefacts of distant peoples. This equivalence will later be underlined when Orla gives Marianne von Platen a gift of a Balinese sarong, thus making of her a utopian double image of the desired exotic Other who yet is also his beloved and familiar other self. This is in keeping with one strand in German nationalist ideology going back to the Romantic era, which held that the Germans were the universal people, theirs was a universal culture which would absorb and integrate the best of world cultures. Such an opening of Heimat to embrace the whole globe exemplifies too Derrida's idea of names or headings which designate at once a negative limit yet also a utopian opening of identity.[4] But if the name is to remain, so too must the limit which simply recedes before the utopian opening. Here the boundary, seemingly expunged in the global Heimat, returns twice over, in the little black circle on the map distinguishing Berlin from the surrounding water and forest and making the city 'abseitig' and in that mutilated border of the Reich: the new forest-encircled Heimat is defined in opposition to the metropolis; the global and the German Heimat are metaphorically equivalent, yet the latter undoes the former, for the global Heimat too is necessarily cut through by the mutilated border dividing the Reich from her eastern neighbours, in particular from Poland. In Viebig's *Das Kreuz im Venn*, the Belgian border was relatively harmless, the only threat coming across it being an increase of traffic through the village. Here a mutilated border suggests damage inflicted on a body and hence a lost wholeness and integrity. The novel nowhere explicitly seeks a restoration of wholeness, but how the metaphor of mutilation might be received by German readers in 1939, the year in which the Second World War began with the German attack on Poland, is a not very moot point. Later on Orla's Man Friday, seaman Bilderman, arrives at the border of the foreign or alien ('fremd') land which projects ('sich hineinschieben') into the Reich (p. 494). The verb is a loaded formulation, suggesting a foreign body pushing into the interior or inside of something else. The reader thus

---

[4] Jacques Derrida, *The Other Heading*, trans. Pascale-Anne Brault and Michael B. Naas (Bloomington, Ind.: Indiana University Press, 1992), 35.

has a triple choice between an unfocused global Heimat signified by oceans and exotic masks from nowhere in particular, and the German Reich as a Heimat of mutilated borders into which a foreign body intrudes, and Heimat as a house on an island on a lake in a forest in East Prussia, such multiple placenta-like envelopes protecting it from the other place, the city of Berlin, and from a wider Germany riven by conflict and shamed by historical defeat.

Turning now from external borders to the physical Heimat, its ecology and economy, here too, as in Viebig's *Das Kreuz im Venn*, the Heimat is internally segmented starting with its function as a threshold between nature and culture. Orla does not return to a childhood Heimat, but like Robinson Crusoe creates a new self-sufficient Heimat by the sweat of his brow. His labour will turn the land he works into a Heimat which can subsist within the larger natural habitat of the forests which are 'die eigentliche Heimat' (p. 386), the real home, of the creatures who fly and seek prey or else swim in the waters of the lakes. Just as the ospreys hunt their prey so too the human beings in this culture fish and hunt animals. But they also husband the habitat for the creatures they kill yet love. The aged fisherman, Petrus, rumoured to be a 100 years old, disappears into the lake and his body is never found; according to the locals he has gone home. As in Viebig's novel, only in death can human beings finally merge with nature though they may live in greater or lesser harmony with the natural environment. Yet even the forests are not a purely natural, time-less realm, but are managed and harvested though over a far longer time-scale than other crops. A key symbolic moment at the end of the novel is the General's decision to fell a stand of huge, more than a century-old pine trees and plant new mixed forest which Marianne will inherit, will nurture as habitat for the creatures, and will then pass on as an inheritance to later generations. The timescale of the growth of trees and their rooted attach-ment to a place construct an opposite image of linked temporal and spatial relations from the frenzied tempo of city life and the circulation of goods in a global market which means that what happens in New York produces crisis in Europe as remote events in a global space impact dis-astrously on the local place. In the pre-modern world time is bound to a particular locale, a place where those engaged in social interactions are all present to one another: a timescale of centuries and the majestic, still presence of trees slowly growing create an aura of slow, organic change. Perhaps for that reason, the forest is a key symbol in German nationalist discourse (as it is too in the olde Englishe oak forest where Robin Hood led his simple life). The decision to fell the trees yet the assurance that the von Platen family will continue to manage the forest puts down a fictional marker of continuity within change which in reality would be smashed a month or so after *Das einfache Leben* came out, when Hitler invaded Poland and so set in train the events which would lead to the final loss to the Germans of East Prussia.

Unlike Crusoe's island, ownership of this Heimat is clear from the start: the house, the land, the lake, and the surrounding forest belong to the von Platen family and will be inherited from her grandfather by Marianne von Platen who is just a child of 13 when Orla, then aged 43, first arrives. But like Crusoe planting corn, so Orla plants potatoes, and his physical labour wins him the right, recognized by the owner, to call the island home. He becomes, as it were, a stakeholder. Orla's integration into this sparse community is confirmed when the local Junker, Graf Natango Pernein, bequeaths him the use for his lifetime of the Pernein estate and country house which will revert on Orla's death to the heir to the title. (Pernein's name signals his Old Prussian descent, a point to be taken up later.) Thus the land belongs by inheritance to aristocrats, but honest labour bestows nobility of spirit upon those who work it. Further segments of the Heimat include agricultural land and a local village, but unlike Viebig's novel which centres on the twin communities of a village and market town rather than on a single individual, Wiechert's Heimat novel shades into the antisocial *Robinsonade* whose hero is the self-sufficient individual. Orla's few friends belong to the old provincial elites. They live in splendid isolation: it takes a journey of sometimes an hour or more to visit next-door neighbours who live miles away through the forest or across lakes. The lower classes figure only as feudal servitors: the forest warden; the old retainer; the house tutor (Wiechert was a private tutor before going to university). Although von Orla's labour wins him spiritual claim to the land, the same cannot be said of the local girls who toil at planting time, their feet naked in heavy shoes because the wet soil would ruin silk stockings (p. 431); unlike Viebig's young women who suffer tuberculosis or betray lovers for blood money, these girls remain picturesque ciphers without inwardness. The class question does emerge when Graf Pernein dies from a blow to the head during a stand-off with some farm labourers tired of working for 'the reaction', but it was a light blow without intent to kill— the count's death was due to his abnormally thin skull—and the chastened labourers disperse quietly. Rather like Thomas Mann's portrayal of the upheavals of 1848 in *Buddenbrooks* (1901), Wiechert here plays down class politics in order to stress local, quasi-feudal bonds so that the death of Graf Pernein is transmuted into an almost natural outcome of weakened stock and the reader is left with a vague, melancholy sense of a metaphoric need to fell and replant. But what that might mean literally remains obscure. Class conflict also figures when on first arrival, Orla takes over the tenancy from a one-time revolutionary, Christoph, who is condescendingly depicted almost with affection. The two men competitively display flags emblematic of their opposing political allegiance at the time of the troubles from which the Weimar Republic was born: Orla's a torn remnant from the pre-war red-white-black flag of the Reich which he was clutching when thrown overboard, the would-be Bolshevik's a torn red flag. 'Stolz weht die Flagge Schwarz-Weiß-Rot von unsres Schiffes Mast' was a popular naval song during the First World War. The confrontation is reminiscent of the two grandfathers, one revolutionary, the other conservative, in Thomas Mann's *The Magic Mountain* (1924) who yet both belong in an overarching European humanism. Arguably, then, Wiechert's novel represents a plea for an end to class-based politics, but from an ultra-conservative position which defends inherited privilege as the guarantee of good husbandry. This is utopianism in the negative sense of failure to face up to bitter realities of urban, industrial Germany which were not susceptible to solution through feudal bonds of sympathy.

A telling absence in the symbolic confrontation between two old warriors is the new swastika flag. More bitter than the division between Bolshevik Christoph and conservative Orla is the generational battle line dividing Orla from his son. Joachim is both militaristic and snobbish: as a young German he feels a sense of betrayal by his father's generation which he longs to avenge. This generational difference is in keeping with historical evidence suggesting that it was the less the front generation than those who were children during the war who formed the breeding ground for National Socialism. Joachim's bitterness is a veiled allusion to the myth of the stab in the back, which blamed Germany's defeat not on her army but on weak political leadership. In a sequence of explicit moral confrontations with Joachim, Orla defends the generation who died in their millions in the war, pleads for a pacific politics to avoid a repeat of such mass slaughter, and upbraids his son's snobbery: Orla has returned from the war full of chastened solidarity with the millions of ordinary men who served and is fired by moral outrage at privileges for officers over their men.[5] His comradeship with Bildermann symbolizes this most basic commitment to the men, whether they died or survived, who fought in the Great War. The new Heimat can almost include an old Communist, then, who is at least moved by idealism, but not Orla's unimaginative son who has no conception of the terrible suffering of those who died and of their parents such as forest warden Gruber and his poor wife, driven mad by the thought of her son burnt to death on a torpedoed warship. The moral commitment to post-war solidarity between the officers and men of the

---

[5] See Jürgen Kocka, *Klassengesellschaft im Krieg 1914–1918* (Göttingen: Vandenhoeck and Ruprecht, 1977).

front generation might salvage something of value and so assuage the threat of meaningless absurdity posed by slaughter on such a scale and to no purpose. But the moral commitment is never translated into a political stance. Instead it takes the form of a male bond between Orla and the devoted Bildermann, extended to embrace also the old General, which leaves class difference untouched. Indeed caste differences add sentimental pathos to the bond. As a social space, this new Heimat is an ultra-conservative utopia ruled over by the military caste of the Prussian Junkers, the landowning squirearchy from whom the officers in the German army were disproportionately drawn. It is not just Orla's labour which wins him acceptance, but the distinction of his name, *von* Orla, and his status as a frigate captain. All this belongs in a hierarchical tradition of Prussian militarism, although as General von Platen muses, the navy was always more associated with the Reich whereas the army was the child of the Kingdom of Prussia, so that the General's friendship with naval Orla represents an opening to change within the East Prussian elite (p. 542). To a reader at the end of the twentieth century this is a sinister not to say grotesque consummation. In the late 1930s, such an ultra-conservative concern with overcoming division between the Kingdom of Prussia and the Reich is strangely out of time, representing a throwback to the particularism which had been one aspect of the discourse of Heimat in the nineteenth century. In the obscure coding of the 1930s it is ambiguous: the positive presentation of Junker nobility obliquely expresses distance from the anti-aristocratic *völkisch* populism of the Nazis and from Hindenburg's mistake in opening the way for an upstart like Hitler, but it also values a code of martial honour, underpinned by older regional and feudal loyalties, turned to the service of the nation. It was just such a combination of honour and nationalism which inhibited opposition among the military elite who had no great love for the Austrian corporal, an inhibition briefly and tragically overcome in the officers' plot of 1944 at a time when it was already clear that Germany could not win the war. Thus Wiechert's novel attacks militarism, revanchism, and hierarchical arrogance in the figure of Orla's son Joachim, yet sustains a code of martial honour in the service of nation which helped to deliver Germany's military elite into the hands of the Nazis.

Rather than a socialistic overcoming of class difference, the friendship between Orla-Crusoe and Bildermann-Man Friday comes close to the ideal of the *Männerbund*, the bonding of men in proto-militaristic comradeship, as, for example, in veterans' associations such as the Stahlhelm or as advocated by ideologues like Hans Blüher (1888–1955), a founding figure in the *Wandervogel* youth movement which had started in the early 1900s with a view to introducing urban youth to the countryside and so had affinities with the Heimat movement. In the immediate aftermath of the war Blüher's magnum opus, *Die Rolle der Erotik in der männlichen Gesellschaft*, came out in two volumes in 1918 and 1919. Blüher, at this point still an admirer of Freud, advocated an ideal of male eros fuelled by the sublimated sex drive as the highest expression of human nobility in contrast to the baser sexual attraction between men and women which subserved the animal function of propagation of the species. (By the mid-1920s Blüher, well in tune with the times, had turned anti-Semitic, though his ideas on male friendship proved too radical for the National Socialists, colliding as they did with the anti-homosexual tendency which came to prevail, especially after the murder in 1933 of Ernst Röhm, the homosexual leader of the SA (Sturmabteilung) who also represented the more radically socialist trend within the movement.) At first sight Wiechert's new Heimat for the heroes who have survived the cleansing flames of war does seem rather close to the *Männerbund*. As Richard Bessel suggests, fault lines in the Weimar Republic divided not only the front generation from their children but also from women in a demography skewed by the death of millions of men.[6] The traumas of war fuelled resentment of women which could take the form of irrational misogyny, as Klaus Theweleit documents from letters and diaries of Freikorps soldiers in the first volume of his study *Männerphantasien*.[7] Moreover, in the post-war world of the roaring twenties, widespread fears of a breakdown of traditional order focused on a new kind of woman who was perceived to pose a threat to male supremacy both in taking jobs from men and in her frenzied pursuit of pleasure. Orla's wife is an absolutely stock figure: the New Woman as vamp. Gloria is a neurotic, sexually voracious drug addict in thrall to the decadent pleasures of the cinema and dancing. A bad mother only redeemed in death, she is metaphorically equated with the city. Thus when Orla sets off to his island, he leaves behind a son, a wife, and the city as the three ills of militaristic revanchism, decadent modernity, and urban anomie to be overcome in the new utopian Heimat. He and Bildermann form a homoerotic if not homosexual duo. (Sailors in uniform were in the 1920s already a popular signifier of homosexuality, but it would take an overly dirty mind to read Bildermann in this way.) On the other hand, Wiechert's novel has none of the cruder misogyny of the extreme right. The notion that women did not suffer as did male heroes is undone in the figure of Frau Gruber who so identifies with her dead son, burnt to death in a torpedoed warship, that it is as if she had been there. Heimat is often symbolized in a maternal figure: poor mad Frau Gruber

[6] Bessel, *Germany after the First World War*, 271–2.
[7] Klaus Theweleit, *Männerphantasien*, i. *Frauen, Fluten, Körper, Geschichte* (Reinbek: Rowohlt, 1980).

symbolizes Germany as a pale mother wounded beyond recovery by the death of her sons; that Bildermann is able to comfort her a little signals distance from the misogynistic extremes of the *Männerbund*. In contrast to Frau Gruber, the hope for a future Germany is embodied in a young girl, Marianne von Platen. But the failure of the plot to reach closure in the traditional happy ending of marriage between Marianne and *either* the father *or* the son indicates present ills in Orla's generation which are too deep to be cured and distance from a resentful younger generation of men. Hope is postponed to an unknown future. Instead of a wedding which would signify the full integration of Orla into the Heimat, the climactic moment is a collective funeral for some twenty unknown soldiers from a local regiment whose bodies have been belatedly recovered from a collapsed trench. Thus *Das einfache Leben* undoubtedly taps into the emotions at play in the comradeship of veterans, but points to a future symbolized in heterosexual love which will bloom again only when the dead have been finally laid to rest. This outcome is yet another facet of a novel based upon a principle of appropriating and attempting to redirect conservative and even reactionary discourse to humanistic ends in opposition to the politics of National Socialism.

Racism is arguably the defining characteristic of the National Socialist movement, differentiating it even from allied movements such as Italian fascism. One common device of Heimat as an ideological discourse is to deploy a bounded location with the effect of silently excluding problematic issues which happen elsewhere, so that the technique of reading for absences is a peculiarly appropriate approach. Thus the controversy over Edgar Reitz's *Heimat*, located in a village with no Jewish inhabitants, centred on its silence on the Jewish question. Jews are a notable absence in Wiechert's novel even though *Das einfache Leben* was published a year after the *Kristallnacht* when the National Socialists launched attacks all over Germany on synagogues and Jewish property. (Given the lack of approval, silence was necessary, of course, if the novel was to be published.) The sheer scale of Jewish deaths in the Holocaust can, however, lead later generations to forget that anti-Slav racism was also a major feature not just of National Socialism but of German nationalism and, indeed, more obviously subserved German expansionist interests than did anti-Semitism. It is notable that, despite the length of *Das einfache Leben*, the Polish question is strikingly absent, making the few mentions of matters Polish all the more significant. The motifs of the mutilated border and of the projection of the strange land into the body of the Reich, an allusion to the Polish corridor giving Poland access to Danzig and the sea, have already been discussed and do send out a nationalist territorial message. The first people Orla meets when he arrives in the region are the forester Gruber and his wife. Gruber mentions local fears of the Poles, the hard life hereabouts due to flight of the young people from the land, and millenarian dread of apocalyptic catastrophe (pp. 391–2). Orla responds that the German people will recover from the confusions of the time, a vague formulation which gives no hint of what form the recovery might take and from what troubles in particular; this is the coded language of 1939 which different readers no doubt decoded in different ways and is certainly open to a German-nationalist reading. That Gruber is a Catholic and that the Gruber children's facial features indicate an inheritance from peoples stretching as far as Asia suggest, however, that Wiechert had no sympathy either with Prussian Protestant ascendancy or with notions of racial purity. One trace of Polish culture this side of the border is the call of 'Jilk, Jilk' which the beaters still use to drive the game out of cover, recalling how a predominantly Polish rural population served German landowners. These linguistic traces are presented as a colourful feature of the specialized vocabulary of the hunt. In the code of the times, this tiny detail conveys distance from linguistic purism as a facet of nationalistic propaganda going back to the doctrine, propagated by Fichte or the Grimm brothers in the nineteenth century, which defined German ethnic identity with reference to the German language. The enrichment of German by traces of the language of her neighbours is in line with the liberal ideal of a German culture open to other influences, though Wiechert's 'Jilk, Jilk' sends only a minimal signal compared with the large French element in the Eifel dialect in Viebig's stories. In sum: here too Wiechert's novel sends mixed signals in appealing by implication to German territorial claims following losses due to the Treaty of Versailles, but in rejecting biological racism.

There would seem also to be a clear rejection of biological racism in the highly sympathetic portrait of Graf Natango Pernein whose name signals descent from the Old Prussians, a Baltic people in the same linguistic group as Latvians and Lithuanians who were displaced by the German invaders in the late Middle Ages. Other contexts could, however, put a more sinister slant on the figure of Natango Pernein. For example, one trend in historical linguistics argued that the Nordic races had spread out eastwards as a *Herrschervolk* (master race) rather than arriving *from* the East as the term Indo-Germanic might seem to imply: on this theory Scandanavian languages and a Baltic tongue such as Old Prussian originated together with the Germanic languages in a Nordic linguistic Heimat in contrast to Romance and Slav languages.[8] Such Nordic ideology went

---

[8] See e.g. Dr Matthaeus Much, *Die Heimat der Indogermanen im Lichte der urgeschichtlichen Forschung* (Jena: Verlag Hermann Costenoble, 1904).

back to the nineteenth century, notably to Julius Langbehn's *Rembrandt als Erzieher* (1890) which valued the North German genius of Shakespeare and Rembrandt. Rembrandt's art was healthy: 'die heilende Kraft der Scholle spricht aus ihm . . . Bauernseele ist Volksseele'.[9] Such ideology reached its apogee in Richard Walther Darré's tracts of 1929 and 1930 respectively, *Das Bauerntum als Lebensquell der nordischen Rasse* and *Neuadel aus Blut und Boden*. When the National Socialists took over power in 1933, Darré became *Reichsbauernführer* (Peasants' or Farmers' Leader) and Minister of Food and Agriculture.[10] Darré preached a mystical bond of identity between the German peasant and the land he tilled and propagated self-sufficiency in farming. In this light, the sympathetic portrayal of Pernein would not signify rejection of racism but commitment to a German imperialism with racist undertones which simply assimilated intermediary ethnic groups such as the Sorbs or Old Prussians into the German *Volk*, as Langbehn had assimilated Rembrandt or Shakespeare to his Low German pantheon. On the other hand, Natango Pernein, as a descendent of the Old Prussians who were displaced by the Teutonic Knights in their colonizing drive eastwards, could represent the residual survival of a wronged people driven from their Heimat; there is a brief, joking allusion to this effect. But Pernein's bequest of his estate and mansion house in recognition of Orla's worthiness of such an inheritance could fall in the ambit of an aggressively nationalistic historical geography which operated with the concepts of *Volksboden* (folk or ethnic soil) and *Kulturboden* (cultural soil) and which, like the Nordic theories, simply expunged claims which intermediate peoples might pose by drawing them in under the hegemony of the Germans as the advanced *Kulturvolk* intrinsically fit to hold power over more primitive peoples. *Volksboden* designated areas settled by Germans, where German was spoken, and where the results of German industriousness were evident. As Orla travels towards his island he moves through a landscape of farmland and villages which become more and more primitive the further east he moves. The excellence of his own husbandry signifies his growing right to claim his island as Heimat because of the labour invested in it. (Such an idea descends from the imperialist and capitalist doctrine underlying Defoe's novel and Locke's concept of private property.) German *Kulturboden* was interspersed among areas controlled by other ethnic groups and was also characterized, as the geographer Albrecht Penck put it, 'by an extremely

---

[9] 'the healing power of the soil speaks from his work . . . the peasant soul is the soul of the *Volk*'. *Rembrandt als Erzieher: Von einem Deutschen*, 4th edn. (Leipzig: C. L. Hirschfeld, 1890), 193.

[10] On Darré and National Socialist agricultural policy see Colin Riordan, 'Green Ideas in Germany: A Historical Survey', in Riordan (ed.), *Green Thought in German Culture: Historical and Contemporary Perspectives* (Cardiff: University of Wales Press, 1997), 3–41 (24–6).

careful form of cultivation, which does not grind to halt when it encounters difficulties'.[11] The difference between *Volks-* and *Kulturboden* was highly subjective and both could serve as foundation for territorial claims. Thus Penck claims that characteristic German soil cultivation extended to the Russian border: 'This was the great frontier of civilization that German soldiers were so aware of as they marched eastwards. It is so vivid that one can observe it oneself from the train.'[12] As indeed Orla does. But whether the more primitive cultivation he observes from his train window heralds the simple life Orla longs for or a backwardness which his labour will overcome so establishing his moral claim to the land is unclear. Once more Wiechert's novel is Janus-faced: the primitive landscapes and villages may be a positive value to be set against the city or a negative value to be transformed by sweat and toil into a German Heimat. In the latter case Thomas von Orla, in whom nobility is harmonized with the peasant spirit of the German *Volk* and who shares the ideal of self-sufficiency propagated by Darré, comes dangerously close to becoming a hero in the *Blut und Boden* mould as a peasant-aristocrat who goes through a double apotheosis as an aristocrat turned peasant, who is then re-ennobled by Pernein's bequest.

Wiechert's novel is unmarred by biological racism, but could it be accused of cultural racism in deploying the emotionally laden iconography of *Blut und Boden* which was bound in 1939 to appeal to an extreme, reactionary nationalism close to if not identical with National Socialism? The novel abounds in strong visual images of landscapes, forests, and manly labour. Thus Orla and Bildermann take on the job of felling the great pine trees for the sheer pleasure of it in a scene close to Heimat kitsch and dangerously reminiscent of the popular yodelling song 'Die lustigen Holzhackerleut'. The pathos is heightened by the contrast between muscular men and a delicate, pure-faced girl when Marianne brings them their well-earned dinner in the traditional double pot and then gazes at Orla's face as he sleeps, tired out by manly labour. The masculinity idealized in Wiechert's novel is culturally regressive: in many phrases scattered through the length of the novel Orla is associated with pre-modern even medieval ideal types of the warrior, the peasant, and the celibate monk.[13] The female body symbolic of the Heimat as object of

[11] 'Deutscher Volks- und Kulturboden', in *Volk unter Völkern: Bücher des Deutschtums*, i, ed. K. C. von Loesch (Breslau, 1926), 62–73 (64), cited in Michael Burleigh, *Germany Turns Eastwards: A Study of Ostforschung in the Third Reich* (Cambridge: Cambridge University Press, 1988), 26.

[12] Ibid.

[13] On the continuing history of the archaic figures of the peasant, the artist–priest, and the warrior in right-wing literature during the Weimar Republic see Ulrike Haß, *Militante Pastorale: Zur Literatur der anti-modernen Bewegungen im frühen 20. Jahrhundert* (Munich: Wilhelm Fink, 1993).

longing is here that of a fragile girl-child and the desire she evokes is tinged with paedophiliac undertones. That the maiden bringing the double pot is a wealthy landowner adds a note of phoney sub-Rococo pastoralism in a tradition going back to Marie Antoinette got up as a shepherdess. Another such moment comes when Orla harvests his first potato crop. The first sandy potato he cradles in his hand is a mythic signifier, in the mode analysed by Barthes, which could feed into the discourse of German nationalism to incalculable effect on a reading public in 1939. (Brecht's poem of 1937, 'Traum von einer grossen Miesmacherin' ('Dream about a Great Grumbler', subtitled 'During a Potato Shortage'), which depicts a huge potato fading away with hunger as Hitler bellows about honour and glory is a comical deflation of such mythic tokens.) Whereas Viebig explicitly thematizes the perspectival nature of Heimat imagery in noting that locals do not perceive their town as picturesque and in the motif of the tourists with their Kodak cameras, Wiechert eschews alienation effects in his descriptive writing and indeed makes Bildermann into the guardian of authenticity who tries to stop a journalist from taking photographs, lest reproducible images in city newspapers tarnish the authentic aura of Heimat. Yet the many pathos-laden moments could be seen as non-racist revaluation of *Blut und Boden*. The sandy potatoes, baked on an open fire and grown by traditional methods by two men who together with their few friends could almost constitute a commune, have that proto-green appeal which has been a utopian aspect of Heimat through all the twists and turns of the mode: small is beautiful. Of course, green communes always risk pandering to the psychologically regressive longing to escape complex problems of the modern world into the simple life. But the very proximity of Wiechert's novel to National Socialist ideals is perhaps a measure of its author's striving to recuperate green values from a regime he opposed. It is the very narrowness of the dividing line which makes the novel interesting as a document of its time.

Marieluise Fleißer (1901–1974)

Although Wiechert had his difficulties with the National Socialist regime, his work was sufficiently coded to avoid being banned. Marieluise Fleißer's literary career was, by contrast, cut short when the National Socialists assumed power and her books were among those burned by the Nazis in 1933 in a demonstrative ritual designed to silence opponents and draw waverers to heel. Although Fleißer's work was not overtly party-political, it was ideologically and aesthetically antithetical to the literature approved by the new regime, quite apart from her association with Brecht which would in itself have drawn official hostility. Fleißer was born and brought up in Ingolstadt where her craftsman father made jewellery and ran a hardware shop. Her mother died when Fleißer was just 17; that and her education away from home in a convent school in Regensburg may have something to do with the lack of mother figures in her work, though there is a frightful prospective mother-in-law in her novel *Eine Zierde für den Verein* (1968; originally *Mehlreisende Frieda Geyer*, 1931). After her schooling, Fleißer went on between 1919 to 1925 to study drama in Munich where she met Brecht in 1924. They became lovers and Brecht encouraged Fleißer to come to Berlin, where he arranged the première in 1926 of her first play, *Fegefeuer in Ingolstadt*. Brecht also took an interest in *Pioniere in Ingolstadt*, encouraging Fleißer to write the play in the first place and suggesting amendments after the unsuccessful première in Dresden to make it more sexually provocative for a Berlin production, which duly came to pass in 1929 in the Theater am Schiffbauerdamm where Brecht's *The Threepenny Opera*, with the musical score by Kurt Weill, had opened the previous year. The amendments look as if they may owe something to Frank Wedekind's play about adolescent sexuality, *Frühlings Erwachen* (1889)—Brecht was a great admirer of Wedekind. They include the heroine's loss of viginity to a soldier in a rhythmically rocking barrel and a schoolboy discussion of the female anatomy, additions on a par with Wendla's on-stage loss of her viginity or schoolboy Melchior's anatomical drawing of the sex act in Wedekind's play. But whereas the sexual explicitness in *Frühlings Erwachen* is in tune with a grotesquely surreal theatricality which oscillates between comedy, tragedy, and farce, the laddish inserts in a woman's view of sexual conflict stood out awkwardly in Fleißer's more understated theatrical language. The provocative additions duly drew scandalized reactions, heightened by outrage at the impropriety of a woman author daring to besmirch German military honour. Disillusioned by her experience of hectic city life and by the humiliation of a very one-sided affair with Brecht who had several other lovers, Fleißer finally made a break in 1929 and became engaged to Hellmut Draws-Tychsen, an editor of the right-wing newspaper, the *Berliner Börsen-Zeitung*. This was a move out of the frying-pan into an even more painful fire, for Draws-Tychsen, a writer of pretentious pseudo-mystical texts full of the exotic primitivism which had long been an aspect of modernism (as witness the masks in Orla's study), was as arrogant, more exploitative, and massively less talented than Brecht.[14] In

---

[14] On Draws-Tychsen see Günther Lutz, *Mareluise Fleißer: Verdichtetes Leben* (Weiden: Obalski and Astor, 1989), 111–19.

1929 Fleißer published a volume of short stories which was well reviewed but sold only 2,400 copies; in 1931 her novel *Mehlreisende Frieda Geyer* came out selling only 1,196 copies, while a volume of travel writing of 1932 sold a mere 374 copies. The downward slope was clear. Through the years in Munich and Berlin, Fleißer had returned intermittently to Ingolstadt where she had a long-standing friendship with Josef Haindl whose family ran a tobacco and spirits business in the town and who wanted to marry her. A failed attempt at suicide, ever more bitter rows with Draws-Tychsen, then the book-burning in 1933, the departure into exile of literary colleagues, and her own financial problems together explain Fließer's return to Ingolstadt in 1933 where she finally gave way to Haindl's pleading and married him in 1935. Subject to a partial publication ban— she was still able in the 1930s to publish the odd story in newspapers, but not in book form—worn out by work in Haindl's business, having suffered a nervous breakdown in 1938, and drawn into auxiliary work in a munitions factory in 1943 as the war effort came to affect virtually the whole population, Fleißer found it impossible to continue writing. After the war, she did write a few pieces, a new play was premièred in Munich, and she was invited by Brecht in 1956 to come to East Berlin, but, bound by loyalty to her now sick husband who died in 1958, Fleißer refused and stayed on in Ingolstadt . The great turn in her fortunes came in the late 1960s when Fleißer's work was discovered and celebrated by a new generation of playwrights, notably Franz Xaver Kroetz and the film-maker Rainer Werner Fassbinder. By the time of her death in 1974, Fleißer's plays were being regularly performed and editions of her work, in some cases substantially revised, had come out to considerable critical and public success. In 1981 Ingolstadt finally recognized a famous daughter and founded a literary prize in Fleißer's honour.

Pioniere in Ingolstadt (1929; 1968)

The first version of Fleißer's play, dating from 1928, has not survived, but a second version, prepared for production in Berlin in 1929 and incorporating last-minute changes to placate the censor (the rocking barrel went out), is published in the collected works edited by Günther Rühle along with the substantially revised version of 1968 which Fleißer undertook partly at the prompting of Brecht's widow Helene Weigel and which was premièred in Munich in 1970.[15] A couple of years earlier, however, the

---

[15] Marieluise Fleißer, *Pioniere in Ingolstadt: Komödie in vierzehn Bildern* (1968 version); *Pioniere in Ingolstadt: Komödie in zwölf Bildern* (1929 version), in *Gesammelte Werke,* i. *Dramen* ed. Günther Rühle (Frankfurt am Main: Suhrkamp, 1994), 127–85; 187–222.

1929 version had formed the basis for an adaptation produced in Munich in 1968, with the playwright Franz Xaver Kroetz in the role of the sergeant and directed by Rainer Werner Fassbinder who also made a television film in 1971. To what extent the 1968 version should be seen as more authentic because less distorted by the input of overbearing male collaborators, first Brecht and then Fassbinder, is a moot point. Discussion here will centre on the earlier version which is of interest in the history of the Heimat mode both in the context of the Weimar Republic and for the later reception of Fleißer's work, but will also touch on changes in the final version to see whether Fleißer had come to a changed perception on matters at issue here.

Fleißer's work is almost all set in her native town of Ingolstadt where she spent most of her life. A town on the Danube in Upper Bavaria, Ingolstadt had been at the turn of the century rather a backwater, a garrison town with a medieval centre and a population of some 15,000 though the development of the arms industry had already begun and by the time of the First World War the dependency on the military of a rapidly growing population was intensified when new factories were opened and the town became a centre for military production. But under the provisions of the Treaty of Versailles Ingolstadt lost its garrison status. The adverse effects on the local economy of the closing down of factories as well as the numbers of demobbed soldiers staying on in the town who then joined the Freikorps and later the SA, the activist wing of the National Socialist movement, help to explain why Ingolstadt, by the mid-1920s the second largest town in Upper Bavaria with a population of around 27,000, became an early stronghold of National Socialism.[16] The flat Danube plain differs in aspect from the famously picturesque region of the Bavarian Alps which has been a setting for Heimat kitsch throughout the history of the mode, and as quite a substantial town Ingolstadt might scarcely seem to furnish a location in the Heimat mode for a play with action set in 1926. But a key aesthetic principle shaping the play, that of restriction or reduction, does create characteristic spatial features of Heimat, producing a sense of bounded enclosure which could protect and nurture but in fact limits and stunts the lives of townsfolk who are reduced to a few characters sketched with minimalist concision in a loose succession of short scenes and in a pared-down language of short, punchy sentences lacking all poetic colour which is the most striking feature of the play. The action centres on flirtations between soldiers in a sapper regiment stationed in the town with a view to building a bridge across the

---

[16] On Ingolstadt as a centre of National Socialism see Geoffrey Pridham, *Hitler's Rise to Power: The Nazi Movement in Bavaria, 1923–1933* (London: Hart-Davis, McGibbon, 1973), 108–14.

Danube and two local girls, the more sexually experienced Alma who has just lost her position in domestic service and the still virginal Berta who is a maidservant in the Benke household. Karl (Korl in the later version), the cynical soldier with a woman in every town to whom Berta loses her virginity in a loveless coupling, Berta's employer Benke (Unertl in the later version), and his son Fabian are the main male characters. Fabian who fancies Berta and is determined to get revenge for the soldiers' success with local girls, damages a ladder by the river where the sappers are building the new bridge with wood paid by the town, but it is the sergeant, Fabian's ally against his rival Karl, who falls in the water and so the revenge falls flat. The soldiers in turn take revenge on Fabian by tying him up a sack and threatening to drown him, but he eventually gets out and gets off with Alma who unlike Berta is ready to market her sex and, after a fling with Karl, recognizes in Fabian a possible good match who can save her from the drudgery of domestic service and from prostitution, though if Fabian turns out anything like his father unpaid domestic drudgery will be her wifely fate. In the penultimate scene, Berta loses her virginity, emerging from the bushes with Karl to the humiliation of being floodlit in the lights being used to complete the bridge-building that night. The virginity broken and the bridge built, the soldiers leave the next day after posing for farewell photographs with their local sweethearts. Even Karl pays for a snapshot. The camera supposedly does not lie, but the photograph of Karl and Berta will convey the illusory image of a happy young couple in the Heimat which the army has served so worthily. Thus whereas Viebig gently ironizes the role of photography in producing Heimat and Wiechert's Bildermann strives to protect the Heimat from being photographed, Fleißer radically demystifies the mythic image of Heimat which photographs construct.

As in the other texts so far examined, space here too is segmented, most of the locations having the quality of a threshold between different facets of the Heimat. The play opens as the sapper regiment marches in, accompanied by military music and with a field stove for cooking out of doors. Their arrival signifies the entry of an outside force into the town in the shape of soldiers from elsewhere who will transform the local economy and ecology by building a bridge across the river, so turning what had been a boundary into a threshold to the outer world. In the final version the scene is set by the town gate as threshold into the Heimat; by implication the bridge over the river will open up a route through the hitherto enclosed town. Several scenes are set on the river bank which is at once a green place of bushes and undergrowth but also a building site with machinery and floodlights, so indicating the transformation of a once rural Heimat under the impact of modernity. The park bench, scene of erotic encounters between local girls and soldiers, marks a location where culture meets nature in the tamed aspect of a small-town park (in the final version the Luitpold park is identified by name), but in contrast to Bäreb's sexual ecstacy in the Echternach gardens in Viebig's *Das Kreuz im Venn* no spring awakening will happen here: Berta is later reduced to an instrument of another's pleasure, denied expression of her feelings, and told to be silent when being taken. Indoor scenes in the Benke/Unertl household merge into the outdoors. In the final version this takes the form of a balcony with washing and a view of town roofs, underlining the sexual division of labour and intensifying an oppressive sense of enclosure. In the 1929 version the living room opens into the *Laube*, that is a porch or small summer house which may be, as here, attached to the main house, typically in the form of an open-sided, roofed corridor running along one side of the house and generally covered with plants such as roses or geraniums. The *Laube* is the ultimate idyllic small-town scene. As the opening edition of the journal *Die Gartenlaube* (*The Summer House*) put it: 'Es soll Euch anheimeln in unserer Gartenlaube, in der Ihr gut-deutsche Gemütlichkeit findet, die zu Herzen spricht.'[17] The title of this family journal, first published in 1853, went on to become emblematic of the so-called Biedermeier ideal of happy families living in domestic bliss which dated back to the politically reactionary post-Napoleonic period and which became the target of a German tradition of comic satire. Fleißer's play is subtitled as a comedy in twelve scenes, but the satire is bitter in taste. For the visually idyllic household is a prison for young people under the shadow of a gross patriarch who exploits his servant and into whom his still charming son seems doomed to turn when the childish idealism has been knocked out of him. The opening of scene 4, the first of several set in the Benke household, establishes the triangle of son, father, and maidservant with minimalist precision: Fabian goes into the *Laube* to catch a fly and smell a rose; Berta carries in supper; Benke says grace then unleashes a pleasurable outburst of phoney rage over dirty crockery. Fabian still has a gentle nature: bending to smell the rose he is surely thinking of Berta, but killing flies like the brave tailor who dispatched seven at one blow in the Grimms' fairy tale suggests incipient manly ambitions. Bound in domestic service, Berta is a heroine at the mercy of a Biedermeier ogre who sadistically indulges his power over a servant, a later stage perhaps of killing flies. Despite the idyllic setting, then, it seems unlikely that a happy ending can reconcile these three. Killing flies,

---

[17] 'You'll feel at home in our summer house where cosy German cheeriness will touch your heart.' Cited in Hermann Glaser, *Kleinstadt-Ideologie: Zwischen Furchenglück und Sphärenflug* (Freiburg: Rombach, 1969), 40.

bullying servants, cold serial collecting of virginities, and, in the 1968 version, murdering rivals are stages in a sinister apprenticeship to a changing manhood on a threshold between older and newer modes of power, which finds its apogee in the military who are seen at their collective worst in the scene in the beer tent. A beer tent is yet another ambiguous place. Neither indoors in private nor in the free open air but enclosed in communal intimacy, the revellers in the beer tent display that tipsy bonhomie which can quickly turn into a mood of mob violence. Military uniforms, ritual humiliation of a scapegoat in front of the crowd, and laddish competition to get the woman cumulatively create a vaguely threatening atmosphere: the jolly togetherness and folksy oompah music become creepily sinister; the canvas of the tent seems but a thin protection against a brutishness ready to break through. Ödön von Horváth's play *Kasimir und Karoline* (1932), set in the Munich Oktoberfest, creates a comparable mood of violence just below the surface linked to aggressive male sexuality.

In a picture still corresponding to the structure of provincial society which Viebig had shown, Fleißer's segmented Heimat is mainly inhabited by young women (more young men appear in the later version) but under the rule of a traditional patriarchy underpinned by a sexual division of labour which leaves ownership of the Heimat, in the shape of property and commerce, in the hands of men and confirms the subordinate position of women, most obviously so in domestic service. But whereas domestic servants or rural farmservants had been typical literary figures at the turn of the century, by the mid-1920s the urban office worker had taken over as the characteristic figure embodying the changing position of women. In a hostile review of 1970 of the revised version of the play, which strengthens the theme of low-paid, or in the case of a wife unpaid, domestic labour, Joachim Kaiser, drama critic of Munich's *Süddeutsche Zeitung*, suggested that since exploitation of maidservants or of dependent workers ('abhängige Hilfskräfte', i.e. unpaid work by family members) was a thing of the past, the play had no relevance in the contemporary Federal Republic, given too that soldiers in the West German army enjoyed massively more citizen's rights than did those serving in the GDR, Russia or, for all he knew, China.[18] Quite apart from the perhaps unduly rosy picture of the West German labour market and army, Kaiser's criterion for plays of correspondence to sociological conditions at the time of performance would cut a terrible swathe through the realist theatrical tradition, excising at one fell swoop classics stretching from Lessing's *Emilia Galotti* through Ibsen's *A Doll's House* to Brecht's *Furcht und Elend des Dritten Reichs*. But what of correspondence to conditions at the original

[18] *Süddeutsche Zeitung*, 3 Mar. 1970, cited in Marieluise Fleißer, *Pioniere in Ingolstadt*, ed. David Horton (Manchester: Manchester University Press, 1992), 107.

time of the writing of the play? It is worth remembering that although the cultural critics of the Weimar Republic built up to mythic status the New Woman freed from domestic enclosure by her emblematic typewriter, more than half of women in employment up to 1933 still worked in agriculture and domestic service, especially in the provinces. Such women were not interesting to metropolitan essayists, but Fleißer's play makes visible the uneven nature of the modernizing process which meant that older social relations survived alongside new developments, yet not simply in parallel for the perception of change made old oppressions all the more bitter and fear of loss of traditional privilege all the more hysterical. Moreover virtually all the low-paid New Women office workers were single, two-thirds of them were under 25, and most lost their job on marriage, marriage remaining the ultimate goal for the overwhelming mass of women, whatever sector they worked in. (It is a pleasing irony that the first woman to be awarded the Marieluise Fleißer prize by the town of Ingolstadt should have been Irmgard Keun whose novels so wittily undid the myth of the New Woman while still celebrating liberating change.)

That in Fleißer's play maidservants personify the Heimat can also be seen, however, as a theatrical rather than a sociological choice, offering a metaphor for the ancient ideal of woman as man's handmaiden brought up to date for the 1920s. Seen in a negative light a maidservant's dependence and servility are qualities which in a different light might transmute into love and nurturing care. This is the double bind which haunts feminist critique of femininity: the feminine qualities which critics of patriarchy value and which men must repress in order to succeed in a competitive world, are the very values which, being internalized, bring women to subject themselves, so remaining complicit in reinforcing male dominance. Fleißer's play shows a woman in thrall to her own femininity and caught between Old and New Men. Benke and Karl represent the old and the new, with Fabian as test case for a possible other way. Benke is a Heimat patriarch, but a patriarch in tune with the market economy: he expects to wring the last ounce of labour out of his maidservant, but wonders whether he should not marry again, since a wife would work without payment. Here is a petit bourgeois man who has no truck with the high bourgeois love match: whether as their employers or their husbands men must retain control over women. Karl, by contrast, is a New Man. He has no wish to own or control women, merely to screw them: he wants to be free and expects women to have the same dégagé attitude as he does. As the eponymous hero in Brecht's poem 'Vom armen B. B.' (1922) puts it: 'In mir habt ihr einen, auf den könnt ihr nicht bauen.'[19] Hence women should keep quiet

---

[19] 'In me you have someone on whom you can't rely.'

and get on with it without a lot of emotional talk. (It will of course be for the woman to look after any resultant babies which a soldier could hardly drag around from one posting to the next.) Berta's faith in Karl, her belief that he cannot be as cold as he seems, leaves her at his mercy. Much more than any pressure on his part, it is Berta's desire to make Karl the gift of her love along with her body which brings about her humiliation. Moreover, Karl's very imperviousness lends him the aura of worldly experience which lures Berta so that she scarcely notices young Fabian's naive ardour. Post-marital Fabian might not turn into a tinpot tyrant like his father, but his aggressive response to sexual humiliation and easy consolation with Alma suggest otherwise. Thus the choice between Fabian, his father's son, and Karl is a choice between the limiting Heimat and escape to a wider changing world. But Berta, reluctant to remain enslaved under domestic patriarchy yet emotionally unable to evince the required new objectivity, is left in a void between worlds, in a no woman's land. *Neue Sachlichkeit* (New Objectivity) designated a mood of cool cynicism which by the mid-1920s came to replace the high pathos of Expressionist painting and literature. Urban novels of the period by women authors tell much the same story of the double bind of feminine values which men lack and no longer even desire in women, values which contribute to women's self-subordination, yet without which the world would be a cold hell. Brecht's play *Der gute Mensch von Sezuan* (1943) diagrammatically analyses such a dilemma and the topic would return in women's writing of the 1970s when Fleißer's work found a feminist readership.

One main difference between the 1929 and 1968 versions is a shift of emphasis from tension between the Heimat and the military, conveyed in Fabian's failed pursuit of revenge, to hatred between ranks, conveyed in Korl's successful and much more violent revenge on the sergeant, giving a very different picture from Wiechert's idealized friendship across ranks. This could be seen as a turn towards a class theme, but both Korl and the sergeant are at the lower end of the military hierarchy; their mutual hatred fuels a struggle for dominance, played out through sex and centred on masculine rather than on class identity. To draw a comparison with the dramatic prototype for such conflict, Büchner's *Woyzeck*, the comparable figure to Fleißer's sergeant is Büchner's drum major, not the upper-class captain, and Korl's success compared with Woyzeck's failure, if anything weakens any sense of class oppression and strengthens an analysis of power relations centred on gender. Moreover, the addition of a whole sub-plot about the theft of wood from the army by members of the local swimming club adds a new dimension to the Heimat theme. Competitive team sport is a key facet in the popular culture of the modern nation state. Fleißer shows how sporting ambition which begins with local patriotism associated with the Heimat contributes to the construction of an aggressively competitive spirit which then feeds into nationalism.[20] As the title and subtitle suggest, sport is also a major theme in Fleißer's novel *Eine Zierde für den Verein: Roman vom Rauchen, Sporteln, Lieben und Verkaufen.* There had been a long association dating back to Napoleonic times between gymnastics—but other sports too—and German nationalism, of which the 1936 Berlin Olympics, designed to burnish the image of the Third Reich, was a climax. Sport helped build up community spirit, which could take a generous liberal form but might also be marred by terrible racist prejudice; a look through the many sporting journals which had sprung up already by the turn of the century demonstrates both tendencies. In the 1968 version of *Pioniere in Ingolstadt* the floodlit taking of a virginity by a soldier is more obviously than ever turned into a spectator sport accompanied by appreciative whistles and yells; this together with the murder of the sergeant and the introduction of the local heroes of the swimming club conveys an analysis of a society on the verge of political disaster couched not in terms of class conflict but of popular culture and the widespread attitudes of ordinary people in provincial Germany.

The Heimat mode responds to economic and social change, whether in a mood of denial or of negotiation. It is notable that the military has figured among the forces driving forwards the process of the change in the texts so far selected, though Orla's new Heimat is an effort to escape war-wrought change. War, it is said, is the mother of invention. In English the added epithet 'civil' engineer implies a status secondary to those primary inventors of the engines of war, the military engineers. To move further afield for a moment, following the Jacobite Rebellion General Wade's straight military roads opened up the Scottish Highlands enabling the clearance from the land of Gaelic-speaking peasants to make way for sheep, game-shooting Sassenachs, and in our time mass tourism as well as transport of oil and nuclear waste, as John McGrath's critical Heimat play, *The Cheviot, the Stag and the Black, Black Oil* (premièred 1973), documents. The military roads also opened the way to writers and musicians such as Walter Scott or Felix Mendelssohn who collectively created the potent Highland myth which influenced Friedrich Lienhard, one of the main ideologues of Heimat at the turn of the century. Military engineering with civilian spin-off is an important material negotiation between the nation and Heimat which Romantic conservatives like Scott either mystified or attempted to hold back. Thus Ludwig II of Bavaria blocked Alpine road construction unless for the purpose of building castles; wilder

---

[20] See Moray McGowan, *Marieluise Fleißer* (Munich: Beck, 1987), 102–6 on women and sport and on sport in the Third Reich.

conspiracy theorists have even suggested that his drowning was engin-
eered by militarist modernizers anxious to exploit the Alpine Heimat,
the irony being that nothing has more stimulated mass tourism than
Ludwig's castles. Nowadays, of course, Greenpeace and other green
groups regularly take on the military and roadbuilding is surrounded by
controversy. Fleißer's play takes up this long interplay between Heimat
and military engineering. The bridge being built over the Danube in
Ingolstadt will serve a double function in speeding up military movement
and encouraging trade, hence the town's willingness to supply the wood
for nothing. The autobahn network was to be one of Hitler's most popular
policies; it helped to bring down unemployment and would enable a
blitzkrieg against France and Belgium. The driving of the autobahn
through the Mosel region to the French border is a major motif in Reitz's
Heimat. The strategic value of bridges also makes them a target for sabotage, as, for example, by the Freikorps during the French occupation of the
Ruhr; the psychopathic Scharrer in Fleißer's novel *Eine Zierde für den
Verein*, an embittered right-winger of the type who might join the SA,
dreams of rape, murder, and blowing up bridges. As well as the material
impact on the physical environment, sociologically too, armies have long
figured as agents of change, with a disruptive effect on local communities.
(The illegitimacy figures in garrison towns are superseded only by those
in university towns.)[21] In the eighteenth century, J. M. R. Lenz had already
taken up the theme of the threat to local virgins of the arrival of a lot
of young men in his play *Die Soldaten* (1776). Not that the virgins always
perceive the arrival as a threat. The army represents mobility and awakens
dreams of escape in young women with otherwise narrow horizons. As
Alma puts it: 'Da ist mir nicht bang. Der Pionier ist im Land.'[22] Soldiers are
good clients, whether for a local landlady like the fair Helene in Viebig's
Das Kreuz im Venn or a local prostitute like Alma who in the 1968 version
even dreams of escape to Berlin in preference to domestic hard labour at
home. Alma's new objective attitude to sex finds Korl's approval, unlike
Berta's old-fashioned yearning for love.

One literary leitmotiv completely lacking in Fleißer's portrayal of
Heimat sexuality, however, is the Carmen theme of the naïve soldier who
falls prey to a femme fatale, which Viebig, still in the ambit of the *fin de
siècle*, does take up. Like the gypsy Carmen who is at home in the Andalusian
mountains, the femme fatale can take the form of a woman shown as the
natural spirit of a locality, the locality being seen at once as a homeland yet

<hr>

[21] Thomas Nipperdey, *Deutsche Geschichte 1866–1918*, i. *Arbeit und Bürgergeist* (Munich: Beck, 1993), 28–9.

[22] 'I'm not worried. The sappers are here.'

as exotic in the eyes of an arriving stranger. That Heimat can also be exotic heightens its allure—the Scottish Highlands exemplify this effect in signfying at once an archaic homeland but in the most exotic detail of kilts, tartans, bagpipes, antlered deer, and wild-haired, wailing women wrapped in shawls. A comparable German tradition appears in the mountain film set in the Alps. Such films tend to have a heroine halfway between femme fatale and mountain nymph, as played for example by Leni Riefenstahl in Arnold Fanck's *Der heilige Berg* of 1926, the year in which Fleißer's play is set. Sexy Pola Negri too played such roles. Female sexuality is linked metaphorically with wilderness and assumes a mythic power which compensates in imagination for women's social powerlessness, hence the appeal of such figures also to women as well their obvious attraction for men. By contrast with the mythic grandeur of the Heimat in mountain films, *Pioniere in Ingolstadt* evinces the new cynical objectivity. Perhaps the single most telling line in the play, present in both versions, is Karl's laconic comment that nowadays girls have to put up with things because there are not enough men: 'Heut muß ein Mädel sich was gefallen lassen, weil es wenig Männer gibt' ('zu wenig Mannsbilder' in the later version).[23] After the slaughter of so many men in the First World War, this is the law of supply and demand in the sexual commerce prevailing in a Heimat drained of both love and erotic mystique. Cynicism is a mood of self-attack based on despair, in which the best qualities of human beings are devalued. It is psychologically expensive yet can be in some conditions the best way to preserve integrity. Fleißer was attacked in the right-wing press for daring as a woman to write about the military world, for having no sense of the true essence of the *Volk*, and for besmirching the Bavarian and German spirit with 'jüdische Geilheit und Dirnentum'.[24] As such hysterical responses show, Fleißer's bitter comedy hit home as a weapon against the inflated values of hyper-nationalism, militaristic manhood, and racist *Volk* ideology propagated by the National Socialists and others on the right of the political spectrum in the late 1920s.[25] It is not surprising, therefore, that her work should have enjoyed a revival in the late 1960s when the Nazi past became a bitter bone of contention between the young Germans and the older generation.

[23] Nowadays a girl's got to put up with things because there are too few men'. Fleißer, *Pioniere* (1929), 206; *Pioniere* (1968), 74. 'Mannsbild' is a South German dialect term.

[24] 'Jewish sleaze and prostitution'. For documentation of press reception see the notes to Fleißer, *Pioniere in Ingolstadt*, ed. Horton, 105–9.

[25] On cynicism, see Peter Sloterdijk, *Kritik der zynischen Vernunft*, 2 vols. (Frankfurt-am-Main: Suhrkamp, 1983); also Alan Rodway, *English Comedy: Its Role and Nature from Chaucer to the Present Day* (London: Chatto and Windus, 1975), 36–7.

3 (Un-)Happy Families
Heimat and Anti-Heimat in West German Film and Theatre

The West German Heimat Film: 'a strikingly authentic reverse image'[1]

Students of German are familiar with a syllabus centred on post-war realist literature dealing with the war and its aftermath of shattered cities and a starving populace, which then modulated in the mid-1950s into a formally more complex, critical reckoning with the National Socialist past.[2] To claim that escapist Heimat films showing happy, if naive, country dwellers in beautiful surroundings such as the Black Forest, the Lüneburger Heide, or the Alps might offer a more authentic image of post-war West Germany than authors such as Böll or Grass would be perverse. Yet the enormous popularity of Heimat films in the 1950s and their continuing success in the video market and as standard fillers in the television schedules suggest that such films did and still do in some sense represent an authentic expression of widespread attitudes among the German population: as the essayist and film critic Siegfried Kracauer put it, every popular film corresponds to popular desires.[3] Film does not, of course, simply emanate from a people as a spontaneous expression of feeling. Of all art forms it is arguably the most institutionally bound, being dependent on a complex process of production and distribution which in Occupied Germany was also politically steered; the different cultural policies pursued by the Americans and the Russians would in part account for the very different film histories in East and West. Through its marketing the film industry builds up a public for popular genres and helps to shape public attitudes by the films it distributes, the choices frequently being informed by an underlying political agenda. Yet success in drawing the public is also dependent on tapping into dreams and desires, assuaging anxieties and

---

[1] Eric Rentschler, 'Germany: The Past that would not Go Away', in Wilhelm Luhr (ed.), *World Cinema since 1945* (New York: Ungar Publishing Co., 1987), 208–51 (215).

[2] On how the later construction of a critical canon may have a distorting effect on perceptions of the 1950s, see Keith Bullivant and C. Jane Rice, 'Reconstruction and Integration: The Culture of West German Stabilization 1945 to 1968', in Rob Burns (ed.), *German Cultural Studies: An Introduction* (Oxford: Oxford University Press, 1995), 222–6.

[3] *Theorie des Films* (Frankfurt am Main: Surhkamp, 1985), 223.

fears, which the cinema does not create, to which it at most gives shape and focus: cinema is indeed a dream-machine, but a machine driven by fuel from the public. The public is not, of course, a monolithic unity and many viewers who found Heimat films unwatchable formed an alternative public for the generation of younger film-makers who began to emerge in the 1960s and who sought to establish an intellectually demanding and aesthetically innovative art-house cinema, the New German Cinema, just when television was becoming the medium of family entertainment, so dealing a death blow to the Heimat film (though not to the Heimat mode which continued in the guise of television series such as *Familie Hesselbach* or *Schwarzwaldklinik*). The new film-makers and dramatists did not simply turn away from Heimat, however, but sought initially at least to reverse the reverse image and so to uncover again bitter truths which Heimat films had screened out. As Volker Vogeler put it: 'Wir haben den alten deutschen Heimatfilm an den Füßen aufgehängt und lassen Blut aus seiner Nase tropfen. Das politische Bewußtsein, um das wir uns bemühen, zeigt uns den Begriff "Heimat" doch in einem ganz anderen Licht als früher'.[4] This chapter, then, tracks a dialectical movement as the Heimat film of the 1950s drew forth its anti-Heimat negation in both theatre and cinema a decade or so on. The last part of the chapter will track the continuing zigzag as the concept of Heimat was retrieved and redefined with the rise of green politics and as reflection on German identity between (lost) province(s) and (divided) nation(s) continued and shifted.

Heimat films have often been compared to the Hollywood western. As Anton Kaes puts it, both genres depicted 'imaginary spaces, pure movie lives, and a strong moral undercurrent'.[5] Closest to the western is the sub-genre of films set in the past and often drawing on the literary Heimat tradition, such as *Der Meineidbauer* (Rudolf Jugert, 1956), based on a play by the Austrian Ludwig Anzengruber (1839–89) and a remake of a 1941 film of the same title directed by Leopold Hainisch. This tells a dark story of betrayal and blackmail: an unmarried woman is cheated out of an inheritance when her partner dies and is forced to return to her gypsy village where her son falls into crime and is killed before the wrong can be righted. With its themes of guilt in the older generation, a criminal

---

[4] 'We have strung up the old German Heimat film by the heels to let the blood drip from its nostrils. The political consciousness we pursue casts a quite different light on the concept of "Heimat"'. Cited in Thomas Hoffmann and Ines Steiner, 'Die sechziger Jahre: Zwischen Jagdszenen und Jägerporno', in *Der Deutsche Heimatfilm: Bildwelten und Weltbilder. Bilder, Texte, Analysen zu 70 Jahren deutscher Heimatgeschichte* (Tübingen: Tübinger Verein für Volkskunde, 1989), 114.

[5] *From Hitler to Heimat: The Return of History as Film* (Cambridge, Mass.: Harvard University Press, 1989), 15.

Fig. 5. *Der Meineidbauer* was one of the few 1950s Heimat films showing the ugly face of the Heimat—out of tune with the times, it was not a commercial success

yet victimized younger generation, and the excluded alien gypsy, *Der Meineidbauer* gave masked expression for audiences of the 1950s to deeply troubling issues by personalizing them in the form of family melo-drama. Such regression to generational or economic conflicts of an earlier age is not unlike US western plots during the McCarthyite 1950s. But like some other darker Heimat films, *Der Meineidbauer* was a box-office fail-ure. It was as if the German cinema audience did not want strong plots, for in contrast to westerns, the great mass of Heimat films avoid charismatic characters or striking cinematography in favour of minimalist plots, happy endings foreseeable from the start, and natural backdrops in which the idyllic outweighs the sublime and the terrible scarcely figures. (One can only wonder at Wolfgang Kaschuba's claim that the German Heimat film is more complex and enigmatic than the western.)[6] The Heimat hero occasionally rides off into the sunset, but more often settles down happily ever after with his sweetheart, for in contrast to the male antagonisms and

[6] 'Der Deutsche Heimatfilm—Bildwelten als Weltbilder', in *Heimat: Analysen, Themen, Persepktiven*, vol. 294/I (Bonn: Bundeszentrale für politische Bildung, 1990), 829–51 (841).

friendships which drive western plots, Heimat films propagate family values and marriage. Such films offer not so much the mythic images characteristic of the western or of the earlier German genre of mountain films of the 1920s and 1930s; rather, they purvey the reverse image of the German present. For it is to absent realities that they offer imaginary balm.

So what did the Heimat films not show? In the West the *Grundgesetz* or Basic Law establishing the constitution of the Federal Republic of Germany was proclaimed in May of 1949 with elections following three months later. Then in October came the foundation of the German Democratic Republic. Konrad Adenauer, the first Chancellor of the FRG who remained in office till 1963, and in the GDR the even longer serving Walter Ulbricht, who became First Secretary of the SED (Sozialistische Einheitspartei Deutschlands (Socialist Unity Party of Germany)) only in 1953 but remained in office till 1971, set their stamp on the era of reconstruction in two German states divided along the Cold War fault line dividing Europe. The entry of West Germany into NATO and the advent of the Warsaw Pact, both in 1955, then the building of the Berlin Wall in 1961 by the East German regime in an effort to halt the flight of labour and a ruinous black market in currency, sealed the seemingly permanent post-war settlement. Total defeat in war left German cities physically shattered and a demoralized population. Over three million men had fallen in the war with comparable numbers of civilian casualties. There were some two million war-wounded and over three million homes had been destroyed; estimates suggest up to 45 per cent of houses were either destroyed or severely damaged and 40 per cent of the road network in the Western zones was out of use at the end of the war. Most of the six to seven million German prisoners of war had returned by the early 1950s, but the rising divorce rate, which levelled off in the mid-1950s only to climb again towards the end of the decade, is a measure of long-lasting stresses which, as Robert Moeller suggests, began with such fundamental issues as who would have enough to eat when during the immediate post-war period much of the population suffered from malnutrition.[7] To such figures must be added the transfer of between eleven and thirteen million people from east to west, east here including the Soviet occupation zone and then the GDR, until the Berlin Wall staunched the flow: estimates suggest that by October 1946 there were already more than seven million refugees in the three Western zones; in the FRG census of 1950 the figure had risen to

[7] Robert Moeller 'Reconstructing the Family in Reconstruction Germany', in Moeller (ed.), *West Germany under Construction: Politics, Society and Culture in the Adenauer Era* (Ann Arbor: University of Michigan Press, 1997), 109–33 (111).

9.6 million.[8] The highest proportion of refugees to total population (33 per cent) settled initially in Schleswig-Holstein where to this day Heimat museums devoted to towns or villages in East Prussia still survive so adding a twist to the strong local Heimat tradition; the highest absolute numbers settled in Bavaria (1,937,000), though there was some levelling out between regions during the 1950s. Such figures help to explain the sense of victimhood among the German population, though they do not excuse the failure to undertake a proper accounting of what the Third Reich meant or to acknowledge the full atrocity of the murder of millions of Jews and the many other war crimes perpetrated especially in Eastern Europe. The Nuremberg trials, conducted from November 1945 to October 1946, and in West Germany the half-hearted exercise in denazification of the Civil Service and other key groups, which the Adenauer government largely succeeded in resisting, tended to stoke more resentment than remorse.[9] The undiscriminating doctrine of collective guilt evoked bitterness or simple indifference in individuals; if all in general are guilty no one in particular can be held specifically accountable. Conversely the Nuremberg trials of leaders allowed for demonization of Hitler and his henchmen and exculpation of the German people who were thus turned from guilty perpetrators into the victims of an evil genius, then of the ravages of total war and of occupying forces perceived as vindictive or incompetent.

In the face of the division of Germany and the Cold War, Heimat films served to re-establish German identity based on a regional sense of belonging and on local traditions. Images of cultural continuity signified by folk festivals, costumes, and music masked the reality of political discontinuity. In *Die Fischerin vom Bodensee* (Harald Reinl, 1956), for example, set on Lake Constance where three countries meet, groups from Austria, Switzerland, and Germany come together for a *Trachtenfest* or folk festival, clad in a colourful variety of costumes with bands playing traditional songs. Such innocent Germanness transcending nationalism is highlighted through contrast with a pickpocket vamp who speaks with a French accent; whether she is francophone Swiss or French matters less than that she is not German. Heimat films specialize in sunsets shot through lakeside reeds, blue skies, and purple heathland or the towering grandeur of the Alps which serve to screen out recent memories of cities in

---

[8] See Rainer Schulze, 'Growing Discontent: Relations between Native and Refugee Populations in a Rural District in Western Germany after the Second World War', in Moeller (ed.), *West Germany under Construction*, 53–72.

[9] Curt Garner, 'Public Service Personnel in West Germany in the 1950s: Controversial Policy Decisions and their Effects on Social Composition, Gender Structure, and the Role of Former Nazis', in Moeller (ed.), *West Germany under Construction*, 135–95.

ruins. Paul May's *Und Ewig Singen die Wälder* (1959) abounds in images of plenty when the old farmer Dag prepares a Christmas feast for his labourers, friends, and family, serving an abundance of bear meat, huge cheeses, beer, and schnapps. Such a scene distracts from memories of material hardship in the war and its aftermath only a decade before. Or closer to the hungry times, in Hans Deppe's *Schwarzwaldmädel* of 1950 one character wins a tombola prize of a huge basket of luxury food and wine. Sloping thatched roofs, kitchen gardens, rustic wood panelling, and cupboards embellished with the warm colours of folk-art flower decoration in a style unchanged for a hundred years or more offer distraction to a public living in new concrete blocks filling the gaps left by bombs. Many films do have brief shots of post-war cityscapes or of American skyscrapers, but only to intensify by contrast the comfort of thatched farmhouses and old inns. The film-makers purveyed a visual universe of signs—landscapes, cloud and sky, vernacular architecture, peasant costumes, shining copper pots and foaming beer tankards, lederhosen, aprons, and swelling bosoms in laced bodices—designed to convey a trans-historical Germanic essence preceding and outlasting the tribulations of history. Photography of Alpine flora and fauna distract attention from history to the cycle of nature.

But Heimat films do not only purvey the reverse image of a timeless, untouched world that is *not* post-war Germany. The bulk of the genre, in contrast to the western, is set in the present day and includes contemporary motifs such as reconciliation of wartime enemies: in *Am Brunnen vor dem Tore* (Hans Wolff, 1952) an Englishman returning to marry the German girl with whom he fell in love when in the occupying forces meets the German pilot who during the war had shot him down only to then save him from his blazing plane and who now just happens to love the same girl. Here the great balm for the audience is the essential goodness of the German pilot who, like the Englishman, was only doing his patriotic duty. Chivalrous rivalry in war turns into friendly rivalry in peace for the love of a girl. The alluringly wealthy English suitor screens out darker aspects of occupation when many women suffered rape and when the borderline between rape and prostitution was fluid; the soldiers who gave away cigarettes and chocolate for sex did not usually return with offers of marriage and life in an English mansion.[10] We will not give away the ending here, but note merely the economics which show the Heimat girl competently managing a newly reopened inn and the German suitor running the BP petrol pump. Prisoners of war scarcely figure directly, but men regularly

---

[10] On this point see Ute Frevert, *Women in German History: From Bourgeois Emancipation to Sexual Liberation* (Oxford: Berg, 1989), 258; also Atina Grossmann, 'A Question of Silence: The Rape of German Women by Occupation Soldiers', in Moeller (ed.), *West Germany under Construction*, 33–52.

return from many years abroad often to be absolved or cleared of some accusation. *Wenn die Heide blüht* (Hans Deppe, 1960), for example, tells of a returnee hero-musician, who after a decade in America is cleared of an accusation of fratricide and, reconciled with his father, settles down in the Heimat with his sweetheart, implausibly sacrificing his brilliant singing career. Refugees or expellees from the East do figure quite frequently, though without explicit indication of the political context. The forest-warden in *Der Förster vom Silberwald* (Alfons Stummer, 1955), the first of a popular series with much Alpine nature photography of baby deer, eagles, and foxes, is a refugee who plays Bach on the organ of the village church, implying a provenance from somewhere in East Germany where that great musician was at home. Presumably a Protestant, the warden nonetheless joins piously in the ceremonial blessing of the dead deer at a Roman Catholic service for the hunt shot against the backdrop of a little chapel in the south German style framed by majestic mountains. *Das Mädchen Marion* (Wolfgang Schleif, 1956) tells of an East Prussian aristocratic widow who leaves the family stud farm to flee west before the advancing enemy. She reflects whether she is not thereby giving up all claims to Heimat rights in an ambiguous sliding between possible meanings of the term *Heimatrecht*, literally legal right of abode, but in context also property rights to the estate or emotional attachment to her native soil. This is the kind of ambiguous appeal exploited by right-wing parties such as the BHE (Bund der Heimatvertriebenen und Entrechteten—literally, union of those driven from their Heimat and deprived of their rights) who achieved some spectacular successes in the early 1950s. Still today reclamation of property has proved one of the thorniest issues since unification of the two Germanies. The widow and her daughter, Marion, together with a foal born during the flight of a retreating German cavalry regiment, find a new Heimat and after a mother–daughter rivalry over the local vet, live happily ever after, the mother getting the vet, the daughter a suitably younger expert horseman who trains the foal, now grown into a winning showjumper. Racist and revanchist undertones are legion: the horse Prusso, sired by Wotan, implies in his name and descent the very spirit of lost Germanic lands; the girl and the horse, broken in by imperious kisses and the whip respectively, are equated as being of good blood and breed; worst of all Prusso is cruelly mistreated by spivvy Polish horse-thieves pretending to requisition the horse as of right, but who are prevented by the animal-loving German vet and decent anglophone military police. Here anti-Polish resentment and the Cold War almost break through the surface.

The mood is not always so revanchist, however, and in a number of films clownish vagabond-musicians serve to transmute refugees into timeless wanderers in the Romantic tradition. These nomadic figures are the archaic embodiment of a landscape; like gypsies or tinkers, the musical clowns are country folk with a whiff of magic about them who are filmed emerging out of the landscape or disappearing into it again like hobgoblins of the hills and heathlands. They suggest a bond with the landscape strong enough to survive wandering and look back to the tradition of travelling apprentices or to the fairground entertainers of an earlier age. In *Wenn die Heide blüht*, for example, the musician-clowns perform a Heimat song for an old man from the Sudetenland, their melancholy comedy drawing the sting from the misery of exile which is softened too by the blonde-haired granddaughter who leans cheek to cheek with the old man. At the close, the hero proclaims that he could do without the landscape but not without the girl: Heimat is rooted in loving human relations, not in mythological connection to the soil, so there can be a second Heimat for those driven from their home. But the sentimental shots of grandfather and granddaughter sitting round a table with friends in a kitchen garden full of flowers and vegetables masks the reality of often bitter economic competition between local populations and refugees and serves too to block out political history. For the Sudetenland, from 1918 on part of the new state of Czechoslovakia, had been a centre of violent inter-war agitation by ethnic Germans under the Nazi leader Konrad Henlein and had provided the pretext for the German invasion of Czechoslovakia in 1939. Alongside a story about a man returning from exile to be cleared of an unjust accusation, the allusion to the Sudetenland but silence over its history served to confirm the essential decency of the German audience, to absolve them of guilt, and to turn them into victims of injustice. Once happily settled in a second, new Heimat, they were generously ready to forgive if not quite to forget.

So far we have been looking mainly at the masked treatment of the past and the effects of the war. But perhaps the most pervasive negotiation in Heimat films looks at once backwards *and* forwards in time, being designed to harmonize economic modernization with the restoration of patriarchal gender and family relations, an ideological agenda which is often embarrassingly obvious. This facet of Heimat films is both a reverse image of the reality of family disruption following the war and parallels key social and economic policies of the Adenauer era, so that many Heimat films can be seen as a utopian reflection of the social market economy and of a paternalistic social order which required hard work and apolitical quiescence from its citizens, to be rewarded by a motor car and a holiday in the Alps. (Increasingly far-flung holiday travel may be another reason for the declining market for the local exoticism of Heimat.) Historians debate whether restoration or modernization is the right term for

West Germany in the 1950s. Arguably both tendencies were in play in a process of 'modernization under a conservative guardianship', as one historian puts it.[11] The guardianship prevailed especially in policy designed to re-establish the 'normal' family unit which the war had disrupted. In 1950, nearly five million out of fifteen million households were headed by divorced women or widows; there were 1,400 women to every 1,000 men in the age group 25 to 39; refugee families fleeing in advance of the Soviet army had been largely headed by women; illegitimacy rates were growing. Construed as a scarcity of men (*Männermangel*) and superfluity of women (*Frauenüberschuß*), such conditions were to be rectified by pro-natalist policies to increase the birth rate and by restoration of the family as the basic social cell, a policy backed by sociologists such as Helmut Schelsky who argued that class distinctions had been levelled out by the war and hence the family should replace class to become the central arena of welfare policy and the motor of social advance.[12] Nazi ideology had emphasized women's maternal role, but the exigencies of war meant that women were massively drawn into the workforce, continuing to play an inestimable role in the late 1940s in the labour of reconstruction in bombed-out cities as the so-called *Trümmerfrauen*. Policy under the Adenauer government aimed, by contrast, to reintegrate demobbed men into the workforce and return women to the household. Thus by 1950 the proportion of women in employment had dropped from 36.1 per cent in 1939 to 31.3 per cent (in the territory of the Federal Republic). But from the mid-1950s, the proportion rose again to reach 33.4 per cent in 1961.[13] Exhausted by the terrible labour of feeding themselves and their families in the immediate post-war years, many women were not averse to a return to the household, though they were less ready to submit to the dominance of a paterfamilias and relations between children and returning stranger-fathers or stepfathers also posed problems. But as Germany's economic miracle got under way, conservative family policy conflicted both with rising need for labour and with growing consumer demand. These developments tended to drive more married women to work to supplement the male family wage in order to acquire household goods such as washing machines and televisions as well as the annual family holiday. Moreover, female emancipation, access to education, and the right to work had been long-term features of modernization which the imaginary Heimat—and the FRG as a liberal democracy—

---

[11] Christoph Kleßman, cited in Axel Schildt and Arnold Schwottek, ' "Reconstruction" and "Modernization": West German Social History during the 1950s', in Moeller (ed.), *West Germany under Construction*, 413–43 (415).

[12] See Moeller, 'Reconstructing the Family', 117–19.

[13] Frevert, *Women in German History*, 333.

could not totally expunge if they were to appeal to the female audience
—and an increasingly educated female electorate. Many Heimat films
reflect the tensions between economic modernization and the conservative family ideal in plots dealing with parenthood and in their portrayal of
male and female types.

Along with such negotiations over gender roles, the other key signifier
of modernization is the motor car. In the course of the 1950s the number
of motor cars in West Germany rose eightfold, reaching over four million
by 1960, the highest rate of increase in the world.[14] Like any popular genre,
Heimat films give expression to the play of desire as the camera ranges
over flowers and sunsets, homely interiors and grand country mansions
with wonderful gardens, sparkling Rhine wine, and euphoric communal
celebration. There was some chance that the male gaze could be deflected
to bosomy blondes in dirndls away from leggy chorus girls or the slightly
threatening elegance of the New Look of 1950s career women. But the
motor car was a too potent symbol, a too alluring object of desire to be
displaced by the horse and cart, and so the rural or mountain Heimat
is everywhere penetrated by the motor car. The environmental threat it
posed, which Clara Viebig had already signalled in *Das Kreuz im Venn* but
which 1950s Heimat films largely ignore, would form a theme in a later
critical Heimat discourse.

If students of German are to find any pleasure in Heimat films, then it is
as documents of their time in which the detective viewer can winkle out
the many traces of popular desires and anxieties in this age of restoration
yet modernization. For example, there are the plots dealing with fathers
learning after many years of offspring they did not know they had. *Wenn
der weiße Flieder wieder blüht* (Hans Deppe, 1953), *Die Fischerin vom
Bodensee* (Harald Reinl, 1956), and *Mariandl* (Werner Jacobs, 1961) all
feature fathers discovering their unknown daughters while in *Ferien vom
Ich* (Hans Deppe, 1963) the hero learns of his son's existence. This motif
provides an answer by wish-fulfilment to various situations: the prisoner
of war who did not get back till the mid-1950s; the illegitimate war baby;
the men often returning from America as hybrid German-Americans who
allude indirectly to fathers in the occupying forces, but also to emigrants
returning. The various resolutions likewise answer various needs. *Wenn
der weiße Flieder wieder blüht* shows at a time of rising divorce that a new
life is possible for men and women who found themselves strangers when
reunited after the war: the hero, now a famous popular singer returning
home after many years abroad, does not stay with his wife and newly discovered daughter but sets off again with his elegant woman manager,

---

[14] See Schildt and Schwottek, ' "Reconstruction" and "Modernization" ', 424.

leaving the Heimat woman about to marry her original sweetheart who will be a good father to her daughter. Here was reassurance that a second marriage, like a second Heimat, can be happy and—like the stepfather vet in *Das Mädchen Marion*—that stepfathers can restore paternal order and will love their stepdaughters, but not too much. The popular singer returning from America, a motif also in *Schwarzwaldmelodie* (Geza von Bolvary, 1956) and *Wenn die Heide blüht*, may also be an altogether darker trace of the many Jewish singers, composers, and entertainers who were driven out of Austria and Germany and ended up in America, such as the famous tenor Richard Tauber, singer in opera and operetta, or the Jewish members of the Comedian Harmonists, a group whose story has now belatedly been told in a film, a television documentary, and a stage play. Another film with a hero returning from America is *Ferien vom Ich*. Here the hero, owner of a large aircraft corporation, is finally reunited with his wife, having proved his fathering skills in a sequence of father–son scenes of fishing, flying, and shopping to buy presents for mummy. This film of 1963 brings the theme of absent fathers up to date by combining the figure of the returning emigrant with the issue of reconciling business success and parenthood.

If Heimat films teach men to be fathers, the lessons for women too are legion. Along with modelling fatherhood, *Ferien vom Ich* offers modern women the ego-satisfaction of a high-status job but also delivers a sub-liminal warning that women who do not make motherhood and reconcili-ation with wandering husbands the top priority risk losing their children. Thus mummy, a successful stage designer with the Vienna Opera House, is here got up in a dirndl to present a properly maternal aspect in the holi-day hotel designed for business people taking time out from the rat race and suffers anguish for a while when it seems as if her son has been spir-ited away by his father. The woman who can have it all as long as family duties come first was a sign that the economic miracle was well under way. *Ferien vom Ich* makes interesting comparison with Edgar Reitz's *Heimat* for the theme of a father returning from America as a wealthy, phil-anthropic businessman is evident in both films, which also both feature aeroplanes bringing modern technology into the Heimat in spectacular fashion. The theme of family roles is often, as here, combined with nego-tiation between tradition and modernity. The eponymous heroine of *Die Fischerin vom Bodensee* likewise turns out to have a wealthy father, which eases the way towards her marriage to a local well-heeled fish farmer who uses up-to-date methods in contrast to the heroine's traditional net-fishing for wild trout in the lake. Here Heimat tradition, figured in the girl, and modernity, figured in her lover, are harmonized through a mar-riage which will also end the anomaly of a woman being in charge of

fishing rights and complete the restoration of the patriarchal order begun
with the establishing of paternal identity. In a comic sub-plot an older
henpecked husband re-establishes his authority as master of the house.
Restoration of patriarchal order goes along with adaptation to the market
economy and the demand for luxury products which traditional methods
could not satisfy, so exemplifying the thesis that commercialization was
replacing earlier associations of Heimat with fate and mythological connection to the soil.[15] (As late as 1996, *Der Fischerkrieg*, directed by Klaus
Gietinger and likewise set on Lake Constance, half undoes the modernizing message when the hero opts for traditional fishing and the Heimat
girl rather than staying true to his fiancée, the Dutch heiress to a fish finger
factory!) *Das Mädchen Marion*, discussed above for its refugee theme,
begins with strong female characters as mother and daughter flee together
in a covered wagon, looking like prettified versions of Brecht's Mother
Courage and her daughter or the Wild West come to East Prussia. Mother
and daughter eventually settle with a widowed farmer's wife in the West.
The women enterprisingly take up weaving to earn extra money, but the
loom, though picturesque, is contrasted with the shiny accoutrements
of modern veterinary medicine and the embryo female craft collective
with green undertones is nipped in the bud when mother and daughter
both find a good man to support them. One year earlier, *Der Förster vom
Silberwald* (1955) offers an equally reactionary message for women
through its heroine who gives up her bohemian life in town as an artist
with a liking for jazz to become the dirndl-clad wife of the forest warden.
Wenn der weiße Flieder wieder blüht is, by contrast, less reactionary
on gender roles: although the hero sets off with his elegant modern man-
ageress leaving the Heimat woman behind with her Heimat man, the
Heimat woman too is elegant and runs a flourishing fashion business
in Wiesbaden. The wish-fulfilment of wealth and success, with careers
open also to women, anticipates the economic miracle in Germany with
America as model which is celebrated a decade on in *Ferien vom Ich*. On
the margins between the genres of Heimat and the review film, *Wenn der
weiße Flieder wieder blüht* reduces Heimat to a stage backdrop as the hero
sings of home surrounded by leggy chorus girls, long-time signifiers of
modernity in contrast to the Heimat bosom. (In a famous essay of 1926,
'The Mass Ornament', Siegfried Kracauer had taken chorus girls' legs as
a key symbol of modern times.) Deppe's later film, *Wenn die Heide
blüht* (1960) is plumb in the Heimat mode, however, and regresses to an

[15] See Ted Rippey, Melissa Sundell, Suzanne Townley, ' "Ein wunderbares Heute": The Evolution and Functionalization of "*Heimat*" in West German *Heimat* Films of the 1950s', in Jost Hermand and James Steakley (eds.), *'Heimat', Nation and Fatherland: The German Sense of Belonging* (New York: Peter Lang, 1996), 137–59 (156).

Fig. 6. This image of rather chaste young lovers wandering through the heathery Heimat is from *Wenn die Heide blüht*—but could come from many examples of the genre

ultra-conservative never-never land of heathland and folk costumes whose fantasy status almost surfaces in the closing sequence showing the returnee hero amidst the blooming heather in a clinch with his dirndl-clad Heimat girl as the modern Other Woman, a sophisticated singer, drives off sadly with her would-be sugar daddy in a large automobile back to the urban world which the audience too, dreaming of Heimat *and* big motor cars, will re-enter on leaving the cinema.

It hardly makes sense to recommend any specific Heimat film over any other: it is the genre in bulk which performs the censoring dream work for the Adenauer era, screening out or distorting traumatic memory and offering wish-fulfilment as Freud argued dreams do. But perhaps two final examples can together offer a spectrum of typical features. *Schwarzwaldmädel* (Hans Deppe, 1950), one of the great successes in German film history, was the first post-war colour film produced in the FRG. The most popular film of the early 1950s, it reached an audience of 14 million by 1952 with showings into the mid-1960s.[16] This film exemplifies the continuity of production and actors between UFA (Universum-Film AG), the main film company during the Weimar Republic and the Third Reich, and West German film in the 1950s.[17] Hans Deppe, who in the decade 1950–60 produced fourteen Heimat films, had begun his career as director in 1934. *Schwarzwaldmädel* exemplifies further continuities in being based on an operetta of 1917, much performed throughout the 1920s and 1930s, and first filmed in 1933. A review of Deppe's 1950 version enthuses over the authentic, immortal music of German operetta.[18] The composer of the immortal music was Leon Jessel, a Jew whose name appears in the film credits, but who, according to Robert Dachs, after surviving in hiding for some time during the Third Reich, was tortured then murdered by the Gestapo in Berlin.[19] Jessel's many other compositions have not survived, only *Schwarzwaldmädel*. The unabashed having of cake and eating it may perhaps explain the great popularity of *Schwarzwaldmädel* in its 1950 version. In keeping with its theatrical provenance, the Heimat location is thoroughly stagey with little more pretence to authenticity than the opening sequence of a ballet on ice performed for an urban audience. The heroine is both a modern young woman with a career *and* a Heimat girl who dons her dirndl back home on holiday in the Black Forest. On her first meeting with the hero at a carnival ball in town she is wearing a traditional folk costume. This sets the theme of Heimat as a leisure activity or game of dressing up. The vagabond-musicians in this film are only pretend tramps, denizens of tinpan alley on holiday from the city who have to steal a ragged costume from a scarecrow to play the part. The main location, as in so many Heimat films, is a country inn which allows for the mixing of locals cashing in on local colour with visitors spending the cash. Within the Heimat, dressing up is intensified

[16] See Willi Höfig, *Der deutsche Heimatfilm 1947–1960* (Stuttgart: Ferdinand Enke Verlag, 1973), 229.

[17] On such continuities see ibid. 143–69.   [18] Cited ibid. 228.

[19] *Sag beim Abschied . . .* Catalogue for an exhibition on popular entertainers of the 1920s and 1930s in Vienna and Berlin at the Museum der deutschen Geschichte, Berlin, Winter 1998 (no date, publisher, place of publication, or ISBN number), 130.

during local festivals when simpler traditional costume becomes full festive display, in *Schwarzwaldmädel* notably the heroine's huge scarlet pompommed hat. In Clara Viebig's *Das Kreuz im Venn* (1908) the tourists' photographs were presented as an illusory image in contrast to the reality of country life at the turn of the century. Here the boundary between image and reality has become hopelessly blurred in camera shots of maiden in pompommed hat against meadow backdrop designed as instant tourist-office posters. The nationwide success of the film no doubt boosted tourism, though it did least well in the Black Forest area where audiences evidently did not recognize themselves. As well as promoting tourism, the film also served the German motor trade with splendid shots of the heroine in her tombola prize of a Ford Taunus, a modern woman driving back home to dress up as a Heimat girl. Here was a feast for the eye, moving through shiny red motor car to red pompoms and swelling bosom amidst pink cherry blossom and green meadows, a commercially successful paradise of pleasure and the very reverse of the hell Germans had just lived through, if indeed they had lived through it.

More aesthetically ambitious, *Dort oben, wo die Alpen glühen* (Otto Meyer, 1956) deploys spectacular photography of Alpine climbing in the mountain film tradition of the 1920s and 1930s. It also treats with some seriousness the theme of modernization as it impacts on rural life in a debate about the drawbacks and benefits of a new road which would bring more cars and tourists into the Heimat. The hero, an accomplished mountaineer and wood-carver specializing in puppets, is not interested in the tourist market and upholds Heimat traditions, his wood-carving placing him in a line stretching back to Ganghofer's hero in *Der Herrgottschnitzer von Ammergau* or to Lienhard's ideal of folk art. The road supporters are the local innkeeper who stands to gain most and the hero's fiancée, an ambitious woman who runs her own farm and who is in love with the innkeeper or perhaps with his business acumen. The plot is initiated by a pair of tourists, niece and uncle, who represent the best and worst aspects of tourism. The uncle has all the up-to-date gear but no knowledge of mountain lore and ends up a laughing stock, though he does learn better in the end as is only fair given that he makes one of the few critical references to Hitler in the whole Heimat film corpus when he retorts that he does not need a 'Bergführer' (mountain guide), having had enough of führers. His niece, however, is an accomplished mountaineer who embarks on a climbing expedition with the hero as guide and promptly falls in love with him. But he first sticks by his faithless yet jealous fiancée, then finally achieves happiness neither with the too emancipated woman mountaineer nor the bossy fiancée but with a younger Heimat handmaiden who helps him with the puppets. The film shows gradations in Heimat identity from the hero and his artless bride who are the pure core, through the innkeeper and his ambitious bride who are the commercial modernizers, to the niece and her uncle, the tourists whom the new road will bring in ever-greater numbers to sustain the Heimat economy. Subliminally, the plot, camerawork, and details such as costumes construct images of more and less desirable masculinity and femininity. At the summit, all too literally, is the hero who during the joint climb is mainly shot from below outlined against the sky and mountain peaks as the woman climber, shot from above, struggles up towards him, aided by his helping hand. Blond and handsome, his outdoor rustic clothes allow for more muscular display than the landlord's Tirolean jacket which compares well, however, with the ridiculous uncle's gear. Women mountaineers, it seems, can expect comradeship but not love, for corduroy climbing pants 1950s style are unalluring compared with the dirndls the Heimat women wear even when out on the mountains. As in *Schwarzwaldmädel*, however, modernity is not simply the enemy. Modern aspirations and traditional values can be harmonized, but in contrast to the earlier film here sacrifices are to be made if the characters are to find the special blend of happiness and security only Heimat can confer. Heroism gets toned down and refashioned when the lead male has an accident on a second climb and is brought back to the village on a bier, in an echo of war-wounded returnees. That a little boy plays a key role in his rescue signifies the need for heroes to turn into fathers if a new generation of men is to be secured. The main costs of security, however, are erotic. The underlying sexual message is repressive and the ideal of gender relations reactionary, for though the landlord takes a strong woman as bride and business partner, they are unsympathetic figures, who compare badly with the hero and his child-bride. The strong but faithless fiancée drove the hero to undertake the second climb which almost killed him, the child-bride nurses him back to health. Compared with the pre-war genre of mountain films, which associated mystical landscapes with 'wild' women played by the likes of Pola Negri or the young Leni Riefenstahl, love in the mountains 1950s style is a tame affair. But a war-weary public were clearly ready to exchange mystical eroticism for the social market economy. The lure of Heimat discourse at its most seductive comes from the perspectivistic angle of vision, from backward yearning or utopian longing, by which the Heimat effect is produced. The Garden of Eden only becomes Edenic when seen with a backward look from after the Fall, although its trace beckons as an all-inclusive paradise. The aesthetic catastrophe of Heimat film, the reduction of myth to kitsch comes from the injection of up-to-date realities into the timeless Heimat so that the sheer incongruity of styles sets the teeth on edge. A Garden of Eden containing a Ford Taunus and cherry blossom elicits not yearning but the surfeit which follows a double portion of Black Forest gateau. The worm-wood served up by the early New German Cinema was a much-needed antidote while the different aesthetic solutions Edgar Reitz brought to bear in his injection of current realities into the Heimat will be the topic of Chapter 6.

Anti-Heimat in Film and Theatre: An Iconoclastic Inverse Image?

Following the decline of the 1950s Heimat film, there was a revival in the 1960s and 1970s of the German art film. The year 1962 is generally taken as the symbolic date marking the beginning of the New German Cinema when a number of younger film-makers signed the Oberhausen Manifesto committing themselves to a break with the past and a new intellectual, formal, and economic beginning.[20] Despite recurrent finan-cial crises, the new film-makers were achieving growing critical successes by the mid-1960s at a time when competition from television threatened the popular audience for film. Then in the 1974 an agreement on co-production between film and television set the financial basis for the breakthrough of German film to international acclaim for directors such as Werner Herzog, Alexander Kluge—the key theorist and patron of the new cinema—Volker Schlöndorff, Wim Wenders, and women directors such as Helke Sanders-Brahms, Helma Sander, and Margarethe von Trotta. Above all there was Rainer Werner Fassbinder, the most product-ive and innovative of the new film-makers. The development of the New German Cinema at once fed into and was a symptom of profound cultural change in Germany. The building of the Berlin Wall in 1961 and the resignation of Konrad Adenauer in 1963 together marked the end of the post-war era and the first phase of the Cold War. After the initial shock waves, the Berlin Wall had an oddly stabilizing effect. In the eyes of a crit-ical younger generation, the Wall established the permanence of the other socialist Germany and encouraged a more probing analysis of the now firmly bounded West Germany which had changed from a post-war occu-pied country into an emerging world power and an economic giant in the Western alliance. (What happened to the more probing analysis of their society attempted by GDR film-makers will be the topic of the next chap-ter.) The 1960s saw the growing radicalization of a generation of people

---

[20]   See John Sandford, *The New German Cinema* (London: Eyre Methuen, 1981).

too young to have direct memories of the Third Reich, as writers as well as film-makers increasingly questioned the moral authority and even legitimacy of the West German State. The Grand Coalition between the CDU/CSU (Christlich-Demokratische Union/Christlich-Soziale Union (Christian Democrat Union/Christian Socialist Union)) and the SPD of 1966–9, which was seen to undermine the possibility of democratic opposition within parliament, created a highly politicized mood fuelled also by the international repercussions of the Vietnam War. This is the context too for Siegfried Lenz's reckoning with Heimat and radical youth in his novel *Deutschstunde*, to be considered in Chapter 5. The growing tensions between the generations culminated in the wave of student protests from 1967 to 1970. The subsequent emergence of terrorism remained limited to a tiny minority but had a huge effect on public attitudes and elicited a draconian state response.

The response of writers and film-makers to past and present political history was mediated through a great variety of aesthetic devices and innovations. These could take the form of extreme anti-realist experimentalism as in some work by Jean-Marie Straub, or the magic realism and exotic settings of some of Herzog's films, or the various modes of alienated or stylized realism as practised by Kluge and Fassbinder. Such formal experimentation drew on earlier traditions such as German Expressionism and its Hollywood outgrowth in the *films noirs* of the 1940s and 1950s to which émigré directors such as Fritz Lang had contributed. The directors of the New German Cinema were critical of the continuity which, despite the dissolution of UFA in 1945, prevailed in the West German film industry, and were critical also of kitschy 1950s Heimat films whose directors were not émigrés but were tainted by an association with National Socialism. Thus along with avant-garde experiment or the appropriation of earlier traditions, a further strategy took the form of a critical transformation of established genres, notably the 1950s Heimat film.[21] A striking feature of the critical counter-culture which emerged in the late 1960s is the strong interchange between theatre and cinema in a number of plays and films which adopted an iconoclastic rhetoric which can be termed anti-Heimat. Influenced by the critical *Volksstück* of authors such as Ödön von Horváth or Marieluise Fleißer, whose work was considered in the last chapter, the playwrights Martin Sperr and Franz Xaver Kroetz, as well as Rainer Werner Fassbinder who was active in both media, revisited the Heimat mode. Sperr and Kroetz both wrote plays

---

[21] For an excellent survey see Eric Rentschler, 'Calamity Prevails over the Country: Young German Film Rediscovers the *Heimat*', in Sigrid Bauschinger, Susan L. Cocalis, and Henry A. Lea, *Film und Literatur: Literarische Texte und der neue deutsche Film* (Munich: Francke, 1984), 50–71.

which were taken up as film scripts, both set their plays in Lower Bavaria, and both acknowledge a debt to Marieluise Fleißer as did Fassbinder. All three also deal with inter-generational family relations, the leading theme in many of the 1950s Heimat films. Reacting against the escapist sentimentality of the cinematic dream-machine, they inverted or travestied the conventions and values of the 1950s Heimat films in an attempt to evaluate national identity in the light of the Holocaust and the social conditions of the Federal Republic. The term 'anti-Heimat' can be ambiguous. What is under attack is the right-wing or escapist *discourse* of Heimat rather than a simple rejection of all things rural. But the attack sometimes took the form of negation so bleak as to amount to a rejection of provincial or rural existence. Other texts, however, do not seek to destroy the idea of Heimat completely and might be allocated to a more differentiated critical Heimat mode.

Murdering the Family: Martin Sperr's *Jagdszenen aus Niederbayern*

If any single work exemplifies the inversion of homely or idyllic motifs to produce a rhetoric of anti-Heimat, then it is Martin Sperr's play *Jagdszenen aus Niederbayern* (premièred in Bremen in 1966).[22] The play was filmed in 1968 by Peter Fleischmann who followed Sperr's text fairly closely, though he changed some names and reduced the number of characters. But in contrast to the vigorous marketing of 1950s Heimat films, Fleischmann's film, for all its innovatory impact in the history of New German Cinema, is currently not easily available and so our discussion here will be of the play. Volker Vogeler's image, cited at the beginning of this chapter, of Heimat hanging upside down to let the blood drip from its nostrils, is an allusion to the carcass hanging from a hook in the village butcher's slaughterhouse, the setting of scene 2 of Sperr's play in which a group of women are busy stirring a pot full of meat to make sausages. Animal carcasses and slaughterhouses had been a frequent figure in modernist film and literature, being often associated with the urban metropolis, whether Chicago or Berlin, in works such as Upton Sinclair's *The Jungle*, Brecht's *Die heilige Johanna der Schlachthöfe*, and Döblin's *Berlin Alexanderplatz*. Or there is the animal carcass juxtaposed in a montage of images of violence in Eisenstein's *October* (1928). Here in a village setting, the motif is part of a sequence which undermines then destroys

[22] *Jagdszenen aus Niederbayern*, in *Bayerische Trilogie* (Frankfurt am Main: Suhrkamp, 1972), 7–59.

any illusion of rural idyll. For confrontation with the process of which the Sunday roast or the tasty sausages are the end products is liable to provoke a queasy response in the urban public for whom the anti-Heimat playwrights wrote. The ostensibly idyllic opening scene, set on Sunday morning in the village square, is already full of dark intimations. The whole village smells of roast pork, so the opening sentence of dialogue establishes. The person speaking is Barbara, mother of Abram, the homosexual who will end up as a beast hunted by the villagers, their already roused bloodlust unleashed by Abram's bloody deed of slaughter when he repeatedly stabs the young woman pregnant with his child just after she has called him 'eine schwule Drecksau' (scene 12).[23] The time is 1948, just after the currency reform which set German economic recovery in train. It is good to have meat again, Barbara comments in an exchange with the gravedigger, Knocherl (literally 'little bone'); it really whets your appetite. As homely details of ordinary life, the carcass or the smell of meat would be harmless enough; sausages or roast pork with dumplings are typical Bavarian fare. But as part of a sequence of images beginning with the title of the play, they take on a blackly symbolic undertone: a war which has seen the slaughter of millions—the gravedigger later lists the weekly tally of corpses at the busiest times during the war—has only just finished, but the appetite for meat is there and the readiness to slaughter animals, whether wild, domestic, or human remains undiminished. In 1950s Heimat films hearty food and drink signified the restoration of peacetime prosperity; Sperr inverts such signifiers to produce a sense of murderous threat.

A key negotiation in the Heimat mode determines who can be integrated or at least tolerated in a community and who must be excluded as radically different. In *Jagdszenen aus Niederbayern* most of the characters at some point come into the frame as candidates for exclusion. A permanent instability at the core of individual relationships is shown to corrode the whole community which can only find an illusory sense of stabilizing group identity in ganging up together against a scapegoat on whom all can for a moment project their anxieties and hatreds. While the kill would be even more satisfying, the expulsion of the scapegoat provides a moment of communal unity in the closing scene showing a village festival complete with beer tables and brass band as all join in the chorus of a hunting song. The scene is redolent with the sinister, beer-swilling bonhomie which Fleißer too evokes in her picture of small-town Bavaria in her Heimat novel *Eine Zierde für den Verein*. The blackly satirical effect is heightened by the echoes from endless similar communal festivities in

[23] 'a dirty pig of a queer'.

1950s Heimat films. The play takes up several further motifs which are treated sentimentally in Heimat films. Here a family of Silesian refugees arouses envious bitterness: not only are they getting jobs and subsidies while locals go short, but they are Protestants, so the complaints run. Compare this with the sentimental song about the Sudetenland in *Wenn die Heide blüht*, or with the Protestant, Bach-playing hero of *Der Förster vom Silberwald*, a film which ends with a celebration of the hunt complete with dead deer. The deer is not yet skinned, of course, unlike the carcass hanging on a butcher's hook in Sperr's play.

In *Der Förster vom Silberwald* the hero's happy acceptance into the community is crowned through marriage. As we have seen, marriage provides for reconciliatory, stabilizing closure in many Heimat films, whether a new marriage or a marriage restored through men returning from long absence. Or there is the closely related theme of the restoration of patriarchal order through returning or new fathers who reaffirm family values. Sperr's plot centres on an iconoclastic destruction of the family as the foundation of Heimat. Maria, mother of Rovo, the stock figure of the village idiot, hopes that her long-missing husband will never return. Yet women without husbands evoke hostility which could provoke exclusion were it not deflected to a better target: Maria attracts contemptuous accusations not only as mother of an idiot but also as a nymphomaniac because she has two single men as lodgers, so bringing the village into disrepute. But when she gets the good news (!) that her husband is dead, she rejoices, for now the way is clear to set up with Volker, one of the lodgers, and to send Rovo away to a home on the spurious grounds that he is not safe in the village—or perhaps not so spurious, for who would be safe in this village? The marriage of Maria and Volker and the exclusion of Rovo will get rid of abnormality and produce a normal household but at the cost of excluding the child and with him the whole rationale of the family household. War-wounded Volker goes along with the plan to exclude the mentally disabled child even though he himself is physically disabled and convinced that his wooden leg stigmatizes him as less than a man in the eyes of women. Ageing widows with deviant sons are also potential outsiders whom the community might gang up on: Barbara, Abram's mother, has become a nomad forced to keep moving on because of her son's antisocial activities which get blamed on an inadequate mother; she longs to settle down and so is ready to disown her son. Or there is the young woman, Tonka, who risks exclusion through being pregnant by Abram, the outcome of his doomed effort to become normal. Nor do those stigmatized as immoral or abnormal bring any touch of hope into this hellish place—one character calls the village a hell. For they are as ready as anyone else to stigmatize others. Thus Tonka, under attack for disgusting immorality, attacks Abram, the father of her child, for his disgusting homosexuality. The planned exclusion of Rovo by Maria, his symbolically misnamed mother, undermines the cult of motherhood as the emotional core of Heimat and the notion of the sheltering village community which can better cope with disability than the cold urban world. Clara Viebig's cast of characters in her stories of village life in the Eifel had included the poor little creature, 'das Miseräbelchen', a mentally retarded boy whom the family and the community sustained even if his death was welcomed as the lifting of a burden.[24] Of all Sperr's cast of characters, Rovo comes closest to being innocent like Viebig's *Miseräbelchen*. The traumatized embodiment of the damaging effects of war, Rovo sees no difference between war and peace having been always harshly treated. Yet Rovo turns on Tonka, calling her a whore. Viebig's *Miseräbelchen* had a friend in the cat Peter who lay across his feet to keep them warm; Rovo gleefully tells Abram how he had swung a cat by its tail and hurled it high in the air. The cat survived the fall, but Rovo will not survive: under threat of being sent away, he kills himself; Abram too will be excluded and hunted like a beast. Yet both characters laugh at the story of the cat, suggesting the sadistic pleasure shared by victims and perpetrators of violence alike, for all combine within themselves both roles. Anyone perceived as different comes under threat; everybody at some time or other is so perceived; everybody so perceives others at some point. This is the law prevailing in Sperr's Heimat. Dog eats dog except when they briefly unite together to hunt in packs. Such images turn the Heimat upside down to show it as the very negation of human community.

The most iconoclastic moment comes in scene 12 when in a frenzied knife attack Abram murders Tonka, pregnant with his child, taking care, so he proclaims, to reach the embryo so that it should feel the father's rage. Much of the play goes towards undoing motherhood in figures such as Maria or Barbara, deviant mothers who reject abnormal or deviant offspring. Here fatherhood self-destructs in a violent negation of those paternal duties of care and protection which complement the rights accruing to the father under patriarchal law. Jehovah absolved Abraham from the horror of child-sacrifice, a foundational moment in human culture which Abram undoes in stabbing an embryo in the womb. The immediate precipitating factor is Tonka's contempt for Abram as a homosexual. Homosexuality is the scandalous transgression which definitively breaks open and would destroy the patriarchal foundation of the village Heimat and its key supporting pillars, the law of compulsory heterosexuality and the principle of identity defined through exclusion of others. In the

---

[24] Clara Viebig, 'Das Miseräbelchen', in *Kinder der Eifel: Erzählungen* (Düsseldorf: Ullstein, 1994), 157–62.

Judaeo-Christian tradition, Abraham is the biblical *Urvater* from whom communal identity flows. Acceptance of a homosexual as father would be a travesty undoing all order, as Abram's bloody deed duly and ritualistically confirms. Exclusion is necessary to sustain order: hunting down the homosexual who has murdered a mother and an unborn child thus serves ideally to confirm the villagers' righteousness; the more horrible the crime, the more powerful the reassertion of the law. Comparison with the scapegoat and the horror of his crime confirms the villagers as living in accordance with the law, and so the all-present threat of exclusion is for a moment lifted.

When Abram murders Tonka he is already on the run, having broken another powerful taboo banning not only homosexuality but also paedophilia, a crime which has become a leading preoccupation in the 1990s both as a social issue and in popular literature, film, and the press. Sex with under-age children is a provocative motif in several works of this period when attacking patriarchy was on the agenda. Interestingly, it was a motif also in Viebig's *Das Kreuz im Venn* where the potential victim's innocence deflected Rotfuchs from his rapacious intent. Yet like Abram, Rotfuchs too was hunted down like an animal. The patriarchal order requires the protection of children from adult abuse in such laws as the age of consent or the incest taboo. Yet the conventional nuclear family, the church, or children's homes, where Rovo would have ended up had he not killed himself, have proved fertile ground for cruelty to children, to say nothing of the effects of war. The radical film-makers and playwrights point up the hypocrisy of moral outrage against individual transgressions in a society where child neglect and abuse are endemic. Rovo has suffered the terrors of wartime bombardment and the ministrations of his superstitious mother who rubs him with nettles for his own good. But what rouses the communal ire is a kiss talked up into attempted homosexual rape. Here again, Sperr inverts the theme in 1950s Heimat films of the protective secondary father who will love a stepchild, but not too much. As one of her lodgers, Abram had come into question as a possible replacement for Maria's lost husband, but his is the wrong kind of love for his potential stepchild. The projection of all guilt on to the absolute other, the paedophile homosexual scapegoat, absolves Volker, the other replacement father who merely wants to get rid of Rovo, not to kiss him. Yet it is rejection by Volker and Maria which precipitates Rovo's suicide, whereas Abram was in Rovo's eyes the only person who treated him as a human being. Sperr does not idealize his homosexual anti-hero, but like Büchner in his play *Woyzeck* (1837; first published 1879) he shows how violence comes into being as a response by abused and violated victims of collective persecution: 'wie die Gewalt entsteht' ('how violence comes about'), as Böll puts in the subtitle to *Die verlorene Ehre der Katharina Blum*. The thesis has its dubious aspects in all three texts, not least in Sperr's play as in Büchner's in eliciting identificatory sympathy with a male perpetrator of violence upon a female victim. (Böll, writing just as Second Wave feminism was peaking, would reverse the gender roles.) In both plays, however, a boy-child is there to suggest an original innocence which in Rovo, older than Woyzeck and Maria's child, has already been brutalized. In this iconoclastic text, the moral core is protest at the suffering of children.

Depending on the frame of reference we bring to bear, Sperr's play raises many troubling questions. To what extent is specifically Catholic, south German culture under attack, or could the analysis apply to any religiously based culture? To what extent is this a play about Germany and the German character? While the analysis of scapegoating could be brought to bear on the mentality of the many ordinary Germans who colluded or actively supported the exclusion of the Jews, even if many did not quite face up to the full implications of Nazi policy, it is perhaps couched in universal terms which leave no room for discriminating judgement or for historically specific political analysis: if human nature is so flawed, then the differential attribution of responsibility becomes meaningless. If the play does indeed imply the interchangeability of victims and perpetrators as well as the universality of the scapegoating mentality, then this could suggest that the Holocaust was not unique, but was merely an extreme exemplification of a universal human tendency. Seen in the light of the 1980s *Historikerstreit*, Sperr's play might thus seem to touch on a key bone of contention: the uniqueness or comparability of the Holocaust. Yet in the context of 1990s ethnic conflicts, the black vision might seem justified. Read as gay literature, the play is a radical protest against continuing state-sanctioned stigmatization of homosexuals which prevailed in both Germanies. In scene 9, Volker admits to having indulged in gay sex in the army and thinks that homosexuality should now be decriminalized. Sperr points here to the hypocrisy of selectively persecuting individuals while ignoring widespread homosexual activity in male institutions such as the army as had happened during the Third Reich and continued after the war. After the murder in 1934 of Röhm, leader of the SA and an enthusiastic proponent of a macho cult of homosexuality, male homosexuals had been one of the groups to suffer persecution during the Third Reich following the addition in 1935 of extended discriminatory measures to Paragraph 175 of the criminal law code, the paragraph criminalizing male homosexuality. Yet in 1957, at the height of the restorative Adenauer era, the Federal Constitutional Court turned down an appeal against Paragraph 175, rejecting the appellants' claim that it violated the principle of equal rights in the Basic Law and condemning male homosexuality as deviance, a judgement backed up as late as 1986 when the court judged that prosecutions under Paragraph 175 during the Third Reich did not constitute National Socialist injustice. It was not till the end of the 1980s that the claims of homosexual victims of National Socialist persecution were finally recognized in principle. In the twelve years from 1953 to 1965 —Sperr's play was premièred in 1966—nearly 38,000 men were found guilty under Paragraph 175, considerably more than those prosecuted during the twelve years of the Third Reich.[25]

In the context of this study, Sperr's play is a truly radical attack on the patriarchal foundations of Heimat discourse. The homosexual anti-hero brings out the silent exclusions which sustain the Heimat community. Sperr's play does not only invert individual motifs from 1950s Heimat films but transmutes the whole prevailing mood of romantic idyll into horror and might even be said to take back the mythical advent of culture. The biblical echo in the name Abram turns the smell of roasting meat in the opening lines of the play into an intimation of human sacrifice just as the women stirring the pot of meat take on a Sweeny-Toddish undertone of Grand Guignol. Such horror could risk falling into reductive absurdity were the play to be produced in a straight realistic idiom. But a stylized or alienated acting technique would highlight the mythic element and the self-consciously literary echoes of Büchner's *Woyzeck* and perhaps also of Wedekind's *Frühlings Erwachen* (1889): a homosexual kiss is an idyllic moment here as in Wedekind's play, while the penultimate tiny scene with the butcher's wife and Knocherl parodistically echoes similar tiny moments of idyll in *Frühlings Erwachen*. On the other hand, a village Jack the Ripper is perhaps nearer the mark than the spring awakening. Jack the Ripper finally disembowels the heroine of Wedekind's Lulu plays (1895–1913), which G. W. Pabst adapted in his brilliant film *Die Büchse der Pandora* (1929). Jack cuts out Lulu's sexual organs with a knife just as here Abram stabs into a womb. A key figure in the cultural history of Munich, Wedekind played Jack many times on stage, just as Sperr plays Abram in Fleischmann's film. Another interesting comparison would be with Fritz Lang's *M—Eine Stadt sucht einen Mörder* (1931) in which Peter Lorre gives an unforgettable performance as the scapegoat with whom the implied spectators are brought to sympathize even though he is a mass murderer of children. A strong subtext in Lang's film is the attack on mothers who may be to blame for producing deviance in their sons through failures or excesses of love. (Post-Freudian mothers can't win.) Wedekind too

---

[25] See Robert G. Moeller, 'The Homosexual Man is a "Man", the Homosexual Woman is a "Woman": Sex, Society, and the Law in Postwar West Germany', in Moeller (ed.), *West Germany under Construction*, 251–284, esp. 282–3.

attacked mothers as the agents who transmit patriarchy across the generations and presented child sexual abuse with a certain nonchalance.
Sperr's play in which a village seeks a murderer thus stands in a tradition
of male critics of patriarchy which has its dubious aspects. Yet these
aspects are at the same time the cutting edge of radical provocation.

Rainer Werner Fassbinder: *Katzelmacher* and *Wildwechsel*

Rainer Werner Fassbinder directed several films in the anti-Heimat
mode including *Katzelmacher* (1969), a rather disappointing version of
Marieluise Fleißer's *Pioniere in Ingolstadt* (1971), and *Wildwechsel* (1972),
based on a play by Franz Xaver Kroetz. Just as Sperr played Abram,
so Fassbinder himself plays Jorgos in *Katzelmacher*, the Greek worker
whose arrival in a Munich suburb acts as the catalyst among a group of
young men and women to bring out already seething hatreds and who
then becomes the scapegoat. ('Katzelmacher' is south German, denigrating slang for a foreigner from the Mediterranean region.) *Katzelmacher* is
one of the earliest works to take up the issue of foreign workers in post-war
West Germany. Initially, the flood of refugees from the East answered the
growing demand for labour as the West German economic miracle got
under way, but the advent of the Berlin Wall blocked the flight of labour
westwards and brought a massive expansion in the already considerable
recruitment of foreign labour from Mediterranean countries, including
Turkey. Thus between 1960 and 1966 the number of foreign workers in the
Federal Republic grew from 300,000 to 1.2 million.[26] Then in 1966/7 came
the first economic downturn since the end of the Second World War. This
was one of the precipitating factors in the social unrest in the late 1960s
and is the context for the theme of xenophobia in *Katzelmacher* and the
claim that foreigners take German jobs. While disaffected students were
taking to the street in protest against their Nazi parents, Fassbinder's film
shows another kind of disaffection among young working-class people
with petit-bourgeois aspirations. *Angst essen Seele auf* (1973), Fassbinder's
most profound treatment of the theme of foreign workers, centres on the
perspective of the outsider and features a touching relationship between
Ali, a Moroccan *Gastarbeiter* who has lost his Heimat, and Emmi, an older
woman whose sad loneliness unmasks the lack of human warmth or

[26] Ulrich Herbert, *Arbeit, Volkstum, Weltanschauung: Über Fremde und Deutsche im 20. Jahrhundert* (Frankfurt am Main: Fischer, 1996), 219. This study usefully locates current debate on German nationality law in the history of foreign labour in Germany.

community in the West Germany of the *Wirtschaftswunder. Katzelmacher* focuses less on the stranger and more on local reactions. Nowadays, Turks constitute much the biggest group of foreign workers, but they were preceded first by Italians, and then by Greeks who still now form the third biggest category, numbering some 351,000.

Like *Jagdszenen in Niederbayern*, Fassbinder's film shows how perceived difference is used by a community to momentarily stabilize its own system. Initially, however, the arrival of Greek Jorgos is destabilizing. It brings to the surface the envy, resentments, and frustrations of characters who are not so much integrated as imprisoned in their 'heile Welt', a 'safe world' which is a perversion of the cherished goal of the 1950s Heimat film. The most striking feature of *Katzelmacher* is the disillusioning filming of location with much use of a still camera creating framed, painterly shots of static figures, often sitting round tables or side by side in a row against an almost blank background. This aesthetic, the very antithesis of 1950s chocolate-box Heimat locations, also contrasts with the longer tradition of sentimental or Biedermeier genre painting of provincial and village localities and interiors stretching back to the nineteenth century. Lacking provincial local colour or big-city excitement, the suburban locales, filmed in black and white, are here drab and nondescript. The characters repeatedly sit on a railing running along the façade of a house which serves as a whitish, flat background for static figures, the framing usually half cutting off two window boxes of black-and-white flowers in contrast with the lurid colours of the 1950s Heimat films. The still camera creates limited vision so that episodes set in local pubs or restaurants do not open up into spacious scenes of jolly festivity as in 1950s Heimat films but convey imprisonment within the static framing. Even the beer looks flat. A blown-up print of what looks like sixteenth- or seventeenth-century Munich on the wall behind the pub table has sinuous lines of rivers, bridges, and old streets which contrast with the cut-off shots of sharp-angled, anonymous, 1960s apartment blocks. This visual rhetoric takes on a blackly comic note in the unhappy cheese plant in one of the flats which, overshadowed by the geometric lines of tables and windows, droops and pines ever more as the film progresses. The spectator is denied visual pleasure in the motor car, the great love object of German economic recovery, and only hears the undifferentiated whine of traffic on the soundtrack, in contrast to the gleaming individual motor cars in Heimat films which propel people into picturesque landscapes and idyllic marriages. Intercut with the many static images are repeated sequences showing two characters, two women or a man and a woman, walking arm in arm towards the camera which moves backwards as they approach past a line of lock-up garages—again we are denied sight of motor cars—to the tinkling notes of a waltz by Schubert known as the *Sehnsuchtswalzer*. The amateur piano-playing evokes a past Biedermeier era of happy families and a culture in which rustic idyll, conveyed in the wistful ländler rhythm, had already by Schubert's time become a token of conservative ideology in an urbanizing world. Combined with the lock-up garages, the effect is of brilliantly comic travesty.

The rotation of a small number of locales with shifting pairs or groups of characters, the swapping of places within sequences, and the repetition of the couples walking in time to the waltz create a musical structure of variations on a theme. The Viennese playwright Arthur Schnitzler (1862–1931) gave one of his best-known plays the title of *Reigen* or *Round Dance* (1896/7) which was then filmed as *La Ronde* (Max Ophüls, 1950). Fassbinder transports the sexual dance from the anonymous, heartless, but exciting city to the claustrophobic, heartless, and boring suburb where everyone knows everyone, at least till the arrival of the Greek. Musical chairs would also be an appropriate metaphor for the desultory partner-swapping, including amateur heterosexual and homosexual prostitution. Here the two figures in Schnitzler's play of actress and prostitute are merged in Fassbinder's Rosy who does it for money to pay for film school, her dream escape route; one of Rosy's customers, who betrays his girlfriend with Rosy, in turn services a gay acquaintance for money. (Such cooling down contrasts with Sperr/Fleischmann's heated treatment of homosexuality.) The rondo structure contrasts with the linear plot of 1950s Heimat films which drives the characters towards reconciliation and marriage. Here the arrival of Jorgos provokes rising sexual tension and aggression: the women are excited by an exotic stranger; the men too, faced with a rival, feel driven to prove their sexual prowess. These reactions convey how racism is pervaded by sexual fantasies which turn the stranger into an object of desire, jealousy, or disgust. 'Katzelmacher' means literally a man who behaves like an unneutered tom-cat fathering many kittens, hence the men's repeated mantra that Jorgos should be castrated and when Marie breaks ranks by having an affair with Jorgos, the other four men beat him up in an aggressive climax—quite the opposite of the integrative endings of Heimat films. In the end, though, nothing has really changed. If there is to be change, then it can only be by escape from this suburban anti-Heimat to the city and film school, as Rosy dreams of, or to the sunny Greece Maria dreams of. Thus *Fernweh* wins out over *Heimatliebe*, and no wonder given how repulsive the Heimat is. *Katzelmacher* is an aesthetic paradox. It depicts a drab world of stunted, impoverished relationships with supreme elegance and wit. The spare, laconic understatement of individual shots along with the overarching rhythmic pulse make this an intensely pleasurable film. The Schubertian sequence becomes ever more delicious with each repetition. And there are idyllic moments, such as a shot of Maria and Jorgos's faces in close-up with two slim criss-crossing branches of a tree behind them. The effect, reminiscent of the decorative, turn-of-the-century *Jugendstil*, contributes to the pervasive aesthetic patterning. Fassbinder would in other films take up the looming chiaroscuro of Expressionism or the artificial lighting and the nightmare shadows of *film noir*. But in this early film all is light and clear. The film is also pervasively comic, not least in resisting steamy eroticism: Fassbinder's unexotic appearance and emphatically unalluring performance as Jorgos comically undo the stereotype of sexual potency which his racist characters project on the Greek stranger. The supposedly exotic stranger, he looks exactly like the local denizens. Similarly, the attack on Jorgos is played unconvincingly as farce. As spectators we are thus denied the pleasures of melodramatic sex and violence, yet there is ample compensation in this deconstruction of Heimat discourse. For the stylized depiction of alienated sex, boredom, hopelessness, and racism avoids naturalist fatalism not in the storyline, but in the fluency and wit of its form.

Where *Katzelmacher* centres on young adults, *Wildwechsel* turns to adolescents. Under-age Hanni gets pregnant by her older boyfriend, Franz, who has already served a gaol term because of their relationship. (In Fleischmann's film of *Jagdszenen aus Niederbayern*, Tonka is renamed Hannelore, a name perhaps echoed in tribute in Kroetz/Fassbinder's Hanni.) The lovers reject abortion as a solution and egged on by Hanni, Franz murders Hanni's father who they fear will denounce them again to the authorities: the murder has come to seem the only way to save their love and the idyllic dream of keeping the baby and setting up their own family. The film closes bleakly: Franz, awaiting trial for murder, hears from Hanni in the closing sequence that the baby was deformed and had died at birth. Both the play and the film invoke the Naturalist explanation of behaviour as a product of milieu. The depiction of milieu in *Wildwechsel* combines elements of regional culture with class-based economic factors and with historical influences which come together to cause the family structure, the conservative base of the social order, to implode. Bavarian Catholicism is pervasively signified in the crucifixes and kitsch religious pictures of the Madonna in Hanni's house, in shots of the local church, and in the crucifix Franz wears along with his rock-and-roll leather gear. Although the young couple break the religious ban on extramarital sex, their rejection of abortion and their idealistic dream of setting up their own family have more in common with the cult of Madonna than does Hanni's father's economic view of the family: having invested time and money in bringing up Hanni, he is enraged that she should throw herself away on a wastrel who does not even have a flat of his own and works in the local chicken factory. Feeding into the father's punitive outrage is not only conventional Catholic teaching and petit-bourgeois class pretensions, but also an authoritarian hangover from the Third Reich and a deep-reaching self-pity: when he was Franz's age, he was fighting on the eastern front; is his daughter now to be taken from him by this callow boy? In the play the father proposes castration as the right punishment for the likes of Franz, yet Kroetz objected to shots in the film implying the father's lust for his daughter. Such Oedipal intimations, whether dreams of castrating the rival or of enjoying the daughter, add a further factor to the self-destructing dynamic within the family. In the closing sequence, in an up-to-date disposal of young love which would do away equally with *Romeo and Juliet*, the young people mouth the clichés of officialdom to deny their love: it was not real love, it was all just physical, they intone. But the wistful thought of a baby boy who would have been called Michael leaves a trace of idealism which makes the outcome all the more bleak. In killing off the baby and with him the next generation, the plot quite undoes the reconciliatory happy ending of the typical 1950s Heimat film, ostensibly reverting to the fatalistic closure characteristic of turn-of-the-century Naturalism which shows characters helpless in the face of social forces. But it does so rather knowingly, more as a citation of Naturalist fatalism than as straight regression to an earlier idiom. When at the end the characters themselves blame Fate, this is a grotesque echo of 'You are my Destiny', the Paul Anka song which punctuates the soundtrack. The film brings out how pop songs of young love and youth in rebellion feed into the lovers' dreams of breaking free. The clashing discourses in *Wildwechsel* thus mix Catholic tradition in travesty in the dream of a holy family on the run from punitive authorities, with rebellious youth or love's young dream celebrated in American pop music, and the echoes of fateful love in the manner of *Romeo and Juliet*. Whereas 1950s Heimat films injected glossy up-to-date realities into a timeless Heimat, Fassbinder does the opposite. In *Wildwechsel* archaic ideals and romantic dreams infiltrate the mentality of the denizens of a drab contemporary Heimat which is anything but timeless, its immediate past history and economic underpinnings being all too evident. The effect of such mixing is an alienating irony which dismantles both the supposed fatality of social forces and the romantic dreams but without entirely extinguishing the humanity of the young people. In contrast to the mood of cynical comedy in *Katzelmacher*, in *Wildwechsel* a compassionate note sounds through the mayhem.

Resurrecting the Family? Franx Xaver Kroetz and the Critical *Volksstück*

Jagdszenen aus Niederbayern and the two Fassbinder films exemplify varieties of a stylized naturalist idiom deployed in scenes of everyday life to travesty Heimat discourse. Subsequently, however, Franz Xaver Kroetz, the author of the play on which Fassbinder's *Wildwechsel* was based, accused Fassbinder of turning his play into pornography of violence. In retrospect, Kroetz's repudiation of the film can be seen as the outcome of growing political worries about his own realist aesthetic.[27] The end of the 1960s when Kroetz began to write was a time of political radicalism. The alliance of the CDU and CSU with the SPD in the Grand Coalition government of 1966–9 led to the rise of extra-parliamentary opposition especially among students who increasingly took to the streets in wide-scale protests against authoritarian structures within the universities, against an older generation perceived as politically tainted by the Third Reich, and in solidarity with international protests, often couched in Marxist terms, against the Vietnam War, Western imperialism, and the capitalist system. Although Kroetz was not involved in the student movement, which was already ebbing when he decided to join the German Communist Party in 1972, his very earliest work was imbued with a spirit of protest which sought to expose suffering and alienation underlying West Germany's economic miracle. Yet his unease at Fassbinder's *Wildwechsel* extended to his own early work generally, as many interviews testify, and arose from the fear that his plays were not politically effective.[28] These fears were if anything intensified by his own success, for his work was certainly effective in drawing the theatregoing public, but not the kind of public he sought to engage. Kroetz emerged as a dominant figure in German theatre with astonishing rapidity. The year 1971 saw the first production beyond small fringe theatres of his work, but by the 1972/3 season he had become the most frequently played German-language dramatist in the German theatres, his work continuing up to the early 1980s to be among the most performed. During this time his preferred form was the critical *Volksstück* until in 1980 his play *Nicht Fisch nicht Fleisch* marked a shift to more experimental techniques. The term *Volksstück* denotes a traditional, popular genre of play with a bucolic setting and often in the mode of farce, which derives its comic effects from regional and class stereotypes, but sometimes also drawing contrasts

---

[27] See Michelle Mattson, *Franz Xaver Kroetz: The Construction of a Political Aesthetic* (Oxford: Berg, 1996), 16–45 on political art and on aesthetic debates about realism.

[28] For a useful bibliography of Kroetz's interviews, see ibid. 203–4.

between rural and urban mores when the countryman goes to town or the townie visits the country. Another common element is dialect. Although the tradition goes back much longer, the *Volksstück* can be considered under the umbrella of Heimat literature. It remains still today a popular form on television, purveying comic stereotypes of village life for an overwhelmingly urban public.

Kroetz's attempt to appropriate the *Volksstück* to left-wing ends raises many questions about how far Heimat literature in a realist mode can be politically effective, if indeed literature ever can be politically effective. Kroetz initially sought to align himself with a tradition of critical realism represented in the work of Marieluise Fleißer and Ödön von Horváth in plays depicting lower-class characters who are in some sense representative of the people at large, though quite how was one of the worries besetting Kroetz in his struggle to find an effective idiom. The aim being accessibility not just to an elite intelligentsia, the language is colloquial, often fragmentary, with pauses, repetitions, clichés, dialect words, pronunciation, and syntax, though Kroetz warned against phoney imitation Bavarian in productions in other parts of the country. Local accessibility through dialect thus caused problems of translation nationally. The rural and provincial settings link in with the anti-metropolitan tendency in the Heimat tradition, whether on left or right, and mark a shift from orthodox Marxist emphasis on the urban proletariat towards rural workers. But in what sense could rural workers represent 'the people' who might unite to become politically effective in the West Germany of the 1970s? In the early 1970s less than 7 per cent of the West German population worked on the land.[29] The average farm was much smaller than in Britain and 50 per cent of farms were less than ten hectares. By the same token, however, the farms being smaller meant that more people were working on the land than in Britain. At the same time the movement out of agriculture in postwar West Germany was among the most rapid in any developed country, the resultant stresses representing a significant facet of social change. But could the urban theatre public recognize their problems in a marginal figure such as the landless farmworker Sepp in *Stallerhof*? What was sure was that redundant farmworkers seeking work in the city would not come to the theatre to learn about their troubles. Kroetz's dilemmas recall the problems facing aspiring left-wing writers which the English critic William Empson identified in his classic study of pastoral writing. Empson distinguishes between proletarian literature, or more widely folk literature,

[29] For figures on agriculture at this time see Günter Kloss, *West Germany: An Introduction* (London: Macmillan, 1976), 59–63; also Graham Hallett, *The Social Economy of West Germany* (London: Macmillan, 1973), 42–51.

which is about, by, and for the people, and pastoral which is about, but not by or for the people, and went on to define pastoral as the process of 'putting the complex into the simple' and as the attempt 'to reconcile the conflicts of an individual in whom those of society will be mirrored'.[30] Most good proletarian literature is really covert pastoral, Empson suggests, and none the worse for that. Empson's provocative comments catch well the dilemmas inherent in Kroetz's enterprise: the very act of writing divides the writer from the people and the public remains stubbornly limited to the educated, urban middle class. Above all, the process of 'putting the complex into the simple' and of finding individual figures in whom the conflicts of society are mirrored is perhaps doomed to failure: the complex is too complex to be reduced to accessible simplicities; individuals cannot represent a whole society; to show a solution to social conflicts mirrored in the individual would be hopelessly utopian; not to show a solution would be a throwback to Naturalist fatalism which showed individuals helplessly caught in the mechanisms of heredity and environment. In its author's eyes this was the trouble with *Wildwechsel*: its marginalized characters reach no social understanding, the inarticulate violence of their response being liable at best to provoke pity, at worst the pornographic thrill Kroetz saw in Fassbinder's film, but certainly not effective political action. Such problems had led Theodor Adorno to reject the whole project of a committed political literature, to downgrade realism as a literary mode, and to privilege modernist aesthetic autonomy as the only revolutionary path worth pursuing in the arts: art liberates through form not content; revolutionary art is difficult and resists easy consumption; accessible popular culture is but a commodity in the market designed to stupify and depoliticize the public.[31] On such a view Kroetz's project for a popular, engaged, political art was misconceived from the start. More generously eclectic in spirit, Empson's is perhaps a fairer approach than Adorno's: Kroetz's plays may not have precipitated the revolution, but might still count as good art, whether labelled proletarian or pastoral. In our context the issue is whether Kroetz succeeds in appropriating the Heimat mode to left-wing argument in his preferred form of the critical *Volksstück*.

A look at three examples may put some flesh on these abstract questions: *Stallerhof* (1971) is the climax of Kroetz's early work in a mode of heightened naturalism; *Oberösterreich*, premièred in 1972, marks a shift to more overtly political form close to socialist realism; *Das Nest* of 1974

[30] *Some Versions of Pastoral*, 4th edn. (London: Chatto and Windus, 1978), 6, 22, 19.
[31] Adorno, 'Engagement', in *Gesammelte Schriften*, xi (Frankfurt am Main: Suhrkamp, 1974), 409–30; on popular art and the culture industry see Theodor Adorno and Max Horkheimer, *Dialectic of Enlightenment*, trans. John Cumming (London: Verso, 1979), 120–68.

continues in the socialist realist vein and promotes a left-wing green agenda.[32] It is an irony of German history that just as the most radical writers and artists in the GDR were struggling to break out from socialist realism, some of the most radical voices in the FRG and Austria were experimenting with realist idioms in an effort to escape from the elitest ghetto of high modernism so valued by Adorno, though by 1974 the so-called *Tendenzwende*, a shift from political protest to a more inward-looking neo-romantic tendency, was well under way. *Stallerhof* poses in an acute form the dilemmas faced by the would-be proletarian writer protesting against injustice, for how can a play about a dysfunctional peasant family with a retarded daughter made pregnant by an elderly farmworker represent the social conflicts of West Germany at large? The main characters in *Stallerhof* are a relatively prosperous small farmer, Staller, his wife, their daughter Beppi who has learning difficulties intensified by her poor eyesight, and an elderly seasonal farmworker, Sepp, who is close to retiring age. Sepp has sex with Beppi even though she is still just a child. Beppi loses her virginity just after having diarrhoea brought on by a trip in the ghost train at a country fair. Sepp cleans her up with his handkerchief then does the deed as laconically as the stage direction describing it: 'Geht schon wieder. Geh her. *Nimmt sie, entjungfert sie*' (Act 2, scene 1).[33] Like the deflowering, the ensuing love affair is depicted on a knife edge between idyll and travesty. In bare outline, the plot of *Stallerhof* echoes the perennial Rococo tale of ardent lover wooing country maiden —Goethe's poem 'Heidenröslein' exemplifies the mode—except that here the youth is close to drawing the old-age pension and the maiden is under age. When the inevitable happens and Beppi gets pregnant, her horrified parents flirt with ideas of murder, whether of Beppi, Sepp, or of the foetus by way of an abortion on the kitchen table. But in the end the only murder is of Sepp's dog. After all, the new child might even be a healthy boy who would compensate Beppi's long-suffering parents for having a retarded daughter as their only child. In *Stallerhof* Kroetz avoids the pornography of violence which he saw in Fassbinder's *Wildwechsel* by alluding to but not showing horrors such as child murder or amateur enforced abortion. And he reverses a key principle in Sperr's *Jagdszenen in Niederbayern* where hints of humane feeling are always drowned out by horror; here hints of horrors that might, but do not, happen underlie a surface veneer of humanity. Sepp is sent off to the city rather than murdered

[32] Franz Xaver Kroetz, *Stallerhof* and *Geisterbahn*, in *Heimarbeit / Stallerhof / Geisterbahn / Kapellenspiel von der heiligen Jungfrau / Michis Blut* (Hamburg: Rotbuch Verlag, 1996); *Oberösterreich*, in *Maria Magdalena: Der Soldat / Oberösterreich / Wunschkonzert* (Hamburg: Rotbuch Verlag, 1996); *Das Nest*, in *Mensch Meier / Herzliche Grüße aus Grado / Das Nest* (Hamburg: Rotbuch Verlag, 1999).
[33] 'You're all right again. Come on. *Takes her and deflowers her.*'

and the play closes with two tiny scenes: in the first pregnant Beppi and her mother pick wild cranberries together; in the closing scene Beppi's labour pains are just starting as she sits at supper with her parents. 'Papamama', she cries (Act 3, scene 6). In the sequel, *Geisterbahn*, this ironic happy ending of new life in the rural Heimat is undone. Beppi stands up to her parents and goes off with Sepp and baby Georg to a new life in Munich, but the little family does not prosper, Sepp dies, and rather than give up her child to the social workers, Beppi kills Georg and is imprisoned. 'Mir ham ein Wirtschaftswunder' (Act 1, scene 4), Staller proclaims in the first play.[34] The second play demonstrates the fate of the socially excluded whom the economic miracle fails to reach.

In the programme notes for a production of *Stallerhof* in Cologne in the winter season of 1972/3 Kroetz writes of his intention to reveal a gap between what the audience has hitherto believed and the reality shown on the stage. *Stallerhof* undoes the double illusion that material prosperity brings happiness and that the economic miracle has brought prosperity for all. To be sure, Staller and his wife are better off than ever before: in the past a girl of Beppi's age, as her mother notes, would have been labouring throughout the summer up on the high meadows, something Beppi does does not have to do, unlike Kathrinchen in Viebig's *Das Kreuz im Venn* who over the summer herds cows out on the meadows, so missing out on school. But half a century on, Beppi is almost illiterate due to poor schooling and ignorant parents while Sepp, the ageing farmworker, represents those who fail to survive in a society based on competition and achievement. *Stallerhof* undoes another kind of illusion, the chocolate-box images of Heimat films, through a disillusioning rhetoric of visual effects such as sweeping out cow-dung from the milking parlour, Beppi's deflowering, or Sepp masturbating in the lavatory. But such moments are juxtaposed with with more idyllic scenes such as Beppi and Sepp enjoying a day out together in the garden of a country inn, in echo perhaps of the paradise garden in Swiss author Gottfried Keller's classic village tale of star-crossed lovers, *Romeo und Julia auf dem Dorfe* (1856). Or there is the scene of mother and daughter picking cranberries. Such juxtaposition of idyll and obscenity has affinities with Wedekind's technique in *Frühlings Erwachen* (1891), but there the heroine dies of a botched amateur abortion whereas here Beppi's mother relents and allows the pregnancy to proceed despite what the neighbours may think. Country life is thus not reduced to the rural idiocy which Marx had attacked in the *Communist Manifesto*, virtually calling for the country to be suburbanized. Kroetz deploys a reverse discourse: humanity is most purely embodied in the

---

[34] 'We've got an economic miracle'.

country 'idiots', Beppi and Sepp, and in *Geisterbahn* the more 'advanced' city proves more deadly than the 'backward' country.

The most striking feature of Kroetz's artistry is the dialogue. Critics have commented on the inarticulacy of his characters as a sign of their defective state as helpless victims. The opening sequence of *Stallerhof* offers a reflection on language which could lead to such a conclusion. Short-sighted Beppi has just received a postcard from Munich and hesitantly half reads, half guesses what it must say, 'Bald kommen mir', she reads, at which her mother slaps her to make her correct the dialect 'mir' to 'wir'.[35] The passage conveys that Beppi's backwardness is largely the result of her short sight and also evokes social determinants of speech such as the denigrating of dialect even by dialect speakers themselves which helps produce the hesitant lack of oral confidence of rural people compared with fast-talking townies. Yet as the play proceeds, the dialect evocative of a region and its history, the laconic clichés, the use of isolated particles such as 'ebn' or 'genau' framed by long silences, understatement at moments of intense emotional stress, truncated sentences omitting pronouns and so highlighting meaning-bearing nouns and verbs, take on a rhythmic expressiveness. The silences speak: they open up space for unspoken meaning which the spectator fills, rather like silent close-ups in the cinema. The effect is two-edged: limited linguistic capacity does signal social deprivation yet at the same time is highly expressive. Such a technique looks back to Büchner's *Woyzeck* where the fluency of a doctor comes across as the idiocy of the educated in contrast to inarticulate Woyzeck's humanity. This is one device of pastoral in Empson's sense: such dialogue is a means of putting the complex into the simple in the figures of Sepp, the simple fool, and Beppi, the wise child. Kroetz's critical realism combines attack on rural deprivation and ignorance while preserving an image of potential human wholeness, this double effect most strikingly achieved in the dialogue.

Seen in the context of the shifting appropriations of the Heimat ideal, *Stallerhof* clearly runs counter to the *Blut und Boden* ideology of the Third Reich which elevated the peasant as the ideal German type and celebrated the fecundity of peasant women. Beppi's surly, brutal father is a model to be avoided, while her mother has not been fecund, and her only child might have fallen victim to the Nazi policy of euthanasia for the mentally retarded. The communal unity of Heimat Nazi style is denied in many details evoking the economic divisions between big landowners, small farmers, and landless labourers as also between town and country. The play does invoke a mythic community which is not located in the local

---

[35] 'We're coming soon'.

Heimat, however, but distanced in the form of *Fernweh*, of longing for an exotic utopia in the 'Red Indian'[36] story Sepp tells Beppi in Act 1, scene 2. A white traveller, a doctor, is invited by the chief to choose one of the women of the tribe, but the doctor chooses an outcast as his concubine, so redeeming her and assuming magical powers in the eyes of the tribe when he survives contact with the tabooed outcast. He then marries her, survives a plot by the tribe to kill him in revenge against their white enemies, becomes the tribal spokesman, and mediates a truce with the white attackers. More episodes will clearly follow. Sepp's story draws on a tradition of children's literature dating back to Karl May (1842–1912), author of immensely popular stories about American Indians which remain among the longest-lasting best-sellers in German publishing history. May's biggest successes, *Old Shurehand* (1894) and the three volumes of *Winnetou* (1893–1910), formed an exotic counterpoint to turn-of-the-century Heimat discourse. May's works celebrate the noble American Indians and he himself, though he shared the pervasive racial stereotyping of his time, had anti-imperialist, pacifist leanings. Sepp's story illustrates how, *pace* Adorno, popular literature can express the utopian dreams and desires of the socially deprived. The story overcomes divisions: the white male scientist (Sepp), who is divided by race and superior culture from the tribe, at once restores tribal unity by redeeming the outcast woman (Beppi) and enters the tribe himself as leader and spokesman. Thus the hero lays claim to the power of discourse to negotiate a truce between warring peoples by reconciling the native American *Naturvolk* (the rural Heimat) and the white *Kulturvolk* (modern educated society). But as we all know, native Americans and white settlers were not reconciled and nowadays Indian reservations have become an exotic tourist attraction concealing the reality that her native peoples form the most deprived and marginalized group in the American melting pot. In Empsonian fashion, the heroic pastoral of Sepp's story offers an imaginary resolution to Sepp's individual conflict which reflects in simplified form wider, West German, social conflicts between town and country, rich and poor, educated and deprived. But in the framework play, the conflicts remain unresolved as the hero is expelled and in the sequel, the squaw fails to survive with her child in the city.

Stallerhof has an open ending: a birth is imminent and like Sepp's 'Red Indian' tale more episodes can follow. *Geisterbahn*, by contrast, closes off the future: the miserable ending recalls the fatalistic streak in the Naturalist theatre of the turn of the century, while the motif of infanticide

---

[36] The 'Red Indian' story becomes all the more offensive if taken to be about actual American Indians rather than as a somewhat grotesque allusion to a popular German literary tradition.

looks back even further to the *Sturm und Drang* era in the late eighteenth century. Sepp and the baby dead and Beppi herself reduced to the status of childish victim, no way forward is left. The year Kroetz joined the DKP (Deutsche kommunistische Partei), 1972, also saw the first production of *Oberösterreich*. This play seeks a way out of the fatalistic impasse by blending together many conventions of Heimat literature with a didactic message as in a Brechtian *Lehrstück* but in the un-Brechtian Heimat mode. There are only two characters, the husband Heinz and his wife Anni, who live in Bavaria, probably near or in Munich for they have a day out at the Starnbergersee. The play opens as they switch off the telly, having just watched a travel programme about the imperial city of Vienna, arousing dreams of travelling to distant places, just as television advertisements awaken desire for any number of goodies to decorate their home and garden. Rather than utopia in the shape of stories about Red Indians, here the consumer culture of late capitalism and the economic miracle have infiltrated *Fernweh*—the longing to wander the wider world—and *Heimatliebe*—love of home—feeding dreams of heritage tourism and a swimming pool in the back garden. 'Illusionen braucht der Mensch', so Heinz proclaims. 'Mir ham doch eh so viel Illusionen, daß mir uns nicht beklagen können', Anni replies.[37] But Anni gets pregnant, putting an end to the dreams as the two add up the costs and what they will have to give up to afford to have a baby. Heinz fails to persuade Anni to have an abortion and in the last scene Anni reads out an item about a man on trial in Upper Austria for murdering his wife because she refused to have an abortion, indicating the fatalistic outcome, signalled in the play's title, which our couple have avoided. For they are agreed that their child must come into a world with hope, the message conveyed being that market-driven dreams are in fact an obstacle to hopes for a better future. Yet the play closes with Heinz playing the Viennese waltz 'Wien, Wien, nur du allein' on his accordion, so keeping alive their dream of visiting Vienna. The play thus combines an attack on consumerism but also on the class inequality which means that unrealizable dreams for some—being able to afford a child *and* a holiday in Vienna—are taken for granted by the better off. In a later interview Kroetz claimed that *Oberösterreich* was a 'Massenstück mit zwei Personen' ('a play for the masses with two characters'); there was no need to multiply the characters since Heinz and Anni share the dreams of the mass of the people.[38] Many moments in the play sketch in the economic and social inequalities intrinsic to capitalism and which extend into the so-called private sphere of sexual relations and reproduction. But

---

[37] 'Man needs illusions.' 'We've got so many illusions, we can't really complain.'
[38] *Theater heute*, 7 (1980), 18.

the unspectacular outcome of a couple settling down to make the best of things conveys little sense of how this unjust world might be changed. The warnings that murdering your wife or infanticide are not the answer are more a response to a German dramatic tradition than to German political realities of the 1970s.

Das Nest of two years later is similar in idiom, but does offer more of a political message. This again starts off with a couple watching television, this time a play, which they both find unconvincing, called *Oberösterreich*. (*Oberösterreich* was hugely successful and was shown on television, but without the framework political discussion which Kroetz had wanted and which would have served to get across more of the economic and political implications of his play.) Such authorial self-deprecation comically conveys Kroetz's perennial worries over failing to get his message across. As an alienation effect, it emphasizes the status of Kurt and Martha as characters in a play with a message and their initial lack of consciousness of their own typicality: the problems they face are the problems of a whole class. Kurt is a lorry driver, Martha does piecework at home making men's ties. They are saving up to afford the child Martha is expecting. As in *Oberösterreich*, they too list all the items necessary for a new baby and what they might save on to afford them in a scene which will get across to a leftish urban audience the difficulties facing ordinary provincial working-class people—the play is set in small-town Upper Bavaria—but might also reach the much wider television audience. The couple believe in self-help as emphasized in a scene in their allotment which invokes a mentality going back to Voltaire's satirical novel *Candide*: Kurt and Martha believe all is for the best in the best of all possible worlds and that all they need do to survive is cultivate their garden. This is the apolitical ideology of the *Spießbürger*. Driven by fear of losing his job with a wife and child to support and fearing competition from cheap imported labour, Kurt colludes with his employer and illegally dumps poisonous waste in a lake where, as fate would have it, Martha goes for a picnic and paddles with baby Stefan whom she dips in the water, causing burns to his delicate baby's skin and to her own legs. After immersing himself in the lake but without ill effects and contemplating suicide, Kurt finally decides to go to the police to report his own and his employer's crime and to seek help from his trade union: 'Die Gewerkschaft, das sind viele.'[39] Where the fatalistic closure at the end of *Geisterbahn* remains in a naturalist idiom, *Das Nest* accords with socialist realism in attacking capitalism, but at the same time showing progressive historical forces in the shape of working-class solidarity through trade unionism. Interestingly, the play focuses not only

---

[39] 'There are many people in the union.'

on capitalist exploitation of labour, but also on environmental damage, so giving a green twist to the red message: the reference to the many in the union is followed up by a closing picture of baby Stefan playing in the garden, so recuperating the small-scale garden from its negative meaning as a symbol of political indifference by juxtaposing it with the simultaneous need for large-scale political intervention. How convincing the ending is is another matter, for the trade unions, more concerned by unemployment than with industrial pollution, have not played a leading role in the rise of green politics, just as state socialism proved as careless of the environment as Western capitalism.

The texts by Kroetz considered so far all centre on family relationships, whether failing families in *Stallerhof* and *Geisterbahn* or families winning through in *Oberösterreich* and *Das Nest*. In *Das Nest*, emergent political commitment is rooted in maternal love as a primary instinct. In *Stallerhof* it is maternal instinct in Beppi's mother which saves the foetus. Paternalism is more of an acquired instinct but once awakened serves in the two later plays as the activating force mediating between the family and the wider economic and political world. In *Stallerhof* Sepp, the lover, is more fatherly to Beppi than her biological father, a combination continuing the provocative motif of under-age sex we have seen in other works at this time, while in *Geisterbahn*, pathos attaches not only to the young mother and her child but also to Sepp as loving father without whose support the little family is doomed. In all the plays the core vulnerable humanity to be protected is embodied in a child and in *Stallerhof*, *Oberösterreich*, and *Das Nest* resort to abortion symbolizes the dehumanizing effects of misconceived moral conventions and of materialist consumerism under capitalism. Whatever Kroetz's intentions, *Oberösterreich* and *Das Nest* offer solutions that 'fit rather nicely into conservative politics', as Michelle Mattson puts it.[40] For the plays sustain traditional family values and roles and anathematize abortion just at a time when the right to abortion had become a focus of the women's movement. *Stallerhof* was premièred in 1971, the same year as *stern* magazine published a declaration by 374 women that they had undergone an illegal abortion. *Oberösterreich*, premièred the very next year, rubs the message home. Of course enforced abortion performed on a mentally backward mother evokes memories of euthanasia policies under the Nazis and no one wants children to be unaffordable by the respectable working class. But in the theatre what is shown on stage takes on symbolic expansion of meaning difficult to control; the pathos Kroetz invests in new life under threat of abortion puts his plays in a tradition at odds with left-wing support of abortion rights

---

[40] Mattson, *Kranz Xaver Kroetz*, 90.

during the Weimar Republic, the last time there had been a big campaign
on the issue centred in Germany's big cities and especially Berlin. In this
respect, these plays are indeed more in keeping with the Heimat tradition,
even with Bavarian Catholicism and its elevation of the unborn child,
than with Marxism or the feminist movement of the 1970s in offering a
mix of anti-capitalist rhetoric with support for family values, a combination which could suggest a right-wing or even fascist tendency.

Such a conclusion would, however, be quite unfair in not taking into
account the historical context. Seen in retrospect, Kroetz's plays interestingly exemplify a crisis in the 1970s in left-wing thinking which, as his
interviews demonstrate, he himself was only too aware of. What Kroetz
called his 'Realismus-Problem', the difficulty in creating figures representative of historical forces, was less an artistic than a historical problem for
a writer dealing with rural or provincial themes at a time when economic
and social change had in any case rendered hopes of proletarian revolution illusory.[41] *Nicht Fisch nicht Fleisch* of 1980, written after Kroetz had
left the DKP, adopts a new theatrical language combining realist detail
and surreal symbolism. The play opens up the domestic Heimat, conveyed in a few props such as a bed and a kitchen sink, to evoke in travesty
a history of humanity's odyssey away from a state of nature to the complex
technological world of today. Classical Marxist faith in technological progress is replaced by a sceptical questioning in tune with green thinking
and a differentiated evaluation of new technologies depending on how far
they can be harnessed to humane ends. The shift from the proletariat and
heavy industry to skilled workers in electronics and the new information
technology is conveyed through the choice of the printing industry as
focus. The play also takes a more critical view of traditional family roles,
attacks the patriarchal pretension of the male characters, and recasts
to some extent the issue of abortion. A shift from Marxist class to feminist gender analysis was especially evident in Kroetz's production of the
play in the Munich Kammerspiele in the 1983/4 season where women's
right to self-determination was more emphasized than in the published
text.

Bauern Sterben of 1986 is an even more radically experimental play
which, as Moray McGowan suggests, adapts the Expressionist *Sta-
tionendrama*, a term derived from the stations on Christ's way to the
Cross.[42] The title *Bauern Sterben* means literally 'peasants dying' or 'peasants are dying' and is a provocative echo of the term *Waldsterben* or

[41] For an extensive discussion of these issues see ibid., ch. 2.
[42] 'Botho Strauß and Franz Xaver Kroetz: Two Contemporary Views of the Subject', *Strathclyde Modern Language Studies*, 5 (1985), 58–75 (72).

'forest dying' which denotes the damage to trees caused by acid rain and is a cause célèbre in German ecological circles.[43] Kroetz's title signals his humanist position in contrast to some more radical ecological warriors who do not privilege the human species. The play conveys the final stations in mankind's passage towards ever greater alienation from nature, a process immensely speeded up in the twentieth century as the global flight from the land spawns vast city wastelands and human beings become ever more denatured. The main figures are a brother and sister who set out on a journey away from a rural Heimat which is already corrupted from within by the father's greed for profits from increased production using chemicals and new technologies and the mother's lust for modern consumer goods. The siblings' departure is preceded by the laying out of their grandmother's corpse in whose stomach an aborted foetus from the sister's womb is sewn, emblematically signifying the death of the maternal Heimat following the corruption of the paternal order in the preceding scene: no life can spring from a dead foetus in a dead womb. The siblings then wander through a devastated world only to return in the last scene, but all that remains of the Heimat is an alien snowy landscape and the father's grave. Deepest Bavarian dialect is interspersed with short passages of standard German, the linguistic distance signifying a double alienation: global modernization brings the loss of attachment to specific localities just as traditional cultures are becoming archaic within the span of a single generation, thus leaving no sense of belonging whether in a global space anywhere between Landshut and Calcutta, as the opening stage directions put it, or in an alienated Heimat which has become an anonymous grave in a snowy wasteland. *Bauern Sterben* has magnified the naturalist fatalism of *Geisterbahn* into an Expressionistic apocalypse. The intervening phases in Kroetz's work of optimistic faith in progress to be achieved through political activism, followed by the more sceptical yet still differentiated analysis of economic and social change in the early 1980s, have given way in *Bauern Sterben* to a nightmare vision of global devastation. The play has the weaknesses of the Expressionist manner. Even accepting the thesis that there is now a global economy, the totalizing claim to speak, in Bavarian dialect, for humanity anywhere, whether in Landshut or Calcutta, is too simplistic. This is the kind of humanism, the claim to speak for a universal humanity, which has been attacked as masking the pretensions of a Western elite who in fact speak only for themselves. Likewise, as Hans Magnus Enzensberger had argued in his essay 'Zur Kritik der politischen Ökologie' (1973), the notion of a single ecological system risks obscuring the very different effects of economic

---

[43] Franz Xaver Kroetz, *Bauern Sterben* (Hamburg: Rotbuch Verlag, 1999).

imperialism in different parts of the world in the post-colonial age.[44] Conditions in Landshut and in Calcutta differ enormously. Moreover, the apocalyptic scenario could seem dangerously close to the reactionary cultural pessimism which fuelled the more right-wing tendencies in the Heimat movement before the First World War, helped to undermine faith in democratic politics during the Weimar Republic, and during the Third Reich fed into *völkisch* propaganda: *Ohne Bauerntum stirbt das Volk (Without the Peasantry the People will Die)* is the title for a wall painting displayed in 1939 in the Lüneburg Heimatmuseum showing gruesome octopus-tentacles stretching out from the city to threaten the substance of the German people.[45] On the other hand, just as Expressionist art was singled out for attack by the National Socialists, so Kroetz's play is not liable to appeal to the new right of today. Rather it exemplifies what might be called a post-Marxist ecological turn, often apocalyptic in mood, which by the late 1970s had become a marked tendency in German intellectual debate; Enzensberger's essay with its echo of Marx's title, 'The Critique of Political Economy', is an early example of the trend.

One continuity through Kroetz's work, however, is the invocation of Heimat defined through family relations, provincial or rural in location, and with an anti-urban bent. These features survive through the phases of his work, but also through constant shifts of mood, from early lament for the Heimat destroyed in *Stallerhof* and *Geisterbahn*, through activist defence of a Heimat worth fighting for in *Oberösterreich* and *Das Nest*, through the political uncertainty of *Nicht Fisch, nicht Fleisch* where family solidarity, shaken but still surviving, remains the basis of residual hope in a world in flux, to the apocalyptic mood of *Bauern Sterben* in which lament has turned into horror modified by cynicism. Commenting on the work of Marieluise Fleißer, we suggested that, although cynicism is a mood of self-attack based on despair, in which the best qualities of human beings are devalued, it may in some conditions be a way of preserving integrity. Scenes 1 and 6 respectively in *Bauern Sterben* convey through the figures of actors and a poet in a hurry an authorial reflection on the hopelessness of political art. Such undoing of earlier aspiration combines with the iconoclastic image of an aborted foetus sewn into the stomach of a dead grandmother which undoes the iconography of mother and child underlying the Heimat discourse of *Stallerhof* or *Geisterbahn* to create a

---

[44] On these issues see Arrigo Subiotto, 'From Everyday to Doomsday: The Critique of Progress and Civilisation in Hans Magnus Enzensberger's Writing', in Axel Goodbody (ed.), *Literatur und Ökologie* (Amsterdamer Beiträge zur neueren Germanistik, vol. 43; Amsterdam: Rodopi, 1998), 69–84 and the other essays in this volume.

[45] Reprod. in Martin Roth, *Heimatmuseum: Zur Geschichte einer deutschen Institution* (Berlin: Gbr. Marin, 1990), 258

work in the cynical mode where cynicism is the downside of dashed hopes. Kroetz's love–hate for Heimat continues into a collection of poems, published in 1996, *Heimat Welt: Gedichte eines Lebendigen*. The title poem, 'Heimat Welt', contrasts Brazil and the bloodstained history of slavery, when over a period of three hundred years four million black people were killed, with Germany and the murder of six million Jews over a period of five years, concluding cynically that slaves at least had a certain value. Yet the longing for Heimat rooted in core parent–child love as a universal human emotion is evoked in the image of the poet's baby being passed along and kissed, like a little fat communion wafer, by the dark-skinned descendants of slaves in Salvador. In keeping with the title of the collection, literally *Heimat World: Poems of a Live Man*, the baby, aborted in *Bauern Sterben*, has come back to life, but in a distant land. The concluding verse reads:

> Viele tausend Kilometer
> entfernt sagt mein Herz
> wenn ich an Heimat
> denke; Vorsicht.[46]

Thus the poet feels more at ease in the wide world than in the narrow Heimat, yet still elevates the inter-generational bond at the heart of Heimat as a universal value. Whether the cynical weighing up of the history of slavery against the Holocaust is an adequate response to German history or to imperialism, and whether the salvation in exotic Salvador of Heimat values through the instrument of the poet's baby convincingly renegotiates Heimat for the 1990s, we leave here as open questions, though we shall return to the issue of Heimat discourse as a medium for reflection on the Third Reich in Chapter 5 and to Heimat in a postmodern vein in the last chapter.

---

[46] 'Many thousand kilometres | away, my heart says, | when I think of Heimat: | beware.' *Heimat Welt: Gedichte eines Lebendigen* (Hamburg: Rotbuch, 1996), 25.

4 At Home in the GDR?
Heimat in East German Film

From the foundation on 17 May 1946 of DEFA (Deutsche Film Aktien-gesellschaft) under licence by the Soviet military administration, film production in the Soviet zone and then East Germany followed a different course from in the West.[1] DEFA's remit, as stipulated by the Soviet authorities, was to participate in the struggle to build up a democratic Germany and to educate the German people, especially young Germans, in the spirit of true democracy and humanity. Such a mission contained the seeds for the best and worst features of East German film history as film-makers committed to the socialist project strove to produce serious, critical, and aesthetically ambitious films in the face of official demands for films in the socialist realist mode. Socialist realism was the artistic credo which emerged from the First Pan-Soviet Writers' Congress of 1934 and was declared binding in the GDR in the 1950s: naturalistic realism deployed in the service of historical truth should show reality moving inexorably towards the communist society; in contrast to the formalism and pessimism of bourgeois elitist art, socialist realist art should be accessible to the masses and should offer role models for the public in the shape of the positive hero.[2] Official pressure was fluctuating, however. It was not permanent warfare but rather a sequence of crises over the years as more liberal or more repressive tendencies prevailed. On the positive side, DEFA produced a number of now classic anti-fascist films in the 1940s and early 1950s which testify to a determined reckoning with the Nazi past, beginning with Wolfgang Staudte's *Die Mörder sind unter uns* (1946), a film which had been turned down by the cultural officer with the American occupying forces but was given the go-ahead by his Russian counterpart. Indeed it is fair to say that up to the early 1960s East German film production compares more than favourably with the film industry in the Federal Republic, with a considerable body of artistically serious films to set against the flood of Heimat kitsch. Along with anti-fascist films, other key genres were historical films on the German labour movement which

---

[1] On the history of DEFA see Wolfgang Gersch, 'Film in der DDR' in Wolfgang Jacobsen, Anton Kaes, and Helmut Prinzler (eds.), *Geschichte des deutschen Films* (Stuttgart: Metzlar, 1993), 323–64.

[2] On socialist realism see J. H. Reid, *Writing without Taboos: The New East German Literature* (Oxford: Berg, 1990), 30–5.

could tend to be propagandistic, films of literary classics such as Heinrich Mann's *Der Untertan* (Wolfgang Staudte, 1951)—an ambitious production which was only released in the West in 1956 in a cut version—and the so-called *Gegenwartsfilm*, realist films with a critical agenda depicting everyday life in the GDR which began to be produced from around 1953 on. It is this last genre which is our concern here. Following the death of Stalin a new direction in cultural policy ushered in a period of successful film production in the 1950s bringing with it growing audience figures, culminating in 1957 with sales of 316 million cinema tickets, the highest figure in the history of the GDR.[3] In 1958 and more massively in 1965, however, the party bureaucracy clamped down on the film-makers. Following the 11th plenum of the Central Committee of the SED in 1965 twelve films were banned, being either withdrawn from the cinemas, not released, or else prevented from completion. This catastrophe was a body blow from which the industry never fully recovered, although some of the best GDR films were produced in the 1970s, such as *Die Legende von Paul und Paula* (Heiner Carow, 1973), *Jakob der Lügner* (Frank Beyer, 1975)—the only DEFA film to win an Oscar nomination—and Konrad Wolf's last film *Solo Sunny*, released in January 1980, which, seen in retrospect, is full of premonitions of a society losing its way.

To reactionary proponents of Heimat from the turn of the century to the Third Reich, Marxism had been anathema: it was the cosmopolitan doctrine of rootless, urban intellectuals bent on turning the faceless proletarian masses into a weapon to destroy German culture. Not surprisingly, such Heimat discourse was in turn anathematized in the GDR, and one of the first steps towards denazification in 1945 was the dissolution of local history societies and the deletion of *Heimatkunde* in the National Socialist mode from the primary school syllabus. Yet by the mid-1950s the concept of Heimat was being reappropriated in socialist guise. For beyond international brotherhood, there was the need for a local identity if the citizens of the GDR were to have a sense of belonging that might withstand the lure of capitalist West Germany. According to a Politburo decree of 1952 local history was to return to the syllabus to encourage in young people identification with the GDR and the readiness to defend their Heimat, a task also falling to local museums which documented the trades and skills of a region, presenting Heimat in the form of economic

[3] Anette Battenberg, Jürgen Herdin, Karen Meyer, and Anette Wagner, 'Heimatfilm in der DDR: Annäherung an eine Fragestellung', in *Der deutsche Heimatfilm: Bildwelten und Weltbilder: Bilder, Texte, Analysen zu 70 Jahren deutscher Heimatgeschichte* (Tübingen: Tübinger Verein für Volkskunde, 1989), 149–72 (152).

and social history.[4] As so often throughout its history, once again Heimat discourse served to mediate also the national idea. Thus one speaker at a conference of 1958 on the topic of Heimat proclaimed: 'Der Begriff "Sozialistische Heimat" befindet sich bei uns heute mit dem Begriff "Sozialistisches Vaterland" in Übereinstimmung. Unser sozialistisches Vaterland aber ist die Deutsche Demokratische Republik.'[5] In contrast to this kind of dry prescription of a duty to feel at home, the DEFA films of contemporary life which began to be made in mid-1950s sought by more subtle means to combine measured critique of the contemporary scene with construction of a liveable sense of identity and belonging for GDR citizens. While there is no such genre as the GDR Heimat film, then, there are GDR films about Heimat.[6]

Heimat is a bounded place or social space connecting individuals with something larger through a process of identification, so providing a sense of security and belonging at times of stressful historical change. What could Heimat mean in a Marxist political context and in East Germany as a front-line Soviet bloc country with the Cold War division running through its capital city? A philosopher in the Marxist tradition, Ernst Bloch, defined Heimat as 'etwas, das allen in die Kindheit scheint und worin noch niemand war: Heimat'.[7] Bloch, who returned from exile to teach at the University of Leipzig before moving to West Germany in 1957, takes up the forward-looking aspect of Marxism as a philosophy rooted in the Enlightenment faith in historical progress. In Bloch's tag, Heimat is a name for the conditions enabling the realization of their potential for all human beings: man being a social animal, such non-alienated whole-ness cannot be achieved by isolated individuals but only in the just society of the future. In contrast to the conservative vision of a lost Heimat in the past, Heimat is here a creative project to be worked on. It can be envisaged as a future utopia or as a guiding idea for the present, a process or direc-tion of aspiration. Bloch's epigrammatic formulation does look back-wards too, in the Romantic tradition, to childhood when we come trailing

---

[4]   For a survey of such policies see Dieter Riesenberger, 'Heimatgedanke und Heimatgeschichte in der DDR', in Edeltraut Klueting (ed.), *Anti-Modernismus und Reform: Beiträge zur Geschichte der deutschen Heimatbewegung* (Darmstadt: Wissenschaftliche Buchgemeinschaft, 1991), 320–43.

[5]   'The concept of the "Socialist Heimat" today corresponds to the concept of "Socialist Fatherland". Our socialist Fatherland, however, is the German Democratic Republic.' From *Um unsere sozialistis-che Heimat: Referate und Diskussionsbeiträge einer Tagung am 20. Juni 1958 in Berlin* (Berlin: Deutscher Kulturbund, Zentrale Kommission Natur- und Heimatfreunde, 1958), 76, cited in Ina-Maria Gerverus, *Auf der Suche nach Heimat* (Munich: Beck, 1979), 12.

[6]   On the distinction between Heimat film and films about Heimat see Battenberg et al., 'Heimatfilm in der DDR', in *Der deutsche Heimatfilm: Bildwelten und Weltbilder*, 149–72.

[7]   'something that appears to everyone in childhood and where no one has ever been: Heimat' *Das Prinzip Hoffnung* (Frankfurt am Main: Suhrkamp, 1977), 1628.

clouds of glory before imprisoning alienation closes in. The hope of over-coming alienation in the communist society accords with the optimistic doctrine of a humanity common to all individuals and peoples and stands at the opposite extreme from racist exclusivity and in some tension too with nationalism. Thus whereas Heimat discourse had served through very different political contexts to mediate German identity between smaller region and larger nation, the socialist Heimat mediates between nation and universal humanity. But the negotiation between a utopian, all-inclusive humanism and a bounded identity as a GDR citizen was complicated by Germanness as a third dimension at once overarching the Cold War division yet bisected by it. The title of Christa Wolf's novel, *Der geteilte Himmel* (1963), filmed by Konrad Wolf in 1964, catches the scandal of a temporal, political boundary which yet divides the sky or heaven, the timeless symbol of utopia, for the closed East–West border necessarily produced exclusivity instead of utopian openness. This idea is translated in the film into many shots of faces bisected by lighting or mirror play to convey self-division and alienation from human wholeness.

Heimat boundaries may open to welcome in and allow out, or remain closed to exclude and keep in. The others who can be integrated or must be excluded are as crucial to the definition of a community as those who belong from the start. In the terminology of deconstruction, Heimat as Self/Same depends on a balancing notion of the Other. Heimat GDR style offers a peculiarly literal example of Derrida's theory that names or headings such as Heimat, which define identity, designate at once a negative limit or boundary *and* a chance or opening up of identity to the future. Yet because the opening which allows for the integration of the other expunges the difference necessary to define identity, the boundary simply recedes.[8] A leading theme in many DEFA films is the peculiarly intimate German self–other division which runs through the GDR subject who is both East German and German. Resolution of the resultant conflict demands at once integration of the other in a GDR open to the future yet also exclusion of the other from a GDR bounded and defined through its difference from the other Germany. Too much openness would expunge the difference and bring the threat that the socialist GDR might lose its guiding idea and collapse into its other; too rigid an exclusion would block the opening to the future. The balancing act of integrating yet excluding is played out through characteristic plots centred on cross-generational tensions which turn on who can be included, but who must be excluded or who, more threateningly, exclude themselves by going west. Since the

[8] Jacques Derrida, *The Other Heading*, trans. Pascale-Anne Brault and Michael B. Naas (Bloomington, Ind.: Indiana University Press, 1992), 35.

balancing act is an ongoing process because the boundary keeps shifting, the best of the DEFA films of contemporary life have problems in reaching closure: their often ambiguous or unconvincing happy endings may be one reason for the perennial attacks by the bureaucracy with its demands for a vision of a society which was no longer shaped by antagonistic forces but had arrived.

A related balancing act mediates between tradition and modernization: the need to show the GDR as open to the future, as a place to *work on* to turn it into Heimat, had to be balanced with the GDR as an already homely place to *stay in*. The result is fascinatingly ambiguous locations which, imbued with a sense of the passage of time, often signify yearning for the past more than faith in the future. This aspect of *mise-en-scène* is one defining mark of DEFA cinematography. Locations showing the traces of history combine with the cross-generational theme to pose the question of whether young people can identify with the older generation, the founding fathers committed to the socialist project, and conversely whether the older generation can remain open to the future which the young represent. For if they do not, then the young might turn definitively into the enemy/other either by going west or by infecting the GDR with social diseases such as criminality or fascism which flourish under capitalism but from which socialist societies are supposedly immune. Two further elements feed in to produce the ambiguities marking location in the DEFA films of contemporary life. Built into Marxist dialectical materialism is a Janus-faced view of modernization as bringing alienation through intensified division of labour yet as a necessary phase in the movement of history towards communism. In particular, factory production threatened traditional craftsmanship, yet also called the proletariat into being by bringing large numbers of workers together who then lived in close proximity in working-class districts and so could develop solidarity both at work and in urban communities which, mythically heightened, might represent an urban Heimat. To this theoretical construct must be added the specific reading of twentieth-century German history as a struggle between capitalism and its fascist outgrowth on the one hand and a revolutionary proletariat which earlier in the century had almost prevailed. The revolutionary potential was there, so the argument runs, and survived through persecution, exile, and war to be realized in the great experiment of the GDR. Urban locations showing old, surviving architecture from the past—whether street corners or Berlin tenements or the factory floor—are thus laden with pathos, signifying at once the unchanging spirit of humanity embodied in the proletariat yet evoking also a terrible history of exploitation, persecution, and loss. Since identity denotes continuity through time, time and change are willy-nilly built into the ostensibly spatial metaphors of Heimat. This doubleness is paradigmat-ically exemplified in many representations of urban locations in GDR cinema which project a yearning backward look towards the suffering yet comradeship of the older generation. Less easy to show is Heimat in the making which will appeal to the young in their own terms. New blocks of flats or smart interiors in a modern style lack aura and do not speak as the old locations do of a transcendent human essence shining through the traces of history. Moreover, Yuri Gagarin and Sputnik always excepted, the signifiers of modernization, new technologies, new motor cars (or more often motor bikes), new interior decoration, new household appli-ances, new media, new music, new styles, new almost anything were at the same time the signifiers of the capitalist West with its consumer cul-ture and youth market: images of the new stood on a knife-edge between signifying openness to the future and alien desires corroding socialism from within.

Thus DEFA films of contemporary life aimed to perform a transaction which would open up Heimat GDR style with its backward yearning for an idealized humanist solidarity to integrate the desires of youth for new pleasures and freedoms. Rock and roll or blue jeans, symbols of rebellious youth even in the West, have a whole extra dimension of meaning in the East where orthodoxy sought to police desires infiltrating through dangerously porous borders. The contested arena as often as not being figured as sexual in Oedipally structured plots of conflict between the gen-erations, the resolution and integration of the young in the Heimat is symbolized by heterosexual union. But heterosexual union being notori-ously unstable, it can only be turned into closure—or arrival, to use the orthodox terminology—at the cost of re-establishing a patriarchal order in contradiction to the desire for openness. The twists and turns of the film-makers as they seek to escape from the horns of this dilemma make the best of the DEFA films a fascinating field of retrospective study. *Berlin um die Ecke* (Gerhard Klein, 1965/1990), one of the banned films of 1965 which was premièred only in 1990, exemplifies such tensions and also the striking value in DEFA cinematic language of locations imbued with symbolic meaning. This film is one of a series of four Berlin films made by director Gerhard Klein and scriptwriter Wolfgang Kohlhaase. Their working title for the film was Berlin Chapter Four. The film centres on a group of young men who work together in a team or *Brigade* in a factory in Schöneweide, an industrial district of Berlin. A loosely episodic plot follows the troubled relations between these young workers and their older colleagues. Faced with stroppy youth as well as lack of spare parts or new machinery, the old struggle against the odds to keep production levels up, while the young break rules and flout petty regulations which in fact hinder production. The young men, having completed their apprenticeship, are resentful at being allocated to a lower wage level than is their due and falsify their worksheets to compensate. When this comes out there is a big works meeting to discuss the situation at which the editor of the factory news-sheet launches an impassioned outburst against such malpractice which in his eyes is a betrayal of the socialist project. Faced with the editor's moralizing zeal, the young men become increasingly resentful at being blamed and treated like children. In the eyes of the young a similar authoritarianism prevails also in pubs and dance halls, for example where there is 'Kravattenzwang' or compulsory tie: 'Ich habe meine Anweisungen', as the doorman at the dance hall puts it in a phrase which could serve as a slogan for the whole culture;[9] the policing of desire is comically evoked in a street scene where the hero is pleading his cause with the heroine while at his elbow a policeman accuses him of going through a red light even though he had been pushing his motorcycle on foot. The main young characters are the hero, Olaf; his friend, the even more disaffected Horst, who at the age of 18 had gone west briefly and now a year or so on wonders why on earth he came back instead of staying in the West with its transistor radios, shoes with cuban heels, and jeans; and Karin, a young woman who has just separated from her husband and who works in a restaurant kitchen but aspires to become a singer and get into film or television. The main old men are the news-sheet editor and Paul, a skilled craftsman who services the ageing factory machines. The plot turns on whether the young men will go or stay: will Olaf in particular finally identify with the old whose Heimat has been almost destroyed by historical upheavals and stay to create, in company with Karin, a new Heimat which can accommodate the desires of the young?

The film opens with Olaf's confession to Horst of how he fancies a woman who had jumped into the water in her clothes and to whom he lent his bathing robe. Desire is evoked in many shots of Olaf and Horst gazing at women which create a contrast between Horst's quick, easy satisfaction of lust and Olaf's sustained yearning for Karin, the woman who jumped into the water. Karin has a double or even triple aspect. When we first see her singing in the dance hall she projects a highly sexy image but remains inaccessible, for this is a performance or projection of an image; were Karin, like the girl Horst gets off with, to have instant sex with Olaf, the image would be at once dispelled and the gaze would simply shift to the next illusory object of insatiable desire. Besides Karin as performer, there is also Karin as working woman in the restaurant or auditioning for

---

[9] 'I have my instructions'.

television bit parts. And then there is Karin, not as projected image, but as herself a sexually desiring subject who asserts against a bullying and jealous husband the right to self-determination and to choose where she will live and whom she will sleep with. That she is always late for her job peeling potatoes because of auditioning and late for auditioning because of peeling potatoes offers a wry model of the tensions between economic necessity and cultural aspirations. By implication, the GDR should enable Karin in her three aspects—as performer of dreams, as citizen/worker, and as desiring subject—to flourish. In a film largely focalized through Olaf, the woman as seen through his eyes thus embodies the cultural ambitions, practical dilemmas, and utopian promise of the GDR. A quick shot of Olaf's bedroom shows a poster of Marlene Dietrich just discernible on the wall behind his bed, so instantly evoking for film buffs that great performer of an ironized eroticism, whose anti-fascist credentials and independence of spirit were legendary. The poster sends a coded message to the party ideologues: artistic freedom to express rather than repress the vagaries of desire is the path to the future which will also take forward the great tradition of German cinema before the rise of National Socialism.

If utopian hopes and longings are conveyed through feminine images in *Berlin um die Ecke*, the sense of a lost Heimat is evoked through the *lack* of a feminine presence. Even though, following the losses of men in the war, there were more households headed by lone women than by lone men in both East and West Germany, in the DEFA films of the 1950s and 1960s older men on their own often bear a strong symbolic charge, their pathos intensified by the lack of women which in turn underlines the utopian value set on young women. The most evocative scenes in *Berlin um die Ecke* centre on the two older men, the editor of the factory newspaper and the maintenance engineer, Paul, who together represent respectively paternal law and paternal love, not in their role as actual fathers, though Paul does have a son, but symbolically as father figures who define the GDR and its historical provenance. These scenes also exemplify the importance of locations which signify *Heimweh* and *Fernweh*: the nostalgic longing for lost Heimat but also the longing for travel, for Heimat should never become a prison but should be open to the wider world. In a crucial encounter following the editor's outburst attacking the youth brigade, Olaf waits in the entrance hall to the tenement where the editor lives and in a scuffle in the dark makes his nose bleed. The two men spring apart when a young girl skips down the steps and passes between them, asking her elderly neighbour if he is all right. The girl lends the scene a trace of Oedipally structured melodrama in which old and young men do battle for control over token women, here a young girl who signifies the future. In a state of shock, the older man makes no complaint and after the girl has left walks off slowly along the corridor and up the stairs, dabbing at the blood on his face. As the editor walks away his shoes squeak; these are not the smart, cuban-heeled shoes Horst longed for but, like the editor's whole outfit, the typical inelegant and old-fashioned garb which by the mid-1960s meant that the citizens of the GDR looked visibly different from their counterparts in the West. The next scene cuts to the editor's flat and a long silent sequence shot with a still camera as he wipes the blood from his nose, dabs helplessly at his coat to try to prevent bloodstains, gazes at his face in a small mirror above the tiny kitchen sink with its one cold-water tap from which he then fills a battered kettle with a whistle stopper for the spout. Along with the anxious rubbing of the worn over-coat to save it from stains, this long shot of a typical kitchen in a flat unchanged since the turn of the century, with its single tap and sparse utensils, conveys the sense of past lives back through decades in a working-class household. These silent objects are the telling details of an unspoken history, unknown in its specific form yet all too well known in its larger trajectory: so much of Berlin was reduced to rubble; the surviving tenements in their pock-marked poverty speak of a past proletarian community destroyed by National Socialism and war but whose spirit the GDR claimed to draw on to fuel the great project. Then when the bell rings, the old man finds Olaf at the door, clearly regretful at what has happened, and the two men begin to talk to one another. The editor's comment that the last time he was attacked was by fanatical young Nazis in 1945 deepens Olaf's guilt, but makes him the more determined to explain that he is a committed worker who does care about doing things well, but is fed up at being bossed about and preached at and condescended to. As the men converse, the editor pulls out a basket of potatoes, pours water in a basin, and begins to peel the potatoes. The scene reaches an evocative and brilliantly acted climax when Olaf asks the question, which the audience too, confronted by a man peeling potatoes after a day's work, also wonders: 'Haben Sie keine Frau?'[10] The editor's silent look leaves Olaf chastened and the audience never does learn whether he ever had a wife, whether she died in bombing raids or as a victim of political violence, or of one of the thousand natural causes flesh is heir to. In the film's symbolism it is the telling absence of a woman which evokes a Heimat lost for a whole generation but to be regained by the young now building a new world.

Heimat regained will not, of course, be the same as the working-class Heimat of the past. The old sexual division of labour with its the female domestic sphere and male workplace is going; Karin peels potatoes for a

---

[10] 'Don't you have a wife?'

wage, not for a husband, and resists her husband's efforts to control her.[11] She too has the same kind of tenement flat as the editor. But her flat in the Wichertstraße in Prenzlauer Berg is furnished to suggest bohemian escape from domesticity and the camerawork emphasizes the spaciousness of the old high-ceilinged flats in contrast to the narrow focus on the kitchen sink flanked by a battered chair and table in the editor's flat. Karin's bohemian flat contrasts too with the flat in a later scene belonging to Paul's son; its sterile modern chic, with no pictures on the wall and no woman to give it either warmth or erotic promise, heightens by contrast both the lost Heimat evoked in the editor's flat and the bohemian dreams of new freedoms which Karin's flat conveys, for, as is still the case, the traditional Berlin flats in areas such as Prenzlauer Berg have more potential style than all the post-war developments, at least so *Berlin um die Ecke* suggests in a subtle play of architectural signifiers of change and continuity which denies any simple message of progress or arrival.

As evocative as the editor peeling his potatoes are the scenes devoted to Paul, the maintenance engineer. Factories and machine production, which under capitalist conditions generate alienation, are at the same time the scene of proletarian solidarity for which the machine itself becomes a metonym as the object bringing workers together. In *Berlin um die Ecke* the machine, which Paul struggles Sisyphus-like to keep in production despite lack of spare parts such as 16 mm nuts, takes on a metaphoric expansion of meaning. Like the hearth in a household, so this clapped-out machine, which so many have laboured on through the decades, is a physical symbol of co-operative labour through time and of a spirit of solidarity stretching back across the gulf of the Third Reich. In the socialist Heimat, the factory as much as the domestic household should be a place of community, not of ill-tempered squabbles. When Paul has a heart attack, he and his machine are virtually equated: when the old man and the old machine have gone, who will continue the struggle to ensure that the GDR creates workplaces and households in which its people can feel at home? The machine's antiquity gives it aura, as age invests Paul too with dignity and pathos. Here is a proletarian equivalent to the rural blacksmith in Edgar Reitz's *Heimat*. After the heart attack Paul goes to a convalescent home where, sitting outside in a sheltered corner amidst the greenery of shrubs and creepers on the wall behind him, he remembers his grandfather who was offered, as a gift of firewood, the wood from a chestnut tree which had to be felled. Since there was not enough space for

---

[11] On the East German policy of integrating women into the labour force see Jutta Gysi and Dagmar Meyer, 'Leitbild berufstätige Mutter: DDR-Frauen in Familie, Partnerschaft und Ehe', in Gisela Helwig and Hildegard Maria Nickel (eds.), *Frauen in Deutschland 1945–1992* (Bonn: Bundeszentrale für politische Bildung, 1993), 139–65.

the tree to fall safely, the grandfather had, at the age of 80, climbed the tree and cut down first the crown then the mighty trunk and lived to tell, at the age of 90, of this exploit to his young grandson, now himself an ageing man who will not live to be 90. The reminiscence is told in voice-over by Erwin Geschonnek, possibly the best-known of all the DEFA actors, as an inner monologue while the camera lingers in a long, still close-up on his face. The resonances of this scene are multiple: it evokes a spirit passing down through generations of working men; communal provision for the old, figured in the gift of firewood, is answered by individual heroic endeavour; the need to fell a mighty tree when its time has come recalls the motif, common to Marxist as to Heimat discourse, of man's struggle with nature but without the mystification of nature found in many Heimat texts. That the heroic endeavour is not shown directly, but as a memory, allows for analogy between the individual exploit in the past and the current communal struggle with the old machine in the factory which has had its day and should be replaced. The past is not idealized, however; the grandfather's savings from a life of labour, 3,000 Reichsmarks which he had kept in a wooden box to pass on to his grandson, were worth nothing after the great inflation in the 1920s. The value of heroic masculinity is heightened by excision of any female presence through camerawork which cuts off the nurse helping the invalid in his chair; only her hands are briefly seen as Paul's vision is turned inward to memories of his grandfather. But, the inwardness of memory robs the remembered heroic act of the monumentalism characteristic of fascist aesthetics which it would risk taking on were it shown directly. The poetic quality both of the words and of the visual image of the old man's face leaves it open to viewers to make their own associations. (The pathos of an ageing face would be a leading motif also in Reitz's *Heimat*, though in the later film it is the face of a woman, Maria.) The contrast between the mighty grandfather and the invalid remembering may have provoked suspicions in the party ideologues that the positive hero was here shown as dying of the unequal struggle with conditions in the GDR. Modes of death were a heavily coded item in GDR culture: three years later much suspicion attached to the even more tragic death at a young age of Christa Wolf's heroine Christa T. in *Nachdenken über Christa T.* (1968). The weight of censorship fell more heavily on the popular medium of film, however, and Wolf's novel was released despite heavy criticism, though initially only in a small print run. In another highly resonant scene, shot against the background of the Spree, Paul tells Olaf of the great ships he watched sailing past on the larger waters of the Baltic Sea when he was convalescing and talks yearningly of the countries one could sail to on the world's oceans. Given the fortress mentality prevailing in the GDR, such an expression of

Fernweh, of the longing to leave the Heimat and travel the wide world, was potentially subversive. Whether the longing for a socialist Heimat open to the world is subversive or utopian depends on the viewer: the metaphors of boundless water and sky recall the lakeside setting of Christa T.'s half-built house, film and novel alike both evoking the need for Heimat to be open to dreams and imagination. Immediately following this scene Paul dies. But just as Wolf's heroine is survived by the narrator whose book is designed to resurrect and reactivate the spirit of Christa T., so Olaf is invited by the editor to write about Paul in the factory newspaper and so keep his spirit alive into the future, just as the larger text of the film, in which Olaf's testimony is given in voice-over, would have done for the values Paul represents, had the censors not banned it and in so doing contributed to stifling hopes for a humanistic and open socialist society.

Berlin um die Ecke was released in 1990 in a deliberately rough, not fully-edited version which in itself conveys the sense of aspirations crushed by a heavy-handed bureaucracy. The most evocative scenes in *Berlin um die Ecke* imbue with a patriarchal aura the GDR Heimat as a project or aspiration in Bloch's sense to which an older generation of men have devoted their lives. If Heimat in its utopian mode is the overcoming of an absence, is the presence of the feminine for the male subject who must at the same time realize an ideal of male solidarity, then it is questionable whether Heimat discourse shaped in such terms could accommodate the changing role of women and the aspirations of the younger generation. The doubts are even more evident in another of the banned films, *Denk bloß nicht ich heule* (1965/1990, Frank Vogel), in which hope for the future is almost undone in the closing sequence. In contrast to the Berlin films, this film is set in the provincial town of Weimar and nearby rural surroundings and so has many affinities with traditional Heimat discourse. Indeed Weimar, centre of the German classical inheritance, can lay claim to be *the* provincial centre of a culture defined in anti-metropolitan terms. Plotted like a *Bildungsroman* or novel of development, it shows the social integration of a young man, a GDR rebel without a cause, under the influence of a benign if rather stern older man and his daughter with whom the hero is in love. The disaffected hero represents the other who must be integrated if the GDR Heimat is to remain open to the future whereas his buddies who are proto-Nazi thugs must be excluded lest they corrode the very identity of the GDR as different from the capitalist/fascist West. But the integration does not quite work and the happy ending is less than convincing. In the penultimate scene, the hero lays claim to the daughter, inviting her to leave her father and follow him. Earlier on the film has many allusions to Goethe in a scarcely veiled plea for an open and un-puritanical ethos. This closing moment is reminiscent of Schiller's *Kabale und Liebe* (1784): various figures in the film could parallel the ghastly creeping Wurm, the servant of power, in the play, just as some of the disaffected young men recall the nastier elements among Schiller's robbers in *Die Räuber* (1781), another *Sturm und Drang* classic. The hero shouts his challenge standing on a stage in the local village hall which had only just been the scene of an act involving performing dogs in human costumes walking on their hind legs. The message to an authoritarian father-state is scarcely veiled. Unlike the heroine in *Kabale und Liebe* who cleaves to her father, the daughter here rushes out in pursuit of her young man but only to offer him a bed on the sofa at home and the assurance that daddy will agree. That this could be a lasting solution ushering in an epoch of happy families seems unlikely.

Denk bloß nicht ich heule and *Berlin um die Ecke* both end with a coming together of hero and heroine which leaves their future life hard to imagine. *Berlin um die Ecke* closes with a cut from the young lovers zooming off on a motorbike into the sunset to a panoramic shot of a group of boys kicking a tin can on the street corner while a grown-up female figure shouts at them angrily from the pavement. Whether Olaf and Karin can turn into home-building parents for such children is a moot point, for desire will stray across containing boundaries and how is the wild woman who jumped into the water to become a nagging aproned mother mediating the paternal law to unruly boys? Legally, reform of marriage law and a programme of rights for women came much sooner in East Germany than in the Federal Republic where, despite the constitutional commitment to sexual equality, the marriage law retained many patriarchal trappings till 1977.[12] Moreover, in contrast to family policies during the Adenauer era which were designed to return women to the home, East German policy aimed to facilitate women's participation in the labour force, so that family policy in the two Germanies took on an ideological edge in the context of the Cold War. On the other hand a long left-wing tradition emphasizing heavy industry and male camaraderie produced a certain helplessness in face of the problems of working women. Following the demise of the GDR, there has been much retrospective criticism of state-driven emancipatory measures which, so it is argued, merely intensified the double burden on women of childcare and paid work, leaving gender roles in the sexual and domestic sphere unquestioned. Be that as it may, many of the DEFA films portray male rebels against paternalistic authority who must be redeemed by older men who look back to a lost Heimat and by young women who

---

[12] On the history of women's rights legislation in East and West Germany see Sabine Berghahn, 'Frauen, Recht und langer Atem: Bilanz nach über 40 Jahren Gleichstellungsgebot in Deutschland', in Helwig and Nickel (eds.), *Frauen in Deutschland 1945–1992*, 71–138.

symbolize the Heimat as a project for the future. In such films the female characters serve as a mirror reflecting the desires of the male subject and the final redeeming ideal: they become the utopian figure of Heimat for the men. But in the 1970s, at the same time as the Women's Movement in the West was gathering force, the focus in an increasing number of DEFA films shifted to female protagonists which made the establishing of a closure in terms of Heimat more problematic. For who could mirror the ideal of homecoming for a female rebel? A father would be too patriarchal altogether, a mother too smothering, a child would reinstate the old definitions of woman through motherhood, a traditional man is the problem in the first place, a new man is incredible. One solution, adopted in Heiner Carow's *Die Legende von Paul und Paula* (1973), is to offer the heroine a new man, a father of young children, but then to kill her off so that she is permanently out of reach, alienated as an ideal which then serves to maintain the boundaries keeping the new man on the straight and narrow. This is equally true of the reverse image of Heimat from a woman's perspective: the death of Christa T. enables the narrator to justify in the name of an alienated ideal the actual boundaries defining the GDR and to keep open the hope that work will continue on a half-built project. The female protagonist might, of course, become a homemaker in company with a woman friend and lover as a focus stabilizing her desires, an aspiration which shines through at times in the writing of Irmtraud Morgner. But homoeroticism was something of a taboo in the GDR and separatist feminism is incompatible with socialism. In sum, woman as the vessel of unfocused and unbounded desire which cannot come to rest, from the eponymous heroine of Christa Wolf's *Nachdenken über Christa T.* (1968) to Konrad Wolf's *Solo Sunny* (1980), is a figure subversive of, and eventually destructive of, Heimat discourse GDR style.

5 Heimat Past and Present— A Land Fit for Youth
Lenz's *Deutschstunde,* Emil Nolde and *Heimatkunst,* Michael Verhoeven's *Das schreckliche Mädchen*

Deutschstunde: A Best-Seller of the Late 1960s

Deutschstunde (1968) by Siegfried Lenz (born 1926 in Lyck in Masuria, East Prussia), tells the story of Siggi Jepsen, a young man who has been arrested for art theft and sentenced to be held in an institution for delinquent youth ('schwererziehbare Jugend', literally 'difficult-to-educate youth').[1] The story is told in the first person by Siggi who shares a name with his author—his full name is Siegfried Kai Johannes Jepsen. As part of his rehabilitation, Siggi has to write an essay on the topic of 'The Joys of Duty' and tells the story, set during the Second World War, of his father Jens Ole Jepsen, policeman in the northernmost police station in Germany, in Rugbüll, on the border between Schleswig-Holstein and Denmark. The story proves so long in the telling, however, that the narrator cannot complete it in the hour or so provided, but instead voluntarily spends several months in solitary confinement, so arousing the interest of educational psychologists such as Wolfgang Mackenroth who embarks on a case study of this unusual inmate to be presented for a diploma. (Mackenroth has a trace of ironic self-portraiture, perhaps, since Lenz worked briefly as a journalist on crime issues.) The bulk of the narrative concerns Jens Ole Jepsen's determination to enforce an order issued by the National Socialist government forbidding a famous local painter, Max Ludwig Nansen, from painting, a duty the policeman 'joyfully' sets about fulfilling. The story continues into the post-war rehabilitation of the painter marked by an exhibition of his work in Hamburg. But the narrator's father, unrehabilitated by the post-war denazification programme to which he was briefly subject as a policeman under the Nazi regime, continues his dutiful efforts to destroy work which the painter had produced during the time of the decree forbidding him to paint. The narrator steals paintings, then, to keep them safe from his father. Siggi's account closes with his arrest

---

[1] *Deutschstunde* (Frankfurt am Main: Suhrkamp, 1979).

for art theft shortly after the opening of the exhibition which a younger generation of painters and photographers, including the narrator's brother Klaas, have greeted with derision. Thus Siggi is left unable to identify with his terrible father but isolated too from a younger generation who seek a total break with the past. A central question the novel leaves with its implied readers in 1968 is: can anything be recuperated from the past or is a tabula rasa needed?

For a reader of today at the turn of the twentieth century, three historical moments come together in *Deutschstunde*: the time of the first story which is set in Rugbüll on the German-Danish border during the Second World War from 1943 onwards; the time of the second framework story, which is set on an island in the Elbe near Hamburg in 1954 and is about the telling of the first; and finally the time of the novel's publication in 1968. The narration of the first story is retrospective, being told from the point of view of the narrator in 1954, but heavily focalized through his more innocent younger self. The framework story adopts in the main an intercalated time structure, that is to say it alternates action and its narration, the action here being the telling of the first story and a few events at the time of the telling, such as the narrator's twenty-first birthday. That the past matters not only in itself but because of its continuing effects in the present is made clear through the convergence of the two strands: the first story ends with the events after the war leading up to the narrator's arrest; the second framework story ends with the completion of the telling of the first story, its handing over in manuscript to the director of the institution, and the narrator's imminent release. But there are occasional glimpses of another shadowy 'I' who belongs somewhere else in time and nowhere specific in place. Thus when Wolfgang Mackenroth first arrives, the narrator remarks: 'er kam mir, wenn ich heute daran denke, wie ein junger Tierpfleger vor, der sich zum ersten Mal in den Käfig gewagt hat'.[2] Such a sentence breaks out of the intercalated format to imply an altogether later, retrospective position—perhaps somewhere in the mid- to late 1960s?

As a serious novel achieving sales comparable to popular best-sellers, *Deutschstunde* was one of the great publication successes of post-war Germany. It had already gone through four hardback printings by the end of 1968 and by early 1970 had reached hardback sales of 200,000.[3] By 1974 over a million hardback copies were in circulation to which must be added sales of the paperback which came out in 1973 and which had

---

[2] 'he seemed to me, when I look back today, like a young animal-keeper venturing for the first time into the cage' (p. 72).

[3] See Winfried Baßmann, *Siegfried Lenz: Sein Werk als Beispiel für Weg und Standort der Literatur in der Bundesrepublik Deutschland* (Bonn: Bouvier, 1978), 159–64 on the reception of *Deutschstunde*.

reached a further quarter of a million readers by 1976. Its success may in part be explained by the political climate of the time, the latest of the three historical moments a reader of nowadays meets in *Deutschstunde*. The novel came out towards the end of the decade which saw the building of the Berlin Wall in 1961, cementing the Cold War division of Germany, and in the same year the trial in Israel of Adolf Eichmann, a leading figure in the implementation of the mass extermination of the Jews, which reopened the whole question of the Nazi past. In 1962 came the *Spiegel* affair, when, following an article critical of the Bundeswehr, the offices of the *Spiegel* magazine were occupied at midnight on the orders of the Defence Minister and right-wing leader of the Bavarian CSU, Franz Josef Strauss, its files seized, and its editors and the author of the article arrested. Such state interference in the press, reminiscent of practices during the Third Reich, brought a further souring of relations between the government and left-liberal intellectuals already concerned about the hardening of Cold War policies and by their perception that only lip-service had been paid to confronting the Third Reich and its legacy, leaving attitudes and institutions in West German political and social life unchanged. In 1963 came the end of an era with the retirement of Konrad Adenauer, an impression strengthened in 1965 when an economic recession interrupted the hitherto seemingly unstoppable momentum of the post-war economic miracle. Then came the elections in 1965, in which a number of leading writers such as Heinrich Böll, Günter Grass, and Siegfried Lenz publicly threw in their lot with the SPD and its leader Willy Brandt. These elections were notable for the emergence on the radical right of the neo-Nazi party, the NPD (Nationaldemokratische Partei Deutschlands) which although it failed to cross the 5 per cent threshold in the federal elections, achieved considerable successes in 1966 in elections in Hesse and Bavaria. In the 1967 Landtag elections, however, the NDP did return four representatives in Schleswig-Holstein with 5.8 per cent of the vote.[4] On the left, a Marxist-based oppositional trend among student radicals and some trade-union circles intensified when the 1965 elections led not to a clear change of government, but to the formation in 1966 of a Grand Coalition between the CDU/CSU and the SPD, an outcome disappointing to left-liberal intellectuals, but perceived even more drastically on the Marxist left as SPD collusion in the status quo which made effective parliamentary opposition impossible and so demanded an activist extra-parliamentary response, the so-called APO (Außerparlamentarische Opposition). In the course of the decade there had been isolated outbursts

---

[4] Timothy Alan Tilton, *Nazism, Neo-Nazism and the Peasantry* (Bloomington, Ind.: Indiana University Press, 1975), 112.

of student discontent which came to a head, however, from 1967 to the early 1970s. The German student protest movement was, of course, part of a wider international protest against the Vietnam War and Western neo-colonialism and was marked by events such as the shooting of the student Benno Ohnesorg by the police during a demonstration in Berlin in 1967 against the Shah of Persia. But also on the agenda were specifically German questions such as the emergency laws passed in 1967 by the Grand Coalition which were perceived as a return to the anti-democratic powers of the Nazi regime, the dominance of the right-wing Springer press whose virulent attacks on the student leader Rudi Dutschke were widely blamed for his shooting in 1968, the authoritarian structure of university education, as well as various individual scandals over former Nazis in prestigious positions in the Federal Republic.

Cumulatively the student protests and their reflection in the press gave rise to the sense of a massive generation gap between younger Germans and an older generation who had failed to confront the past with intellectual honesty following the political catastrophe of the Third Reich and hence failed also to undertake the root-and-branch changes needed in the present. As Gordon Craig has documented, education policy in schools was a key arena in which the battle over the past and its understanding was fought out, or rather all too often not fought out, so leaving young people in a state of grotesque ignorance.[5] The title of Lenz's novel signals the didactic intent: this is to be a German lesson for citizens who are challenged to go forth from reading the novel in 1968, just as in 1954 Siggi goes forth after writing down his memories, now aged 21 and so of responsible age as a citizen of the Federal Republic. Siggi hands over his manuscript to the director of a penal institution as a message to a member of the older generation set in authority over the young. But the novel perhaps addresses especially Siggi's generation who were children during the war and who could thus play a key role as intermediaries between the young protesters of the late 1960s who, like Siggi in 1954, are just coming of age in 1968, and their elders, the directors of penal institutions or universities, who were of responsible age during the Third Reich. The concept of generation is, of course, an abstraction and even within the five or so years of the war, a gulf divides the child Siggi from his elder brother Klaas who deserted from the army, as had Siegfried Lenz himself. (Lenz is of an age with Klaas rather than Siggi.) Not the least of dutiful Jens Ole Jepsen's crimes is to have tried to drag his youngest child into the futile final struggle to stop the advancing allied forces as he had earlier reported his undutiful

---

[5] See, *The Germans* (Harmondsworth: Penguin, 1991), 75–7 on the history syllabus in West German schools from the 1950s to the 1970s.

elder son to the authorities. (His behaviour is constantly contrasted with that of Joswig, Siggi's guard in the institution, who oversees an order forbidding smoking by passing on a few fags on the sly whereas the policeman failed to wink at a few paintings on the sly, to say nothing of his betrayal of his own son.) At the close of the first story, Klaas and his friends, more alienated even than Siggi, disagree with him over how to view the painter Nansen. The younger generation is thus shown to be divided in itself, an important factor in the reception of the novel at a time of political uncertainty and of youth protests with no clear single sense of direction.

The high sales of *Deutschstunde* during the crisis of the late 1960s can in part be explained because it offered a positive response to the protests from students over the individual and institutional authoritarianism of their fathers and their universities and the failure in the post-war Federal Republic to properly reckon with the individual and institutional crimes of the past. These issues come through above all in unregenerate Jens Ole Jepsen: the figure of a village policeman and father brilliantly combines the individual, the familial, and the institutional so that a text set in a village on the northernmost German border could nonetheless speak generally to the West German public. As the narrator puts it, what is needed is not an institution for 'schwererziehbare Jugend' but for 'schwererziehbare Alte' (difficult-to-educate old people). Moreover, the novel offered highly sympathetic figures for readerly identification in Siggi, Klaas, and their sister Hilke as the victims of an obsessively vindictive father who claims to act in the name of duty but is clearly playing out his own resentments. A presentation of the Third Reich showing young Germans among the prime victims allowed for admission of widespread collusion in terrible crimes, but also offered the salve of recognition for the suffering of Germans. (This combination is a factor too in the reception of Edgar Reitz's *Heimat* and in the controversy it aroused and is also true of *Das schreckliche Mädchen*.) Their status as victims of the crimes of their elders explains and to a degree justifies the alienated young people at the end. At the same time, that one of Klaas's friends gives violent expression to his resentments in knocking Siggi unconscious offers a clear enough warning: Chapter 2 touched on the theme of resentment following the First World War as a factor in the rise of National Socialism; Lenz's novel offers a warning that the victims' resentment, however well justified, can take on politically dangerous colours. In the 1970s the danger was confirmed in the turn to left-wing terrorism among a tiny minority of disaffected youth; the longer running, larger danger of right-wing extremism fuelled by resentment gives Lenz's novel an edge still today, though the resentments now have new sources. The popularity of *Deutschstunde* with its measured plea for recognition of past crimes and the need for reformist change in the present was in keeping with what proved to be the majority popular feeling as expressed in the elections of 1969 which produced a coalition government between the SPD and the liberal FDP (Freie Demokratische Partei (Free Democratic Party)) under the chancellorship of Willy Brandt, an outcome confirmed also in Schleswig-Holstein where the NDP dropped below the 5 per cent barrier, dropping below even 1 per cent in 1972.

Competing Images of Heimat

This was, then, the political context of Lenz's *Deutschstunde* and its early reception. Less easy to pin down is what might be called the emotional climate and here the complex handling of the theme of Heimat in *Deutschstunde* may help to explain its popular appeal. One source of bitter disagreements and resentment following the Second World War was the poisoning of memory and personal past history by a monstrous politics. This is a leading post-war theme in such representative works as Böll's *Billard um halbzehn* (1959) and Grass's *Die Blechtrommel* (1959) and *Katz und Maus* (1961). Grass's works in particular evoke their narrators' lost Heimat of Danzig, now the city of Gdansk in Poland. In contrast to Grass's subtle mourning for a youth, for a personal past, for memories of childhood places all blighted by the crimes of the National Socialist regime in which so many ordinary Germans had actively or passively colluded, many Germans especially among those who had fled to the West or been expelled from former German territory, resented the loss of their Heimat, refused calls to take responsibility, demanded the right to remember without having to feel guilty, and finished up by feeling simply resentful at the perceived denial of that right by authors such as Böll or Grass. Such resentment is an aspect of the inability to mourn which has been diagnosed as a symptom of post-war Germany.[6] The most vivid childhood memories often turn on holiday places which offer that ecstatic sense of release from school and a heightened perception of an unfamiliar place which then becomes loved but must be left behind to become an object of longing till next year. The popularity of Böll's *Irisches Tagebuch* (1957) marks perhaps the displacement abroad, and to a people more sinned against than sinning, of the yearning for Heimat. *Deutschstunde* tells of people who live near the sea, but like *Irisches Tagebuch*, the setting

---

[6] Alexander und Margarete Mitscherlich, *Die Unfähigkeit zu trauern: Grundlagen kollektiven Verhaltens* (1962; Munich: Piper, 1967).

also appeals to urban readers' holiday memories in the many evocations of landscapes, seascapes, and the huge skyscapes of Schleswig-Holstein which since the nineteenth century had been a place for German holiday-makers. This is true too of Grass's vivid evocations of seaside sights, sounds, and smells. The poisoning of such memory is unforgettably conveyed in *Die Blechtrommel* in the image of the horse's head washed up on the beach writhing with corpse-fattened eels and Oskar's mother's subsequent bulimic self-destruction on a surfeit of tinned fish. For the wider German public who bought *Deutschstunde* in such numbers the novel told an exciting story, it modelled in miniature the intergenerational conflicts of the time, but it also evoked in Proustian fashion memories of time past conjured up through sights and smells, sounds and tastes. Such memory rooted in bodily sensations is a fundamental facet of Heimat as the longed-for lost realm of childhood. Lenz's wonderfully evocative descriptions of clouds passing across the sky or of herrings sizzling in the pan tap into the memories of a public before mass air traffic who still went for holidays on the North Sea or the Baltic.

Thus *Deutschstunde* observes many conventions characteristic of Heimat novels such as the emphasis on location and landscape. The first chapter begins with the island in the Elbe, the place of telling, and closes with a precise statement of the location of the story to be told with its double centre of Rugbüll, the realm of the policeman, and Bleekenwarf, the realm of the painter. The Heimat is delimited by a national border, here with Denmark, like Belgium in *Das Kreuz im Venn* or Poland in *Das einfache Leben*, in each case the foreign country playing almost no part. Much more significant is the umbilical cord of the road to Husum, the local centre as was Aachen in Viebig's novel. As later emerges, the road and the telephone also connect the Heimat with Berlin: Viebig's local mayor finally goes off to Berlin; Lenz's policeman serves Berlin locally. In Viebig's novel, the marginal artist or intellectual almost falls prey to the high moorland just as Wiechert's von Orla momentarily senses imminent death in his watery realm. Here the threats come from a death-dealing regime and its foes, though some episodes do still convey the dangerous margin between culture and nature. The intellectuals in Viebig's and Wiechert's novels resist the temptation to consummate their love of the Heimat through the channel of a local virgin; whether Lenz's painter has succumbed to the temptation or merely transformed the local virgin, Siggi's sister Hilke, into a dancing maenad on canvas is left obscure. Along with observance of many conventions of the mode, Lenz constantly reflects upon these very conventions so that Heimat appears as disputed territory: whose values and which images of Heimat are to prevail? As we saw in the last chapter, towards the end of the 1950s Heimat as where you go on your holidays became a leading motif in ever more vapid Heimat films offering dreams of a holiday romance in a setting of mountain or moorland. One of the locals in Rugbüll, the aged Captain Andersen, has often played small parts in films as the archetypal old sea dog: harbour towns and sea shanties are common motifs in the popular Heimat mode. (Captain Andersen is a trace anachronistic since this film genre only became a mass mode in the 1950s, though sea shanty music played on the accordion or ship's piano is much older.) In contrast to the cinema-goers who could simply and pleasurably consume images of meadow flowers, bodiced bosoms, or old tars with a lifetime written in their wrinkles, readers of *Deutschstunde* cannot simply consume Lenz's clouds or her-rings because the evocative descriptions are constantly interspersed with reflection upon the literary or visual production of images so that readers of necessity must think about the rhetorical power of images, about who is producing them, about where they are coming from and at whom they are directed. Siggi often explicitly asks himself how he should picture the landscape as backdrop to his story, so indicating the rhetorical force of images. Thus Lenz potentiates the theme of Heimat as an image which had appeared already in Viebig's *Das Kreuz im Venn* in the motif of tourists' photographs.

The novel also makes clear that besides films there had been a long tradition in Schleswig-Holstein of polemical writing about Heimat which by the 1920s was more and more coloured by resentments and racist pre-judice. As a disputed border region, Schleswig-Holstein had more than its share of Heimat prophets such as Adolf Bartels or Gustav Frenssen, both of whom welcomed the new Nazi regime as did a higher proportion of the public in Schleswig-Holstein than anywhere else in Germany: in the elec-tion of July 1932 in which the NSDAP achieved its biggest electoral success in a free election, Schleswig-Holstein recorded the highest vote for the National Socialists—51 per cent compared with 37.3 per cent in Germany as a whole—and in Nordfriesland, the region in which *Deutschstunde* is set, many constituencies recorded much higher figures—68.6 per cent in Husum, for example. In the immediate area where the novel is set the vote for the National Socialists actually rose from 64.5 per cent in July to 68.2 per cent in the November elections although nationally it had fallen.[7] Lenz may also have had in mind the disturbing continuation in post-war Germany of local celebration of Adolf Bartels, a notorious anti-Semitic propagandist, by bodies such as the Dithmarscher Heimatfront or the

---

[7]   See Thomas Steensen (ed.), *Nationalsozialismus in Nordfriesland* (Nordfriisk Instituut and Institut für schleswig-holsteinische Zeit- und Regionalgeschichte: Bräist/Bredstedt, NF, 1993). This study also looks at the widespread failure in parish records and local history to face up to the past.

headmaster of the Adolf Bartels Mittelschule in the town of Heide who promised in 1958 to continue to teach his pupils in the spirit of Bartels.[8] Per Arne Scheßel, Siggi's maternal grandfather, is a local author of books of Heimat lore whose teaching may be deduced from the mentality of his daughter, Siggi's mother Gertrud Jepsen. A red-gold blonde who would no doubt look well in a Heimat film, Gertrud Jepsen is a racist with a horror of physical disability as of anyone who looks alien in any way; her depressive illness is symbolic of a mentality so narrowly turned in on itself as to make life almost impossible. In this way Lenz alludes to the Nazi policies on racism and euthanasia and to the cult of Nordic health of which Gertrud is such a grotesque travesty as she is of the maternal Heimat. For Gertrud is a mother lacking warmth and unable to love freely. Nansen's wife Ditte is a more sympathetic Heimat woman, but in a self-consciously arty mode: in her heavy woven skirts she looks like a Heimat prophetess. (Such clothes look back to a trend in the reform movements of the turn of the century which valued the two extremes of nakedness and of peasant style, both on grounds of an appeal to nature; weaving, knitting, quilt-making, wooden beads, unvarnished wood tables, rustic pottery, and so forth belong in this aesthetic which is comparable to the English arts and crafts movement.) Ditte too, however, is permanently ill and unable to have children and so fails to embody maternal Heimat in the Nazi sense. Gertrud Jepsen is the daughter of a local notability in such a tradition, but snobbery sours her relations with her own daughter, Hilke, whose working-class boyfriend Addi not only has the un-German surname of Skowronnek and is epileptic, a sin against healthy *Deutschtum* in Gertrud's eyes, but also plays the accordion, a vulgar musical instrument in Gerturd's view. (Middle-class admirers of traditional Scottish fiddle or mouth music tend likewise to be contemptuous of popular accordion bands.) Her attitude uncovers the lie of Heimat as a united *Volk* rooted in their locality, the *Volksboden*: class distinctions remained potent throughout the Third Reich whose leaders sought alliance with capital in running a war economy based on exploited local labour as well as imported slave labour. That Gertrud, daughter of the Heimat expert, has such an attitude is all the more ironic since for a public in the 1960s and still today the harmonica or the more technically developed accordion, which Gertrud sees as the instrument fit only for gypsies, instantly evoke Heimat music and film. As noted in the previous chapter, wandering musicians, marching along against a backdrop of mountain or moorland, or in a North German maritime or harbour setting, commonly figure in

---

[8] Steven Nyole Fuller, *The Nazis' Literary Grandfather: Adolf Bartels and Cultural Extremism, 1871–1945* (New York: Peter Lang, 1996), 184.

Heimat films and continue to be a massively popular feature of German television. The tradition has recently taken a new twist in the Bavarian rock group Die Alpinkatzen, headed by Hubert von Goisern who combines yodelling with a rock idiom (to hear is to believe) and plays the accordion surrounded by Bavarian Alps or with a Greenpeace boat in the background.[9] So far, then, Heimat appears in *Deutschstunde* as the place of childhood recalled yearningly in memory; as the never-never land of kitschy films; as a culture of popular songs and accordion bands; as the utopia of a return to nature which intellectuals pursued in artists' colonies practising arts and crafts; as the *Volksboden* to be cleansed of the artistically or physically degenerate and of racial aliens.

Within these in part competing, in part mutually reinforcing connotations, Max Ludwig Nansen, the painter of images of the Schleswig Heimat, is shown to be more in tune with popular Heimat feeling than Gertrud Jepsen, daughter of the Heimat expert, when during his birthday party he encourages Addi to play his accordion and everyone joins in a congo of figures dancing through the painter's garden like the travelling musicians in a Heimat film. In this scene Lenz offers his readers a moment of almost Dionysian ecstasy as the people at the birthday party are lifted out of time into a heightened communion, a ritual of dance and music or a spontaneous *Gesamtkunstwerk* of the kind Nazi ideologues and the earlier prophets of Heimat, such as Lienhard, preached. The scene is the equivalent of Bäreb's excursion in Viebig's *Das Kreuz im Venn* to the Feast of St Willibrord and the subsequent ecstatic consummation in a scented garden. The dance contradicts mean-spirited Gertrud Jepsen, justifies Addi and Hilke, and signals a bond between Addi's 'vulgar' music and the 'high' art of one of the greatest painters of the century, an art the Nazi regime so relentlessly suppresses and seeks to destroy through the willing instrument of a vindictive policeman. Had Lenz allowed the ecstatic dance to stand as the truth of a *Volk* unity set against the divisive policies of the Nazis, then he might have been accused of propagating the same sentimental lie as many 1950s Heimat films which purveyed reconciliatory myths at the cost of excluding divisive contemporary realities and remaining silent on unatoned and unatonable evils such as the genocide of travelling Romanies. But the utopian moment of ecstasy is punctured by the arrival of the policeman with an order of seizure for Nansen's paintings produced in the last two years. Moreover, later, just as he is about to be arrested at the post-war exhibition of Nansen's paintings, Siggi recognizes in one painting a depiction of Nansen's garden not as the scene of

---

[9] Compact disc: *Hubert von Goisern und die Alpinkatzen, 'Aufgeigen stått niederschiassen'* (BMG Ariola Musik: Vienna, 1992); a concert filmed in 1995 has been shown more than once on television.

festive dancing but estranged in a vision of sinister beauty. Instead of faces there are dangling masks, a symbol of concealment. What lies behind the mask of a human face remains unknown. Masks symbolize human behaviour which has become a performance driven by some larger script or ritual whose meaning, however, remains unknown to the actors: hidden among the garden flowers are eyes which look spellbound at the seemingly knowing narrow slit eyes of the masks; it is unclear who is spying on whom, whose gaze is that of the victim, whose that of those whom the script empowers to victimize. As Siggi looks at eyes looking at eyes, he too is being watched and is arrested and discreetly pulled away, just as a decade earlier the policeman arrived at the birthday party to seize Nansen's paintings. In Siggi's mind the masks become interchangeable with flower heads, emblematic of natural beauty and innocence, but which he wants to strike from their stems with his stick, a victim become the destroyer of flowers. This complex moment undoes any sentiment about Heimat and its representation to convey on the one hand the mysterious painted vision of mysterious painted masks in an Edenic scene imbued with threat and inviting the destruction of beauty as a lie; yet the flowers are beautiful and their destruction would be senseless. On the other hand, the scene also juxtaposes the unmysterious operations of the state and its minions at two moments in time: the policeman's eager enforcement of orders from a criminal regime; the uncomprehending and misdirected efforts of the post-war German state ready to punish the young victims of the past for their present reactions, rather than their elders, the perpetrators of past evils. In this way Lenz offers a straightforward condemnation of the Third Reich, a warning to post-war authorities to think of the historical causes of present youth disaffection, but an admission too of a final bafflement in the face of the extremities of which human beings are capable and an aching sense of utopian dreams blighted. This is perhaps the deepest sense of Heimat in the novel: the blighted dream. Such a summing-up label can only point towards a meaning which is produced not by any explicit statement but by the tension generated between evocations of landscapes and skies, of paintings, and of fleeting memories on the one hand and on the other the policeman's unrelenting, complacent, impervious malice and the terrible hurts which the war cumulatively inflicts.

The young psychologist Mackenroth is working on the topic of art and criminality, a formulation which alludes with oblique irony to a main theme in the novel. Ostensibly the phrase refers to art theft, of which Siggi is guilty, as was also on a much larger scale though for different reasons the Nazi regime which burned, profitably sold on, or hid away work by artists it disapproved of as well as looting art from Jewish citizens and

from collections all over Europe. The destruction of art pales to insignificance, of course, compared with the genocide of European Jewry, other
policies of mass murder, and the savage conduct of the war especially on
the eastern front. Such a history, it might be argued, eludes artistic representation. Thus Theodor Adorno famously questioned the moral viability
of literature post-Auschwitz. Indirectly, then, Mackenroth's topic of enquiry invites the reader of *Deutschstunde* to question the legitimacy of art
or literature as a response to criminality on such a scale. A novel in the
Heimat mode is especially problematic because its narrow focus cuts out
so much; this accusation was a main factor in the controversy surrounding Edgar Reitz's *Heimat* which will be discussed in the next chapter. The
focus in *Deutschstunde* on young Germans as victims arguably distracts
attention from much greater crimes; the effect in a rural area of sporadic
Allied bombing in wounding Siggi's brother Klaas leaves the effects of the
German eastern campaign on the populations of Poland and Russia
or even of the Allied bombing of Hamburg or Dresden on urban populations shrouded in silence, to say nothing, literally, of concentration
camps, though Lenz does, through the views of Gudrun Jepsen, draw the
Nazi racist policies into the frame. Undeniably, then, the narrow focus of
Deutschstunde depends on a knowledgeable readership to draw connections. Yet lack of knowledge is precisely one of the problems *Deutschstunde*
implicitly addresses and no amount of connection-drawing can grasp
'the whole picture' from the basis of a village in Schleswig-Holstein.
Arguably, however, there is no 'whole' picture waiting to be grasped: history can always only be told partially through different modes of representation, fictional or historical, realist or symbolic, and following an
agenda of interests which will determine choices of what to include and
exclude. It is then for readers, on the basis of their knowledge and of their
own political or moral values, to judge the validity of such choices in any
work of art. Our agenda in this study of Heimat determines in turn the
main point of interest here: does the demonstration in *Deutschstunde*
that the cultural discourse of Heimat fed into the political ideology of
National Socialism and helped construct and sustain popular prejudices
on which the regime fed mean that Heimat literature and art, before, during, *and* after the Third Reich are irremediably tainted by the criminality
of that regime? If so, then *Deutschstunde*, whose popularity came in some
measure from tapping into the nostalgic longing for Heimat, has perhaps
cut away the ground of its own legitimacy. This issue is played out through
the figure of Nansen whose work Siggi defends both against his zealous
father and the young people after the war who see only the superannuated
style of a painter with Nazi sympathies. The topic of art and criminality
calls to mind, then, the issue of responsibility which artists might bear for

a criminal regime. As citizens, artists may be called to account as much or as little as any other individuals. The more difficult question concerns their art and is part of the wider discussion of the role of culture, as distinct from politics or economics, in accounting for the Third Reich. Not surprisingly this question has exercised many writers and artists and *Deutschstunde* may be seen as continuing a tradition initiated by Thomas Mann's *Doktor Faustus* (1947). Mann's novel too is structured as the narrative by an amanuensis and friend telling the life of a creative artist, a musician whose music gives complex expression to the spirit of the times. *Doktor Faustus* closes with the statement of a hope beyond hopelessness that the musician's work, silenced during the Third Reich, might yet be heard and its meaning understood by a future audience. Likewise, Lenz's novel closes on the hope that a post-war public should see and understand the work of a painter so in tune with the times that he welcomed the very regime which then persecuted him.

Emil Nolde and *Heimatkunst*

In contrast to Mann's Adrian Leverkühn who is a montage of features drawn from many sources, Lenz has based his fictional character, with little concealment and many clues, on one person, the Expressionist painter Emil Nolde (1867–1956). That Nolde had been for a while a committed Nazi adds a controversial edge to the plea for understanding, which is further complicated by the problematic relation between fact and fiction in the hybrid mode of fictionalized biography. Biography, autobiography, and their fictionalized counterparts all pose such problems, as signalled already in the famous title of Goethe's autobiography, *Dichtung und Wahrheit*.[10] 'Truth' cannot simply be equated with 'fact', but deviations from fact in a fictionalized biography, presumably in the cause of some deeper truth, can give pointers towards the underlying rhetoric of a work of fiction. In a critical biography of Nolde, Robert Pois comments:

> Nolde's suffering during the war was minor indeed compared to the agonies endured by millions at the hands of people to whom the painter wanted to lend support. Out of conscience we cannot romanticize it as Siegfried Lenz in his otherwise fine novel, *The German Lesson*, unfortunately tended to do.[11]

[10] On such issues see William Sprengemann, *The Forms of Autobiography: Episodes in the History of a Literary Genre* (New Haven and London: Yale University Press, 1980).
[11] *Emil Nolde* (Lanham, New York, London: University Press of America, 1982), 198. The biographical information about Nolde is largely drawn from this study.

To explain this criticism, a brief account of Nolde's biography is necessary. Moreover, quite apart from his status as model for a fictional character, Nolde is of interest here, since more perhaps any other modernist painter of his generation, Nolde might be termed a Heimat painter even though his work is not in the style to which the term *Heimatkunst* was originally applied. Nolde was born on a farm near the small town of Rottebül, now in Denmark, in an area of North Schleswig which following the Prussian victory over Denmark in 1864 was incorporated into Prussia and hence also into the German Reich in 1871. His original family name was Hansen, but in 1901 he took the name of the village of Nolde near his birthplace. The change of name was at once an assertion of self-created artistic identity and a signal of the rootedness of his art in the Heimat. When this region reverted to Denmark after the First World War, Nolde, then living in Utenwarf in Denmark though with many visits to Berlin, became a Danish citizen. In 1920 he was a founder member of the Danish North Schleswig branch of the National Socialist Party which was later incorporated into the German party in 1940 following the invasion of Denmark. A committed German nationalist even though his mother and his wife were Danish, Nolde moved back to Germany in 1927 and built Seebüll, the house and studio which now form the Nolde museum located close to the Danish border near the small town of Neukirchen. Nolde's letters and the version of his memoirs which came out in 1934 make clear his distress at the separation of his native Heimat from the German fatherland, his perception of his own art as German and specifically Nordic in inspiration as compared with southern Mediterranean art, his belief in racial purity, and his anti-Semitic and generally chauvinist attitudes. Xenophobia was commonplace in the kind of closed, rural milieu which Nolde came from, but his anti-Semitism was also fuelled by resentment against the painter Max Liebermann and the art dealer Paul Cassirer (of whom Otto Dix painted a famous portrait), leading figures in the Berlin art world in the first decades of the century, who were both Jewish and who had in 1908 and again in 1910 rejected Nolde's painting for exhibition at the Berlin Secession, the umbrella organization of the artistic avant-garde. Nolde's anti-Semitism went along with a reactionary anti-urban attitude reminiscent of the ideas propagated by Heimat ideologues such as Lienhard and Bartels.

Nolde's long-standing commitment to National Socialism availed him little. After an initial battle for dominance between Alfred Rosenberg, the leading cultural spokesman of the Nazi party and the founder in 1929 of the Kampfbund für Deutsche Kultur which rejected modernism in favour of a true German *Volk* art, and Joseph Goebbels, the Minister of Propaganda, who favoured co-opting modern art and even commandeered a few Noldes to hang on his walls at home, Nolde fell victim to the policies anathemizing modern art. In 1933 he was ordered along with other artists and architects to leave the Prussian Academy of Arts, a step he tenaciously refused to take, only to be finally excluded in 1941. In 1937, forty-eight works by Nolde were included in the notorious exhibition *Entartete Kunst* (Degenerate Art), which opened in Munich and then travelled throughout Germany.[12] Nansen's first names, Max (Beckmann, Burchhartz, Ernst, Pechstein, Pfeiffer Watenphul, Rauh) and Ludwig (Gies, Kirchner, Meidner) gesture towards other artists so honoured. In the same year, over a thousand of Nolde's paintings were seized from museums and other collections, some of which were sold in auction abroad while others were publicly burned on 20 March 1939, a moment which Lenz obliquely recalls in the episode of the burning of Siggi's hidden treasures in the windmill. Although in 1936 an order forbidding Nolde from engaging in artistic activity had been issued, he began in 1938 to work on a series of watercolours which he called his 'ungemalte Bilder' (unpainted pictures), lightly disguised in *Deutschstunde* as Nansen's invisible pictures. He continued to work on this series despite a further order in 1941 forbidding him to paint and after the war went on between 1945 to 1951 to paint over a hundred large oil paintings for which the 'unpainted' watercolours served as studies. In 1946, the Schleswig-Holstein government appointed Nolde as Professor of Art and in the following years major exhibitions were mounted in Germany and abroad, but alongside such honours Nolde's last years were marked also by controversy over his earlier political stance.

What of Nolde's painting, however, as distinct from his politics? No other painter's work attracted such debate during the Third Reich, finding throughout the 1930s the support of some despite the attacks of others. As late as 1940, Nolde was still being argued over in the Reichssicherheitshauptamt, the SS agency responsible for the Gestapo. In 1933 paintings by Nolde had been included in an exhibition, mounted in Berlin by an association of young artists, which was designed to illustrate the unity of spirit between modern art and National Socialism and also in 1933 even Rosenberg had praised some of his seascapes. Nolde's own evident surprise at his failure to find favour is understandable given that he himself regarded his work as Germanic art expressing a folk spirit rooted in the Nordic Heimat. In 1924 Nolde painted a landscape dominated by a white windmill, standing like a strange creature against a backdrop of deep blues, greens, and purples of sky, land, and water, its almost black sails like arms held up against flaming orange clouds, whether to conjure

---

[12] See Stephanie Barron (ed.), *'Entartete Kunst': Das Schicksal der Avantgarde im Nazi-Deutschland* (Munich: Hirmer Verlag, 1992).

forth or ward off is unclear.[13] (In *Deutschstunde*, the flames will engulf the windmill.) This was one of many works figuring windmills, as for example a striking lithograph of 1926, the year when one Jörgen Hansen published a book of educational theory with the title *Die beseelte Landschaft: Ein Beitrag zur Reform des erdkundlichen Unterrichts* which can serve here to illustrate the discursive context of Nolde's windmill pictures, landscapes with cottages, or garden flowers against a backdrop of sea or sky.[14] Hansen's pamphlet is a typical example of ideas in circulation for decades urging the importance of geography in giving children a sense of their own locality and its culture as an essential basis of identity before they embark on a wider syllabus. Such local geography was termed *Heimatkunde*. The cultural landscape, Hansen suggests, shows forth how the human beings who work upon nature are shaped by the landscape they inhabit so that their artefacts, fields, or gardens in turn are harmoniously imbued with the spirit of the wider landscape. But beyond the visible, the peculiar character of a landscape, its essence or atmosphere, is an invisible spirit which reveals itself to an artistic mode of apperception. The invisible landscape finds expression in sounds and smells—Lenz draws on such effects—as well as visible colours and shapes. The horizon marks the boundary between the visible and the invisible, hence, so Hansen remarks, mountain folk do not flourish on the plains, nor could a Fresian be comfortably transplanted to the mountains. Hansen's high-flown plea for 'Expressionismus in der Geographie' then modulates into a pedagogic statement of the three stages in a geography lesson—landscape, man, and culture—to culminate in an evaluation of the visible and invisible landscape so that pupils should feel drawn to the German land with its different ethnic groups, their Heimat. Had the arguments over Nolde gone the other way, Hansen's remarks could have served as an introduction to a catalogue of Expressionist *Heimatkunst* designed to demonstrate the persistence of the Heimat spirit through a changing aesthetic idiom. (Ernst Barlach or Paula Modersohn could also exemplify such a claim.) The visual arts even more than literature had provided the original terrain for advocacy of *Heimatkunst*, above all in the influential tract by Julius Langbehn discussed in Chapter 1, *Rembrandt als Erzieher* (1890). *Rembrandt als Erzieher* propagates a *Heimatkunst* which should give expression to a powerful individual personality and to an ethnic or tribal spirit (*Stammesgeist*),

---

[13] Owned by the Ada and Emil Nolde Foundation, Seebüll; reprod. in Werner Haftmann, *Emil Nolde* (New York: Harry N. Abrams, n.d.).

[14] Jörgen Hansen *Die beseelte Landschaft: Ein Beitrag zur Reform des erdkundlichen Unterrichts* (The Spiritualized Landscape: A Contribution to Reforming Geography Teaching) (List and von Bressendorf: Leipzig, 1926), section v, 'Die Landschaft'. Hansen provides a bibliography of articles and books in a similar vein.

thereby also expressing the German *Volk* soul: 'Die irrende Seele der Deutschen, welche sich künstlerisch jetzt in allen Erd- und Himmelsgegenden umhertreibt, muß sich wieder an den heimatlichen Boden binden; der holsteinsche Maler soll holsteinisch . . . malen.'[15] Nolde/Nansen, the Schleswig painter with a strong personality, fits the bill. Langbehn's assertion that whether they liked it or not the Dutch and the Danes were Low Germans, would have been balm to Nolde, the *Grenzmensch*, or border person, as he called himself, who so suffered under the loss of his Heimat to Denmark. Langbehn called for a new art not in *imitation* of, but in the *spirit* of, Rembrandt and was scornful of what he called tendentious imitation folk art. But he was popularly perceived as looking for a return to an old German style modelled as much on Dürer as Rembrandt and it was this direction which ultimately prevailed. Thus Nolde, whose masterly *Entombment* of 1915 echoes but does not imitate one of the greatest paintings in the history of German art, the Deposition in Grünewald's Isenheim altarpiece, fell foul of an ultra-conservative hatred of modernist abstraction and distortion. Rather than Nolde, the Nazi regime chose to stand patron to the mock-Renaissance art of Adolf Ziegler, who was appointed president of the Kulturkammer (Chamber of Culture) and to whom Lenz briefly alludes in *Deutschstunde* and who became known, because of the exactitude of his draughtsmanship in nude depictions, as 'der Meister des deutschen Schamhaars' ('the master of German pubic hair').

What most aroused Nazi enmity was not Nolde's landscapes, but his fascination for the exotic or primitive or ritualistic in painting human figures. Like Wiechert's von Orla who sought the simple life but had travelled the world and decked his study with masks, Nolde had traversed the globe on a journey commissioned in 1913 by the German Colonial Office to visit German New Guinea, crossing Russia, Siberia, Manchuria, then sailing to Korea, Japan, then on to China and Hong Kong, then to Manila, the Palua Islands, North-Eastern New Guinea, and New Ireland, these latter then called Kaiser-Wilhelm-Land and Neu-Mecklenburg. After six months in Melanesia, he returned by way of Indonesia, Burma, Singapore, reaching Port Said at the outbreak of the war. Lenz alludes in *Deutschstunde* to a striking sequence of paintings of Russians derived from studies made during this journey. Nolde's love of Oriental splendour comes out in the turbans and robes in his religious painting which also depicts Christ and his disciples with strongly marked Jewish features, his

---

[15] 'The wandering soul of the Germans, now traversing all corners of the globe, must again bind itself to the Heimat earth; the Holstein painter must paint in the Holstein way.' *Rembrandt als Erzieher: Von einem Deutschen*, 4th edn. (Leipzig: C. L. Hirschfeld, 1890), 19.

Fig. 7. Emil Nolde, *Schwüler Abend* (*Sultry Evening*, 1930), Nolde-Stiftung Seebüll

anti-Semitism being directed not at the mythic hero of a world religion, but at modern, urban Jews in Germany. Nolde's ideas on race and culture are a mix of confused prejudice not a worked-out philosophy, but if there is a defining feature, it is the idea of racial and cultural purity. Thus, like Langbehn who hero-worshipped the Jewish philosopher Spinoza but railed against 'mulatto' or mixed-race art, Nolde protested against the colonial exploitation of primitive peoples whose intact culture was threatened with adulteration or extinction and painted many powerful portraits of exotic subjects yet attacked 'mulatto' art in the same terms as Langbehn. Yet what was Nolde's art but a 'bastard' mix of cultural influences, to use another of his epithets? In his oeuvre as a whole the contrast between the Heimat and the exotic serves to mutually reinforce the expressive effect of both poles. But in the end, Nolde's Expressionist manner undoes the distinction between Heimat and the exotic, as Lenz brings out in the description of the garden painting with masks or the painting of Siggi's sister, Hilke, which so horrifies Gertrud Jepsen. This latter alludes to the recurrent motif of dancing girls in Nolde's work who, whether Semitic or Germanic in type, are in their ecstasy equally estranged and erotically charismatic, effects achieved by Nolde's wonderfully rhythmic handling of colour, as for example in the *Candle Dancers* of 1912. Nolde's

Sultry Evening, an oil painting on wood of 1930, depicts low-lying, black-roofed cottages whose walls reflect in a slighter darker tone the intense flame-red of clouds reflecting an unseen setting sun. The darker red seems to emanate from inside the buildings from a light source which pierces eerily in a brilliant almost-white, through windows like eyes answering the conflagration in the sky. (The windows in the tower of the eponymous castle in Kafka's novel look at first sight like eyes.) The two great bands of red are divided by spreading blackness which has engulfed a darkly irradiating green ground, almost wholly obscured behind but still visible in front of the cottages, while at the side, filling a third of the canvas, are the huge, heavy, mauve, and bluish-black delphinium blossoms. Here is Heimat infused with strangeness, the flowers evoking an anxiety which could turn to horror, the mood on the edge of apocalypse. Nolde's work exemplifies paradigmatically Heimat as an antithetical mode of seeing in terms of identity and difference: in Nolde's pictures, the familiar Heimat is infused with strangeness and distance so that belonging turns to longing or to horror. Similarly, Lenz conveys the familiar landscape through which Siggi, nicknamed Witt Witt after the call of a local bird, moves like a young creature in its habitat. But the flat landscape is ideal terrain for the spying eyes of a policeman ready to drive his own son, like a wounded animal, into the hunters' clutches. Thus the invisible landscape in *Deutschstunde* evokes both longing and horror.

Nolde's biographer, Robert Pois, is surely right to suggest that Lenz's Nansen is a romanticization which does not conceal but certainly under-plays Nolde's racism and persisting commitment to National Socialism. Yet Nolde's paradoxical *Heimatkunst* bursts out of the narrow-visioned ideology of Heimat and of his own racist notions. Along with the many allusions to other versions of Heimat, it serves Lenz well as an intertext through which to convey a complex reflection on German history and personal identity. The romanticization does not lie in the descriptions of painting, then, but in the depiction of Nansen as a powerful personality (shades of Langbehn's ideal Heimat artist) and as a paternal protector to Siggi, Klaas, Hilke, and the two children whom he and Ditte foster. In *Deutschstunde* Heimat is gendered in patriarchal mode, the matriarchs being in their different ways inertly sick. Nansen and Jens Ole Jepsen battle over who is to promulgate the laws governing the Heimat: Nansen would be his own master and sheltering patron to the young; the police-man serves masters who rule from Berlin and who arrive in motor cars or speak down the telephone, those lines of connection between the Heimat and the Reich. This struggle brings out the contradiction between Heimat and nation which all along bedevilled a discourse designed to strengthen the nation by appeal to older and antithetical loyalties. The awkwardness comes out in geographer Jörgen Hansen's clumsy syntax when he strives to blend Heimat and nation: 'Auf diese Weise soll den Schülern Land und *Volk*, besonders das deutsche Land mit seinen verschieden Stämmen, die Heimat, menschlich nahe gebracht werden.'[16] The real father and his masters massively fail the children, and even the ideal father's paternal aura fades somewhat as the power struggle between the policeman and the painter reaches a final vulgar phase of fisticuffs and the children are quite forgotten. A hinted identity between the two comes out in Nansen's picture of the clownish figure in the red cloak, from which another figure, recognizable as Klaas, turns away in fear; the mockery of the clown is a warding off of Nansen's empathy with the absurd policeman, both men being gifted with second sight. Yet a paternalistic undertone infuses *Deutschstunde* to the end when Nansen has become a remote figure seemingly untouched by Witt Witt's troubles, not least in the author's affectionate portrait of Siggi so that the novel expresses a double plea: that the fathers' generation should now nurture the young whom they have so grievously injured; that the sons should discriminate in judging their fathers' generation. Emil Nolde's Heimat art demands just such discriminating judgement in giving expression to psychic needs and utopian dreams, to visions of cultural and human diversity, to the power of symbols and mythic beliefs, and to difference within identity: Nansen and his Balthasar echo Nolde's many paintings of juxtaposed men and their demons. That National Socialism could seem to Nolde and others to answer such dreams and fears is the difficult case to which Lenz has offered his discriminating response.

Michael Verhoeven: *Das schreckliche Mädchen* (1989)

If *Deutschstunde* is a German lesson, Michael Verhoeven's film of 1989, *Das schreckliche Mädchen* (*The Nasty Girl*) is a history lesson which twenty years on takes up the story of young Germans exploring the Nazi past, this time not in memory but through the prism of local history and from the point of view of a later generation and of a girl rather than a boy. Here too the main story is recalled retrospectively but the heroine, being born after the war, has no first-hand memories of the Third Reich. Instead the film shows her efforts to research into her town's Nazi past and the hostile reaction of friends and neighbours and other vested interests

---

[16] 'In this way, land and people, especially the German land with its different tribes, the Heimat, should be brought humanly close to the pupils.' Hansen, *Die beseelte Landschaft*, 18.

ranged against her. The emphasis is not now on recollection but on present-day reactions to historical revelations of an ever-receding past which still, however, exerts its baneful effect. The film echoes Alexander Kluge's influential film *Die Patriotin* (1979), where the heroine was a rather naive young history teacher; here the heroine is by the end anything but the naive daughter, pupil, then wife of teachers who are much her inferiors in civil courage. The casting of Lena Stolze, who had twice played the role of Sophie Scholl in films about the White Rose resistance group—one of them, *Die Weiße Rose* (1982), directed by Verhoeven himself—implied for the cinema-going public a parallel between a young woman of enormous bravery who was legally murdered during the Third Reich by a criminal regime and a young woman, bold in her search for the truth decades later, who comes close to being illegally murdered by honest townsfolk. The main story is filmed in colour and begins in 1978 when the heroine who has two years earlier won a prize essay competition for German school-children, set by Karl Carstens, President of the Federal Republic, enters a second competition, this time on the topic of her home town, *Meine Heimatstadt im Dritten Reich*. This main story is sandwiched, however, between the disjointed fragments of an earlier pre-history told in black-and-white flashback and going back to the 1950s, and a later framework set around 1983 when the heroine's researches, now published in book form, have become a cause célèbre. The framework consists of state-ments, interspersed through the main story, by the heroine, members of her family, and other townspeople speaking directly to camera in inter-view mode. Thus the film mixes the modes of fictionalized reportage and film biography with a strong autobiographical element since it is the heroine's view of things which is being recounted, as is signalled in fleet-ing moments when she looks directly to camera in the midst of the earlier narratives. Such an alienation effect breaks through the illusion of reality with the effect of a direct appeal to the cinema audience, comparable to the implied parallel between fictional Siggi's manuscript and Lenz's text as an intervention in public debate. Siggi's story proved long in the telling, taking months to write rather than a couple of hours. Here the essay too proves so long in the writing that Sonja misses the deadline for the com-petition and, a marriage, two babies, and four years or so on, extends the essay first into a University dissertation which, lacking the support of her professor, is not presented and turns instead into a book. The length of the telling, in this case over years, is the result not of the twists and turns of memory, but of the obdurate blocking tactics the heroine meets every-where she turns in her searches through the church, press, and local government archives.

Like the allusion to Nolde in *Deutschstunde*, here too Sonja Wegmus, née Rosenberger, the heroine of the film, is based on a real person, Anna

Rosmus, who in 1983 published an account of widespread collaboration with the National Socialist regime by citizens in the town of Passau.[17] In the film Passau has become Pfilzingen but is easily recognizable by its baroque splendours. Lenz put a policeman at the centre of his study of local history with the role of culture and the arts as the other leading theme. Verhoeven's film, set in a substantial provincial town, brings a wider range of institutions into the frame in an analysis of sociological, economic, and political factors both during the Third Reich and in the post-war period. The heroine uncovers information about two particular cases: the denunciation by two priests of a local trader, Nathan Krakauer, ostensibly for fraud, but since Krakauer is Jewish he is taken off to a concentration camp never to return and his property is seized; the other case is the denunciation by a local woman of Pfarrer Schulte who in his sermons had spoken out against the regime and in particular against the race laws. Pfarrer Schulte was executed. A third case is that of a now elderly communist who was imprisoned in a local labour camp, then deported to a death camp, but survived to be liberated by the Americans, only to be interned again for a while at the beginning of the Cold War under suspicion as a communist and who is now trying to document his claim for a pension as a victim of political persecution; with silent irony it is left unclear whether the claim will cover both incarcerations. He and Sonja Wegmus become allies. Of all the characters in the film, the old communist speaks with the strongest dialect accent which signals that lefties need not be city folk but can belong in the Heimat, even if they are somewhat thin on the ground in provincial Bavaria.

The figure of the six million dead in its sheer enormity can recede into abstraction. Verhoeven's film aims to break through the abstraction, not from the side of the Jewish victims—this is not a Holocaust film—but from the side of the ordinary German population. The local history of individual cases can render more concretely how the final enormity, executed in camps mainly located on foreign soil, followed from a myriad of individual actions and interests played out at home. This and its handling of post-war denazification policies and of continuing everyday fascist attitudes in the heroine's idyllic Heimat town give the film its political edge. A leading theme is the role of the press, of education, of local government, of the Church, and of local business interests both in collusion with Nazi policies during the Third Reich and in covering up the past after 1945. Especially interesting is the criticism of denazification policies. The woman who denounced Pfarrer Schulte 'just to shut him up' and who protests, rather convincingly, that she had no idea that he would be executed,

---

[17] See Hans-Dieter Schütt, *Anna Rosmus, die 'Hexe' von Passau: Deutschland, Deutschland über alles—wächst kein Gras* (Berlin: Dietz, 1994).

was interned for a while after the war; the judge in the Volksgericht, the notorious People's Court during the Third Reich, who passed the death sentence lives on as an honoured citizen with a generous pension. Yet he certainly did know what would happen. (Verhoeven had also pursued the legal profession in his film *Die weiße Rose* and the disgrace that the guilty verdicts passed on members of the *Weiße Rose* had not been annulled; that they subsequently were is in large measure due to Verhoeven's film.) Denunciation is of course morally repugnant, but the differential implementation of denazification depending on social status is politically disgraceful. What the two priests who denounced Nathan Krakauer may have known or not known is unclear, but they surely knew more than their simple parishioner, yet they were never called to account and are now leading citizens of Pfilzingen. The film also attacks tokenism: thus the former mayor Zumtobel (literally in dialect 'to the devil') served as scapegoat to be sent to the devil, allowing others, such as 'der braune Heinrich' who turns out to be Professor Juckenack, off the hook. Juckenack's grotesquely multiple functions as priest, professor of theology and of history, newspaper editor, head of the ecclesiastical and newspaper archives etc. signal his representative status for local notabilities in general and for institutional collaboration with the regime. This is in keeping with the stress also on economic interests and on corruption in local government. Seizure of Jewish property led to lucrative pickings for the local business community; in the post-war world, corruption continues in the underhand dealings over planning permission and building contracts for a bypass cutting through the green, rolling landscape of the Heimat. The recent corruption is less murderous than what happened during the Third Reich, but some of the responses to the heroine's revelations suggest violence ready to break out. The incipient violence signals a further leading argument in the film, the continuation of right-wing extremism fuelled by Cold War politics and by resentments over divided Germany and the lost Heimat in the East. The heroine's father is a *Heimatvertriebener*, one driven from his Heimat of Silesia; 'Silesia is ours' figures as a slogan on a handkerchief during the heroine's wedding as in the attacks on the wedding car and later on her house. The culture of denunciation in the former GDR and the continuing violent resentments despite the end of the Cold War and German unification give Verhoeven's film a contemporary interest. The film undoes the easy stereotype of the 'evil Nazi' by showing the involvement of ordinary and otherwise quite sympathetic characters. Thus the heroine can reveal not only that the awful Professor Juckenack was responsible for denouncing the Jewish trader—something that gives her and the spectator a certain amount of pleasure—but that the sympathetic priest Pater Brummel was also involved, which explains Sonja's initial reluctance to name names for fear of simply perpetuating a cycle of denunciations, though in the end she does speak out. The film conveys a differentiated picture of acts of minor or major resistance by a minority of people, of minor and major collaboration by many, of silent dislike, apathetic indifference, or passive support for the National Socialist regime, of greater and lesser knowledge of the wider national implication of local events. This variegated mix prevails also in the post-war period so that the film comes across as a warning of what horror can come out of 'ordinary' communities not just in Germany, but in the new Europe or indeed anywhere. It serves too to counteract monolithic accusations of evil rooted in 'the German character' which keep surfacing as, for example, in the controversy over Daniel Goldhagen's indictment of ordinary Germans in his book on the Holocaust, *Hitler's Willing Executioners* (1996), by showing a complex interplay of individual actions with local institutional and wider national political factors not susceptible of easy answers.

Perhaps bravely, given the extreme sensitivity of the material, Verhoeven has cast his film as a satire, using black humour and irony to expose the machinations of those still in authority who wish their past to remain undisclosed. What could have been a dry tale of 'lost' files and legal battles is given a sharp and stylish treatment, mixing the genres of the heroic or mythical quest with that of the documentary and including elements of the thriller in the neo-Nazi attacks on Sonja. The result was considerable international acclaim including a Silver Bear at the 1990 Berlin Film Festival and an Oscar nomination as best foreign film. Along with the intercutting of different time strands and of narrative with mock interviews, another satirical device is the use of interior scenes in colour superimposed against background monochrome images of the baroque townscape of Passau. These unsettle the idea of coming to terms with the past by suggesting the shadow of history over the supposedly rehabilitated present. The Wegmus living room foregrounded against the local market is comically sinister in effect, showing a household vulnerable to attack from a seemingly idyllic community. Another ironic device subverts Sonja as heroine or martyr on a dangerous quest. Sonja's vision of herself as a latter-day Joan of Arc lampoons the Catholic Church and prevents the film from becoming a celebration of heroism or from exploiting the parallel with Sophie Scholl. There was always the risk, to which Verhoeven's own film had contributed, that Sophie Scholl's memory could be abused by her transformation into an icon so that her exemplary bravery might serve as an alibi providing comfort, especially to Christians, that some Germans had offered resistance. Verhoeven shows both ecclesiastical collusion and the brave resistance of Pfarrer Schulte, but the

inclusion of the old communist serves as a reminder that the main
opposition to National Socialism did not come from the Church, while
the shot of Sonja standing under the sheltering hand of a saintly statue
in the façade of the cathedral indicates the long history of ecclesiastical
appropriation of human bravery or suffering to propagandistic purposes
through the device of sanctification. This is the fate Sonja rejects at the
end of the film when she refuses to become a local heroine who will save
the honour of her Heimat and nation. The rush to cover her with honours,
like the scapegoating of mayor Zumtobel, is a tokenism of saints and
devils which allows everyone else off the hook. Shots of Sonja against a
looming, oversize photograph of the Federal President Karl Carstens convey an analogous message of how a worthy project, a school essay competition, can be turned to the purposes of national propaganda. Carstens
had less than happy relations with Germany's intellectuals or indeed with
heroines, having in 1974, when he was the CDU parliamentary chairman,
accused Heinrich Böll of publishing under the pseudonym of Katharina
Blüm (*sic*) a book inciting violence. Böll had in fact published under his
own name a story entitled *Die verlorene Ehre der Katharina Blum oder:
Wie Gewalt entstehen und wohin sie führen kann*, which like Verhoeven's
film is a study of scapegoating and of right-wing attitudes and institutional corruption.[18]

Sonja refuses the role of local heroine, but she is also determined not to
run away from the local bully boys to Munich, the big city where she could
be safely anonymous, and in her closing unsaintly and foul-mouthed outburst refuses to be driven, or elevated, out of her Heimat. The film thus
addresses a central theme of the Heimat mode: the expulsion and subsequent, here ironic, recuperation of an errant member of the community. Persecution and expulsion but without recuperation were a defining
feature of several anti-Heimat texts of the 1960s and 1970s which were
designed to expose the racism and more general fear of alterity in German
society; thus the outsider in Martin Sperr's *Jagdszenen aus Niederbayern*
is a homosexual. In similar mood, the killing of Sonja's pet cat and the
abusive phone calls that Sonja receives are warnings that she should
leave, or they imply that she is not properly German. But Verhoeven's
blackly humorous film does not entirely undermine the ideal of Heimat as
an inhabitable social space and as threshold between nature and culture.
Thus Heimat appears mainly in travesty, but occasionally straight. The
film observes conventions we have come across already in linking a locality to a regional centre, here Munich, and then to the nation, though
threads now link the Heimat to the European Community when Sonja

18 See J. H. Reid, *Heinrich Böll: A German for his Time* (Oxford: Berg, 1988), 183.

wins a trip to Paris and and has to explain to other young Europeans that her Bavarian Heimat may be social but is definitely not socialist, an allusion to the right-wing Bavarian Christan-Social Party. A number of moments allude satirically to stock elements of the 1950s Heimat film, as when Sonja yodels in celebration at finally getting her hands on the Zumtobel file. Or there is the sudden, dazzling transition from black-and-white flashback to a painfully colourful present as Sonja bounds towards the camera, the orange flowers on her dress clashing horribly with grass of an unlikely poisonous shade of bright green. But a few unironic scenes show Sonja in harmonious unity with the Heimat, as when she is collecting wood for her grandmother. In these scenes, the irony disappears and a naturalistic filmic representation of the outdoors is fleetingly restored. The wood-gathering establishes Sonja's relationship with her grandmother, a positive figure who lived through the era Sonja is researching and who is bravely unswerving in support of her granddaughter's endeavours as she had earlier bravely protested against the removal of crosses from schoolrooms. (This detail must be set against the negative example of Juckenack, but does indicate that conservative Catholics were less prone to join the National Socialists than some other population groups.) These scenes convey the diligence and stubborn persistence of both women. Such stubbornness is traditionally associated with peasant figures and may be contrasted with flexible adaptation to a changing world of urban cosmopolitanism. It is a double-edged virtue. In the critical Heimat tradition of the 1960s and 1970s, and indeed in the *Volksstück* or in Oscar Maria Graf's Bavarian novels of the 1920s, characters were often, for good or ill, stubborn and inflexible in the face of interference from outside; this is the attitude the grandmother displays in protesting against the removal of the crosses. But people in small communities may also be obsessive in their hatreds, like the policeman Hans Ole Jepsen in *Deutschstunde*. Sonja's stubborn attitude is very much a positive characteristic, though at times it borders on obsession, as her husband suggests, and arguably it even elicits violence. But it also uncovers a significant propensity to political extremism, which being brought out into the open can be countered, a diagnosis which some political developments in Germany in the 1990s have since confirmed.

Verhoeven's film follows after the feminist movement of the 1970s and in contrast to the patriarchal Heimat in *Deutschstunde* or the manly tree-felling in *Das einfache Leben* or even Viebig's Heimat, embodied in women and girl-children but ruled by men, Heimat here expressly descends through the female line. (Sonja's father is after all a *Heimatvertriebener*.) Much comic satire undermines any idealization of motherhood or the family, however, and Sonja is a modern woman devoted to causes other than just to her children or the ironing. But an occasional wisp of fairy-tale atmosphere invests Sonja and her grandmother with the aura of wise women. Wood-chopping as a symbol of the continuity of the generations—as tree-felling was in *Das einfache Leben*— is lightly ironized when Sonja, in crude grandmotherly disguise, looks forward to a grandmotherly future self, but the motif still taps into the powerful symbolic cluster of the forest: Sonja has something of a young witch whose connection with the woods and her work for her grandmother show an intimacy with her Heimat and in turn motivate her research into history. This gives the lie to the accusation that she has betrayed her Heimat. More of a betrayal are the underhand dealings which allowed a motorway to be driven through the landscape. This green message conveys that the Heimat under threat is worth the struggle. Sonja's access to her town's history is important because her connection with that place is important to her; without the truth about the past, there can be no re-evaluation of a Heimat still threatened by the depredations of the opportunists who will collude for profits with any regime. The satire is not merely critical, then, but aims also to be constructive. The long last shot which continues through the closing credits shows a rolling landscape cut through by a motorway in the background and in the foreground the *Gnadenbaum* or miracle tree. Hung around with its traditional votive offerings, the *Gnadenbaum*, like St Willibrord's festival in Viebig's text, signifies centuries-old Heimat lore mixing superstition with piety. The sacred tree is an ancient symbol here deployed parodistically. An alternative to the cathedral with its patristic tradition, the tree's presiding spirits are not saints but young witches casting spells to catch a lover, the moment of Sonja's first kiss comically echoing mythic awakenings of an Isolde or a Brünhilde and many a fairy-tale heroine. (Her second, post-Paris French kiss comes as something of a shock to her erstwhile awakener whose turn it is now to be awakened.) Among the endless legendary and literary resonances of the tree, it is tempting in our context to see a fleeting echo of the painter's magical garden in *Deutschstunde*. Nansen's painting depicted slit-eyed masks and a pair of eyes peering from amidst flowers. There the eyes were probably those of a schoolboy or of his wounded brother. In *Das schreckliche Mädchen*, masked men threaten the heroine with stones and bombs. Our last sight of her is as a young mother clutching her baby daughter and finally as just a pair of eyes peering from the foliage of a sacred tree, leaving the question of whether there will ever be a Heimat fit for nasty little girls.

6 Homeward-Bound
Edgar Reitz's *Heimat* for the 1980s

Edgar Reitz's epic film *Heimat* was premièred at the Munich film festival on 30 June and 1 July 1984. It appeared on German television (ARD) split into eleven film-length episodes from 16 September to 14 November 1984. In 1986, it was broadcast for the first time on British television (BBC2) with subtitles from 19 April to 29 April, divided in the same way. It is estimated that one or more episodes were watched by 25 million Germans on television.[1] In Britain, viewing figures of around 2.5 million were recorded, unprecedented for a subtitled art film of apparently off-putting length. Precedent suggested the BBC could have expected around 300,000 viewers.[2] Though German and British reviewers were largely positive, indeed some were rapturous,[3] the film also aroused controversy.[4] As Colin Townsend documents, the film drew from *Sunday Times* critic Sean French the remark that the revisionist protrayal of a decent German officer was at times a bit hard to take, and it early on aroused disquiet also in France. Townsend also makes the point that the film's episodic structure leaves gaps such as the crucial years of 1933 to 1935 when the process of *Gleichschaltung* (bringing into line) was being driven through in every institution and level of German civil society.[5] Even in rural Schabbach the local school would have felt the force of these policies which are not shown in the film. The film was also received by academics in the light of the 1980s *Historikerstreit*, discussed in the Introduction, and was accused of evading the horrors of German history in favour of a nostalgic representation of a harmless rural idyll, far from the locales of the Holocaust.

---

[1] See 'Kein Stammpublikum', *Tagesspiegel*, 20 Nov. 1984, 25.

[2] See 'Heimat Revisited?', *London Standard*, 2 May 1986, 31.

[3] See e.g. Bob Williams, 'Germany cues the Queen', *The Times*, 19 Apr. 1986, 17; also F. Thorn, 'Geschichte auf dem Handteller: Zur Rezeption von Edgar Reitz' "Heimat" in London', *Süddeutsche Zeitung*, 1 Mar. 1985, 14; Christopher Dunkley, 'Switch on to a Universal Masterpiece', *Financial Times*, 23 Apr. 1986, 19; and John Pym, 'A German Masterpiece', *Financial Times*, 15 Feb. 1985, 5.

[4] See e.g. Gertrud Koch, 'Kann man naiv werden? Zum neuen Heimat-Gefühl', *Frauen und Film*, 38 (1985), 107–9, and Jim Hoberman, 'Once in a Reich Time', *Village Voice*, 16 Apr. 1985, 52, 56. For a differentiated defence see Martin Swales, 'Symbolik der Wirklichkeit: Zum Film *Heimat*', in Rüdiger Görner (ed.), *Heimat im Wort: Die Problematik eines Begriffs im 19. Und 20. Jahrhundert* (Munich: iudicium verlag, 1992), 117–30.

[5] 'Edgar Reitz's *Heimat*: Poetic Evocations of a Nazi past' in Graham Bartram, Maurice Slawinski, and David Steel (eds.), *Reconstructing the Past: Representations of the Fascist Era in Post-War European Culture* (Keele: Keele University Press, 1996), 186–201.

However, suggestions that *Heimat* amounted to an uncritical return to the false reconciliation and conservative family values of 1950s Heimat films tended to ignore both the aesthetics of the film, which when examined reveal a rather more differentiated stance, and one of the most important contexts of Reitz's film, namely the Green movement in the Federal Republic of the 1970s and 1980s. The Greens first entered the Bundestag in 1983, though environmental consciousness had been growing throughout the 1970s as the post–1968 left had fractured into extremists and pragmatists, and into various interest groups. The cultural and economic values of E. F. Schumacher's *Small is Beautiful* (1973), the political culture of *Basisdemokratie* (grass roots activism) and of local citizens' initiatives or *Bürgerinitiativen* pervaded the new Green thinking. By the 1980s the attempt to recuperate for the left the concept of Heimat was in full swing, following the developments traced in Chapter 3 when attacks on the restorative values of the 1950s Heimat film gave way to a less strident critical Heimat mode in literature and films such as Werner Herzog's quasi-mystical *Herz aus Glas* of 1976. In the 1980s, Heimat as an environment under threat and dissociated from the problematic nation becomes a locus of community values. Seen in this context, Reitz's film, though it does convey a village community sympathetically, avoids blinkered provincialism by tracing the impact upon the rural world both of national history and of the wider process of modernization. It is this facet in a complex film that we shall start with in looking at how the film handles the passage of time and the course of history.

Technology in Paradise: A Modern Heimat?

Reitz's historical saga begins with the return of Paul Simon from the First World War to his home in Schabbach, a village in the Hunsrück, a high-lying segment of land between the Rhine and the Mosel, and to his parents, the blacksmith Matthias and the redoubtable Katharina who represent the oldest generation. There then follows the history of a village from 1919 to the early 1980s traced through two families interconnected by marriage and embracing a wide range of minor characters such as one-eyed Hänschen who accidentally lost an eye and wants to be a sharpshooter or Karl Glasisch whose hands bear the stigmata of damage by mustard gas during the war and who introduces all the episodes, shuffling through heaps of old photographs to remind the viewer of the characters and of the passage of time. If any one character embodies the Heimat and binds the episodes together it is Maria, Paul's wife, who stays on in the village of Schabbach after Paul suddenly deserts her and takes off to America, returning only after 1945 as a rich businessman. Paul's desertion is in part motivated by his lingering feelings for Appolonia, an outsider in the village whom he loved but did not marry, choosing instead the Heimat woman, Maria. Other main characters of the middle generation are Maria's sister Pauline, who is married to Robert, a jeweller in the nearby town of Simmern, and Paul's brother Eduard who marries Lucie, a Berlin madam whom he met in a brothel on *Kristallnacht*, 9 November 1938, the night when the regime launched a concerted attack on Jewish citizens and their property. (By this device Reitz arguably sidelines the *Kristallnacht*, an omission drawing much criticism.) Eduard serves as village mayor during the Third Reich, his bad health saving him from war service. But Eduard is not a convinced Nazi, unlike Maria's father Wiegand and her brother, the main baddies. Central figures in the third generation are Paul's and Maria's two sons, Anton who serves on the eastern front but survives to set up an optics factory after the war and disaffected Ernst who eventually makes a business of selling off Heimat antiques. Maria also has a son, Hermann, by her lover Otto Wohlleben, an engineer turned bomb-disposal expert who finally falls victim to his craft. Hermann, a musician, increasingly dominates the final episodes, having an affair with Klärchen, a refugee and hence an outsider in the village, then finding a patron in his stepfather Paul on his return from America. Hermann will be the central character of the sequel, *Die Zweite Heimat*.

Through various devices, the film contrives to suggest that the seemingly 'open' beginning, Paul's return like the prodigal son to his father's house, marks a historical caesura in the life of the village. The year 1919 appears as the point at which the rural environment begins its transition from traditional rural economy, untouched by the developments of cities and the momentous events of history, to become fully integrated into modern society with the old working methods and cyclical family structures gone for ever. Of course this elides the great historical upheavals of the nineteenth century which so affected the rural environment for the sake of creating a good beginning to the story. However, if the contrived beginning could be criticized as historically disingenuous, then the sense of time in the film is nevertheless at odds with the conservative Heimat films of the 1950s which can be peculiarly timeless, or irritatingly partial, when they represent contemporary society. In Reitz's epic, different conceptions of time exist concurrently; different time-lines are dominant at various stages of the century.

Idyllic cyclical or seasonal time is always already disrupted and exists in the film mainly as a trace memory. Thus the haymaking sequence is interrupted by an American aviator's forced landing in the field due to running out of fuel. The clash of two powerful bundles of associations—the modernist sequence of America, aviation, and the dollar; and the eternal agricultural cycle of the whole family pitching hay onto a cart drawn by oxen—is not entirely elegiac in character for the two bundles are brought together in an unlikely fashion in this early sequence to convey the uneven pace of modernization. The aviator's fuel, for example, is fetched in several milk churns. The dual nature of technology is expressed in Paul's response: for him, aviation embodies a utopian promise, though it also reveals the extent of his alienation from the rural landscape. As he flies above the Hunsrück he gains the visual perspective of the outsider he has already become since returning from the Great War, a perspective confirmed in his departure. Technology can liberate the rural community from the back-breaking labour of the past, but technology also threatens to destroy the rural community and will eventually culminate in the horror of modern warfare.

Throughout the film, but especially in the person of Paul in the episode entitled 'Fernweh' (which might be translated as wanderlust), technology is shown to contain both utopian promise and a threat to the traditional Heimat life. Thus Paul's radio, a truly collective village enterprise, funded by Wiegand, built by Paul, and set up by Eduard, Glasisch, and Hänschen at the old ruined Baldenau castle for the benefit of the villagers, initially unites the Heimat community, but at the same time connects that community with faraway cultural events such as the broadcast of Schubert's song 'Der Lindenbaum' from Vienna. It brings what is distant into the village. Reitz emphasizes the utopian moment of balance between old and new by the romantic setting for this episode of a medieval ruined castle, the kind of refuge which abounded in Viebig's Eifel stories, set just across the Mosel from the Hunsrück. Implicit in the development of radio technology for the village is, however, the future erosion of the communal —the radio will atomize the community, which divided into separate households in individual homes will listen to radio programmes connecting the hearth directly to the Reich by bringing the voice of the Führer to the remotest locations. Even in this early example, Wiegand comments as Paul initially tunes into Mass at Cologne Cathedral that he need not have attended church that morning, indicating the implications for communal life. For Paul, the radio is initially a kind of community project, but it serves to fuel his isolation within the community, and his sense of dissatisfaction, his *Fernweh*.

Heimat exists in Reitz's film at the intersection of several time-lines. Idyllic cyclical time exists mainly as a disrupted trace, as in the kitchen scene, where Paul's welcome home in the Simon kitchen is shot through with references to, and visions of, the ghosts of the war. Paul's inability to respond to his family and his forever-fractured relationship with his Heimat set the tone for 'Fernweh', as he struggles, and fails, to build a Heimat life. The time-line of public everyday life modifies the cyclical idyll in *Heimat* and consists of collective events such as the unveiling of the war memorial in 'Fernweh' or the villagers' response to the announcement of the outbreak of the Second World War in 'Auf und davon und zurück' ('Up and Away and Back Again'). Whereas the cycle of the seasons and the observation of great public events both have communal character, bio-graphical time emerges according to Mikhail Bakhtin with the emergence of the modern capitalist society in the nineteenth century.[6] In 'Fernweh' Paul's introspection following his experience of war marks him out as an alienated individual. We follow his biographical life events through the film: the returning soldier, the young father, the émigré, the industrialist, the wealthy sponsor of his stepson's avant-garde music; but this is even more the case with Maria, born in 1900 and described as the villagers' 'living calendar'. The idea of such a living calendar suggests the inter-twining in *Heimat* of private, biographical time with historical time, for though the film does not foreground political history, its focus on social history necessitates the narration of historical developments through the lives of individuals. Here tension between place and time characteristic of the Heimat mode finds paradigmatic expression.

Though Reitz appears to be charting the disintegration of the Heimat in the face of the onward march of history and particularly of modern technology which is obviously about to change for ever the agricultural working practices of the region, technology's Janus face is evident in the example of air-flight, which from 'Fernweh' on expresses both utopian possibilities for the alienated sons of the Heimat and the betrayal of such potential by its use in warfare.[7] The Janus face of modern technology is also evident in other forms of development that take place in the rural Heimat. For what Reitz achieves in his spatial-temporal Heimat is pre-cisely what was missing from 1950s Heimat films, which often juxtaposed the trappings of modern life with the locales of the rural idyll, but with-out any sense of how history and technology really impacted on rural communities. Reitz's *Heimat* has at its core the confrontation between modernity and the rural environment and community. And despite the elegiac tone of parts of the film—the lingering shots of the landscapes of

---

[6] 'Forms of Time and of the Chronotope in the Novel', in M. M. Bakhtin, *The Dialogic Imagination: Four Essays*, ed. Michael Hoquist, trans. Caryl Emerson and Michael Holquist (Austin, Tex.: University of Texas Press, 1981), 214–17.

[7] Reitz allowed the Heimat title to be used for a local television report about the campaign against American nuclear weapons which were stationed in the Hunsrück, perhaps the clearest example of the betrayal of the utopian potential of flight.

the Hunsrück; the celebration of rural types such as Mathias the black-smith and Katharina the matriarch—Reitz finds an accommodation between modernity and the rural Heimat. For technology is not merely an instrument of destruction but is actively celebrated in 'Fernweh' through the excitement of the radio picnic and the enthusiasm of Eduard the amateur photographer, but to an even greater extent later in the film, when Anton's high-tech optics factory is celebrated as a source of new employment and a new skill base for the rural community, in contrast to Wilfried's monstrous abuse of the environment by the use of agrochemicals. Agriculture is shown here to have little social value in that it provides no significant employment for the region, and mechanization means that the smallholdings of earlier decades are transformed in the post-war period into giant agro-prairies giving yet more power to large landowners. By showing a clean factory and dirty agriculture, which far from saving the rural Heimat is poisoning it, Reitz avoids both the reactionary cultural pessimism which had fuelled the rise of National Socialism and the *völkisch* cult of the peasant. Here is a green stance for the times, by implication seeking a reformed agriculture and open to careful industrial developments enabling a mixed rural economy.

In the middle section of the film, the spatio-temporal Heimat is further defined by the building of the motorway which both connects the village to other parts of the Reich and yet at the same time enables travellers to bypass the village. The French woman who rides through Schabbach on her way from Paris to Berlin in Episode 2 would not come into contact with the village community at all in the era of the major road. As Karl Glasisch comments at the beginning of Episode 5, 'Früher ging die Straß von Dorf zu Dorf zu Dorf. Heut geht sie dran vorbei . . . sie führt von Bunker zu Bunker zu Bunker und nimmehr von Dorf zu Dorf.'[8] It is clear from his comments as well as from the nature of the construction process that the road is not simply an amenity for the German people, it is motivated entirely by the desire to prepare for war. The purpose of the road is to facilitate the rapid movement of troops and military equipment. On the other hand the road does facilitate human contacts and economic developments. During the construction of the road, Schabbach sees an influx of Saxon men from the Todt engineering corps who, like Fleißer's sappers in *Pioniere in Ingolstadt*, stay in the village while they are building the motorway. The construction period certainly has a major effect on the village, opening out the rural Heimat to many more influences. In biographical terms, it is especially significant for Maria who falls in love with the

---

[8] 'In the past the road went from village to village. Today it bypasses us . . . it doesn't lead from village to village any more, but from bunker to bunker.'

Fig. 8. Otto Wohlleben and Pieritz pose for Anton's camera during the building of the motorway

engineer Otto Wohlleben and has his child. Socially the roadbuilding functions as part of the economic upturn; the construction workers form a new market for local traders such as Robert and Pauline, eagerly buying expensive jewellery. They even threaten the moral structures of the rural Heimat when Martina, too, sees them as a ready-made market for her services as a prostitute. Lucie, the former Berlin madam, steps in to preserve her new provincial lifestyle just as she likes it, but Martina and the construction workers are nevertheless an exotic urban influence on the Hunsrück Heimat. Reitz's picture of changing sexual mores in the suite of military roadbuilding is thus less downbeat than that of Marieluise Fleißer.

Reitz uses means of communication like the road and the telegraph to indicate how the rural Heimat first undergoes a rapid and rather disorientating integration into a nation, due primarily to the Nazi desire to plan and prepare for war. Then, in a typically Janus-faced gesture he reveals how the very same technological phenomena will in peacetime eventually cause the dislocation of the Heimat from locales of political and social significance. Heimat becomes much more integrated with distant places, but risks both reverting to provincial irrelevance and losing its distinct identity. Reitz's film was made before the revolution in information technology and the information superhighway, but his differentiated exploration of the effects of modernity on the rural Heimat anticipates some of the ways in which spatial relations are affected by technology. Virtual spaces and the global village pose specific problems for the re-evaluation of the rural Heimat. But although Schabbach at the end of the film saga appears to have lost its historical momentum somewhat, a late twentieth-century solution is suggested (albeit rather tentatively) both in Anton's medium-sized optics factory, a model of manufacturing in harmony with the local environment, and in Hermann's avant-garde alienated Heimat art, where the sounds of the Heimat, natural and cultural, can be transformed into concrete music which represents transcendence of, but also a debt owed to, Heimat.

The effects of modernity on the Heimat are thus expressed in various complex and differentiated forms. In almost every case, the effects of technology are shown to be deeply ambiguous. Certainly, there is evidence that the traditional way of life in rural spaces is under threat. However, that life is itself not unequivocally celebrated and is in any case represented as always already superseded. 'Heimat', as Reitz put it, 'is such that if one would go closer and closer to it, one would discover that at the moment of arrival it is gone, it has dissolved into nothingness'.[9] Technology is not merely the destroyer, or even the simple saviour, of the rural Heimat, but one of Reitz's most notable successes in his film saga is to explore in detail the various different effects technology has on twentieth-century Heimat life. Just as, for example, the concept of Heimat as a fixed system of inside and outside is actively being reread, so one of the particular effects of technology on the Heimat under discussion in the film is the issue of the public and private spheres, and the way that technology causes a shift in balance between them. Such a shift is instrumental in the emergence of the key political contexts of the twentieth century. The first radio in Schabbach, as we have already seen, is a kind of community or village project. In a typical ambiguous twist, it serves both to connect Paul with faraway places and to disconnect him from the Heimat, creating the *Fernweh* that leads to his emigration. But radio has other implications beyond unsettling the *Heimweh/Fernweh* dynamic for Paul. Radio itself appears first to be a communal experience in the early example of the radio picnic, but later atomizes the population into discrete units—the nuclear family—sitting around wireless sets. Such a threat to *communal*

[9] Franz A. Birgel, 'You Can Go Home Again: An Interview with Edgar Reitz', *Film Quarterly* 39/4 (Summer 1986), 5.

life in turn creates a *collective* or *mass* public: the era of mass political movements is seen to benefit directly from a technological development which first appears to unite the villagers communally, then to disperse them into a private sphere, and then to make of that private sphere a public arena within which the politics of mass movements is disseminated. The power of radio to penetrate into the home and family is celebrated in a characteristic mix of glorification of modern technology yet reactionary idealization of peasant life, in a painting by Paul Mathias Padua, *Der Führer spricht*, showing a family sitting under a portrait of Hitler listening to the radio. At the outbreak of war, Hitler's speech is heard not only in private homes but also on a public address system by ranks of air cadets standing to attention. The radio, the military, and the declaration of war are all marked by collectivity in this sequence. In the evocation of the wartime radio request show in Episode 7, 'Die Liebe der Soldaten', Reitz again reveals the extent to which the private and personal is compromised by the collective in the twentieth century through war and mass ideologies.

This is precisely the kind of far-reaching treatment that differentiates *Heimat* from the 1950s Heimat films, which seek to provide resolution and rarely pose such questions. The impact of modernity on the rural Heimat is perhaps the most successful aspect of the film. Shot through with ambiguities and undecidable contradictions, technology is at once a force for destruction and restoration of a functioning twentieth-century Heimat. It defines people as private individuals, yet locates them within mass movements. It is frantically promoted by the Nazis and yet apparently despised within Nazi mythology. It holds utopian promise, which is betrayed in military application. Finally, technology appears to be a possible bridge between nature and art, and though the Heimat is changed irrevocably by the developments of modernity, technology itself may well help to create a future workable rural Heimat in the late twentieth century.

Heimat as Image

Reitz's appropriation of the Heimat tradition in his film saga is an audacious move given the reactionary reputation of the 1950s Heimat film and the iconoclastic anti-Heimat trend in the New German Cinema. Thus Ruth Perlmutter accused him of reverting to the 1950s Heimat film tradition and promoting uncritical and vague nostalgia for a rural idyll.[10]

---

[10] 'German Revisionism: Edgar Reitz's *Heimat*', *Wide Angle: A Film Quarterly of Theory, Criticism and Practice*, 9/3 (1987), 21–37.

However, just as his representation of technology departs significantly from the kind of treatment found in 1950s films (see Chapter 3), Reitz's references to the Heimat film tradition amount to much more than homage or pastiche. Indeed, throughout *Heimat*, allusions to a filmic tradition are literally framed in a highly self-referential manner. Reitz seeks not to create a 1980s version of the 1950s Heimat film, but to allude consciously to, and therefore reflect critically on, that tradition. *Heimat* is full of references to the very process of image making, whether filmic or photographic. At all stages of the film, the viewer is thus invited to be wary, not only of the 1950s tradition but also of *Heimat* itself, rather as in *Deutschstunde* Siggi constantly reflects on his evocations of Heimat, underlining that they are produced as verbal images just as the painter or photographer produces visual pictures. Christopher Wickham comments: 'By means of self-reflexive devices, *Heimat* directs attention to its own constructedness as text and repeatedly dismantles the illusion of represented reality'.[11] The photographs at the beginning of each episode in the television version of the film, the references and allusions to photography, to the cinema, to film-making even, are evidence of Reitz's deliberate effort not only to draw attention to the place *Heimat* occupies in the German film tradition, but also to differentiate his work from other examples of the Heimat genre. The notoriously slippery concept of Heimat is forever image in Reitz's film, forever framed, seen reflected and refracted in windows, seen inverted in the old-fashioned cameras used by Eduard, and seen represented in other films and interpreted by Maria and Pauline when they go to the cinema in Simmern.

The first episode is striking for its framed images of the rural scene through windows. Maria's first sighting of Paul as he returns from the war is a reflection in a window that she is cleaning, a potentially 'mythical' scene disturbed by a technique of alienation alerting spectators to the various levels of meaning and myth-making. Maria is engaged in women's work, the image of a dutiful Heimat woman, Paul is the mythical returning soldier seeking to reclaim his Heimat, but the framing of the images in the window, and the reflections and refractions of the image interfere with this comfortable mythology. Eduard's photographic images are also particularly striking in that he is engaged in what amounts to a kind of community project to record details of the rural Heimat. However, these records are not only shown in their inverted form as he views them through his lens, they are also seen to be capable of misrepresentation as in the example of the radio picnic at Baldenau castle. The photographic image is instrumental in challenging Heimat myth-making in the film by

[11] 'Representation and Mediation in Edgar Reitz's *Heimat*', *German Quarterly*, 64/1 (Winter 1991), 43.

emphasizing the means of production used to create visual images. The spectator is shown how Eduard rigs up a piece of string to activate the shutter of his camera, how the group is assembled, how the scene looks to the camera—upside down—and finally how the snapshot looks—it is black and white of course. As well as this possibly symbolic use of the upside-down image (the film inverting reality, a warning to the spectator?) there is an interesting distortion of 'reality' when Glasisch contrives to be next to Wiegand in the photograph. Wiegand despises Glasisch because of his lowly status in the village and is prejudiced against him because of the unsightly scarred skin on Glasisch's hands which he finds disgusting. On the photo they appear together, Glasisch's hands on Wiegand's shoulder, yet the spectator knows that their relationship is different. This is a further example of how Reitz signals to the spectator that there are many layers of 'truth' and as many realities contained in visual fiction as in written fiction. We are supposed to mistrust the images before us and are warned to be especially wary of the Heimat myth of reconciliation.

The cinema itself is shown as capable of distortion in examples of propaganda film: on the eastern front, Anton films for two different audiences, the public that watches news bulletins in cinemas, and top Nazis who have clearance to view more sensitive material. Two different narratives of the war are prepared for their respective spectators; the audience of *Heimat* can see that the camera narrates rather than records reality. Before Anton is old enough to be a soldier, he has a keen interest in both photography and cinema. In one sequence, he shows a news film to a group of friends. It includes a speech by Hitler, but Anton does not have the equipment required for sound reproduction, and so he can show images only. The children argue about the Führer, but the partial reproduction functions again as a clear caveat to viewers about the unreliability of images.

When Maria, Otto, Pauline, Robert, Martina, and Specht go to the cinema in Simmern to see Carl Froelich's *Heimat* (1938), their response and the selection of clips cited by Reitz are not necessarily what one might expect, given the thematic content of Froelich's film. *Heimat* is read somewhat against the grain by Maria, Pauline, and the rest of their party. The film is based on Hermann Sudermann's 1893 play of the same title. It stars Zarah Leander as a woman artist, Magda, who returns to the Heimat with her illegitimate child from a working exile in the United States. Her father tries to recuperate her into the Heimat environment by forcing her to marry the father of her child, who, however, wishes to deny his daughter and have her sent away to maintain their social status. In the film, though not in the play, Magda loves a different man, who accepts her child. The film is rather interesting in that it thematizes the problems of a woman artist, who is not demonized despite her deviation from Heimat family values. Though she ultimately returns to the Heimat in a happy ending, there is some critique of the restrictive morals that made her want to leave in the first place. The men who initially appear to determine her fate, her father and Keller, the father of her child, are also represented rather negatively. However, the focus for the spectators is the family: the evening out at the cinema is a couples' evening, and this tends to shape their response to the film. Reitz cites a selection of clips which emphasize the restoration of the family and the more conservative Heimat values. The film acts as a prelude to an evening that celebrates relationships, and the more progressive and differentiated aspects of Froelich's film are not further discussed.

Reitz emphasizes the role of spectators in reading and interpreting a cinematic text as well as the power of film-makers to construct a certain narrative. Both 'caveats' point towards a self-reflexive text which tends to undercut itself at moments of high mythology, often revealing a layer of framing to act as a distancing device. So, for example, in Episode 4 Otto Wohlleben watches Mathias and Katharina ploughing, and Maria bringing them food and wine—a true Heimat image, comparable to the idyllic moment when Marianne brings dinner to the tree-fellers in Wiechert's *Das einfache Leben*. But there photographers are chased off by faithful Bildermann, whereas here Otto is watching through a surveying instrument which he is using to build the motorway. So the timeless Heimat image is viewed through a self-reflexive frame, and the frame itself is a technical instrument which appears antithetical to the Heimat of the 1950s films. There may be a remote echo too of Brecht's poem 'Wenn der Anstreicher durch die Lautsprecher über den Frieden redet' which evokes how Hitler's strident tones, transmitted by radio, disrupt the rural idyll: 'Die Baumfäller stehen horchend in den stillen Wäldern | Die Bauern lassen die Pflüge stehn und halten die Hand hinters Ohr | Die Frauen bleiben still, die das Essen aufs Feld schleppen . . .'.[12] Otto's death, blown up by a bomb in a field, disperses any aura of the idyllic in his love affair with Maria.

Many of the key images of the Heimat are framed by windows, mirrors, through the viewfinder of a camera, through Otto's surveying instrument. But still other images of the rural landscape, always a key feature of Heimat films, are distanced not by placing a literal frame around them, but by holding the image still—not in a freeze-frame, but simply by

---

[12] 'The tree fellers stand listening in the quiet forests | The peasants leave their ploughs and hold their hands behind their ears | The women bringing food to the fields stand still . . .'. *Große kommentierte Berliner und Frankfurter Ausgabe: Gedichte 2* (Frankfurt amd Main: Suhrkamp, 1988), 11.

lingering for a long time over a shot that is virtually static. Such images punctuate the narrative and although they might tend to have a rather mythologizing effect, this is unsettled both by the unusual length of a static image in a feature film (sometimes ten seconds or so) and by the juxtaposition of images of historical change. For example, still landscape shots of the sky, the fields, the trees and bushes frequently include telegraph wires. During the picnic scene at the ruined castle, there is a striking image of the sky bisected by the wires being used to set up the new radio. Telegraph wires have since their advent figured as signifiers of modernity, bisecting as they do the dome of the sky with its connotations of eternity. Thus even in Clara Viebig's early Heimat writing, telegraph wires already signify change.

Reitz's Heimat is always consciously filmic, always framed. He uses metafictional comment on the process of image production to try to ensure that the viewers remain somewhat distanced from the mythologizing which occurs in 1950s Heimat films. His self-referential approach in referring to cinema and photography, his use of windows and mirrors to create frames for his shot composition, his disruption of mythical images of the Heimat with wires and telegraph poles all point to a Heimat that is very clearly mediated, that is never 'just there' but which is always being represented to the viewer in ways that are clearly signalled.

Gender Mythology in *Heimat*

Heimat discourse came into being as a lament for a rural environment many had left behind in the great migration to the cities of the late nineteenth century. The invocation of Heimat in film and literature often transmits the idea of loss; the Heimat is a lost rural home at the turn of the century; it is a 'lost land' in the case of East Prussia after the war; it is a lost domestic and political wholeness in the traumatic post-war period. Reitz's film is not necessarily different in that it too is motivated to reclaim a 'lost' history, 'lost' memories. Reitz himself is an urban migrant; he took his chance as a young man to escape the repressive Heimat and go to university in Munich. Much of the emotional impact of *Heimatkunst* may thus derive from the loss of local, or even national, identity but Heimat is also associated metaphorically and literally with a (lost) place of childhood, and hence with the loss of, or separation from, the mother, which in psychoanalytic theory begins with the trauma of birth. *Heimatkunst* can therefore be seen as a kind of psychological regression to childhood, a reaction against the 'loss' of the mother. Heimat is thus frequently associated with women. In Heimat films and literature, it is often the task of a maternal woman to embody, or represent, the Heimat for men. Heimat appears in such texts to be rather like the Hegelian concept of a natural 'nether region' which is the realm of women and the family, and which men need to sustain them, but which they must also transcend if they are to function as full members of civil society. Women and especially mothers sustain access to the Heimat for their husbands and sons. Men are thus able to move between the two spheres, whereas the women who provide the bridge between the spheres are unable to transcend the Heimat.[13]

Just as women in a difficult liminal role maintain links to the world outside the Heimat for the benefit of their menfolk, but are unable to move beyond the Heimat sphere into civil society, Heimat itself is also in an ambiguous liminal position between nature and culture. A cultural construct, defined as much by legal and moral value systems as by mere rural or provincial location, it nevertheless is apparently close to nature, operating on the threshold of nature and culture. Women, especially maternal women, are in an analogous position, their affiliations to the sphere of culture and political life masked by a supposed closeness to the sphere of nature and the family and by their function in sustaining the Heimat sphere for the benefit of men. In her article 'Is Female to Male as Nature is to Culture?', Sherry Ortner concludes that it is reductive to ascribe women to the realm of nature for many reasons, but not least because they are responsible for socializing children and are thus clearly a vital part of the cultural sphere. However, she does allow that women are regarded as closer to nature than men.[14] The Hegelian conception of women as tied to the nether world of domesticity, or indeed Rousseau's idea of women being symbolically close to nature, and thus worthy of adulation yet unable to function as full citizens, appears to be particularly appropriate to the position of women within the discourse of Heimat.[15] This is why the murder of a mother and her embryo in the womb is iconoclastic in effect in Martin Sperr's anti-Heimat play *Jagdszenen aus Niederbayern*.

The psychological associations between Heimat and motherhood function partly because of the bourgeois social construct of close mother–child bonding, and partly because women generally have become associated with nature. The metaphor of the Earth as a mother figure has persisted since ancient times and is culturally extremely widespread. Since the Western environmental movement of the 1970s and 1980s, which has

---

[13] Patricia Jagentowicz Mills, *Woman, Nature and Psyche* (New Haven: Yale University Press, 1987), 12.

[14] Sherry Ortner, 'Is Female to Male as Nature is to Culture?', *Feminist Studies*, 1/2 (1972), 485–507.

[15] See Genevieve Lloyd, *The Man of Reason: 'Male' and 'Female' in Western Philosophy*, 2nd edn. (London: Routledge, 1993), 77.

Fig. 9. Maria, the eternal Heimat woman in the 1930s kitchen, complete with Ernst's model aeroplane hanging from the light bulb

implicitly and explicitly revived the representation of nature as female, it has had a renewed currency, for example in the figure of Gaia.[16] Reitz's film is conceived very much in the light of 1970s green thinking and holds up as an ideal the optics factory that can work in harmony with the environment, benefiting from the clean air of the Hunsrück and at the same time causing little environmental damage. So the ideal of nature as bountiful mother-provider to be treated with respect is in evidence, as is a critique of practices which have a dubious or negative environmental impact such as agricultural pollution and Ernst's stripping of older village buildings to provide rustic accessories for city theme bars. The Simon house, which Ernst is ready to dismantle given the opportunity, is closely identified with Maria herself. In her later years she lives there alone, and Ernst's desire to take it apart and sell it piecemeal is seen by Anton in particular as a kind of violation of their dead mother. Though Reitz consciously sets out to undo or at least unsettle much of the mythology

[16] See e.g. Rupert Sheldrake, *The Rebirth of Nature: The Greening of Science and God* (London: Century, 1990), which rejects the mechanistic construction of nature in favour of the organic mythology of a primal mother which characterized the view of nature in earlier and less environmentally damaging cultures.

surrounding Heimat, the gendering of the term as feminine and its association with the maternal are not challenged in his film. Women characters tend to be either maternal Heimat women (Maria, Katharina, Martha), or erotic but dangerous 'other' women (Appolonia, Martina, Klärchen). Arguably, then, the gender roles are conservative compared with the liberal values in Sudermann's turn-of-the-century portrayal of an emancipated woman in his *Heimat* or even with Froelich's 1938 film which sought an ambiguous reconciliation of female emancipation with patriarchal order. On the other hand, paternity is not emphasized, though this has some basis in the historical reality of missing men due to the two world wars. But in Reitz's *Heimat* it is not only fathers who tend to be absent but also daughters, though there is no demographic explanation for this. Even those young women that could be developed into strong daughter figures remain minor characters who are neglected in comparison to Maria's sons Anton, Ernst, and Hermann.

The pattern of women embodying the Heimat for men who then transcend this 'nether region' to find wider outlets for their talents and aspirations is repeated through the generations in *Heimat*. Paul, on returning to his Heimat after the First World War, is positioned at the centre of the narrative choosing between two women, Maria and Appolonia. Maria is the blonde Heimat archetype, Appolonia the dark erotic gypsy, an outsider in the village, mocked and abused by the villagers for her supposed gypsy origins and her relationship with a French soldier. Paul is attracted to Appolonia, who asks him to leave with her, but though he feels alienated from his Heimat, he cannot find the courage to go with her. He chooses Maria, a woman who bears him children and encourages him in all his technical endeavours, and indeed exhorts him to be himself, pursue his ambitions, in short to transcend his Heimat. Maria's encouragement finally backfires when he can bear the restrictive Heimat life no longer and leaves for America without warning to found an electronics firm. Maria not only sustains his access to the Heimat, but becomes a kind of muse to Paul like Appolonia in that she supports his ambitions, and thus unwittingly inspires him to look beyond his surroundings and achieve the transcendence of the Heimat that in Reitz's film is reserved for male characters; women remain stuck in the shadowy 'nether region'. Though Maria speaks in Episode 4 of starting again somewhere far away, she never gets that opportunity. Even Pauline's plan that they should travel to America to see Paul, when they are both old and unencumbered by family responsibilities does not come to fruition.

Paul's choice between Maria and Appolonia prefigures Hermann's situation as a teenager in the 1950s caught between Maria—his possessive Heimat mother—and Klärchen—his erotic muse, a refugee who remains an outsider. Maria's role of providing access to the Heimat is important for her menfolk, but they, unlike the women who remain rooted in the province, must ultimately transcend their Heimat in order to take their place in civil society. In Reitz's film, it is technology, and most strikingly art, which is the route to transcendence for the male characters. Indeed technology feeds into art in the form of Hermann's electronic music. Both technology and art are deeply indebted to the rural Heimat: Hermann's music, for example, explicitly acknowledges the influence of the Heimat in its use of recorded natural sounds like birdsong. His choral piece, which ends Reitz's film saga, is a particularly striking example of male transcendence of the Heimat through art, which both incorporates and expresses a notion of Heimat and its significance. The text is made up of Hunsrück dialect words, and the recording takes place in the caves near Schabbach. This piece, then, embodies both Hermann's debt to Heimat and his desire to move beyond it. Moreover its representation of Heimat is a neat juxtaposition of natural qualities (the cave, the acoustics) and cultural affinities (dialect words), getting close to a workable sense of what Heimat is. In that sense, it is an extremely fitting end to the film series.

However, the choice of the caves as a setting for Hermann's recording is also a monument to his relationship with his muse Klärchen (it recalls a night-time tryst), and therefore a reminder of her persecution by his mother. Hermann is bitterly alienated from his Heimat as a result of the punishment of Klärchen, who is expelled as his seductress following the discovery of their affair and her illegal abortion. He appears, however, to find a way of coming to terms with the oppressive and yet clearly influential Heimat by incorporating Heimat material in an alienated form into his music. Technological distortion and other forms of manipulation assist Hermann in both expressing and transcending the Heimat which is so ambiguous in its meaning for him. Reitz's climactic final scene in the cave is a powerful drawing together of some of the threads of his notions of Heimat (nature, local culture, technology, art, the alienated artist, the muse, and the mother) and also functions as another self-referential indication that he himself as director is doing just what Hermann is doing: incorporating his Heimat in an artistic text as a gesture both of indebtedness and transcendence. But the gender mythology which throughout the film remains disturbingly similar to the conservative Heimat films of the 1930s and 1950s is still palpable even in this final triumphant moment through the figures of Klärchen and Maria who are alluded to in the cave setting and in the dialect text.

Maria's sudden transformation from understanding and cheerful young woman to a bitter and repressive middle age is part of the critical undermining of Heimat mythology, but it also has implications for the representation of gender in the film. Her bitter struggle against Klärchen the outsider who threatens to take her son away from the Heimat and lead him into a transcendent phase of artistic creation completes a rather disturbing identification of Maria with all the negative and positive elements of Heimat. Nothing in *Heimat* really undermines such problematic gender identifications. Though on the one hand the focus on Heimat matriarchs is potentially progressive, on the other hand women are rather fixed in their roles, functioning either as Heimat mothers or erotic muses. What is lacking is an example of how a young *woman* might transcend the Heimat through art or technology; how she might come to terms with her Heimat affiliation and yet be more than just a mother or muse for a man.[17]

Self and Other

Heimat as a system can function with clear distinctions between the inside and the outside. Indeed, one could argue that Heimat must have an Other in order to function itself. The Other might be an internal other, or an exotic external other, which in turn might be the object of loathing, or the object of desire. In some instances, there is a focus on the external other, the exotic or foreign, to create a Heimat system where real tensions between Heimat and Other are in fact to do with internal others—gypsies or Jews. Of course the tensions are not necessarily racial but can be to do with other forms of alterity, whether sexual or moral in a wider sense, a city dweller, or refugee, or other outsider. Many Heimat texts have plots which involve a threat to the security of the Heimat and then the removal of that threat whether by expelling the source of the threat, or more commonly in the 1950s films, by integrating the potential threat into the Heimat and thus masking real tensions and exclusions.

Along with Reitz's clear tendency to make metafictional references and explore the effects of technology on the rural Heimat, his film can also be differentiated from the rather conservative Heimat films of the 1950s by his careful examination of the relationship between Heimat and its Others. He does not merely show a Heimat system set apart from an 'outside' and defined negatively by alterity, or indeed adopt the crass 'have your cake and eat it' juxtapositions of some 1950s films. Rather he suggests a complex interaction between Heimat and Other, by no means

---

[17] *Die Zweite Heimat* (Reitz, 1992) has a strong focus on women artists such as Clarissa, Helga, Evelyne, Olga and Frau Moretti, who all have their own specific Heimat problems to be overcome, and whose different attitudes to art and to love take them in very different directions.

showing the Heimat as purely positive. Reitz reveals in a much more honest way than the 1950s films that Heimat is (also) defined on the basis of exclusions. The threat of actual expulsion from the Heimat is carried out only once, though a significant number of characters have problems conforming to Heimat mores and either leave or are more or less forced to leave. The first episode 'Fernweh' indicates right from the beginning of the saga that such issues are to be dealt with in a more sophisticated manner; the title 'Fernweh' suggests that there are not just fortunate people in the Heimat and those who would like to belong but do not—there are also those who supposedly belong but in fact long to leave. A 1950s Heimat film might show a disaffected character longing to leave, or actually leaving, but in such films the character would almost inevitably return, and moreover be reintegrated into a contented Heimat life. This contrasts sharply with Paul whose return from the United States is a disaster; he has completely lost the ability to communicate with Maria, his Heimat wife, does not stay for the funeral of his mother, and is seen by everyone as an incorrigible outsider.

As the saga begins, Paul is the mythical returning soldier walking all the way home from France. However, even after this first return to the Heimat as a young man it becomes clear that he cannot speak about his experiences and is unable to integrate into Heimat life again. Though he later tries to settle in his rural Heimat with his mother, his new wife, and his two sons, he is increasingly unhappy and finally leaves. His radio hobby distances him from his family and he spends evenings alone tuning into radio stations from all over the world. The virtual emigration soon takes place in a literal sense, when he goes to America and starts an electronics business. Paul is not only alienated from the Heimat by his war experiences, he is also disturbed by the treatment suffered by Appolonia who is virtually forced to leave having been racially abused and also ostracized for having a baby by a French soldier. Paul chooses Maria, the Heimat woman, over Appolonia, the exotic woman, and regrets his choice as he begins to feel more trapped by the Heimat. Before she leaves for good, Appolonia asks him to go away with her, but Paul alights from the train they are in as she travels on. The beginning and end of the first episode are marked by clear symbolic representations of the confinement that Paul feels in the Heimat. As he sits in the kitchen surrounded by his family unable to speak, he focuses on the fly paper that hangs from the middle of the kitchen and frees a fly that is not yet dead. At the end of the episode, his last act before leaving for America is to set a trap for a pine marten. From rescuing a trapped creature, through choosing Maria over Appolonia, to setting a trap himself, Paul can finally endure no longer the restrictions of the Heimat that caused Appolonia to be repulsed, a hated figure, and which confine him to the nether world of rural family life. Global connections through his radio set compound the *Fernweh* of the title.

Appolonia is not the only person close to Paul who is mistreated because of her failure to be counted as a Heimat insider. Glasisch Karl has also fought in the First World War and has returned with skin problems due to gas attacks. He too is virtually ostracized because of his alterity, and is particularly despised by Maria's father, Alois Wiegand who will not touch him. His role as narrator flicking through old photographs at the beginning of each television episode is an indication of Reitz's attitude to the system of inclusion and exclusion, which is at the heart of any Heimat. Significantly, he chooses as narrator a marginalized figure, a character who never leaves his rural home after returning from the First World War, yet cannot be said to be completely integrated into the Heimat as he is despised and treated as an interloper. Karl is also the only villager that really appreciates Hermann's highbrow electronic music and understands the significance of the alienated reworkings of Heimat sounds. Outsiders such as Appolonia, who is racially abused, and Karl, whose damaged skin is the marker of his alterity, allude to the role of racist exclusions in creating a comfortable Heimat for the insiders. However, it is a matter of some controversy that Reitz did not focus on any Jewish characters; the fate of the Jews in the Hunsrück and indeed in the rest of Germany is alluded to but not explored in any depth. Analogues of racism like Karl who is differentiated by his skin do indicate Reitz's ambition to look at Heimat critically but clearly do not go far enough as an exploration of racism in particular as a motivation for exclusion.

Whatever the limitations of Reitz's project to explore Heimat critically without the strident condemnatory tone and baggage of the anti-Heimat texts of the late 1960s and early 1970s, it is clear that he has succeeded in reaching a mass audience with a sophisticated and subtle examination of the Heimat complex. His Heimat is by no means represented as purely positive; there is a succession of alienated young characters who are either unable to integrate, or who are denied the opportunity. Paul, Appolonia, and Karl in the early stages of the saga are later joined by Ernst, another marginal figure, and Hermann, who is thoroughly alienated after the expulsion of his muse Klärchen. But even Maria does not have an unambiguous relationship with the Heimat complex she is so closely identified with. She too complains of feeling trapped, of wanting to start her life again somewhere far away. In one of the film's most successfully differentiated explorations of the question of Heimat and Other, Maria and Pauline go to see Detlef Sierck's 1937 melodrama *La Habanera*. The film tells on one narrative level the story of how a Swedish woman—Zarah Leander again—beguiled by the mystique of Puerto Rico, falls in love with

Fig. 10. Maria watches as Pauline tries out the Hispanic hair style of Zarah Leander in *La Habanera*

a Hispanic bullfighter, who on marriage turns out to be a brute. The island itself is figured as a hothouse of disease, until a Swedish doctor comes along to cure the population. He rescues Leander and her son who go back to Sweden with him. However, Maria and Pauline do not read the film as a critique of the Hispanic Other, a celebration of Leander's recuperation into an ordered (white European) Heimat; rather they dwell on the moments when Leander is most captivated by the exotic charms of Puerto Rico and its people. The two women identify more with her fascination for the Other than with her later disappointment and desire to escape. They also recreate Leander's exotic Puerto Rican hairstyle, though her hair is only styled to look Hispanic in two scenes.

The film was made by Detlef Sierck who emigrated to the United States, changed his name to Douglas Sirk, and became an influential director of melodrama and a particular influence on Rainer Werner Fassbinder. Sierck's film is clearly not at one with its ostensible, xenophobic message but has ambiguous undercurrents of transgression. His representations of alterity slide away from the rather dubious overt 'meaning' of the film. Maria and Pauline clearly read *La Habanera* not for its surface message of safe and pure Heimat over diseased and dangerous Puerto Rico, but find in the film an outlet for their own unfulfilled desires to experience other places and other cultures, perhaps even to be other themselves and escape the restrictions of having to represent the German Heimat for men who are at least able to oscillate between realms, even if this ultimately results in a certain alienation.

Conclusion: *Heimat* as Art Film?

Reitz's filmic reading of the slippery concept of Heimat has caused many areas of difficulty in the film, not all of them successfully resolved. Though the Germans as a people are not demonized in the film, there is a somewhat artificial separation of non-Nazis and Nazis, and it is certainly the case that Maria's father and brother, Alois and Wilfried Wiegand are demonized as token village Nazis. The absence of Jews from the film is unsatisfactory, though Reitz's decision to focus on German memories can be justified. There were, however, Jewish people in the Hunsrück who fled or were deported to camps, though had Reitz tried to include such characters, he would have had to work hard to avoid the obvious pitfall of tokenism. The representation of gender in the film perpetuates many of the most vexing clichés of an earlier uncritical Heimat discourse. Nevertheless, these flaws need to be considered together with the many achievements of the film, the greatest of which is probably the depiction of the interaction of technology and the Heimat. For the main criticisms of *Heimat* depend on a view that the film seeks to represent first and foremost an idyllic Heimat that would feed the nostalgic desires of an uncritical viewing public. This claim is difficult to substantiate when one views the film in its proper context, which is the environmental concern so influential in the German political and cultural scene of the 1970s and 1980s. Technological advance in the village is at the core of the film from first to last. From the early landscape shots disrupted by telegraph wires to the high-tech, clean optics industry and from the very first radio broadcast in the Hunsrück to Hermann's electronic Heimat music, technology is seen not simply as destructive, but in the film's double vision is also the potential saviour of the Heimat.

The cinema screen is indeed an appropriate space for rereading a word such as 'Heimat': a term still of vital importance in defining German culture, yet so full of contradictions and ambiguities that Reitz's film was considered an almost foolhardy venture. However, his technique of reading the term against itself, of exploring its history and exposing its paradoxes is more remarkable for its successes than for its failures: the exploration of a vast genre; the exploration of modernity in interaction with the Heimat; the emphasis on art and mediated expression of Heimat; the contribution to the historical and historiographical debates of the 1980s; and the constant oscillation between Heimat as a necessary site of nurture and a cruel and stifling place of repression. These are the considerable achievements of a film which for all its flaws has still arguably done more than perhaps any other individual film to express the complexities of German identity and history not only for a German but also for an international spectatorship.

7 Heimat Regained, Dissolved, or Multiplied?

This study has concentrated in the main on literature and film. But from the turn of the century to the 1990s, Heimat discourse has always stretched beyond the arts to include sociology, ethnography and folk studies, local history, geography and regional studies, tourist publications, and a whole host of other kinds of texts, not least significant being *Heimatkunde* as an interdisciplinary school subject designed to develop pupils' knowledge not only of their own locality but also of the troubled history of the concept of Heimat in the wider history of Germany. Renegotiation of Heimat in the late twentieth century was a feature of the 1980s which continued into the last decade of the century, fuelled by the continuing reverberations of the *Historikerstreit*, by the popular success of Edgar Reitz's *Heimat* sequence, and as an exercise in identity-building following unification of the two Germanies. In 1990, the Federal Political Education Centre brought out two fat volumes dedicated to the theme of Heimat, with suggestions for school syllabuses, a wealth of essays on a whole range of topics, and extensive bibliographies.[1] The recuperation of Heimat has thus been part of the normalization of life first in both Germanies, and now in the unified Federal Republic. Such re-evaluation stretches further back, of course, with important contributions coming from sociologists such as Hermann Bausinger or Ina-Maria Greverus. In her book of 1972, *Der territoriale Mensch*, Greverus argued that human individuals, if they are to thrive as self-determining agents leading active and fulfilling lives, need a sense of spatial orientation within a flexible political and social framework.[2] On her definition Heimat is not a pre-existing heritage, but must be constantly produced and appropriated by the individual. Greverus's individualist thesis contrasts with the Marxist concept of Heimat, expressed just a year later in East Germany in Günter Lange's study *Heimat—Realität und Aufgabe*. Common to both, however, is the notion that Heimat is not a fixed, static place, but rather a social space which must be constantly adapted or recreated, through individual effort, as Greverus argues, or as an 'Aufgabe und Errungenschaft' to use

---

[1] *Heimat: Analysen, Themen, Persepktiven*, vol. 294/I; *Heimat: Lehrpläne, Literatur, Filme*, vol. 294/II (Bonn: Bundeszentrale für politische Bildung, 1990).

[2] For a sample of her work see Ina-Maria Greverus, 'The "Heimat" Problem', in Helfried Seliger (ed.), *Der Begriff 'Heimat' in der deutschen Gegenwartsliteratur* (Munich: iudicium Verlag, 1987), 9–28.

Lange's terms.[3] Somewhere in between Greverus's individualism and Lange's collectivism lie the citizens' initiatives and community-based activism which have been a key feature of local politics, especially of the green variety.

In such thinking Heimat ceases to be conceived *either* as the place of origin *or* a utopian place of arrival, becoming instead a frame of mind: the commitment of citizens to the process of making a liveable social space. Man may be territorial, but the territory keeps changing. One of the earliest examples of recuperation of Heimat through decoupling it from attachment to a fixed place is Heinrich Böll's essay of 1965 'Heimat und keine'.[4] Böll suggests that Heimat as a place may change so radically as to become no longer singular: Cologne turns into two Colognes, the shattered city of 1945 becoming a second Heimat for the author, totally different from, yet as coloured by sentimental personal memory as, pre-war Cologne, his birthplace and first Heimat. The Federal Republic in 1965 is a third Heimat, more static and less to Böll's taste than the second, fixed as it is in its Cold War identity. Provocatively, Böll argues that the destruction of the great German cities in the West was as much an exiling, 'eine Vertreibung', performed by the Allied bombers, as that suffered by those driven from the lands in the East. Nor were the emigrants driven out in the 1930s by the National Socialists any less bereft of Heimat than the exiled who fled in the 1940s before the advancing Russian army or were driven out of post-war Poland or Czechoslovakia. The title of Böll's essay could suggest deconstruction through multiplication: if Heimat, supposedly the unique place of origin, can be multiplied, then the outcome may indeed be 'keine', a negation of the concept. But if Heimat is a frame of mind inducing an active relationship between human beings and their environment, then multiplication may salvage values worth retaining in an age of more rapid change and greater mobility than ever before. Like Böll's Cologne, places change radically within the course of a lifetime. But so do people who may develop attachments then nostalgias for second or even third Heimats. Thus Edgar Reitz titled his second film sequence, set in the city of Munich rather than the rural Hunsrück, *Die Zweite Heimat*. Of course Heimat cannot be totally sanitized of connection with territory without becoming vacuous and the term 'second Heimat' necessarily bears within it the allusion to a first Heimat.

As Böll's essay indicates, the most politically fraught territorial implications in German Heimat discourse since 1945 have concerned the lost

---

[3] 'Task and Achievement', Günter Lange, *Heimat—Realität und Aufgabe: Zur marxistischen Auffassung des Heimatbegriffs* (Berlin: Aufbau, 1973), 55.

[4] In *Werke: Essayistische Schriften und Reden*, ii. *1964–1972*, ed. Bernd Balzer (Cologne: Kiepenheuer & Witsch, n.d.), 113–16.

lands in the East and the divided Heimat. Many standard works in the post-war canon of German literatures, both East and West, could be assimilated into an extended Heimat mode, including Grass's *Die Blechtrommel*, Christa Wolf's *Kindheitsmuster*, or Uwe Johnson's tetralogy *Jahrestage*. In these examples, characters driven out of a first Heimat seek to make a liveable space, or second Heimat, for themselves or for a next generation. *Jahrestage* has indeed figured as a key text in Norbert Mecklenburg's study of provincial literature; where in Viebig's world the local village is set over against Aachen, Johnson sets Mecklenburg over against the metropolis of New York.[5] Johnson's heroine Regine Crespahl is a latter day exile in New York, but from the mid-nineteenth century and earlier the USA has been a land of immigration for Germans who have reflected upon their lost first Heimat.[6] But exiles have also gone on to realize the American dream, a history reflected in the planter-settlers making a new Heimat in Wild West films or in Oskar Matzerath's fire-raising revolutionary grandfather in *Die Blechtrommel*, who if he did not drown fleeing from the police, may have escaped to America and made a fortune selling fire insurance. As we saw in Chapter 3, the need to move on and find a second Heimat had been a key theme already in many 1950s Heimat films, which in that respect at least were not backward-looking, but celebrated the American-backed economic miracle with none of the dark ironies of Grass's portrayal of post-war Germany.

Reclaiming Heimat?

The countervailing tendency, in contrast to multiplying Heimats, to mourn a lost first Heimat or to seek restoration of German cultural and eventually political unity, never died out, of course. During the 1950s, for example, poetry by now largely forgotten authors such as Agnes Miegel (1879–1964) was popular. Born in Königsberg (now Kalinengrad), Miegel published poems in praise of her home town and her East Prussian homeland throughout her long literary career. In a collection of 1901, a sequence of poems celebrates the conquest and Christianization of Prussia in the thirteenth century by the Teutonic Order and invokes the aristocratic heroism and peasant blood of the folk hero Henning Schindekopf

---

[5] Norbert Mecklenburg, *Erzählte Provinz: Regionalismus und Moderne im Roman* (Königstein/Ts: Athenäum, 1982).

[6] See Cora Lee Nollendorf, 'Fernweh—Heimweh: Attitudes of German-Americans before 1900', in Jost Hermand and James Steakley (eds.), *'Heimat', Nation, and Fatherland: The German Sense of Belonging* (New York: Peter Lang, 1996), 25–56.

who, ensconced as marshal in the Order's castle in Königsberg, presides over the conquered lands.[7] In a collection of 1952, the poet in 'Mutter Ostpreußen' mourns a lost Heimat and celebrates in 'Königsberg' the town 'die zur Mutter selber wir uns wählten' ('which we ourselves chose as mother') and the land 'dem wie Vaterherzen wir vertraut' ('to which we are familiar as to a father's heart'), closing with an evocation of the stars guiding to eternity those who made the supreme sacrifice: 'der Tod fürs Vaterland!' ('death for the fatherland!').[8] The maternal Heimat town and paternal Heimat province are subsumed into the larger fatherland for whom warrior heroes lay down their lives. Rather than the maternal Heimat giving birth to her sons, here the children choose the maternal city. A poem entitled 'Urheimat' celebrates the mythic moment of origin in a virile act of fructification as the colonist's plough cuts its first furrow, transforming virgin land into Heimat. Such metaphors allow for German claims to conquered territory as their Heimat. A whole section in this collection, entitled 'Stimme der Heimat' ('Voice of the Heimat'), celebrates such loaded mythological and geographical items as Patrona Borussiae (patron saint of Prussia), the rivers Weichsel and Memel, and heroes such as Henning Schindekopf and seven centuries on General Paul von Hindenburg, victor over the Russian army and saviour of East Prussia at the battle of Tannenburg in 1914, who in 1933 as President of the Republic handed over power to Hitler. In *Billard um halbzehn* of 1959 Böll chose Hindenburg rather than Hitler as the figure embodying Germany's militaristic history which made the descent into the barbarism of the Third Reich possible. This novel along with Grass's *Die Blechtrommel* marked a seismic shift heralding a reckoning with the past which would intensify in the course of the 1960s, driving writers such as Miegel out of the literary canon which pupils and students studied.

That writers like Miegel were so popular in the 1950s needs to be remembered, however, as part of the cultural history forming the context for later publications such as Martin Walser's *Seelenarbeit* (1979), a novel which, in making the lost city of Königsberg into a key motif, breaks what had become a taboo for left-liberal intellectuals. Martin Walser was born in 1927 in Wasserburg on Lake Constance in the south-west corner of Germany, the region where many of his best-known works are set. Walser belongs to that group of high-profile authors such as Böll, Grass, and Lenz who have over the decades intervened actively in public debate in Germany. Thus as early as 1961 Walser publicly supported the SPD in the elections of that year. Towards the end of the 1960s, however, he moved

---

[7] *Gedichte* (Stuttgart: J. G. Cotta'sche Buchhandlung Nachfolger, 1901), 74–5.
[8] *Gesammelte Gedichte* (Düsseldorf: Eugen Diedrichs, 1952), 137–45 (145).

further to the left in sympathy with the extra-parliamentary opposition which developed at the time of the Grand Coalition government when the alliance between the two main parties seemed to have made parliamentary opposition ineffective, and in the first half of the 1970s, though he never became a member, he stood close to the DKP, the German Communist Party, while also showing solidarity with left-wing literary activists who at that time were forming campaigning groupings such as the Dortmund-based *Werkkreis der Literatur*; thus Walser figures as a mentor for the heroine of Karin Struck's radical feminist text of 1974, *Klassenliebe*. If any one author of the post-war period might be seen to function as a seismograph, responding to subterranean shifts presaging historical change, then it is Walser. Towards the end of the 1970s Walser's position began to change again in keeping with the shifting public mood as he took up green issues and in the 1980s increasingly broached the issue of divided Germany. He made a notable contribution in October 1988 to a series of speeches on the German question by high-profile writers and intellectuals which were delivered in the Kammerspiele theatre in Munich and then printed in the weekly newspaper, *Die Zeit*. Refusing to have any truck with those who sought to rationalize a division cutting through a nation with a common history, Walser closed his speech with an unambiguous—and amazingly prescient—*plaidoyer* for unification of the two Germanies:

> **Das Volk! Populist wird man geschimpft, wenn man meint, die Deutschland-Frage könne nur vom Volk beantwortet werden. Eine Abstimmung in der DDR, eine bei uns. International überwacht. Das Selbstbestimmungsrecht der Völker praktiziert. So einfach wäre das.[9]**

In his speech Walser backs up this call for unification by citing East German writer Wulf Kirsten's picture of small town life, *Kleewunsch*, and poems such as 'die erde bei Meißen' evoking landscapes along the Elbe. Or there are the lines from Kirsten's poem 'wenig gereist', 'flußtalerkühl kommen die abendgerüche vors haus; | von den hügellehnen fallen die jahreszeiten | wie herzliche grüße aus der verwandschaft, | zuverlässigste chronologie'.[10] Kirsten's association of kinship relations with seasonal time is a common characteristic of Heimat discourse. Such an invocation

---

[9] 'The people! You are attacked as a populist if you dare to suggest that the German question can only be answered by the people. A referendum in the GDR, one here too. With international observers. The right of peoples to self-determination put into practice. It would be as simple as that.' 'Über Deutschland reden: Ein Bericht', in *Über Deutschland reden* (Frankfurt am Main: Suhrkamp, 1988), 76–100 (100).

[10] 'little travelled': 'river-valley cool, the evening smells reach the house; | the seasons descend the slopes of the hills | like heart-felt family greetings | most reliable of chronologies.' Cited ibid. 95.

of Heimat to underpin nation contrasts with Walser's essay of 1967, 'Observations on our Dialect'. Writing twenty years earlier at a time of often bitter critique of Heimat discourse by authors like Sperr or Lenz, Walser defends local attachments but he does so in order to dismantle nationalist demands for reunification by demonstrating the impossibility of convincingly translating into dialect a government proclamation on the German question including the sentence 'Die Bundesregierung bleibt bemüht, die Einheit des Volkes zu wahren.'[11] In particular the word 'Volk' proved difficult—the dialect speaker would just say 'mir' ('wir' in High German), but the dialect 'mir' implies an already existing community speaking its dialect which does not include the citizens of, say, Leipzig. The possessive 'our' in Walser's title in itself lays claim to a local, non-national identity. By contrast, in his speech of 1988, the homely simplicities of the provincial Heimat and the comfort of familiar landscapes serve as mythic signifiers of the kind Barthes analysed to enrich the abstract concept of nation and to purify it of any aggressive taint. Here Walser now speaks of 'das Volk' ('the people'), like the crowds who formed when the Wall was first breached who proclaimed 'Wir sind das Volk'. But his essay also foreshadows the rhetorical shift, which came a few days later, to 'Wir sind ein Volk' ('one people'). Walser has continued to provoke debate in the 1990s, notably in his speech on receiving the Peace Prize of the German Book Trade in 1998 and in a subsequent television interview in which he made a plea for normalization of German national identity.[12]

A text on the cusp of Walser's shift from green-tinged, Marxist regionalist to increasingly nationalistic proponent of reunification is his novel *Seelenarbeit* which came out in 1979. *Seelenarbeit* draws on the Heimat mode as a vehicle to reflect on German national identity and enjoyed, like many other novels in the tradition, great success with the reading public, appearing for six months at the top of the best-seller list in the *Spiegel* magazine. Once again, as so often throughout the tradition, the local patriotism of Heimat serves at the same time to mediate larger issues of national identity. The hero of *Seelenarbeit* is Xaver Zürn who lives in a village near Lake Constance with his wife Agnes and their two daughters, Magdalena and Julia. Xaver works as chauffeur for Dr Gleitze, engineer and director of an industrial firm which had been originally located in Königsberg but which relocated to the West at the end of the war, although the leading members of the family had long since moved

---

[11] 'The Federal government remains determined to preserve the unity of the people.' 'Bemerkungen über unseren Dialekt', in *Heimatkunde: Aufsätze und Reden* (Frankfurt am Main: Suhrkamp, 1972), 51–57.
[12] Martin Walser, *Friedenspreis des Deutschen Buchhandels* (Frankfurt am Main, Börsenverein des Deutschen Buchhandels n.d.).

westwards, some acquiring hunting estates in the Alps, some spending the war safely in neutral Switzerland, and one brother even moving before the war across the Atlantic to America, so signalling the international nature of the capitalist class who underwrote and profited from the German war effort. Gleitze's wife comes from Vienna where her father, who had been a judge during the Third Reich, draws a generous pension despite the death penalties he passed in the service of the National Socialist regime. In contrast to these wealthy members of the industrial and bureaucratic upper crust, originating from places as far apart as Königsberg and Vienna and now scattered across the globe, the Zürns and the Ehrles, Xaver's paternal and maternal relatives, are of local peasant stock.

The novel draws both on caricatured Freudian theory and on Marxist class analysis. A key theme is the Oedipal relationship between Xaver and his employer. For Xaver, Gleitze is an admired father figure, yet at the same time he has fantasies of castrating this oppressive employer who dominates his imagination and treats him like a child. The dialectic of consciousness which Hegel describes between servant and master is another leading intertext as Xaver longs for recognition from Gleitze as confirmation for his own sense of identity, but feels constantly misrecognized by him.[13] Deeply implicated in these questions of identity is class difference: whereas the servant is obsessed with his master, the master scarcely notices the servant, but sits in the back of the limousine listening to Mozart through headphones, prompting the reader to wish that Xaver could develop a touch of Figaro's self-confidence and that Gleitze might adopt a less lordly demeanour at the democratic close of the twentieth century. The jokey play with the grand Freudian and Hegelian theories takes on a much darker colour, however, through the historical allusions to the doomed German defence of Königsberg in 1945. The great truth Xaver wants to share with Gleitze is the revelation that his brother Johann died of shrapnel wounds trying to save Gleitze's Heimat from the Russian army. In contrast to the glorious death for the fatherland which Agnes Miegel celebrates in her poem 'Königsberg', Walser has Xaver hear three different versions of his brother's death, the third and fullest account revealing that the shrapnel tore into Johann's intestines causing the contents of his bowels to spill out into his stomach cavity so that his dying words were, 'Das stinkt'.[14] This horror is linked in a complex metaphoric field to Xaver's problems with his bowels, both of these bodily motifs being in turn associated with the mental costs paid, the psychic work or 'Seelenarbeit' which the lower classes must perform, in serving the

---

[13] Hegel, *Phenomenology of Spirit* (Oxford: Oxford University Press, 1977), 111–19.
[14] *Seelenarbeit* (Frankfurt am Main: Suhrkamp, 1979), 71.

interests of upper-class masters, whether in wartime fighting for a homeland owned by capitalists or in peacetime sustaining capitalist profits.

So far, so Marxist, this line in the novel being strengthened also by the introduction of material about the Peasants' War as it affected the southwest region of sixteenth-century Germany. Class division through the ages has left its traces in the local landscape and its architecture of fortified castles, villages, peasant cottages, and more prosperous farmhouses, the Gleitzes' villa being the latter-day equivalent of a lordly castle. Walser, who wrote his doctoral dissertation on Kafka, smuggles in many jokey allusions to his master's great anti-Heimat novel *Das Schloß* (1922; published 1926), most notably Xaver's two difficult daughters who bear a suspicious resemblance to the Barnabas girls, Amalia and Olga, just as Gleitze has traces of Klamm. Kafka's novel is structured round the topography of village and inaccessible castle which the hero K. never succeeds in penetrating. Like K. who in the end has to settle for sharing the maids' room, so Xaver settles for sharing a bed with Agnes and for life in the village, giving up both the struggle for recognition by Gleitze and the fantasies of castrating him. Many critics saw in this a scurrilous unmasking of the Marxist world-view as childish Oedipal fantasy.[15] While there is a grain of truth in that, Walser's analysis in the novel of class antagonism and of different class interests extending through the ages to capitalist collusion with National Socialism and continuing in post-war exploitation is presented with great seriousness. Xaver's fantasy of castrating an individual boss is less an attack on the Marxist understanding of history than a dig at such recent activities of West German terrorists as the murder in 1977 of Hanns-Martin Schleyer, chairman of the West German Confederation of Employers. Like Schleyer, who during the war had been the commander of a slave-labour camp in the East, so one of the Gleitze brothers in Walser's fictional case study of relations between capitalism and National Socialism had been an industrial adviser to Hitler, his 'commis voyageur' or travelling salesman as Gleitze's wife sarcastically calls him. But murdering or castrating individual bogeymen does not serve justice. Hopes of a more rational, organized, working-class opposition to capitalism are also disposed of in the figure of Xaver's cousin, a blustering and ineffectual trade union activist. While preserving a historical vision of Marxist hue, then, the novel retreats from class politics which demand large-scale, abstract identification with people categorized in terms of relations of production, promoting instead a more concrete attachment to a locality and its history, though retaining awareness of how economics and class

[15] On the critical reception of *Seelenarbeit* see Alexander Mathäs, *Der kalte Krieg in der deutschen Literaturkritik: Der Fall Martin Walser* (New York: Peter Lang, 1992), 128–38.

have shaped and still shape both local history and landscape. In essence the novel substitutes for the grand narrative of Marxism a kind of leftish-flavoured *Heimatkunde*. Thus Xaver remembers how his grandfather hanged himself when a good fruit harvest, instead of bringing prosperity, produced a glut in the market, threatening his family with penury. At the same time, Xaver is able to empathize with other people through his sense of compassion for their loss of Heimat so that the larger-scale identification with others is mediated through the more immediate Heimat-bound identity. This goes along with an assertion of the rights of ordinary Germans to mourn for their war dead, like Xaver's mourning for his clever brother who died so miserably defending the Gleitzes' Heimat. Walser carefully insulates the right to mourn for Germans who fell defending Königsberg from revanchist claims to Kalinengrad by allocating to the city such an unsympathetic bunch of exiles as the Gleitzes who are doing fine where they are with their limousines, and villas, and American connections. But the careful mediation of larger identifications, whether political or national, through Heimat sentiment clearly opens up the whole question of Germanness as an overarching identity, albeit sustained by pillars based each in a different Heimat.

The novel evokes the Heimat in a myriad of details of cultural inheritance, of towns, cities, and landscapes, of driving out and returning home. Nor could any reader miss the irony of Xaver's twin love of Heimat and of the motor car, the machine which threatens to despoil the very roads he so loves driving though, those winding sideroads which hug the contours of hills and valleys, unlike the new roads designed to cut brutally through the fragile pre-Alpine landscape. The novel also elaborates on family life. Xaver's beloved wife Agnes has ancestors stretching all the way back to the archetypal housewife in Goethe's verse epic *Hermann und Dorothea* (1796) who never missed the chance to pluck a caterpillar from her cabbages as she walked through her kitchen garden, though, like her husband, Agnes also performs wearing psychic labour and is not just a cipher for Heimat values. Like the allotment garden in Kroetz's play *Das Nest*, discussed in Chapter 3, here too the garden takes on symbolic meaning. Agnes cultivates her extensive orchards along with flower and vegetable gardens to make the home Xaver returns to from his peregrinations as chauffeur. But this benign cultivation of nature is under threat from new roads planned to slice through the region and the Zürns are due to lose some ground and half their redcurrant bushes. Cultivating one's garden is thus revalued from being the emblem of political apathy to signifying the need for engagement to counter threats to one's locality. The daughters too, each stroppy in a different way, help to save the picture of family life from a too saccharine sweetness and a too traditional gendering of

Heimat as feminine. *Hermann und Dorothea* expressed a sense of cultural Germanness expanding out from local attachment long before the existence of a German state. Looking back from our time of writing in 1999, Walser's novel of 1979 anticipates 1989 in proffering a liveable German identity filtered through the web of a densely evoked Heimat. Thus the Heimat discourse of the locality continues to sustain a national sense of identity. Since 1989, however, the rise of *Ostalgie*, a nostalgic regret for past social networks and local values, is creating a sense of a loss for many citizens of the former GDR who felt little attachment to the communist regime but have not felt at home in the new Germany either, faced with the imposition of capitalist competition and the return of people such as Walser's Gleitzes claiming their property and shutting down local factories to save western-based firms from competition. It will be interesting to see whether, after the fact, *Ostalgie* is conjuring a lost Heimat into being.

Postmodern Nomads: The End of Heimat?

Interesting too is whether a politics of garden cultivation must suffice in the era of globalization: is that all there is in the face of an ever-expanding, ever more abstract universe? Xaver Zürn pities his boss Gleitze, speculating that he would be less obsessive about Mozart operas were he not bereft of his Heimat in Königsberg. Gleitze travels to opera houses all over Europe to catch Mozart productions, but also listens to opera in the back of his limousine, insulated by headphones from contact with the human being driving the vehicle. Listening in a mobile space bubble to sounds emanating from a virtual space filled with the ghostly traces of instruments and voices transported from some other time and somewhere else could stand as a symbol for the postmodern condition. Anthony Giddens uses the word 'disembedding' to characterize what he sees as one key force driving the dynamism of modernity, namely 'the "lifting-out" of social relations from local contexts and their rearticulation across indefinite tracts of time-space'.[16] For postmodern man, or 'late modern' in Giddens's usage, time and space are ever less connected through the situatedness of place, the process of disconnection being launched at the beginning of the modern era by the advent of mechanical clocks and global maps, proceeding through railway trains and motor cars, telegraph and telephones, and now accelerating at dizzying pace with the advent of e-mail, hyper-space, and the World Wide Web. The explosion of media,

---

[16] *Modernity and Self-Identity: Self and Society in the Late Modern Age* (Cambridge: Polity Press, 1991), 16.

first of print, then photography, film, radio and television, cables and satellite increasingly substitutes virtual for actual reality, image for essence, enabling communication without face-to-face presence in a place. Mozart's music becomes available beyond the walls of the Munich Residenz theatre or the Musikverein in Vienna, while on the other hand the two men, enclosed together in the motor car, might as well be in different continents for all the communication that takes place. Walser's emphasis on the body, however, whether its vulnerability to shrapnel or to constipation induced by travel, makes the point, to borrow terms from a letter to the *Guardian*, that to enter 'hyper-space' we must pass through 'meat-space':

> **We must all make a journey from cradle to grave and the relationships on which our humanity is founded in between—though enlarged by information technology—still revolve around such quotidian necessities as food, shelter, health and social care.**[17]

Heimat has mediated, often for ill, sometimes for good, between locality and nation through the twists and turns of German history in the twentieth century. It remains to be seen whether Heimat can now mediate between 'meat-space' and 'hyper-space' without falling into reactionary mode.

Heimat values are what make places and peoples different in contrast to the perceived homogenizing tendencies of modernity. At the same time Heimat discourse butresses group identity. This interplay of identity and difference can take on many political shades depending on the historical context. In her book *Nomadic Subjects*, the feminist critic Rosi Braidotti, born in Italy, raised in Australia, educated in France, and working in Holland, evokes a polyglot condition without mother tongue or vernacular. The nomadic, multicultural subject does not only recognize differences between landscapes or cultures, but differences within cultures and localites, indeed within the self, eschewing the illusion of unity. On the other hand, Braidotti also notes that the end of the Cold War and the growing emphasis on common European identity and institutions have gone along with an explosion of regionalisms, localisms, and ethnic wars. Thus the notion of difference is Janus-faced: it may be mobilized in the service of resistance by the oppressed against the hegemony of the powerful, as small nations resist powerful neighbours, or colonies resist empires; but difference can harden antagonistically into a new assertion of divisive identity which in turn oppresses others, as witness the history of the Balkan peoples emerging from the shadow of the Ottoman, then

---

[17]   Prof Hartley Dean, *Guardian*, Friday July 9 1999.

Austrian, then Soviet Empires; the tribal antagonisms which have flared up in post-colonial Africa; or indeed the history of Ireland under the British shadow. One answer might be to press forwards with the fracturing of all identity to become a nomadic subject-in-flux in a globalized hyper-space, leaving behind apocalyptic visions of peasants dying which so troubled Franz Xaver Kroetz in his lost Bavarian Heimat. But postmodern utopianism, as much as postmodern apocalypse, ignores the very different allocation of powers and resources across the globe and within nations and regions, right down to households. Braidotti, for example, wants to retain the category of sexual difference and hence of women as corporeal, sexed beings rather than embracing a postmodern, genderless condition. Just as sexual difference is still a crucial factor affecting distribution of powers and resources between people, so embodied subjects, whatever their sexuality, still inhabit actual physical places as well as virtual social spaces. Nor can one just choose to be a subject-in-flux, trying on interim identities like changing fashions. As long as that is so, then some kind of Heimat discourse, even if only post-Heimat, may well continue to serve as a vehicle of reflection on the embodied subject who (still) inhabits places, however sequentially, and who must negotiate quotidian existence and such things as the right to an abode, to work, to vote, and to a passport. Such a material basis is necessary, for entry to hyper-space necessitates access to the technology and nomads require passports if they are not to be sent back whence they came.

In his musings on Heimat Xaver Zürn thinks with pity of an acquaintance, a Turkish guest worker, feeling that nobody should be driven from their Heimat by economic necessity. But such easy pity can slide into the view that everybody should go back to where they belong, whether that be Anatolia, which would entail ethnic cleasing, or Königsberg, which would require a European territorial war. Less drastic but still problematic is the either/or view that, to take the Turkish example as the biggest category of foreigners in Germany, guest workers must choose between remaining Turkish or becoming German. At the time of writing dual nationality remains a fraught issue in the debates over reform of the German nationality law, dating from 1913, which gives ethnic Germans in Eastern Europe an automatic right to German nationality withheld from ethnic Turks who may have lived in Germany for decades or have been born there. Dual nationality would answer the aspirations of many who live in Germany but do not wish to give up their Turkish identity and citizenship. This is one context for Emine Sevgi Özdamar's novel of 1992, *Das Leben ist eine Karawanserei · hat zwei Türen · aus einer kam ich rein · aus der anderen ging ich raus* which strikingly expresses a sense of hybrid identity. In evoking a nomadic existence, the title might suggest the very opposite of

Heimat literature. But in conjuring up a childhood the author draws on the nostalgic longing for a lost world characteristic of the Heimat mode even as she unsettles it. The novel thus stands in a resonant tradition of novels such as Grass's *Die Blechtrommel* and Rushdie's *Midnight's Children*, which intertwine childhood memory with political history and Heimat with nation.

The novel tells of a girl born in Malatya in Eastern Anatolia but who grows up first in Istanbul, then the small seaside town of Yenicehir, then Bursa, Ankara, a spell with her father in far Eastern Anatolia near Mount Ararat, Ankara again, Istanbul, and who finally takes the train to Germany. In between she also goes on a visit to her maternal grandfather's farm just outside Malatya. The novel begins at a late stage of her pre-birth development in the womb (shades of Oscar Matzerath) going up to around the age of 18 when she sets off for Germany. The nameless heroine, her brothers, Ali and Orhan, and her sister Schwarze Rose (Black Rose, transliterated from the Turkish Karagül) live together with their parents and paternal grandmother. The family moves from place to place as her father Mustafa seeks work through the economic ups and down of Turkey's post-war development up to around 1965. Initially a bricklayer, he then runs his own small business as a builder, interrupted by several financial crises when he has to flee creditors. In quasi-allegorical mode, Mustafa's work parallels the ups and downs in the building of post-war Turkey while his name Mustafa and his membership of the Republican People's Party point back to Atatürk (1881–1938), founder of the modern Turkish nation whose birth name was Mustafa Kemal.[18] The army was midwife to the birth of modern Turkey and still serves as the bulwark for the secular state. Appropriately enough, then, the narrator's earliest memory from inside the womb of a train journey with soldiers allegorically combines a maternal but mobile Heimat with a military fatherland.

The text flows on with no chapter breaks, though line gaps mark moves as the family moves from place to place. This structure is indicated in the title. A caravansari is a traditional inn or hotel with a big courtyard where groups of travellers stop for rest and refreshment. The picturesque image of a travelling life centres on the stopping places rather than the road as such. The happiest stopping place is the old town of Bursa, the earliest Ottoman capital. The unhappiest is a terrible desert place on the outskirts of Ankara, capital of the Republic, which is not a street, but just a scatter of half-built houses with no facilities and no neighbours, only the motorway in the distance on one side and on the other the ridge of a new golf course

---

[18] On recent Turkish history see Nicole and Hugh Pope, *Turkey Unveiled: Atatürk and After* (London: John Murray, 1997).

for American diplomats and military. (Roadbuilding and the military are perennial motifs signalling the intrusions of modernity into Heimat.) As the protagonist finally sets off in the train to Germany, the overarching model of life on the road is confirmed. But the actual caravansaries or stopping places evoke life on the street. Even the train is called the Hurenzug; whores are key figures of street life who like other workers will turn nomadic under economic pressures. Life on the street has different connotations from life on the road. It suggests a close network of communal relations at the heart of which is the family household, but a household open to children's comings and goings and full of connections with neighbours. The novel conveys the development of an identity dispersed among such a community whose members pass the child along as she passes along the street, sustaining her with their watching eyes. Her sense of self is more outside than inside as she goes to school through the streets of Bursa, past the barber's shop, the carpenter's, and the fruit stall: 'Ein Auge gab uns zum anderen Auge, und wir kamen, in ihren Augen getragen, bis zur heiligen Eiche.'[19] The tree marks the start of the steep street leading up to the school. Taken together, the street and the road, the caravansaries and the intervening journeys, sketch an ideal of identity continuing through time and from place to place: they evoke a sustaining base of selfhood in communal networks or connections, but also the capacity to move on and to deal with change and not to be simply submerged in communalism, in other words a mobile sense of Heimat, which, however, collapses in the heroine's adolescence when towards the end of the novel she suffers a nervous breakdown.

Place is a primary factor both in the narrator's growing sense of identity and its ultimate collapse. For the places are also social spaces infused with historical meaning. Among the comic names the narrator gives the streets she has lived in is the Bürokratenstrasse. The bureaucratic elite is part of Atatürk's legacy. Driving through the revolution which set Turkey on a westernizing path but also looking back to an older imperial tradition, the bureaucrats are now the prosperous elite who most benefit from a modernizing process carried out on the backs of the population flooding into the mushrooming cities from rural poverty. Architecture signals the fissures and differences running through the narrator's childhood Heimat: after the newer, grander stone house on the bureaucratic street the family move to the traditional wooden house on the steep street, the happiest of the caravansaries. When mad auntie Saniye complains that

---

[19] 'One eye passed us to the next and we went along, carried by their eyes, to the sacred oak.' Özdamar, *Das Leben ist eine Karawanserei · hat zwei Türen · aus einer kam ich rein · aus der anderen ging ich raus* (Cologne: Kiepenheuer and Witsch, 1994), 131.

they are leaving her behind in the bureaucrat street, the mother says 'wir sind so nah, wenn du furzt, hören wir es in unserem neuen Haus'.[20] The unevenness of social and mental change in Turkey is conveyed in small scale within the household in the figures of the modern mother, her body, her clothes, her hennaed hair, her visits to the cinema, compared with the more traditional grandmother, the teller of old tales and legends with her hanging grandmotherly breasts. Buoyed up in the medium of family attachment, the protagonist can integrate the span between the traditional and modern informing the hybrid cultural mix she enjoys of village tales, *Madame Bovary*, and Hollywood cinema. Well-nigh impossible to integrate, however, are modernity and tradition at their worst, the psychological stress being heightened by the extreme gap between the two. This too is conveyed through architecture: the place which brings her mother close to breakdown is the isolated wasteland of half-built houses without even a street on the edge of Ankara which contrasts miserably with the bombastic new mausoleum for Atatürk at the city centre. These two facets of modernity cannot be integrated or turned into a liveable space; both promote alienation in contrast to the traditional wooden houses on the steep street with their open windows and doors which allowed passage to the sound of a fart from a couple of streets away.

If a building site outside Ankara is modernity at its worst, tradition at its worst is revealed in the story of the protagonist's maternal grandmother who unwittingly offended her husband and was dragged along the ground, her hair tied to his horse's tail. This terrible episode alludes back to the customs of nomadic and semi-nomadic tribes when a married woman who returned on a visit to her family thereby expressed dissatisfaction with her husband, an insult demanding retribution.[21] Though the grandmother did not die at once, she never recovered and died soon after of pneumonia. A symptom of the depression the protagonist's mother suffers in the no man's land outside Ankara is her weeping over her long-dead mother, but it is to her terrible yet beloved father that she nonetheless turns for help, a plea which he unstintingly answers, begging forgiveness of his daughter for an old wrong. And yet the old man still takes the best fruit from his granddaughter's hand to teach her that patience is woman's crowning virtue. The novel closes on an unresolved dilemma: traditional rural patriarchy is marred by terrible cruelties

---

[20] 'we're so near, when you fart we'll hear it in our new house'. Ibid. 159.
[21] See Lale Yalçin-Heckmann, 'Gender Roles and Female Strategies among the Nomadic and Semi-Nomadic Kurdish Tribes of Turkey', in Sirin Tekeli (ed.), *Women in Turkish Society: A Reader* (London: Zed Books, 1995), 219–32.

and by the denial of women's subjecthood, yet a selfhood sustained through older family and communal connections is a good which is threatened by a modernizing process leading to alienation and to new kinds of social and mental divisions in communities which for all the differences of wealth and prosperity once had a sense of mutual need and support.

A minor theme in this novel which will be central in the sequel, *Die Brücke vom Goldnen Horn* (1998), is the oppression of the Kurdish minority in Eastern Anatolia. Özdamar's evocation of a childhood in Turkey thus dismantles the myth of unified Heimat in showing Turkey riven by ethnic divisions and economic stresses which drive her people into exile. Crucial too in the dismantling of any reactionary appeal to origins is the medium of the German language in an autofictional text narrated in German by an adult about a Turkish-speaking earlier self. Thus the autobiographical subject is riven by the linguistic abyss between the German writing self and the Turkish protagonist. Yet the Turkish language, distanced comically, shines magically through the German medium in the form of many transliterations of Turkish idioms in this linguistically hybrid text which also mixes in fragments of Koranic Arabic and of Hollywood American with greetings left in Turkish. The German mother tongue has frequently served in nationalist Heimat discourse as *the* medium of identity or else dialect has signified the local Heimat in contrast to High German and the nation. Özdamar's hybrid language and her nomadic subject who yet finds interim ground under her feet in the communal street life provides one model for a Heimat discourse in our post- or late modern times. Özdamar's post-Heimat evocation of a childhood in Turkey gives voice to a generation who came to Germany as adults, or at least as adolescents. In *Die Brücke vom Goldnen Horn* Özdamar follows her protagonist in the late 1960s to a 'Wohnaym' (Wohnheim) in West Berlin, a job with Siemens, and to oppositional politics first in Berlin, then in Turkey. By contrast, *Schwarzer Tee mit drei Stück Zucker* (1991) by Renan Demirkan (born 1955 in Ankara) deals with migrants who came to West Germany as young children. Central to this novel are the contrasts both between father and mother and between first-generation parents and second-generation children in negotiating a sense of identity informed by nostalgia for the lost Turkish Heimat but longing too to find a new identity in Germany without losing cultural roots.

And then there are the volumes of interviews conducted by Feridun Zaimoglu (born 1964 in Bolu, Turkey), many of them with a third generation of young men and women who were born in Germany: *Kanak Sprak. 24 Mißtöne vom Rande der Gesellschaft* (1995) and *Koppstoff. Kanaka*

Sprak vom Rande der Gesellschaft (1998).[22] 'Kanak', originally meaning 'man' in Hawaiian, then indentured labourer or low, uneducated person, here denotes Turkish-German people and their patois or creole (Sprak), with Kanaka as a feminine form. The interviews evoke many different spaces. The Turkish homeland is not Heimat for 'mutated' Turks or Deutschländer and Deutschländerinnen (jargon for Turkish-Germans born in Germany). Nor is the Turkish ghetto in German cities, inhabited by men in badly cut suits proud of wiping their bottoms with their right hand and by their wives walking seven paces behind, 'die teigwaren-mamma, die aufgeblähte honigkuchenmutti'.[23] The ghetto is rejected by an alienated younger generation whom one speaker sees as lumpenprole-tariat, the product of global economic forces: 'Deshalb sind sie kanaken, deshalb bin ich ein kanake, deshalb bist du ein kanake. Wir sind bastarde . . . Den wechsel vom ackerland zum fließband haben wir nicht ver-daut'.[24] This speaker rejects the notion of either choice between or fusion of two cultures: 'Der kanake ist so etwas wie ein synthetisches produkt, das sich und die fabrik haßt, in dem [*sic*] es gefertigt wurde . . . Also ist der kanake zugleich ein fundamentalist. Jeder unserer jungs steht für eine miniphilosophie'.[25] Among the mini-philosophies are the youth subcultures—in Kanaka Sprak 'süppkültür'—of rappers and fleamarket disc jockeys who mark territory through style: 'die alemannen, bruder, das geb ich auch mal mit, haben nullkommanull stil, und vom stil is'n schritt zum respeckt . . . also muß man nen supereigenen sektor entwick-eln mit'm schild, auf dem in alarmrot steht: zugang nischt, weil stil. Stil is'n hammer'.[26] As a *Heimattracht* signalling local pride, so the dandyism of rappers or drug-dealers signifies street-credibility, though these ter-ritories and styles keep changing. Yet this speaker concludes in the end: 'Die Message is, daß's null message gibt . . . unsre jungs sind wie olle schneemännekens und schmelzen weg wie nix gutes, und am ende haben sie für's schiß gelebt.'[27] The same 'null message' comes from one speaker

[22] *Kanak Sprak: 24 Mißtöne vom Rande der Gesellschaft* (Hamburg: Rotbuch Verlag, 1995); *Koppstoff: Kanaka Sprak vom Rande der Gesellschaft* (Hamburg: Rotbuch Verlag, 1998). Page numbers follow-ing quotations from the volumes will be preceded by *Kanak* and *Kanaka* respectively.

[23] 'pastry-mamas and honeycake-mummies'. *Kanak*, 102.

[24] 'That why they are kanaks, why I'm a kanak and you're a kanak. We're bastards . . . We haven't man-aged to digest the change from fields to factory floor'. *Kanak*, 112; 113.

[25] 'The kanak is a kind of synthetic product which hates the factory in which it was produced and itself . . . That's why the kanak is at the same time a fundamentalist. All our young men stand for some mini-philosophy or other'. *Kanak*, 110–11.

[26] 'the germans, man, let me tell you this too, have nilpointnil style, and it's just a step from style to respect . . . and so you've got to develop your absolutely personal sector with a street sign in red for danger: no entry, because of style. Style is a hammer'. *Kanak*, 121.

[27] 'The message is that there's no message . . . our boys are like bloody snowmen, they melt away like nothing and in the end all they've lived for is shit.' *Kanak*, 122.

who has just mainlined, 'mann, glück dauert halt nur ne runde, und denn marsch zum nächsten glück, wo saft fließt durch mich, mann, wie honig, aber s'is 'n ewiges verschwinden von mir hier drin auf ner scheiß matratze.'[28] Likewise, in the film *Trainspotting* the drug-addict heroes reject Scottish Heimat discourse against a backdrop of particularly dreary Highland scenery and return to Edinburgh where for one of them space will contract to a shitty mattress to die on. One speaker analyses the interplay of 'Sistem' and 'Süppkültür': 'Kritik-Pop und AIDS-Pop und Anti-Aleman-Pop und dein Kanak-Attack-Scheiß stehn schön Schmiere fürs System, weil ihr und wir und alle Welt Lärm machen für Monete'.[29] *Süppkültür* is just the shit people carry into the system on their shoes or 'das Bettelbrot, das der Deutsche seinen better-minded-kids ins Maul stopft'.[30] With more of an energetic survival instinct than the addict disappearing on his mattress, this speaker, training for film and television, is ready to don masks, play roles, and profit from the system without any claim to an alternative, subcultural identity: 'Denn sonst biste n Süppkültür-Verrecker, und Deutschland hat auf dich geschissen.'[31] Instead of identity, postmodern performance is the name of this game. The end of identity means the end of Heimat too, it would seem, whether the homeland, the ghetto, a wider German society, or the subculture: 'ich aber bin nich mehr da, wo ich herkomme, und nich, wo ich hier herumlungere . . . Diese Scheiße mit den zwei kulturen steht mir bis hier'.[32] Another speaker proclaims, asserting that he himself is his place: 'Bin hier die gegend.'[33] Or there is the woman who has no wish to live in Turkey and rejects mourning for the lack of Heimat as ridiculous: 'Ich weine nich herum, daß ich keine Heimat habe, wie so viele andere. Ich finde das lächerlich.'[34] Yet at the close, this speaker does express the aspiration to make a place where people like her might feel at home:

> **Wir werden nie ein Teil der deutschen oder der türkischen Gesellschaft sein. Wir können höchstens der Teil unserer eigenen Gesellschaft sein. Für uns ist nichts vorbereitet. Wir müssen um alles kämpfen, was wir haben**

[28] 'happiness only lasts one round, man, then the march to the next happiness when the juice is flowing through me like honey, but it's an ever-lasting disappearing for me in here on a shitty mattress.' *Kanak*, 107.

[29] 'Critical pop and Aids pop and Anti-German pop and your Kanak-attack-shit in the end all just support the system because you and me and everybody are ready to make a noise for money'. *Kanaka*, 17.

[30] 'the beggar's bread that the Germans stick into the mouths of their better-minded kids'. *Kanaka*, 19.

[31] 'Otherwise you can just die in your sub-culture and the Germans will have shat on you.' *Kanaka*, 19.

[32] 'but I'm not any longer there where I came from, nor here where I lounge around . . . I've had enough of all this shit about two cultures'. *Kanak*, 95.

[33] 'I am here the place.' *Kanak*, 96.

[34] 'I don't go about weeping because I've no Heimat. I find that ridiculous.' *Kanaka*, 41.

wollen: um Aufenthalt, um Sprache, um Bildung, um Staatsbürgerschaft, um Anerkennung, um Respekt, um alles. Und wollen wir eine Heimat, dann müssen wir sogar darum kämpfen.[35]

And so with the pronoun 'wir' returns also the desire for a place or space called Heimat where 'we' can comfortably be together to manage the quotidian necessities of life and to claim the rights of the citizen.

---

[35] 'We will never be a part of Turkish or of German society. At most we might be part of our own society. Nothing is prepared for us. We have to fight for everything: for right of abode, for language, for education, for citizenship, for recognition, for respect, for everything. And if we want a Heimat, then we've got to fight even for that.' *Kanaka*, 46.

Chronology

1890   Julius Langbehn's polemical essay *Rembrandt als Erzieher*

1893   *Heimat* (play by Hermann Sudermann)

1897   *Kinder der Eifel* (Clara Viebig)

1898   *Die Dithmarscher* (Adolf Bartels)

1900   First publication of the journal *Heimat: Blätter für Literatur und Volkstum* edited by Friedrich Lienhard

1901   *Jörn Uhl* (Gustav Frenssen)
       Publication of Adolf Bartels's first racist literary history

1902   Friedrich Lienhard's influential article 'Los von Berlin?'

1903   First publication of the Catholic Heimat journal *Hochland* edited by Karl Muth

1904   Foundation of Bund Heimatschutz (Union for Heimat Protection)

1908   *Das Kreuz im Venn* (Clara Viebig)

1914   Outbreak of the First World War

1918   Armistice signed between Germany and the Allies
       Weimar Republic proclaimed

1919   Treaty of Versailles signed

1920   Foundation of the Nazi Party (NSDAP)
       Death of Ludwig Ganghofer, prolific author of trivial Heimat novels

1923   French invasion of the Rhineland

1926   *Volk ohne Raum* (Hans Grimm)

1929   *Pioniere in Ingolstadt* (Marieluise Fleißer)
       Das Bauerntum als Lebensquell der nordischen Rasse (Richard Walther Darré)

1930   *Neuadel aus Blut und Boden* (Richard Walther Darré)

1933   Hitler becomes Chancellor (30 January)
       Cancellation of the Weimar constitution; one-party state proclaimed (14 July)
       Closure of the Bauhaus

1936   Emil Nolde is banned from engaging in artistic activity

1937   *La Habanera* (Detlef Sierck, later known as Douglas Sirk)
       First of seven Great German Art Exhibitions opens in Munich (18 July)
       Exhibition of 'Entartete Kunst' ('Degenerate Art') opens (Munich, 19 July)

1938   *Anschluß* of Austria (13 March)
       Sudetenland is ceded to Germany ('Appeasement' policy)

Reichskristallnacht (vandalism of Jewish shops and synagogues, 9 November)
Heimat (Carl Froelich's film of Sudermann's play)

1939   German troops march into Prague
Hitler–Stalin Pact (23 August)
German invasion of Poland (1 September)
Britain and France declare war on Germany (3 September)
Das einfache Leben (Ernst Wiechert)

1942   At the Wannsee Conference Heydrich announces the 'Final Solution of the Jewish Question' (20 January)

1943   Clearance of the 'Warsaw Ghetto' (19 April–16 May)

1944   Von Stauffenberg plot against Hitler fails (20 July)

1945   At Yalta Conference Roosevelt, Stalin, and Churchill agree the division of Germany into four zones of occupation (4–11 February)
Hitler commits suicide (30 April)
Capitulation of the Wehrmacht (7–9 May)
At Potsdam Conference the Allies agree on the denazification, demilitarization, and decentralization of Germany (17 July– 2 August)

1946   Nuremberg trials concluded (October)
DEFA established (Deutsche Film-AG, GDR film production company)

1947   Marshall Aid announced

1948   Currency reform in the Western zones (20 June)
Berlin Blockade (June 1948–May 1949)

1949   *Grundgesetz* proclaimed by Western allies (23 May)
Foundation of the Federal Republic of Germany (FRG)
Foundation of the German Democratic Republic (GDR)

1950   *Schwarzwaldmädel* (Hans Deppe)

1954   ARD begins television broadcasts

1955   *Der Förster vom Silberwald* (Alfons Stummer)
FRG enters NATO
Formation of Warsaw Pact

1956   54 Heimat films made, including *Drei Birken auf der Heide* (Ulrich Erfurth); *Dort oben wo die Alpen glühen* (Otto Meyer); *Der Meineidbauer* (Rudolf Jugert); *Schwarzwaldmelodie* (Géza von Bolváry)
Foundation of Bundeswehr

1957   *Berlin Ecke Schönhauser* (Gerhard Klein)

1958   Law on Equality between the Sexes comes into force (FRG)

1960   Adolf Eichmann is kidnapped by Israeli agents (executed 1962)
Wenn die Heide blüht (Hans Deppe)

1961   Berlin Wall is erected (13 August)

1962   Oberhausen Manifesto of the New German Cinema declares war on 'Papas Kino'

1963 ZDF begins television broadcasting
Adenauer resigns as Chancellor and is replaced by Ludwig Erhard
President Kennedy visits the Federal Republic and West Berlin
Der geteilte Himmel (Christa Wolf)

1964 Film version of *Der geteilte Himmel* (Konrad Wolf)

1965 *Berlin um die Ecke* (Gerhard Klein)

1966 Grand Coalition formed between CDU/CSU and SPD
Number of foreign workers in FRG has grown to 1.2 million
Jagdszenen aus Niederbayern (Martin Sperr)

1967 Economic downturn

1968 Assassination attempt on SDS leader Rudi Dutschke
Bundestag passes Emergency Laws (30 May)
Action Committee for the Liberation of Women founded in West Berlin
Film of *Jagdszenen aus Niederbayern* (Peter Fleischmann)
Deutschstunde (Siegfried Lenz)

1969 First SPD/FDP coalition led by Willy Brandt
Katzelmacher (Rainer Werner Fassbinder)

1970 Baader-Meinhof terrorist group founded (renamed Rote Armee Fraktion 1971)
Federal Republic signs the Warsaw Treaty recognizing the Oder-Neiße Line

1971 Brandt is awarded the Nobel Peace Prize for his *Ostpolitik*
Fifteen film-makers (including Rainer Werner Fassbinder) found the Filmverlag der Autoren
Stallerhof (Franz Xaver Kroetz)

1972 Radikalenerlaß (Decree on Extremists) is agreed by Brandt and the Länder
Leading members of the Rote Armee Fraktion are arrested
Heinrich Böll is awarded the Nobel Prize for Literature
Olympic Games are held in Munich. A team from the GDR is allowed to compete
The Basic Treaty between the FRG and the GDR is signed
Wildwechsel (Rainer Werner Fassbinder, based on Kroetz's play)
Oberösterreich (Franz Xaver Kroetz)

1973 Federal Republic joins UN

1974 Brandt resigns as Chancellor and is replaced by Helmut Schmidt
Das Nest (Franz Xaver Kroetz)

1975 Baader-Meinhof trial begins

1977 Industrialists' leader Hanns-Martin Schleyer is kidnapped and later killed
Andreas Baader, Gudrun Ensslin, and Jan-Carl Raspe are found dead in their cells

1979 American TV series *Holocaust* is broadcast in West Germany
Seelenarbeit (Martin Walser)

1980 Founding of the Greens as a federal political party

1982 Death of Rainer Werner Fassbinder
Helmut Kohl (CDU) becomes Chancellor

1983   The Greens enter the Bundestag

1984   *Heimat* (Edgar Reitz)

1985   President Reagan visits the Bitburg war cemetery

1986   Ernst Nolte and Jürgen Habermas exchange hostile articles at the start of the Historians' Dispute (*Historikerstreit*)

1989   Opening of the Berlin Wall (9 November)
       Das schreckliche Mädchen (Michael Verhoeven)

1990   German Monetary Union (1 July)
       German reunification in accordance with Article 23 of the *Grundgesetz* (3 October)
       First all-German elections with Kohl re-elected Chancellor

1992   *Die Zweite Heimat* (Edgar Reitz)
       Das Leben ist eine Karawanserei · hat zwei Türen · aus einer kam ich rein · aus der anderen ging ich raus (Emine Sevgi Özdamar)

1995   *Kanak Sprak: 24 Mißtöne vom Rande der Gesellschaft* (Feridun Zaimoglu)

1998   *Koppstoff: Kanaka Sprak vom Rande der Gesellschaft* (Feridun Zaimoglu)
       In Federal German elections, Gerhard Schröder (SPD) is elected Chancellor

Further Reading and Viewing

Introduction

We recommend as a general reader Rob Burns (ed.), *German Cultural Studies: An Introduction* (Oxford: Oxford University Press, 1995). Also useful as a general introduction to one of the most important political and cultural contexts of Heimat is Colin Riordan (ed.), *Green Thought in German Culture: Historical and Contemporary Perspectives* (Cardiff: University of Wales Press, 1997). On the concept of Heimat and its expression in literary, filmic, and other discourses, we recommend the two volumes published by the Bundeszentrale für politische Bildung, *Heimat: Analysen, Themen Perspektiven*, vol. 294/I and *Heimat: Lehrpläne, Literatur, Filme*, vol. 294/II (Bonn, 1990). The most useful English language texts on Heimat as a social movement are Celia Applegate, *A Nation of Provincials: The German Idea of Heimat* (Berkeley and Los Angeles: University of California Press, 1990); Jost Hermand and James Steakley (eds.), *'Heimat', Nation, and Fatherland: The German Sense of Belonging* (New York: Peter Lang, 1996); and William H. Rollins, *A Greener Vision of Home: Cultural Politic and Environmental Reform in the German Heimatschutz Movement 1904–1918* (Ann Arbor: University of Michigan Press, 1997). Klaus Lindemann (ed.), *'Heimat': Gedichte und Prosa* (Stuttgart: Reclam, 1992) is a useful introductory anthology. Christopher J. Wickham's recent publication *Constructing Heimat in Postwar Germany: Longing and Belonging* (New York: Edwin Mellen Press, 1999) came too late to be considered in detail in our volume, which is mainly concerned with popular film and literature. It offers an interesting discussion of avant-garde texts in relation to the Heimat mode.

Chapter 1

In addition to the works discussed in this chapter, some of Clara Viebig's other works have been reprinted by the Rhein-Mosel Verlag. In particular *Das Weiberdorf: Roman aus der Eifel* (Briedel/Mosel: Rhein-Mosel Verlag, 1993) and her later collection *Heimat: Eifel-Novellen* (Briedel/Mosel: Rhein-Mosel Verlag, 1996) would also be worth study. Other significant Heimat writers of the time include Ludwig Anzengruber, whose *Der Meineidbauer*, on which two Heimat films were based, is at the time of writing available in a Reclam edition with *Lernmaterialien* (Ditzingen: Phillipp Reclam Jun., n.d.). At the trivial end of the *Heimatliteratur* scale, works by Ludwig Ganghofer in print at the time of writing include *Der Klosterjäger* (Munich: Droemer, 1984), a historical Heimat novel, and *Edelweißkönig* (Munich: Droemer, 1984).

For a specialist study of the *Heimatliteratur* of this period, see Karlheinz Rossbacher, *Heimatbewegung und Heimatroman: Zu einer Literatursoziologie der*

Jahrhundertwende (Stuttgart: Ernst Klett, 1975). We also recommend Barbara Krauß-Thiem's study of Viebig, *Naturalismus und Heimatkunst bei Clara Viebig* (Frankfurt am Main: Peter Lang, 1991) and Steven Nyole Fuller's biography of Bartels, *The Nazis' Literary Grandfather: Adolf Bartels and Cultural Extremism, 1871–1945* (New York: Peter Lang, 1996).

Chapter 2

David Horton's 1992 edition of *Pioniere in Ingolstadt* (Manchester: Manchester University Press, 1992) offers much useful context. For further primary reading we recommend Marieluise Fleißer's novel *Eine Zierde für den Verein: Roman von Rauchen, Sporteln, Lieben und Verkaufen* (Frankfurt am Main: Suhrkamp, 1975; originally *Mehlreisende Frieda Geyer*, 1931). We also suggest Ödön von Horváth, *Kasimir und Karoline* (Frankfurt am Main: Suhrkamp, 1994) as a further example of the critical *Volksstück*. A useful secondary collection of essays is Alan Bance and Ian Huish (eds.), *Ödön von Horváth Fifty Years On: Horváth Symposium* (London: Institute of Germanic Studies, 1988). For a general study of the *Heimatliteratur* of this period, see Uwe-K. Ketelsen, *Völkisch-nationale und nationalsozialistische Literatur in Deutschland 1890–1945* (Stuttgart: Metzler, 1976).

A related field of study which we have not studied here is the 1930s mountain film, a genre pioneered by Dr Arnold Fanck, initially a director of Alpine documentaries, and later taken up by his protégé Luis Trenker. Leni Riefenstahl made her name as an actress in such films. A number of *Bergfilme* have been released on VHS video format, particularly those by and starring Luis Trenker which have been brought out by Toppic, a label owned by Polyband (Polyband Gesellschaft für Bild-und Tonträger mbH & Co.KG, Am Moosfeld 37, 81829 München). They include *Berge in Flammen* (1931); *Der verlorene Sohn* (1934); *Der Berg ruft* (1937); *Im Banne des Monte Miracolo* (1945); and *Duell in den Bergen* (1950). A number of films starring Leni Riefenstahl are available to buy on video. *Der weiße Rausch* (1931) available on Arcade Video, order number 51431; and *SOS Eisberg* (1933), part of the series UFA Klassiker, order number 3986, were both directed by Arnold Fanck. The collaboration between Fanck and G. W. Pabst, *Die weiße Hölle vom Piz Palü* (1929) also starring Riefenstahl is available on video and DVD, and her own film *Das blaue Licht* (1932) has also recently become available. Both of these films are also included in a Riefenstahl boxed set which also contains both parts of *Olympia* (1938), *Tiefland* (1954), and *Die Macht der Bilder* (Ray Müller, 1993), a documentary about her work.

Chapter 3

As well as regularly appearing in the German television schedules, a number of 1950s Heimat films have been released commercially as VHS video cassettes. These have been great commercial successes, and so though they tend to be deleted very quickly, there is a good chance that further examples of the genre will become available, or that certain films will be re-released. Available at the time of writing are a number of films issued as part of the Taurus Video Heimatfilm-Kollektion, including Alfons Stummer's *Der Förster vom Silberwald* (1954); Paul May's *Und ewig singen die Wälder* (1959); Harald Reinl's *Die Fischerin vom Bodensee* (1956); and Herbert B. Fredersdorf's *Der Schandfleck* (1956). *Wenn der weiße Flieder wieder blüht* (Hans Deppe, 1953) is available as part of the Taurus Video Romy Schneider-Kollektion. Taurus Video no longer exists but enquiries can be addressed to Kinowelt Home Entertainment GmbH, Schwere-Reiter-Str. 35, Geb. 14, 80797 München. The anti-Heimat films and critical Heimat films of the 1960s and 1970s are much harder to find as commercial video releases, particularly those by less well-known directors such as Peter Fleischmann. Consequently in addition to the Rainer Werner Fassbinder film *Katzelmacher* (1969) available from Filmverlag der Autoren, PolyGram Video VHS 085 698-3, we recommend the critical Heimat films of Werner Herzog, including *Herz aus Glas* (Tartan Video, TVT 1216, 1976), and of Herbert Achternbusch, who is particularly interesting for his use of dialect. His film *Servus Bayern* (1977) is available on VHS video.

A very useful general collection on the Federal Republic in the 1950s is Robert G. Moeller (ed.), *West Germany under Construction: Politics, Society and Culture in the Adenauer Era* (Ann Arbor: University of Michigan Press, 1997). The most comprehensive study of 1950s Heimat films is Willi Höfig, *Der deutsche Heimatfilm 1947–1960* (Stuttgart: Ferdinand Enke Verlag, 1973). A useful concise study is Manuela Fiedler, *Heimat im deutschen Film: Ein Mythos zwischen Regression und Utopie* (Coppengrave: Coppi-Verlag, 1995). On the 1960s and 1970s films see Timothy Corrigan, *New German Film: The Displaced Image*, rev. edn. (Bloomington, Ind.: Indiana University Press, 1994) and John Sandford, *The New German Cinema* (London: Eyre Methuen, 1981). Thomas Elsaesser's Fassbinder study *Fassbinder's Germany: History, Identity, Subject* (Amsterdam: Amsterdam University Press, 1996) is also recommended.

Chapter 4

Some GDR writers who came to the West have engaged with the Heimat mode, see for example the first volume of Horst Bienek's novel sequence, *Die letzte Polka: Roman* (Munich and Vienna: Carl Hanser Verlag, 1975) which evokes Germany in 1939 just before the outbreak of war and is set in Bienek's home town of Gleiwitz (where the Nazis concocted their excuse to invade Poland). Wulf Kirsten's poetry celebrates the region around Meißen and village life. In poems which are a variation on the pastoral tradition for our times he conveys with great intensity the threat of ecological damage, for example *Der bleibaum: gedichte* (Berlin, Weimar, 1977); *Die erde bei Meißen: gedichte* (Leipzig, 1986). See also Wolfgang Ertl, 'Zur ökologischen Problematik in Wulf Kirstens lyrischem Werk', in Axel Goodbody, *Literatur und Ökologie* (Amsterdam: Rodopi, 1998), 123–38.

Chapter 5

Michael Verhoeven's *Das schreckliche Mädchen* (1989) is available with subtitles as an Avant Garde VHS video (*The Nasty Girl*, number VC3391). There is also a VHS video available of ARD's television production of *Deutschstunde* (ARD Video).

Lenz's earlier short stories *So zärtlich war Suleyken: Masurische Geschichten* (Frankfurt am Main: Fischer Taschenbuchverlag, 1993) and his later novel *Heimatmuseum* (Munich: DTV, 1981) are both worth study. For a secondary study of Lenz's work, see Claus Nordbruch, *Über die Pflicht: Eine Analyse des Werkes von Siegfried Lenz* (Hildesheim: Olms, 1996). On Emil Nolde see Robert Pois, *Emil Nolde* (Lanham, New York, London: University Press of America, 1982); also Stephanie Barron (ed.), *'Entartete Kunst': Das Schicksal der Avantgarde im Nazi-Deutschland* (Munich: Hirmer Verlag, 1992). On Anna Elisabeth Rosmus's struggle with Passau and its history, see her work *Out of Passau: Von einer, die auszog, die Heimat zu finden* (Freiburg: Herder, 1999). On the National Socialist history of Passau, see Winfried Becker (ed.), *Passau in der Zeit des Nationalsozialismus* (Passau: Universitätsverlag, 1999).

Chapter 6

Edgar Reitz's *Heimat* has recently been released on VHS (PAL) video format in Germany by Absolut Medien, Rosenthalerstr. 38, 10178 Berlin, order numbers 9551 to 9555. *Die Zweite Heimat* is also available in VHS (PAL), Absolut Medien, order numbers 9601 to 9607. Absolut Medien are also on-line at http://www.absolutMEDIEN.de. For extracts from his production diary and an interesting interview on *Die Zweite Heimat*, see Edgar Reitz, *Drehort Heimat: Arbeitsnotizen und Zukunftsentwürfe*, ed. Michael Töteberg (Frankfurt am Main: Verlag der Autoren, 1993). Reitz is making a third Heimat cycle. A letter from Reitz available on http://www.xs4all.nl/~rrr/heimat/reitz.html gives a broad sketch of the project which will focus on German reunification, with a number of the characters from the first two films meeting again in Schabbach. The time frame is to be the fall of the wall in 1989 to New Year's Eve in 1999. See Eric Santner's *Stranded Objects: Mourning, Memory and Film in Postwar Germany* (Ithaca, NY, and London: Cornell University Press, 1990) for a critical and differentiated discussion of the issue of memory and history in German film, including Reitz's *Heimat*. A special issue of *New German Critique* (Fall 1985), no. 36 contains a dossier of review extracts with an introduction by Miriam Hansen, and articles by Michael Geisler, Eric Rentschler, and an extract of a discussion between Friedrich Kahlenberg, Gertrud Koch, Klaus Kreimeier, and Heide Schlüpmann.

Chapter 7

Martin Walser's earlier short collection of essays, *Heimatkunde: Aufsätze und Reden* (Frankfurt am Main: Suhrkamp, 1968) is particularly interesting on dialect. More recently, in a speech on receiving the peace prize of the German Book Trade in 1998 Martin Walser sought to justify a German patriotism for today based on the ideal of Heimat. For a differentiated contribution to the heated debate which this unleashed see Gert Heidenreich, 'Heimat als Fremde. Rede am 21. März 1999 im Deutschen Nationaltheater Weimar in der Reihe Reden über Deutschland und Europa' in *Zwei Reden in Weimar*, edition München, edited by Andrea Welker (Munich: Edition der Provinz, 1999), pp. 7–53. Emine Sevgi Özdamar has also published a volume of short stories, *Mutterzunge: Erzählungen* (Berlin: Rotbuch Verlag, 1993). On Turkish-German linguistic, literary, and cultural issues, see David Horrocks and Eva Kolinsky (eds.), *Turkish Culture in German Society Today* (Providence: Berghahn Books, 1996) and Sabine Fischer and Moray McGowan (eds.), *Denn du tanzt auf einem Seil . . . Positionen deutschsprachiger Migrant-Innenliteratur* (Tübingen: Stauffenburg, 1997). We also recommend the work of Herta Müller, a Romanian German. Her works are written in a striking hyperrealist style and thematize the position of German minorities in Eastern Europe. Interestingly, she undoes the village-metropolis opposition by evoking the oppressiveness of village life in Romania under Ceauşescu. Berlin, by contrast, precisely because it is alien, is a more comfortable place to be. See her novel first published in 1989, *Reisende auf einem Bein* (Reinbek bei Hamburg: Rowohlt, 1995), and also her essays and sketches *Barfüssiger Februar* (Berlin: Rotbuch Verlag, 1990). Also recommended is the collection of essays on Müller edited by Brigid Haines, *Herta Müller (Contemporary German Writers)* (Cardiff: University of Wales Press, 1998). For an example of the phenomenon of *Ostalgie*, see the recent ARD/Arte television production of *Der Laden* (Jo Baier, 1998) based on Erwin Strittmatter's novel (available on three VHS video cassettes from ArtHaus, order number 00334). An interesting point of comparison would be Volker Braun's retrospective on the GDR and the ideal of community, *Die vier Werkzeugmacher* (Frankfurt am Main: Suhrkamp, 1996).

Bibliography

Primary Texts discussed

Fleißer, Marieluise, *Pioniere in Ingolstadt: Komödie in vierzehn Bildern* (1968 version); *Pioniere in Ingolstadt: Komödie in zwölf Bildern* (1929 version), in *Gesammelte Werke*, i. *Dramen*, ed. Günther Rühle (Frankfurt am Main: Suhrkamp, 1972), 127–85; 187–222.

—— *Pioniere in Ingolstadt*, ed. David Horton (Manchester: Manchester University Press, 1992).

Kroetz, Franz Xaver, *Stallerhof* and *Geisterbahn*, in *Heimarbeit / Stallerhof / Geisterbahn / Kapellenspiel von der heiligen Jungfrau / Michis Blut* (Hamburg: Rotbuch Verlag, 1996).

—— *Oberösterreich*, in *Maria Magdalena: Der Soldat / Oberösterreich / Wunschkonzert* (Hamburg: Rotbuch Verlag, 1996).

—— *Das Nest*, in *Mensch Meier / Herzliche Grüße aus Grado / Das Nest* (Hamburg: Rotbuch Verlag, 1999).

Lenz, Siegfried, *Deutschstunde* (Frankfurt am Main: Suhrkamp, 1979).

Özdamar, Emine Sevgi, *Das Leben ist eine Karawanserei · hat zwei Türen · aus einer kam ich rein · aus der anderen ging ich raus* (Cologne: Kiepenhauer and Witsch, 1994).

Sperr, Martin, *Jagdszenen aus Niederbayern*, in *Bayerische Trilogie* (Frankfurt am Main: Suhrkamp, 1972), 7–59.

Viebig, Clara, *Kinder der Eifel: Erzählungen* (Rastatt: Moewig bei Ullstein, 1994).

—— *Das Kreuz im Venn: Roman aus der Eifel* (Briedel/Mosel: Rhein-Mosel Verlag, 1997).

Walser, Martin, *Seelenarbeit* (Frankfurt am Main: Suhrkamp, 1979).

Wiechert, Ernst, *Das einfache Leben: Roman* (Berlin: Ullstein, 1998).

Zaimoglu, Feridun, *Kanak Sprak: 24 Mißtöne vom Rande der Gesellschaft* (Hamburg: Rotbuch Verlag, 1995).

—— *Koppstoff: Kanaka Sprak vom Rande der Gesellschaft* (Hamburg: Rotbuch Verlag, 1998).

Films discussed

Deppe, Hans, *Schwarzwaldmädel* (FRG, 1950).

—— *Wenn die Heide blüht* (FRG, 1960).

Fassbinder, Rainer Werner, *Katzelmacher* (FRG, 1969).

—— *Wildwechsel* (FRG, 1972).

Grimm, Hans, *Ferien vom Ich* (FRG, 1963).

Klein, Gerhard, *Berlin um die Ecke* (GDR, 1965–90).

Reinl, Harald, *Die Fischerin vom Bodensee* (FRG, 1956).
Reitz, Edgar, *Heimat: Eine deutsche Chronik* (FRG, 1984).
Schleif, Wolfgang, *Das Mädchen Marion* (FRG, 1956).
Stummer, Alfons, *Der Förster vom Silberwald* (Austria, 1954).
Verhoeven, Michael, *Das schreckliche Mädchen* (FRG, 1989).
Vogel, Frank, *Denk bloß nicht ich heule* (GDR, 1965–90).

Secondary Texts

In addition to the recommendations for further reading, we suggest the following select bibliography of secondary material.

Augstein, Rudolf, et al., *'Historikerstreit': Die Dokumentation der Kontroverse um die Einzigartigkeit der nationalsozialistischen Judenvernichtung* (Munich and Zurich: Piper, 1987).
Bastian, Andrea, *Der Heimat-Begriff: Eine begriffsgeschichtliche Untersuchung in verschiedenen Funktionsbereichen der deutschen Sprache* (Tübingen: Niemeyer, 1995).
Bergmann, Klaus, *Agrarromantik und Großstadtfeindlichkeit* (Meisenheim am Glan: Anton Hain, 1970).
Bienek, Horst, *Heimat: Neue Erkundigungen eines alten Themas* (Munich: Hanser Verlag, 1985).
Der Deutsche Heimatfilm: Bildwelten und Weltbilder: Bilder, Texte, Analysen zu 70 Jahren deutscher Heimatgeschichte (Tübingen: Tübinger Verein für Volkskunde, 1989).
Ecker, Gisela, *Kein Land in Sicht: Heimat—weiblich?* (Munich: Wilhelm Fink, 1997).
Emmerich, Wolfgang, *Germanistische Volkstumsideologie: Genese und Kritik der Volksforschung im Dritten Reich* (Tübingen: Tübinger Verein für Volkskunde, 1968).
Görner, Rüdiger (ed.), *Heimat im Wort: Die Problematik eines Begriffs im 19. und 20. Jahrhundert* (Munich: iudicium verlag, 1992).
Greverus, Ina-Maria, *Auf der Suche nach Heimat* (Munich: Beck, 1979).
Haß, Ulrike, *Militante Pastorale: Zur Literatur der anti-modernen Bewegungen im frühen 20. Jahrhundert* (Munich: Wilhelm Fink, 1993).
Hinz, Berthold, *Art in the Third Reich*, trans. Robert and Rita Kimber (Oxford: Basil Blackwell, 1979).
Jacobsen, Wolfgang, Kaes, Anton, and Prinzler, Helmut (eds.), *Geschichte des deutschen Films* (Stuttgart: Metzlar, 1993).
Kaes, Anton, *From Hitler to Heimat: The Return of History as Film* (Cambridge, Mass.: Harvard University Press, 1989).
Maier, Charles S., *The Unmasterable Past: History, Holocaust, and German National Identity* (Cambridge, Mass.: Harvard University Press, 1988).
Mecklenburg, Norbert, *Erzählte Provinz: Regionalismus und Moderne im Roman* (Königstein/Ts: Athenäum, 1981).
Peukert, Detlev, *The Weimar Republic: The Crisis of Classical Modernity*, trans. Richard Deveson (Harmondsworth: Penguin, 1991).

Pohlheim, Karl K., *Wesen und Wandel der Heimatliteratur am Beispiel der österreichischen Literatur seit 1945* (Bern: Peter Lang, 1989).

Pott, Hans-Georg (ed.), *Literatur und Provinz: Das Konzept 'Heimat' in der neueren Literatur* (Paderborn: Schoningh, 1986).

Rapp, Christian, *Höhenrausch: Der deutsche Bergfilm* (Vienna: Sonderzahl Verlagsgesellschaft, 1997).

Schütt, Hans Dieter, *Anna Rosmus, die 'Hexe' von Passau: Deutschland, Deutschland über alles—wächst kein Gras* (Berlin: Dietz, 1994).

Seliger, Helfried W. (ed.), *Der Begriff 'Heimat' in der deutschen Gegenwartsliteratur* (Munich: iudicium verlag, 1987).

Tilton, Timothy Alan, *Nazism, Neo-Nazism and the Peasantry* (Bloomington, Ind.: Indiana University Press, 1975).

Index

KAFKA
A GUIDE FOR THE PERPLEXED

The Guides For The Perplexed Series

Related titles include:

KAFKA:
A GUIDE FOR THE PERPLEXED

CLAYTON KOELB

continuum

Continuum International Publishing Group

The Tower Building   80 Maiden Lane, Suite 704
11 York Road   New York
London SE1 7NX   NY 10038

British Library Cataloguing-in-Publication Data
A catalogue record for this book is available from the British Library.

ISBN: 978-0-8264-9579-2 (hardback)
         978-0-8264-9580-8 (paperback)

Library of Congress Cataloging-in-Publication Data
A catalog record of this book is available from the Library of Congress.

Typeset by Newgen Imaging Systems Pvt Ltd, Chennai, India
Printed and bound in Great Britain by CPI Antony Rowe Ltd,
Chippenham, Wiltshire

CONTENTS

ACKNOWLEDGMENTS

Some material in Chapter 1 appeared previously in somewhat different form in *Monatshefte*, Vol. 68, No. 4, 1976. Permission to reprint is gratefully acknowledged.

This book has benefited greatly from the judicious editorial advice of Janice Hewlett Koelb. The author is particularly grateful for her patience and good counsel.

It is a pleasure to acknowledge the support of Margaret and Paul A. Johnston and of the Guy B. Johnson Professorship which they endowed. The Johnson professorship fund has aided in various aspects of this project.

ABBREVIATIONS OF FREQUENTLY CITED WORKS BY KAFKA

(Complete publication information is provided in the Bibliography)

8vo   *The Blue Octavo Notebooks.* Edited by Max Brod. Translated by Ernst Kaiser and Eithne Wilkins.

Castle   *The Castle.* Translated and with a preface by Mark Harman.

Colony   *The Penal Colony: Stories and Short Pieces.* Translated by Willa and Edwin Muir.

ComStor   *The Complete Stories.* Edited by Nahum N. Glatzer.

Diaries   *Diaries 1910–1923.* Edited by Max Brod. Translated by Joseph Kresh and Martin Greenberg, with the cooperation of Hanna Arendt.

Father   *Letter to His Father/Brief an den Vater.* Translated by Ernst Kaiser and Eithne Wilkins.

Felice   *Letters to Felice.* Edited by Erich Heller and Jürgen Born. Translated by James Stern and Elizabeth Duckworth.

Friends   *Letters to Friends, Family, and Editors.* Translated by Richard and Clara Winston.

Meta   *The Metamorphosis.* Translated and edited by Stanley Corngold.

Milena   *Letters to Milena.* Translated and with an introduction by Philip Boehm.

Missing   *Amerika: The Missing Person.* Translated and with a preface by Mark Harman.

Office   *The Office Writings.* Edited by Stanley Corngold, Jack Greenberg, and Benno Wagner. Translations by Eric Patton with Ruth Hein.

SelStor *Kafka's Selected Stories.* Translated and edited by Stanley Corngold.

Tag   *Tagebücher (Kritische Ausgabe).* Edited by Hans-Gerd Koch, Michael Müller and Malcolm Pasley.

Trial   *The Trial.* Translated and with a preface by Breon Mitchell.

CHAPTER ONE

WHY YOU MIGHT BE PERPLEXED

Franz Kafka would have found it highly amusing to know that one day his work would be the subject of a *Guide for the Perplexed*. He would have rejoiced in the irony inherent in applying the title of a classic work of sacred hermeneutics composed by Moses Maimonides, the most revered and influential Jewish scholar of the Middle Ages, to a commentary on the modern secular fictions their modest Jewish author referred to as his nocturnal scribbling. But he would have also understood immediately the aptness of the project for a writer who made a career out of resisting interpretation. 'Are you perplexed?' he might well have asked his readers. And in response to an affirmative reply, he would surely have sighed, 'Ah, that's a relief. Me too.'

Kafka the writer spent his entire adult life attempting to come to terms with the world through his writing because Kafka the man found that world utterly bewildering. As his friend Milena Jesenská once put it,

> this whole world is and remains a riddle to him. A mystical secret. Something he cannot attain and something he holds in high regard, with a moving, pure naïveté [. . .]. He stands [. . .] and gazes [. . .] in wonder, at everything, even this typewriter, and these women. (*Milena* 244–45)

It was perhaps because everything he encountered in his life—a typewriter, a gas lamp, the women in his life, his work, his own body— puzzled him so deeply that he felt an urgent need to depict that puzzling world in fictions that were both fantastically outrageous and at the same time realistically banal. Kafka's attitude was that the ordinary, everyday world, if examined carefully enough, is far weirder than anything we might dream up out of our own fancy. And even if we manage to conjure up something very weird out of our restless dreams—a salesman turned into a gigantic insect, perhaps, or a war-horse turned into a lawyer—the weirdness of the quotidian world swallows it up and digests it without a burp.

Readers of Kafka therefore tend to be perplexed. How could it be otherwise? Nothing in Kafka's world seemed simple to him, and consequently almost nothing about Franz Kafka's life or works seems simple to us. Everything—the stories, the letters, the 'diaries,' his personal relationships, even his attitude toward his work as an author—everything is complex, ambiguous, or sometimes downright confusing.

The fiction tends to dramatize this complex ambiguity, and not surprisingly it leaves some readers cold. Here is the reaction of a mystified and frustrated reader of the twenty-first century as posted on the Amazon.com website:

> In the interest of full disclosure I did not finish the whole book. To be honest I couldn't bear to read another page of it. [. . .] I just didn't enjoy a single moment that I spent with my nose in this book. The stories I read were boring and full of uninteresting characters, subject matter and plot-less storylines that tended to meander everywhere and go nowhere. To top that off the charac-ters were generally placed in bad situations with no hope of a positive outcome and a lack of desire to look for one. The stories and characters are basically just overly morose and depressing. I slogged on this for as long as I could but found myself constantly wondering why I was reading it since I was enjoying none of it.[1]

I cite this honest and revealing reaction, not to take issue with it, but to let it stand for one perfectly legitimate point of view about Kafka's work. Some people have no taste for it, not because they fail to understand it, but because they understand it perfectly well and hate it. As the punch line of an old joke puts it, 'Even if that was good I wouldn't like it.' The charges leveled against Kafka here—that the storylines lack coherence and direction, that the characters are often placed in hopeless situations, and that the stories are consequently depressing—are not misreadings. They are perfectly sound observations about the nature of many of Kafka's fictions. Kafka himself would not have disagreed.

If there is argument to be made against such a condemnation, it can only be this: inconclusiveness, hopelessness, and so on need not necessarily be faults in a certain kind of fiction. That was Kafka's view of literature from very early on in his career. 'I think we ought to read only the kind of books that wound and stab us,' he wrote to a friend. 'If the book we're reading doesn't wake us up with a blow on the head, what are we reading it for?' (*Friends* 16). The Amazon reviewer rejects Kafka's work because he does not enjoy reading it, but Kafka rejected precisely the books that the reviewer would presumably prefer, the 'books that make us happy' (*Friends* 16). Kafka's very Kafkaesque view was that happiness was not the purpose of books. 'Good Lord, we would be happy precisely if we had no books' (*Friends* 16).

The Amazon reviewer, however, does not feel that he has been awakened by reading Kafka. He feels he has been put to sleep. This disappointment is not the result of a disagreement between highbrow culture and ordinary folks. There are those among intellectuals and scholars who find Kafka boring, and there are those among general readers who find him as arousing as Kafka would have wished. Indeed, the reason that Kafka appears nowadays on so many university reading lists is that he has been hugely popular with all sorts of audiences around the world. In post–World-War-II New York, for example, he was something approaching a fad. Perhaps he never quite reached the standard set by John, Paul, George, and Ringo a few years later, but he was in that league. One writer remembers the frenzy, akin to Beatle-mania, that could develop in those days around the quest to obtain access to Kafka:

> Seeing how young I was, everyone gave me advice. Get Christopher Caudwell, they said. [. . .] But above all, at any cost, I must get Kafka. Kafka was as popular in the Village at that time as Dickens had been in Victorian London. But his books were very difficult to find—they must have been printed in very small editions—and people would rush in wild-eyed, almost foaming at the mouth, willing to pay anything for Kafka.[2]

So why were people rushing about Greenwich Village wild-eyed, willing to pay anything for Kafka? What could there be in these books—these frustrating, fragmentary, unhappy books—that would warrant such enthusiasm?

3

The answer is, and must be, that some people are powerfully drawn to Kafka for the same reason others are powerfully repelled. The perplexity felt by every reader initiates in some not so much frustration as fascination. Each text becomes a mystery that cries out for solution even though no solution is available. Theodor Adorno expressed the matter this way:

> Each sentence says 'interpret me', and none will permit it. Each compels the reaction, 'that's the way it is', and with it the question, 'where have I seen that before?': the *déjà vu* is declared permanent. Through the power with which Kafka commands interpretation, he [. . .] demands a desperate effort of the allegedly 'disinterested' observer [. . .]. [He] overwhelms him, suggesting that [. . .] life and death are at stake.[3]

We readers become passionately attached to Kafka's stories, then, because they prod us with a 'shock of recognition' (in Herman Melville's phrase) and afford us the pleasure of finding in them the same perplexities that confront us at one time or another in our daily lives. No solutions to problems are offered, but the problems are served up with such vivid intensity that we accept them as our own, identify with them, and make them part of our consciousness.

Stories that work their way into our consciousness and find a more or less permanent home there have a special name: we call them 'myths.' When used in this manner the term does not indicate primarily that a story is not factual; it suggests rather that it has taken on such a broad cultural significance that it has become a common possession of an entire community. The story of the Trojan War is such a myth, as are the stories of Tristan and Isolde, Romeo and Juliet, Captain Ahab and the white whale, and the man who woke up one morning to find himself transformed into a gigantic bug.

The poet W. H. Auden was perhaps the first to see that Kafka's stories had a mythic quality, but the novelist Hermann Broch was the first to give a plausible explanation of how they acquired this remarkable characteristic.[4] He finds a productive approach to the question by coming at it from the underside:

> For the modern myth, which so many poets have the ambition to write, does not exist: there exists only something which could properly be called countermyth. For myth is cosmogony; it is description of the primordial forces threatening and destroying

4

man, and myth opposes the symbolization by Promethean symbols, no less gigantic and heroic, demonstrating how man can overcome what is apparently insurmountable and how he can live on this earth; nothing of this applies today . . . [Ours is] the situation of extreme helplessness, and Kafka, not Joyce, has done it justice; in Kafka we find the beginnings of an adequate countermyth in whose repertory the heroic symbols, the father—and even the mother symbols—are of small importance or even superfluous because what really matters is the symbolization of helplessness per se, which means the symbolization of the child.[5]

Kafka's fictions take on the quality of myths (or countermyths, as Broch would have it) by doing exactly the opposite of what earlier versions of myth had done. Kafka mythologizes helplessness; he mythologizes failure; he mythologizes . . . perplexity. And he does so by reminding us that, big and strong as we may sometimes feel, we are all in the larger scheme of things little better than feeble infants. This sense of infantile vulnerability is akin to religious feeling, as anyone knows who has called upon the aid and comfort of God the Father or Mary the Virgin Mother. Kafka's friend Max Brod may well have experienced such a feeling when reading, or hearing Kafka read, these mythic tales. If so we can understand why he thought his friend's work was fundamentally religious in tone.

Broch suggests that the mythic figure behind all Kafka's mythmaking is the child because children embody the qualities of powerlessness and vulnerability that we find in so many of Kafka's protagonists. In fact, we do not ordinarily find children among his major characters— Karl Rossmann, the hero of *The Missing Person* (*Amerika*) is a notable exception—although we do find many creatures, human and animal, with childlike characteristics. Very often his stories are told from the viewpoint of someone who, though an adult, has the unsophisticated, perhaps even childish view of an outsider with respect to the situation in which he or she is placed. Sometimes Kafka contextualizes adult characters in such a way as to foreground their permanent status as children. This is notably true of Gregor Samsa in 'The Metamorphosis' and Georg Bendemann in 'The Judgment,' grownups who still live with their parents and operate mainly in the parental orbit.

But even when children or childlike characters do not figure prominently among the people in the story, the story always tries to put the reader in the position of a child. All of Kafka's stories are children's stories. The audience addressed may be persons of any chronological age, but in spirit all his readers are reduced to the status of powerless, vulnerable creatures facing a narrative that 'shoots towards' them, as Adorno puts it, 'like a locomotive in a three-dimensional film.'[6] We child-readers have no clear idea just what is happening, but whatever it is strikes us with a special kind of terror. Our fear is 'mythic.' It is contained in a form that allows us to deal with it as a common cultural experience.

Kafka seeks to create in his readers this aesthetically formed sense of baffled helplessness. Indeed he appears to have had this goal in mind at every moment in the composition process. We can get at least a partial idea of how that process worked by examining the manuscripts, which offer for some of the works a reasonably reliable record of the writer's initial ideas and the (usually minor) second thoughts he had about them. One lesson we learn from such an examination is that Kafka took special pains to ensure that his narratives would remain puzzling in this mythic way. He never announced explicitly that he followed such a policy, but we can deduce it from the pattern that emerges from the passages he deleted from the novel drafts. In fact the material he cut out is often demonstrably clearer than the text that replaces it.[7]

Many useful examples come from *The Trial*. One of the earliest revisions involves Josef K. and the three bank employees who were present at his arrest. K. is worried about them, and he calls them into his office now and then in order to observe them. 'He had always been able to dismiss them totally satisfied,' says the published text (*Trial* 21). Originally Kafka had not ended the paragraph there but continued thus:

> The thought that in this way he was actually perhaps facilitating their surveillance of him, which might well have been their assignment, seemed to him such a ridiculous idea that he put his head in his hand and remained thus for several minutes until he came to his senses. 'A few more thoughts like that,' he said to himself, 'and you'll be a complete fool.' But then he raised his somewhat grating voice even louder.[8]

The deleted passage does more than make readers aware of an incipient paranoia in K.: it shows that K. himself is aware of it.

There can be little doubt as to why Kafka crossed out this passage: it was too straightforward. One can say this with confidence because the author replaced it with other material that brings up precisely the same idea far more indirectly, in what amounts to a little parable of K.'s anxiety:

> When, at nine-thirty that evening, he arrived at the building where he lived, he met a young fellow at the entrance smoking a pipe. 'Who are you,' K. asked straightaway and brought his face close to that of the fellow [. . .] 'I'm the caretaker's son, sir,' the fellow answered [. . .]. 'The caretaker's son?' asked K., tapping the floor impatiently with his cane. 'Is there something I can do for you, sir? Shall I get my father?' 'No, no,' said K. with a note of forgiveness, as if the fellow had done something truly wrong, but he was willing to forgive him. 'That's all right,' he said, and passed on; but before he went up the stairs, he turned around once more. (*Trial* 21)

This paragraph simply relates events as they happened, not as interpreted by K., without offering any comment on them. In other words, it illustrates the hero's increasing anxiety without discussing it. The information it gives about K.'s incipient paranoia is not spoon-fed to the reader; instead the reader must extract it from the incident itself by reading the emotional temperature of this miniature dramatization.

The passage is far more subtle and ambiguous than the material it replaces. Indeed it is so subtle that, were it not for the assistance of the deletion, one might be in some doubt about its function and meaning.[9] The paragraph forms a virtually independent scene within the chapter, so there is no immediate context to give the reader certainty about the significance of the passage. And this must have been Kafka's intention. He evidently wanted the reader to be in some doubt, since he could have relieved our doubts by simply retaining the deleted material.

Several of the passages excised from *The Trial* contain remarkably clear-sighted observations by characters, especially K. himself, which Kafka must have thought were simply too insightful. During his conversation with Fraulein Bürstner early in the novel, K. seems to be struggling to make small talk, and in the course of his struggle he offers a self-analysis: 'I have no talent for seriousness and therefore have to make jokes serve both for seriousness and joking. But I was arrested, and that was serious.'[10] Nothing even remotely similar to this is retained in the revised text. K.'s comments in the deletion may or may not be accurate, but either way they are too direct for the purposes of the novel.

Kafka also eliminated some particularly insightful remarks by K. near the end of the novel. While the hero is being escorted to his place of execution by two mysterious figures, apparently officials of the court, they pass by a number of policemen. One of these approaches the rather suspicious-looking group, and at first Kafka had K. observe: 'The state is offering me its help [. . .]. What if I transferred my case to the jurisdiction of state law? It might come to the point where I'd have to defend these men against the state!'[11] But Kafka deleted this observation, thus erasing its implied distinction between the laws of the state and the 'Law' of the court that has tried and apparently condemned K. In the revised version, K. says nothing. Instead he behaves in a most peculiar fashion:

> The men hesitated, the policeman seemed about to open his mouth, then K. pulled the men forward forcibly. He turned around cautiously several times to make sure the policeman wasn't following, but when they had a corner between them and the policeman, K. started to run and the men had to run with him, although they were gasping for breath. (*Trial* 229)

The implication that the policeman might interfere, might even help K., remains open but is not forced upon the reader.

The deleted sentence, 'The state is offering me its help,' was surely too unambiguous for Kafka. It provides a clear interpretation of an event that is not clear, that admits of other interpretations—particularly in the revised version—and raises a series of questions. Could K. call on the officer for help and expect to get it? Does K. actually assist his executioners to avoid a confrontation with the police? The passage suggests such things as these, but in the absence of the deletion it does not state any of them directly.

We can see the principle of increasing ambiguity at work also in several cases where the excisions seem to be principally a matter of imagery. In one instance, Kafka went so far as to nearly eliminate an image entirely. The desk in lawyer Huld's office is elaborately described in the first version:

> The desk, which took up practically the whole length of the room, stood near the windows, it was set up in such a way that the lawyer had his back to the door and the visitor, like an actual intruder,

had to cross the entire width of the room before he got to see the lawyer's face, unless the latter had been considerate enough to turn around toward the visitor.[12]

On second thought Kafka deleted the whole passage and replaced with a single short sentence: 'K. felt he could picture the tiny steps with which the visitors approached the massive desk' (*Trial* 104).

The clarity of the original image is unquestionable, especially since Kafka provided a kind of built-in interpretation by the inclusion of the phrase 'like an actual intruder.' We should also note that the deleted sentence presents the image from the outside, as it were, while the revision gives what K. imagines. The second version is thus both more immediate and less preprocessed than the first. It gives less concrete information, but the information it gives is a direct representation of K.'s puzzled and indeed even childlike anxiety. The contrast of the 'tiny' steps and the 'massive' desk helps us share the character's sense of his own insignificance.

The longest of the deleted passages from *The Trial* also seems to have been motivated principally by a desire to render the imagery less univocal. At the end of the exegetical conversation between K. and the chaplain in the 'Cathedral' chapter, Kafka at first composed a number of paragraphs in which light imagery is very prominent. In this deleted passage there are nine uses of the words *Lampe, Licht, dunkel* (lamp, light, dark) and other terms referring to light or darkness. And the action described by the excised material is symbolic along these lines: the chaplain leads K. from a place of total darkness (the cathedral proper) into a place of partial darkness (the sacristy) just as his parable 'Before the Law' had led K. from total ignorance to partial ignorance. And just as K. is not much enlightened by the story or its interpretation, so is he not much aided by the extremely dim light of the sacristy.

Almost all of this is removed in the revision. Reference to the lamp and the darkness in the cathedral are severely limited; there are only three uses of terms referring to light instead of the nine in the rejected passage. The trip to the sacristy is eliminated entirely along with its very clear (one might even say obvious) symbolism. The much reduced light imagery that remains after the deletions is actually much more effective. Such light as there is, as for example the gleam of silver on the statue of a saint (*Trial* 223), has the paradoxical effect of making the darkness seem even darker.

Our darkness seems darker as well, and no wonder. Taken together with other, similarly motivated deletions from *The Trial* and *The Castle*, the pattern of Kafka's revisions shows a tendency to favor leaving us in the dark. But why would a writer do such a thing? Why would he want to make the reader's task more difficult?

I suspect Kafka would have rejected the question. For him, the reader's role was not to understand the story in the sense of deciphering its encrypted message; it was to be 'stabbed' by it. He wanted us to read his fictions the way the prisoners in his imaginary penal colony were supposed to read the rules they had broken, that is, to read through our wounds. With that goal in mind he took pains to make sure that simple acts of interpretation would always fail. He wanted his readers to experience his stories as threatening, painful, and ultimately inscrutable so that those readers might share his experience of the world. And indeed many readers, once they have a taste of the world as it tasted to Kafka, find their future experiences permanently altered. Henceforth their world will always taste a little 'Kafkaesque,' because his myths now structure their reality.

There can therefore never be a simple formula for eliminating a certain puzzlement from our encounters with Kafka. He deliberately foreclosed that possibility. There is no Rosetta Stone for these hieroglyphics, and this Guide does not pretend to offer one. But many years of experience wrestling with Kafka's texts suggests that there is one secure way to make them seem less forbidding: one needs to know something about Kafka's life. This is not to say that biography offers a magic key that will unlock all mysteries; it does not, because Kafka did not want his mysteries unlocked; but the personal context out of which the stories arose at least gives us a secure point of departure from which we may creep up on them. It affords us a sense of the conditions, both emotional and historical, out of which these bizarre tales arose.

Every author of fiction necessarily draws on his or her own experience, at least to some extent, in making up stories. This is true even in the case of fictions dealing with fantastic events and characters in imaginary universes, as for example with Tolkien's hobbits, elves, and orcs in Middle Earth. It no less true for Kafka's fictions of people changed to animals and animals changed to people, of animals who stay animals but think and talk and act like people, of inanimate objects that act as if they harbored conscious intentions, and of persons who behave like soulless automata. Indeed it is perhaps more true of these than of any other modern works of literature.

All of Kafka's inventions, even the most outrageous, came out of a mind formed by experiences that were in many respects quite ordinary for a person of his time, place, and social status. But these ordinary events interacted in extraordinary ways with Kafka's unique personality. We need to know something about that personality and about the incidents that affected him so deeply. Armed with that information we may begin to approach his stories in the spirit in which they were written—a spirit of unrelenting but productive perplexity.

CHAPTER TWO

A SHORT LIFE OF FRANZ K.

Franz Kafka was born on July 3, 1883 in Prague, a Bohemian city
that had its roots in the Holy Roman Empire but belonged during
Kafka's youth to the Austro-Hungarian Empire. Kafka was thus
officially an Austrian. But he was a special sort of Austrian in that
he was a Jew, and despite the relative prosperity of the Jewish
community under Franz Josef I, Austrian Jews were still in many
ways second-class citizens.[1]

   Although ethnically Jewish and the son of a Czech-speaking
father, Kafka did not grow up speaking Yiddish or Czech. His whole
household—with the exception of the servants—adhered to a consci-
entious program of speaking the local variant of standard German
(*Hochdeutsch* with a few minor Austrian peculiarities), and that naturally became his mother tongue.[2] He picked up enough Czech from
the kitchen, the nursery, and a few lessons that he could understand
it well and speak it passably. He could even write it when pressed.
Others thought his Czech was quite good, but he did not consider
himself fluent and never felt really comfortable with the language. He
could also understand a certain amount of Yiddish, not primarily
because he was a Jew, but because Yiddish and German are closely
related languages. When he became interested in Yiddish as an adult,
he had to approach it as something slightly alien.[3] He learned enough
Hebrew to get through his bar mitzvah, but it was only toward the
end of his life that he studied the language earnestly.

   Kafka was thus a person of highly mixed ethnic and cultural heritage.
He is claimed by the Austrians (he grew up a subject of the Austrian
Emperor), the Czechs (he was a Czech citizen after November 1918),
the Israelis (he had plans to move to Palestine and would have qualified
for Israeli citizenship if he had lived long enough), the Germans

(he spoke German, wrote in German, and allied himself with German literary culture), and the international Jewish community (to which he belonged by right of birth). Every one of these claims has more than a little legitimacy, and every one of them has sparked controversy.

1. FAMILY AND BOYHOOD (1883–93)

Kafka's mother Julie (1856–1934) was born into the large and distinguished Löwy family.[4] She was proud of her background. Her father was a prosperous brewer in Podiebrad on the Elbe River, and many of her ancestors had been eminent in one way or another. Among them were several notable for their piety, including his mother's maternal grandfather, whom she remembered 'as a very pious and learned man with a long, white beard' (*Diaries* 152). Even more learned was her great-grandfather: 'Christians and Jews held him in equal honour; during a fire a miracle took place as a result of his piety, the flames jumped over and spared his house while the houses around it burned down' (*Diaries* 153).

It is noteworthy that Kafka chose to discuss his forebears in terms of his mother's maternal line, in which there were many learned people, even rabbis. The interests of those on his mother's paternal side ran more to commerce and therefore were less congenial to the bookish Franz. He says nothing at all in this notebook entry about his father's family, with whom he felt he had little in common. Just how little of his father's heritage Kafka thought he had in him is strikingly evident in this excerpt from the *Letter to His Father*:

> Compare the two of us: I [. . .] a Löwy with a certain basis of Kafka, which, however, is not set in motion by the Kafka will to life, business, and conquest, but by a Löwyish spur that impels more secretly, more diffidently, and in another direction, and which often fails to work entirely. You, on the other hand, a true Kafka in strength, health, appetite, loudness of voice, eloquence, self-satisfaction, worldly dominance, endurance [. . .]. (*Father* 11–13)

Franz asserts solidarity with his maternal background in four ways. First, he calls himself a Löwy, not a Kafka, which is surely a polemical stance for a man named Kafka to take. Second, after admitting to 'a certain basis of Kafka' he claims that whatever there is of Kafka in him has no real power: the 'Löwyish spur' in him actually takes command of his Kafka aspect. Third, he proposes that the Löwy side secretly pushes his small residue of Kafka in some un-Kafka-like direction. And fourth, to top it all, he dismisses his Kafka heritage as something that frequently 'fails to work' at all. In other words, Kafka did not see himself as very Kafkaesque.

This almost total identification with the mother's family is perhaps not particularly surprising. There was very little to brag about on the paternal side. His father Hermann (1852–1931) came from Wossek, a tiny southern Bohemian village where he was born the son of a humble butcher. Little Hermann helped out in the family business from a very early age, delivering meat in the early mornings, sometimes (as he claimed) walking barefoot through the snow. Hermann managed to get enough schooling to learn the elements of reading and writing in German, a foreign language for his Czech-speaking family.

But studying was not his strong suit. He had a bent for business, and at age fourteen he was already living independently as an itinerant peddler. He must have done well. Upon completing a stint of military service, he married in 1882 a bride from a more prosperous and respected family. He was able to set up shop in Prague as a dealer in fashion accessories—gloves, scarves, and so on—catering to a relatively affluent clientele. Perhaps he got some financial support from his wife's relatives, but there can be no doubt that Hermann was an effective salesman. He pulled himself up out of poverty to a position of bourgeois stability and comfort, with the means to purchase an excellent education for his son and to see all three of his daughters married to men who, though not wealthy, were certainly of higher social standing than that into which he had been born.

Part of Hermann Kafka's plan for social improvement was to minimize the family's Jewish and Czech affiliations and maximize its Germanness. Anti-Semitism was not the official policy under Franz Josef, but it flourished nonetheless, and the state did nothing to curtail it. It could hinder the advancement of anyone who was too obviously Jewish. Cultural policy made a few laudable gestures toward fostering diversity, but on the whole it favored the German language and institutions formed on German models. These facts of life in the Austro-Hungarian Empire were powerful motivations for Hermann's domestic policy. He insisted on keeping his own Czech mother tongue on the fringes of his household, and he limited his participation in religious life principally to high holidays. He took an aggressively assimilationist line. The printed invitations he sent out on the occasion of his son's bar mitzvah spoke volumes on this topic: 'I cordially invite you to the confirmation of my son Franz.' The only hint that there might be something not entirely Christian about the event appeared in the notation that it would take place at the Zigeuner Synagogue.[5]

Young Franz, like his sisters after him, received an education designed to further his father's high social aspirations: it was therefore very German and not very Jewish. As a little boy he attended the Deutsche Knabenschule (German Boys' School), an institution whose very name announced its adherence to German standards. The boy hated the place, and he dreaded especially his morning walk to school in the company of the family cook, who seemed always ready to denounce his bad behavior to the dreaded school authorities. The alarming world of Kafka's fictions can be glimpsed in this dramatic account of the walk to school:

> It was getting late, the Jakobskirche was striking 8, you could hear the school bells, other children would start to run—I always had the greatest terror of being late—now we had to run as well and all the time the thought: 'She'll tell, she won't tell.' It turns out she never told, not once, but there was always the possibility she might, an ever-growing possibility [. . .] which she never gave up. (*Milena* 54)

Even discounting the literary artifice in this letter written 30 years and more after the event, we may safely trust that that emotional core of the memory is accurate.

The story of going to school with the cook hints at a fact of the young boy's life that was typical for the late nineteenth century but not so typical of today: children frequently saw little of their parents. In the Kafka family *both* parents spent nearly all their waking hours minding the store, while the children were cared for by servants. The parents appeared at meal times and on other rare occasions of high solemnity. Father Hermann contributed mainly commandments, warnings, and outbursts of anger. The bond between father and son—which was as powerful as it was corrosive—was forged in the sporadic but intense fires of hyperbolic paternal rhetoric.

Kafka's views about the relation between parents and children, as he expressed them in later years to his sister Elli, surely bear the stamp of his own childhood experience:

> In the family, clutched in the tight embrace of the parents, there is room only for certain kinds of people who conform to certain kinds of requirements [. . .]. If they do not conform, they are not expelled—that would be very fine, but is impossible, for we are dealing with an organism here—but accursed or consumed or both. The consuming does not take place on the physical plane, as in the archetype of Greek mythology (Kronos, the most honest of fathers, who devoured his sons; but perhaps Kronos preferred this to the usual methods out of pity for his children). (*Friends* 295)

Kafka's assessment that it would be better to be killed and eaten than to suffer 'the usual methods' of childrearing shows how profoundly damaged he felt. Growing up in the Kafka family seemed to him a process of being psychologically engulfed and consumed—though of course he turned out to be an altogether indigestible meal, even for his voracious father.

2. GYMNASIUM AND UNIVERSITY (1893–1906)

At age ten Kafka entered the Altstädter Deutsches Gymnasium (Old-City German Secondary School), so named after both its language of instruction and its location in the rear of a stately building in the center of town.[6] Hermann Kafka's shop was located on the ground floor front of the building, a circumstance that must have made the boy feel even more acutely the 'tight embrace of the parents' that he would complain about later in the letter to Elli. The principal motivation for the choice of this school was probably not its location, however, but its humanistic curriculum. Such schools regularly supplied recruits for important government jobs, and Hermann clearly was hoping that the next Kafka generation of could take a step up from shop keeping into the administrative professions. In this ambition his son did not disappoint him.

Kafka did, however, regularly disappoint himself—not because he failed, but because he always expected failure. He laid the blame for this expectation at his father's doorstep:

> I was always convinced—and I positively had the proof of it in your forbidding expression—that the more I achieved, the worse

the final outcome would inevitably be. Often in my mind's eye I saw the terrible assembly of the teachers [. . .] meeting in order to examine this unique, outrageous case, to discover how I, the most incapable and, in any case, the most ignorant of all, had succeeded in creeping up so far as this class, which now, when everybody's attention had at last been focused on me, would of course instantly spew me out [. . .]. (*Father* 93)

Among the many enigmas that confronted Franz as he made his way through the world was the unfathomable mystery of his own competence. No doubt the father's hectoring played a role in his lack of confidence, but so did the son's inborn anxiety and puzzlement in the face of the ordinary. 'Life for him is something entirely different than for all other human beings,' his friend Milena Jesenská once wrote (*Milena* 243). And what was perhaps most puzzling for him was the simple process of getting along and 'doing business.'[7] This awe at other people's ability to cope with the world was his particular gift and his particular curse, and it was part of his character even in boyhood. He assumed that he could never 'do business' like the other boys at school and was amazed when in fact he got business done.

The daunting curriculum he felt certain would defeat him was typical of German humanistic secondary education. It was based principally on classical languages and literatures, and much of Franz's time at school was taken up with grammar drills and with translating passages from ancient texts. Some scholars have claimed that this education had little effect on him, but such an assessment seems hasty.[8] Numerous figures from classical myth and history turn up in his writings: Odysseus, the sirens, Poseidon, Prometheus, Alexander the Great, Alexander's horse Bucephalus, and so on. His most famous story takes up the central theme of Ovid's great poem about transformations, the *Metamorphoses*.

Religious instruction was also provided, but it did nothing to amend the negative feelings toward Judaism that Franz had developed at home. According to a report given later by Gustav Janouch,[9] Kafka thoroughly dismissed his religious education. When Janouch mentioned that Scripture was taught in school as part of the history of the Jews, Kafka allegedly 'smiled bitterly' and replied, 'Just so! The history of the Jews is given the appearance of a fairy tale, which men can dismiss, together with their childhood, into the pit of oblivion.'[10] Kafka the Gymnasium student was quite ready to toss what he was being taught into that pit. His indifference or, at times, outright antipathy toward Judaism would undergo a reversal in later years, but as a school boy he was far more interested in radical politics than traditional religion.

At age sixteen he already felt drawn to radicalism, both political and cultural. He began to read radical literature and to wear a red carnation as a symbol of his solidarity with the left.[11] He also felt drawn to literature and to friends of a literary bent, such as a schoolmate named Oskar Pollak.[12] During high school and the first years at university, Kafka harbored an intense affection for this young man, and for a number of years Pollak was his chief confidant.[13] Pollak's intense interest in the arts and in the Teutonic element in German culture struck a chord in Kafka, who was eager to follow where Pollak might lead him. It was Pollak, and perhaps he alone, to whom Kafka showed his first attempts at writing, and it was Pollak who was his first long-term correspondent.

One of Pollak's suggestions was that Kafka look into *Der Kunstwart*, an arts journal Friedrich Nietzsche had helped to found. Possibly this periodical incited Kafka's interest in Nietzsche. Or perhaps the boy's respect for Nietzsche spilled over onto the magazine. Opinions differ on the quality of what Kafka read in the *Kunstwart*, but there is no doubt that it helped to foster Kafka's budding interest in literature.[14] Although nothing remains of what he wrote in this period, we do know that he wrote some things that Pollak read. It is possible, even probable, that these early writings would have displayed a Nietzschean influence more clearly than what we see in the works of his adulthood. We will never know. What we do know is that his support for the philosopher was still strong in early adulthood. It played a key role in triggering one of the most important events in Kafka's life: his friendship with his fellow university student Max Brod (1884–1968).

Brod and Kafka were both attending the Charles University in Prague, where Franz matriculated in 1901. After trying out a number of different courses of study (including chemistry, art history, and German literature), Kafka settled on the law, much to the relief of his parents. This practical choice did not, however, prevent him from pursuing his literary interests on his own time. He was an avid theatergoer and regularly attended talks and poetry readings. In October of 1902, the 18-year-old Brod gave a talk on Arthur Schopenhauer in which he attacked Nietzsche as 'a swindler.'[15] Kafka couldn't let this stand without rebuttal. After the talk he engaged the speaker in a rambling conversation that lasted through their departure together from the meeting and into their walk home. Brod wrote:

That evening [. . .] he was more communicative than usual; [. . .] the endless conversation that went on while he was seeing me home began with a strong protest against the extreme uncouthness of my way of putting things. From that we went on to talking about our favorite authors, and defended them against one another.[16]

How much influence Nietzsche exerted on Kafka in subsequent years remains a matter of scholarly debate,[17] but there can be no debate about Max Brod's influence, not only during the rest of Kafka's life, but beyond. The friendship that began that night would provide the single most important source of support for Kafka's literary career. Brod, too, was studying law, and like Kafka he would later lead a double life as a bureaucrat and as a writer.

Brod himself notes that, unlike Kafka's relationship with Pollak, in which Franz was the instigator, Brod took the lead in seeking closer ties with Kafka. As the junior partner—Brod was a year younger—he always looked up to Franz. He looked up quite literally, since Kafka was considerably taller and more physically attractive. 'Kafka was the stronger partner in our friendship, if through nothing else than his calm and reserve, even though a foundation of equality of rights was cheerfully acknowledged on either side.'[18] Slowly during the years from 1902 to 1904—the very years in which Kafka wrote a series of revealing letters to Pollak—Kafka changed his allegiance from one friend to the other. In 1904 the letters to Pollak stop and the letters to Brod begin.

Another beginning took place in that year: Kafka probably began work on the first piece of fiction that has survived, the 'Description of a Struggle.'[19] Although Kafka was still a law student who was struggling through his examinations, he apparently found time for the literary work he much preferred to legal studies. Indeed, there is no reason to believe that he hadn't been writing at least on and off ever since those first efforts shown to Pollak during their days at the Altstädter Gymnasium. The 'Description' just happens to be the earliest effort that managed to avoid loss or destruction. Understandably, he made little progress on this or any other fiction while he was in law school, and what was begun in 1904 had to wait a couple of years for further development.

His last years at the university were especially stressful. He had increasing difficulty getting respectable grades, and the pathological fears of academic failure he had harbored in the Gymnasium now appeared entirely justified. At the conclusion of his last semester of courses in the summer of 1905, he treated himself to a long vacation at Zuckmantel, a health resort in Austrian Silesia. No doubt he hoped to fortify himself for the final exams that lay ahead of him. While taking the cure, he had a romantic liaison with an older woman. In a notebook entry from July 1916, he wrote: 'I have never been intimate with a woman apart from that time in Zuckmantel. And then again with the Swiss girl in Riva. The first was a woman, and I was ignorant; the second a child, and I was utterly confused' (*Diaries* 365). There will be more to say about 'the Swiss girl' later; for now we need only note that Kafka, even if he was 'ignorant,' was not indiscreet. He never divulged any details about his adventure in the healing atmosphere of Zuckmantel, and we still do not know the lady's name.[20]

Upon returning to Prague in the fall, Kafka faced three difficult oral exams that he had to pass in order to earn his J.D. degree. He would have to spend essentially the whole year cramming and performing. Under the *pro forma* direction of Alfred Weber (the brother of famed sociologist Max Weber), he took and passed the first of them (Rigorosum II) in November, the second (Rigorosum III) in March of 1906, and the third—the Rigorosum I on Roman, German, and canon law that he dreaded most of all—on June 13. He passed with a grade of 'satisfactory,' which was undistinguished but adequate. Five days later he was granted his degree, and his school days were finally over. Feeling he deserved a holiday, he went back to Zuckmantel for July and August—back to the arms of the same woman he had loved the previous summer.

3. FIRST EMPLOYMENT AND EARLY LITERARY EFFORTS (1906–10)

In the fall of 1906 Kafka took up a one-year clerkship in the court system, the normal practice for those seeking a career in government service. Such service did not seem the most likely career path for a young Jew with literary aspirations,[21] but no doubt the experience was at least marginally useful in his later employment. It was also probably at this time that Kafka began work on another piece of fiction, a novel that Max Brod later titled 'Wedding Preparations in the Country.' The protagonist is named Raban, a name that alludes to the author both in the repeated vowel *a* and in its similarity to *Rabe*, the German translation of the Czech *kavka* ('crow' or 'jackdaw'). The chief female character, Betty, may well have been modeled on the lady-love from Zuckmantel. But one can go only so far in reading this fragment as evidence of Kafka's personal history. The hero of the story is planning to marry Betty, but it seems highly unlikely that either Kafka or his summertime lover had any such intention. In any case, Kafka never got further than what looks like the intended second chapter of his wedding story before abandoning the project.

At some point between the winter of 1906 and the summer of 1907, Kafka read at least some of his work in progress to Brod. It may have been this reading that prompted Brod to mention Kafka as an important writer in a review he wrote in February, 1907, for the Berlin paper *Die Gegenwart*. Much to Kafka's amazement he found himself already recognized in print as a major literary figure before he had ever published a single word. He wrote a note to his friend in response:

> It's just unfortunate [. . .] that it will now be an indecent act for me to publish anything in the future, since that would completely destroy the delicacy of this first public appearance. And I would never be able to achieve anywhere near the luster you have ascribed to my name in your sentence. (February 12, 1907, my trans.; cf. *Friends* 23)

Brod's skill as a prognosticator was, in this case at least, far better than Kafka's.

In this same period Kafka seems to have returned to 'Description of a Struggle.' There is a line in that text where a character describes himself: 'I am twenty-three years of age, but as yet I have no name' (*ComStor* 41). If this represents, as seems likely, Kafka's fictional response to Brod's laudatory mention of his name in the Berlin newspaper article, then he must have returned to work on the piece sometime between midwinter and midsummer of 1907.[22] Once again, however, he was unable to bring the story to a satisfactory conclusion.

He did bring to a conclusion, satisfactory or not, his stint as a legal clerk, and he needed a paying job. 'If my prospects don't improve by October,' he told Brod,

I'll [. . .] learn Spanish along with French and English. If you'd like to do this too, it would be nice [. . .]; my uncle [Alfred Löwy] would have to find us a position in Spain or we could go to South America or the Azores, to Madeira.[23] (mid August 1907, my trans.; cf. *Friends* 25)

Before facing the nearly overwhelming task of finding work, he took an August vacation at the home of his uncle Siegfried Löwy, a physician in the rural town of Triesch (now Třešt) southeast of Prague.[24] There he engaged in activities suitable for a young bachelor on holiday: 'riding around on the motorbike a good deal, swimming a lot, lying nude in the grass by the pond for hours' (*Friends* 25–26), and socializing very seriously with a couple of girls he would identify to his best friend Max only as 'A.' and 'H. W.'

The second of these was Hedwig Weiler, an attractive Viennese Jewish girl of nineteen with cheeks 'constantly and boundlessly red' and 'plump little legs' (*Friends* 26). Franz also noticed in particular the planes that formed the tip of her nose and remarked to Brod that 'such are the roundabout ways by which I recognize a girl's beauty and fall in love' (*Friends* 26). The attraction was apparently mutual, and the ensuing relationship was intense enough that it led to an exchange of letters that lasted into the late fall of 1907.[25] They remained lovers, or at least attempted to do so, even after they parted from their holiday romance in Triesch.

Hedwig was in many ways Kafka's opposite. She was short, plump, practical, outgoing, and deeply committed to political action. She does not appear to have had the slightest inclination toward morbid introspection. Kafka's tendency in that direction became evident relatively early in their correspondence:

I have no social life, nothing to distract me; every evening I'm on the little balcony above the river; I don't even read the *Arbeiterzeitung* [Social Democratic Workers' Newspaper] and I am not a good person. [. . .] You can see I'm a ridiculous person; if you like me a little, you're just being merciful; all I have going for me is fear. (August 29, 1907, my trans.; cf. *Friends* 27–28)

He was not happy. She obviously could tell, and she was therefore reluctant to visit him in Prague. She failed to show up for a promised rendezvous. He wrote in response that 'we have danced a quadrille between Prague and Vienna, one of those figures in which couples bow so much they do not come together [. . .]. I do not feel at all well' (*Friends* 31).

He had reason not to feel well. The search for work was not yielding good prospects, perhaps due in part to his undistinguished record at the university. He had hoped for his uncle to descend like a *deus ex machina* from Madrid with the offer of a glamorous job in some foreign land, but the uncle's help, when it came, was of a far less exotic sort. Uncle Alfred had called upon his connections with an Austrian-Italian insurance firm headquartered in Trieste, which was then part of the Austrian Empire. The Assicurazioni Generali had a branch office in Prague and was willing to take on young Kafka, though under less than favorable working conditions. Franz had no choice but to submit his application and accept what they were willing to offer. He joined the firm on October 1, 1907.

At first he tried to make the best of it, professing to find the work interesting though he actually found it oppressive, and hoping to be posted in the future to one of the company's offices in lands far from Prague. He wrote to Hedwig after one week in the new job that he was studying Italian and had 'some hopes of someday sitting in chairs in faraway countries, looking out of the office windows at fields of sugar cane or Mohammedan cemeteries' (*Friends* 35).

But Kafka's budding hopes for a happier future, both in his job with the Italian insurance company and in his relationship with Hedwig, soon withered on the vine. A few weeks after telling her that 'insurance itself interests me greatly' (*Friends* 35) and that he might get transferred to a faraway place, he confessed: 'I can't say whether I am going to be transferred soon and far away; hardly before a year is out. Best of all would be to be transferred right out of the firm' (*Friends* 37). Indeed, he was already looking for another job, though he had to do so very discreetly to avoid upsetting the people who had gone to great trouble to get him hired at the Assicurazioni. He hoped for something with the postal service.

Relations with Hedwig fared scarcely better than those with the firm. She had provoked his displeasure (perhaps intentionally, perhaps not) by reporting enthusiastically about her male friends in Vienna. She even went so far as to send a poem written by one of them for Kafka's critical assessment. He gave it, and it was not favorable. He subsequently retaliated by telling her he wanted to write more often but was too busy with 'a whole crowd' of boisterous companions, including 'cabaret singers, and they have taken away my few evening hours in the merriest fashion' (*Friends* 38–39). By the late fall of 1907 the blossom of their love had been thoroughly frosted. In one of his last letters he congratulated her on having 'a goal that cannot run away from you like a girl and that, even if you try to fend it off, will make you happy' (*Friends* 41). Telling her how lucky she was to have an objective that could not run off 'like a girl' was a nasty cut, knowingly inflicted and doubtless just as knowingly received. There was little hope of further intimacy between them.

If the surviving documents tell an accurate tale, Kafka was not able to write much fiction during these difficult months. His literary career advanced nonetheless. Brod managed to convince his friends Franz Blei and Carl Sternheim to publish a few pieces in the first issue of their literary magazine *Hyperion*. Kafka, obliged to deliver his contribution for the March 1908 issue near the end of 1907, gave the editors eight short prose sketches. The longest was just two pages; most were tiny snippets. The group appeared under the title 'Meditation.' Kafka plundered at least some sketches from material he had composed back in his student days.[26] A few can be found in 'Description of a Struggle,' but the complex history of that document allows no firm conclusions about when much of it was first composed.

From almost any standpoint the collection was a distinctly mixed bag. The Prague writer Franz Werfel allegedly predicted that 'Meditation' wouldn't 'get any further than Bodenbach'—that is, not any further than the Bohemian border.[27] Werfel was no fool, and one ought to forgive his abysmally erroneous judgment. The evidence he had before him would hardly support greater optimism. No one would pay these pieces any heed today if they did not have the magical name 'Kafka' attached to them. All in all, 'Meditation' represented a markedly unimpressive debut for the author whom Brod had announced as one of the foremost among contemporary writers.

This first publication was therefore no major event—not for the literary world, nor for the author, who had other matters on his mind. He was constantly searching for a new job and almost constantly searching for female companionship. Both quests were frustrating, but in the second instance there were more options. It was clear that Hedwig was not coming to Prague to be with him and that he was not going to Vienna, but men of Kafka's time, place, and social station who lacked a genuine lover could always purchase a counterfeit. Franz did so with some regularity. He wrote to Brod:

> I'm in such urgent need of finding someone who will give me a friendly touch that yesterday I went to the hotel with a street-walker. She is too old to be melancholy any more, but she feels sorry, without being surprised, that people aren't as nice to street-walkers as they are to kept women. I didn't comfort her since she didn't comfort me either. (July 29–30, 1908, my trans.; cf. *Friends* 45)

Neither the incident itself nor its unsatisfactory outcome was unusual for Kafka at this stage of his life, though such transactions always left him feeling irritated at both the participants and their spiritually empty interaction.

In summer 1908 Kafka's clandestine job search finally yielded results. Through an old school friend, Ewald Přibram, whose father had risen to a position of prominence in the business world, Franz was able to get his foot in the door at the Workers' Accident Insurance Company for the Kingdom of Bohemia, a semigovernmental agency. Otto Přibram was chairman of the board, from which lofty position he could readily pull a string or two. Furthermore, as luck would have it, Kafka had taken a course in workers' insurance that spring taught by some officials in the company. He had acquitted himself well in the course and made a favorable impression on his future supervisors. Ordinarily the company discriminated harshly against Jews (even Přibram soft-pedaled his own Jewish identity), but an exception was made for the promising young Kafka, thanks to the personal recommendation of the chairman. He started as 'temporary assistant' on July 30, 1908, with admittedly rather slim hopes for advancement. As it turned out, he would rise to a position of high responsibility and remain with the company for the rest of his working life.

The most important feature of the new job was the better working hours: a single shift of six hours from 8 a.m. till 2 p.m. The pay was slightly higher (3 crowns per day as opposed to 80 per month), but the compensation package mattered far less to Kafka than the enormous luxury of being quit of the office in time to eat his dinner, take a long nap, and enjoy an evening free for socializing, or writing, or—under the most favorable circumstances—both. One can hardly overstate the importance of that afternoon nap: it enabled Kafka to indulge in his 'nocturnal scribbling' and become, at least from time to time, the writer he wanted to be.

Unfortunately the increased leisure did not immediately lead to increased literary output. Quite the contrary. During the first years at the Workers' Accident Insurance Company he produced, as far as we know, only a few scraps of fiction, a book review, and a piece of reportage about airplanes—but a most impressive quantity of technical writing for the insurance company. He did his job well, and it was much appreciated by his supervisors, but it took its toll. In the evenings he found himself unable to do much at all. 'God knows why, I no longer have any stamina' (*Friends* 51). Even his socializing was limited, focused mainly on Max Brod and a few other intimates.

His mood remained dark for many months. A few fleeting interludes of good spirits served only to highlight his despair. He told Brod that

only the greater or lesser extent of this despair determines the nature of my present mood. And I'm in the café, have read a few nice things, feel fine [. . .]. But that doesn't alter the fact that for the past two years I get up in the morning without a single memory that has the power to console me [. . .]. (December 10, 1908, my trans.; cf. *Friends* 47)

Matters continued thus, day after day, week after week, month after month. Although he resented the effort it took, he was succeeding in the office and was proud of what he accomplished there. His immediate supervisor, Eugen Pfohl, considered Kafka one of his best employees and gave him glowing reports. But that professional success could hardly make up for the utter lack of progress in what Kafka considered is genuine calling or for the loneliness that seemed to engulf him. Neither his friendship with Brod nor a series of encounters with prostitutes could ameliorate his sense of solitude.

In summer 1909 he apparently gave up on 'Wedding Preparations.' He turned the manuscript over to Max, calling it 'my curse,' and refused to apologize for its incompleteness: 'If some pages are missing, which I was well aware of, it's quite all right, and even more telling than if I had torn the whole manuscript up.' (*Friends* 56).

That spring he had published a couple of snippets extracted from 'Description of a Struggle' in *Hyperion*, where 'Meditation' had appeared.[28] The pieces had little importance for Kafka or for the literary world. The author was not happy when he saw them in print, and this dissatisfaction may have prompted him to try once again to get the 'Description' story into better shape; but that project eventually collapsed.

Feeling ever more worn down, he concluded his first year with the insurance company by asking his employer for a raise in salary and some time off to recuperate from his fatigue. Both requests were granted. Max and his brother Otto had been thinking about a trip. The short holiday was eventful in that Brod came up with a scheme to get his friend writing again: he proposed that they both take notes and write up little articles about an air show in nearby Brescia. They could then compare notes and decide who had done the better job. The writing-contest idea may have seemed like a holdover from elementary school, but it was effective. Brod managed to get Kafka's reportage published a few weeks later in the newspaper *Bohemia*.[29] Though perhaps inconsequential, it was the only serious writing Kafka had done in months,[30] and it did prod Kafka back toward his vocation.

4. TRYING TO LIGHT THE FIRE (1910–12)

Perhaps the prodding was too gentle, or perhaps the pressures of the office were too great. In any case Kafka did little writing until spring 1910, when two important events occurred. First, the insurance firm promoted Kafka to the rank of *Concipist*, an official responsible for drafting legal documents. The promotion conferred both increased responsibility and civil service status. Second, and more important for us, Kafka committed himself in earnest to keeping the series of notebooks (he sometimes called it his 'diary') in which readers today are particularly interested.[31] The two events were not unrelated.

If the insurance company intended him to be a *Concipist* of business documents, it only echoed his own intention to be the *Concipist* of his own brand of literature. One of the earliest entries documents an important moment in Kafka's artistic development:

Finally, [. . .] I hit upon the idea of talking to myself again. I always came up with an answer when I really questioned myself, there was always something to be pounded out of me, out of this heap of straw that I have been for five months and which seems fated to be set afire during the summer and burned up more swiftly than the onlooker can blink. If only that would happen with me! (*Tag* 13–14; my trans.)[32]

The point of the diary was not primarily to keep a record of his life and its intimate secrets but to create an occasion to write—to write about anything at all—in the confident expectation that the result would somehow be illuminating. Such illumination as his writings would provide, however, seemed all too likely to result from their being burned by their author. We know that rejected pages did occasionally meet such a fate.[33] But by wishing that he himself might also be set afire, Kafka opened up another possibility: the chance of literary success by means of absolute self-immolation.

Here is Kafka's plan for his literary career: the self is to become fuel for the hot blaze of composition. Indeed, he would never believe in the truthfulness of his writing save when it roared from page to page in a fire hot enough to consume—and yet at the same time preserve and even enhance—the heap of straw on which it fed. Where else but in a burning bush would genuine spiritual truth be found?

We can see Kafka the *Concipist* in action in some of the early undated notebook pages, probably from the summer of 1910. He tried draft after draft of a text on the theme of the harm done to a certain first-person narrator by his education.[34] There are six different versions, one after the other. But as was so often the case, none of them satisfied their author, and none lit the heap of straw on fire. He gave up on that idea and moved on to something else.

Late in the summer he applied to the institute for a raise; they gave him almost everything he asked for. He went on an autumn trip to Paris with Max, but he got sick and had to return to Prague after only nine days: 'the doctor declared himself horrified by the appearance of my backside,' which was afflicted by a painful 'skin eruption' (*Friends* 67). There was no explanation for what had caused it, though Kafka suspected his travels were at fault. The incident would have had no importance whatsoever had it not been a portent of the increasingly terrible struggle Kafka was to have with his own body. Nearly his whole adult life would be dominated by illness and measures to fend off illness.

Kafka ended the year 1910 in deep melancholy and with a sense of failure. On December 17, he sent Brod a 'fragment of the novella' that he said he was laying aside (*Friends* 70). The novella was 'Description of a Struggle,' and the fragment was a small piece of a revision he had begun in 1909. In March Kafka had handed over to Brod the earlier draft (halted in 1907), not sure what its future would be. 'What pleases me most about the novella, dear Max, is that I have it out of the house' (*Friends* 64). Now in December he decided to scrap the revised version, too, except for half a dozen pages to be saved for later publication as an independent composition (subsequently titled 'Children on a Country Road').

On that same day he wrote in his notebook that he had 'put aside and crossed out so much, indeed almost everything I wrote this year.' He surmised that what he abandoned was 'five times as much as I have in general ever written' (*Diaries* 30). If his estimate was correct, then he wrote far more in this period than any of the surviving evidence would suggest. Granting that he did write so much, we must grant also that he unwrote it all so thoroughly that it might as well never have existed. It was his typical gesture of writing and retracting, a gesture he would repeat again and again during his relatively brief life. He retracted far, far more than he was willing to let stand before the public. Indeed most of what eventually made him world famous was material he had retracted.

The gloomy mood that prevails in the diaristic portions of the notebooks, especially at this time, is often hard to reconcile with the picture of Kafka painted by those who knew him well. Max Brod was well aware of the contradiction and took note of it at the time:

> *Le cœur triste, l'esprit gai*—this description fits him excellently and explains how it was that, even when he himself was in the most depressed state, he never, except perhaps in the hour of extreme intimacy, had a depressing, but rather a stimulating effect on those with whom he went about.[35]

Nearly everyone who had contact with him found him charming. His friend Max noted, with both objective accuracy and perhaps a hint of wistful envy: 'At all periods of his life women felt themselves drawn to Franz—he himself doubted he had this effect, but the fact cannot be disputed.'[36] Indeed, Kafka never lacked female attention—when he was in the mood to accept it.

The notebook regime had the desired effect in that its not-yet-filled pages enticed Kafka to write, or, when he neglected to do so, its still-unfilled pages stood as an objective reproach for his failure.

The notebook attests as well to his reading of Goethe, Kleist, and Dickens, perhaps hoping to find in them some spark to ignite the still unburned heap of straw. He was especially interested in Goethe's diaries and Kleist's letters, because he looked to these authors primarily for parallels with his own family situation and his difficulties in pursuing his calling as a writer. Kleist was a particular favorite, mainly because Kleist, too, had to struggle against family expectations and against the need to earn a living. Kafka could empathize completely. 'They ask him at home: Well, how are you going to earn a living, for that was something they considered a matter of course. You have a choice of jurisprudence or political economy' (*Diaries* 39).

Dickens was perhaps a different matter. Kafka's early work, particularly the America novel, bears traces of an attempt to emulate the British master. But even with Dickens it was the life of the writer as much as his work that held a fascination for Kafka. The first mention of Dickens in the notebooks speaks of 'reading about Dickens' and focuses on the author's experience of the genesis of a story within himself. What most attracted Kafka about the author of *David Copperfield* was the personal intensity with which the writer invested his stories:

> Is it so difficult and can an outsider understand that you [the author] experience a story right from the outset from within from the far point to the approaching locomotives of steel, coal, and steam, and you don't leave it even now but want to be chased by it and you have time for it, therefore you're chased by it and run before it on your own steam wherever it pushes and wherever you lure it. (*Tag* 38; my trans.)

It was a similar personal intensity that drew Kafka's attention to the works of Goethe, who had so much public success so early in life and had to balance his literary aspirations against his responsibilities as an official in the government of Sachsen-Weimar. That sort of balancing act naturally elicited Kafka's interest and sympathy.

Keeping such a balance was proving difficult for the young insurance attorney, even with a 'single-shift' job. Much of 1911 went by without anything happening to kindle the blaze he hoped for. Brod tried another of his schemes to get his friend to write: on a trip at the end of the summer to various destinations including Paris, he suggested that he and Franz keep parallel travel diaries. Kafka agreed, and though he called it a 'poor idea' (*Diaries* 433) he dutifully kept his end of the bargain. With that success behind him, Brod then proposed that the two of them write a joint novel about a pair of friends taking a vacation together.

A single chapter of this collaborative venture, *Richard and Samuel*, was written, and Brod managed to get it published the following year.[37] Subsequent chapters never materialized, however, and the idea of joint authorship appeared to die a permanent death. 'But lo and behold,' as Kafka once wrote, 'even that is only appearance' (*SelStor* 383; trans. modified). In a bizarre turn of events, Brod would indeed become Kafka's collaborator, although under the most terrible of circumstances. His coauthor would already be dead and buried. In spite of such a substantial disadvantage, the Kafka-Brod collaboration would deliver to the public some of the most influential works of twentieth-century literature.

In the fall of that year Franz found himself drawn into a family business operation conceived by his brother-in-law. His sister Elli had married a man named Karl Hermann in late 1910, and the new husband was hoping to exploit a business opportunity in the growing field of asbestos production. He received the enthusiastic support of his in-laws, and with their help The Prague Asbestos Works Hermann & Co. began operation in November of 1911. Franz endorsed the scheme, at least at the outset, and it was apparently his idea that some of the Kafka family money invested in the business be funneled through him. He 'borrowed' from his father sufficient funds to purchase a partnership in the firm. In this way control of the business could remain with the Kafka family, while at the same time leaving Elli's husband Karl as the titular head.

Franz was supposed to take an active, daily interest in the business, and indeed he promised to do so; but he quickly realized that he much preferred the role of silent partner. Whatever enthusiasm he had in the planning stage was quickly ground away by the nasty reality of asbestos manufacture. By the end of the year he deeply regretted ever having become involved:

The torture that the factory causes me. Why did I acquiesce when they made it my responsibility to work there in the afternoons. Now no one is using force on me, but my father forces me by his reproaches, Karl by his silence and my own guilt feelings. I don't know anything about the factory [. . .]. (*Tag* 327; my trans.)

He felt that 'through this empty effort spent on the factory' he was robbing himself of 'the few afternoon hours' that belonged to him. The loss of these precious hours, he feared, would inevitably result in 'the complete destruction of my existence' (*Diaries* 156). Dealing with the asbestos factory was therefore a deadly threat to his efforts at writing. Around this time, however, a new element entered his life that helped to preserve and foster those efforts.

On October 4, 1911, Kafka attended a dramatic performance given by a troupe of itinerant Yiddish players. Something about it struck a resonant chord in him. From then on, for about half a year, Kafka immersed himself in the Yiddish theater and in Yiddish language and literature. He attended many performances and developed personal friendships with members of the troupe. The leader of the group, Jitzhak Löwy,[38] would become a close if only temporary friend; and one of the actresses, a certain Mrs. Tschissik, would be the object of an intense but ineffectual crush.

The performances were crude, as Kafka realized, but artistic merit had little to do with his intense involvement. The performances opened up a doorway into a mode of Jewish existence that Kafka had never experienced before. Even in the very first performance he felt he was coming into contact with 'people who are Jews in an especially pure form because they live only in the religion, but live in it without effort, understanding, or distress' (*Diaries* 64). Such had not been his way of being a Jew, and it certainly was not his father's way, but it was enormously attractive. Both the characters in the plays and the actors who portrayed them partook of this disarmingly unconstrained form of Jewishness. The actors had the additional merit in Kafka's eyes of being artists who practiced a largely unappreciated and unremunerated art. In a metaphorical sense at least, theirs was an art of starvation. Kafka understood that sort of art:

> The sympathy [*Mitleid*] we have for these actors who are so good, who earn nothing and who do not get nearly enough gratitude and recognition, is really only pity [*Mitleid*] for the sad fate of many noble endeavors, above all our own. And that's why it's so immoderately strong, because externally it seems directed toward strangers but actually belongs to us. (*Tag* 98; my trans.)

Given the depth of his feeling it is hardly surprising that his 'Mitleid' rather quickly metamorphosed into personal affection.

The friendship with Löwy became close enough that Kafka invited him home to the family apartment. Löwy got along well with sister Ottla, but not at all well with father Hermann. The actor represented everything that Hermann Kafka loathed about the traditional East-European Jewish village culture out of which he himself had risen: its separateness from the main stream of European life, its embrace of and pride in that separateness, and above all its grimy poverty. As far as Hermann was concerned, the shabby Löwy's presence in the middle-class Kafka home was an affront. It was possibly even unsanitary. 'If you lie down with dogs, you get up with fleas,' he said, and even went so far as to compare the actor with 'Ungeziefer,' that is, with vermin (*Father* 25).

The insult would have remarkable consequences. The possibility that a human being—even a human being of talent and accomplishment—might somehow also exist in the form of vermin unfit to set foot in his father's house percolated in Franz Kafka's imagination for many months. He could not let go of it till he found a way to deal with the contradiction in literary form.

But that would come later. Several more immediate consequences developed from Kafka's acquaintance with the Yiddish plays and the actors who presented them. The experience incited Kafka to write. He filled page after page of his notebooks with accounts of the performances, his reactions to them, and his interactions with the performers. His revived interest in his Jewish roots led him to study Heinrich Graetz's *History of Judaism*, though he had to do so almost from the point of view of an outsider: 'it was at first stranger to me than I thought, and I had to stop here and there in order by resting to let my Jewishness collect itself' (*Diaries* 98–99). From this fresh perspective he began writing about the relationship of largely assimilated German-speaking Jews such as himself to the Yiddish language, a Germanic dialect regularly referred to as 'Jargon' (a German word borrowed from French) by many speakers of standard German, Jew and Gentile alike. He delivered his 'Introductory Talk on the Yiddish Language' as a warm-up for an evening of dramatic readings by Löwy on February 18, 1912.

The talk on Yiddish marks an important milestone in Kafka's life: a public reconciliation with his Jewish heritage and a public affirmation of an aspect of that heritage he had scarcely known before meeting the traveling actors. Kafka used the term 'Jargon' throughout the presentation (not 'jiddische Sprache,' as the translation might imply), but he did so in such a way as to take the sting out of its belittling dismissiveness and afford it dignity and respect. He surely spoke for himself when he assured the audience that they could, with the proper attitude, understand this 'lingo' quite well, despite the fact that it might sound utterly alien on first hearing:

> But if you relax, you suddenly find yourselves in the midst of Yiddish [*Jargon* here and in every subsequent case]. But once Yiddish has taken hold of you and moved you—and Yiddish is everything, the words, the Chasidic melody, and the essential character of this Eastern European Jewish actor himself—you will have forgotten your former reserve. Then you will come to feel the true unity of Yiddish, and so strongly that it will frighten you, yet it will no longer be fear of Yiddish but of yourselves.[39]

What frightened Kafka—and what he expected would frighten the audience as well—was the discovery that something that seemed foreign and external actually already resided deep within the self, where it might under certain circumstances reveal itself as very much at home. That discovery was scary, but it was also exciting; and it had implications that went far beyond the initial issue of Jewish ethnic unity, important though that issue surely was. It held the promise that an amazing world of wonders might lurk undetected in the depths of one's own being. One day Kafka would become the explorer and chronicler of that world, and his name would become synonymous with its alarming structure.

The talk on 'Jargon' was the climax of Kafka's preoccupation with the Yiddish theater and its actors. Shortly thereafter the troupe left town. Franz never saw the beloved Mrs Tschissik again, and his subsequent contact with Löwy was sporadic and ultimately unsatisfactory for both of them. They simply grew apart.[40] But the energy and excitement that had built up during the fall and winter carried over into the spring, and in March Kafka felt ready to launch a major new project: a novel set in America.

It was not entirely new. As a boy he had wanted to write such a novel and had actually worked on it now and then during his school days.[41] Now, however, he set out to treat the theme afresh with the skill and experience of a mature man, and with a revitalized sense of his own abilities. 'Today, while bathing, I thought I felt old powers, as though they had been untouched by the long interval' (*Diaries* 192).

On March 16, he made himself a promise: 'Tomorrow, today, I'll begin an extensive work [. . .]. I will not give it up as long as I can hold out at all. Rather be sleepless than live on in this way' (*Diaries* 196).

He appears to have kept to his vow. From spring to fall of 1912 he turned out page after page of a work he planned to call *Der Verschollene—The Missing Person*. As so often happened, all this work eventually failed to meet his standards. He destroyed the draft. But in the light from the funeral pyre of this rejected version Kafka began another with the same premise and the same title. The fire he had been hoping might ignite inside him was beginning to blaze up in earnest.

5. TO MARRY OR TO BURN (1912–13)

According to the King James Version, Paul says in First Corinthians that 'it is better to marry than to burn' (I Cor. 7.9). It is not very likely that Kafka knew the text, but it is not impossible. He read at least portions of the New Testament. Whether he knew Paul's apothegm or not, the alternative it proposes is one that was painfully familiar to him. If we allow Kafka's fire metaphor to operate in tandem with Paul's, we may imagine that the always ambivalent Franz would have understood precisely this choice as the existential dilemma of his maturity. As a series of decisions made over a period of years clearly demonstrates, however, he would have felt uncertain whether to accept Paul's valuation or reverse it.

The idea of marriage attracted him enormously: by founding his own household with a good Jewish wife he would establish his independence from his parents, make a place for himself in the world, and at the same time fend off a bleak future as a lonely bachelor. But a visit in September 1912 from his Madrid uncle Alfred Löwy, a successful man of the world who never married, confirmed many of his nephew's fears. Kafka wrote down how Alfred described a typical evening among the local dignitaries at an exclusive French pension:

I know everyone well already, sit down in my place with greetings to all, but because I'm in a peculiar mood speak not another word until I say good-bye when I'm leaving. Then I'm alone on the street and really can't see what this evening was good for. I go home and regret not marrying. (*Tag* 435; my trans.)

Even a luxurious bachelorhood like Uncle Alfred's obviously had grave disadvantages.

But so did marriage. In fact, when Kafka looked at the matter head on, the idea of marriage terrified and repulsed him. His highest aspiration was to burn in the blazing heat of literary creation, and that required hours of solitude every day. Marriage would bring an end to solitude; that was the whole point of marriage, after all; but it would also bring an end to art. For an artist it was better to burn than to marry.

The America novel he was working on had a close but paradoxical relationship to this dilemma. It never saw the light of day, but we can safely assume that it explored the same fundamental issue we find in the later version that survived: the relation of a person to his family and community. We can be sure of this, because the key idea in his America project—dating all the way back to his boyhood—was the traumatic severing of that relation through exile in a foreign land. Such a story is the inverse of a fantasy of marriage: it is a fantasy of having no family at all and of repeatedly losing any social connection that might serve as a substitute for a family. Kafka's imaginative exploration of what it would be like to have no relatives whatsoever posited a radical but plausible alternative to the daunting prospect of forming his own household.

Kafka followed through on his promise to keep going with the project for as long as his strength held out. He even took it with him on his summer vacation. Once again he traveled with Brod, this time to Leipzig and Weimar. Brod had arranged for them to meet in Leipzig with representatives of the newly founded Rowohlt publishing firm, to whom he had diligently touted Kafka as a rising star. One of the partners, Kurt Wolff, would shortly leave the firm to found his own company, taking Kafka with him. Wolff would be Kafka's only publisher during his lifetime, and their brief meeting in Leipzig formed the basis of a relationship that would assure Kafka's access to the German-speaking reading public all over central Europe. At this stage, however, the relationship consisted of little more than Kafka's halfhearted promise to submit something for Rowohlt to consider.

After one day in Leipzig the travelers moved on to Weimar, where they spent six days breathing in the atmosphere of Germany's most famous cultural center. Goethe and Schiller had both lived there, Schiller only for a short time in retirement but Goethe for most of his long life. Goethe's house and garden had been carefully preserved since his death in 1832, and they attracted throngs of tourists, Kafka and Brod among them. As usual, Franz almost immediately fell into a holiday crush. The girl was Margarete Kirchner, the exceptionally pretty teenage daughter of the man who took care of Goethe's house.

Kafka must have known it was hopeless from the outset. She had no interest in him, and no wonder: he was a shy, elderly gentleman of 29 years, Margarete's senior by the colossal span of over a decade. He must have seemed to her more like an embarrassing uncle than a suitor, but he tried to be a suitor all the same, buying her gifts and trying to make dates. She raised his hopes by promising to appear for this or that rendezvous and then dashed them by standing him up. When he left Weimar he wrote to her, and she sent him a few polite, noncommittal notes in return. One contained some pictures of her in various poses, along with a greeting from her mother—just to underscore the fact that this correspondence meant nothing personal. The photos were clearly not encouragement; they were a consolation prize for his abject failure; but he cherished them all the same, unable to suppress a sigh in praise of her beauty (*Friends* 83).

Max and Franz parted at the conclusion of their stay in Weimar. Brod returned to Prague and Kafka went on to spend three weeks at Jungborn, a health resort in the foothills of the Harz Mountains. Kafka thought his fragile health required some intervention, and an institution like Jungborn seemed just the tonic he needed. It was a trendy place in many ways, not unlike resorts one might find today along the coast of California, specializing in vegetarian diets, deep breathing, spiritual reorientation, and nude sunbathing. It promised to marshal the forces of nature to reintegrate and rebalance the energy centers of the body.[42] To the constantly ailing Kafka, all this seemed like a very good idea.

Along with the health regimen, Kafka maintained his artistic discipline. The resort had a 'writing room' where silence was enforced, and there he read quite a bit and wrote a little on his novel. Whatever progress he made on the manuscript was all in vain, of course, because shortly thereafter he destroyed every page. Working on the project in this place of natural healing did have a lasting effect, however, in that the subsequent version of the America novel would eventually lead its hero to a fictive Jungborn-like institution in 'Oklahoma.'

With his holiday behind him, Kafka had to get down to work, both at the office and at his own writing desk. He had promised, even if reluctantly, to send a manuscript to Wolff at Rowohlt, and therefore he needed to put something together out of the material lying in his drawer. The sense of obligation quickly gave way to frustration, however; he felt defeated before he even started. He wrote to Max, 'I am stopping,' and asked him not to be angry about it (*Friends* 84). But Brod would not be so easily prevented from getting more of his friend's work into print. He pushed Kafka to persevere, and on the evening of August 13, the two friends met at Max's house to go over the final order of the pieces for a book that was to be called, like Kafka's very first periodical publication, *Meditation*.

A relative of one of Max's in-laws happened to be visiting the Brods. She was a 24-year-old woman from Berlin named Felice Bauer. She didn't stay long, since she had to catch an early train the next morning. Kafka and Brod walked her back to her hotel, and that seemed to be the end of it. A few days later Franz wrote:

> Miss Felice Bauer. When I arrived at Brod's on 13 August, she was sitting at the table and looked to me like a serving girl. I wasn't at all curious about who she was, but rather took her for granted at once. Bony, empty face that openly wore its emptiness. Open throat. A blouse thrown on top. Seemed dressed for home, although as later became clear she by no means was. (I alienate her a little by such a close physical inspection. What a state I'm in now, for certain, alienated in general from everything good [. . .]) Almost broken nose. Blonde, rather straight unattractive hair, strong chin. As I was sitting down I looked at her closely for the first time, by the time I was seated I already had an unshakeable opinion. (*Tag* 431–32; my trans.)

He might have added, as he did when he wrote about Hedvig years earlier, 'such are the roundabout ways by which I recognize a girl's beauty and fall in love' (*Friends* 26).

Kafka was indeed falling in love, in his own extraordinarily roundabout fashion. He seemed to focus obsessive attention on every defect in the object of his affection, noting only a few features that might be considered attractive. But whether his thoughts about her were positive or negative, they kept nagging at him in the days that followed. He sent the *Meditation* manuscript off to Rowohlt, meager though it was, relieved to have the business at least temporarily out of his way. It left his mind free for further meditation on the woman from Berlin and on all the fantasies that she had awakened in him.

He explored ways to get back in touch with her. On September 20. he finally worked up the courage to send a letter, carefully typed out on company letterhead. 'In the likelihood that you no longer have even the remotest recollection of me, I am introducing myself once more: my name is Franz Kafka [. . .]' (*Felice* 5).

The correspondence with Felice, from almost the instant of its inception, released a surge of creative energy that would decisively shape the course of Kafka's existence. Two days later, in the night from September 22 to 23, 1912, he wrote the first piece of fiction that satisfied him: 'The Judgment.' On the night of the 23rd he started another story, but this one went nowhere and he quickly abandoned it. On the 25th he started from scratch on a new version of the America novel and kept working on it night after night, as if the story were chasing him and he had to keep running to stay ahead of it. By October 2 he had finished the opening chapter, which he read to Brod the following day.

The frantic pace continued, even though his precious free time was mostly taken up in the first weeks of October with obligations at the hated asbestos factory—obligations that cast him into a suicidal depression and increased even further his alienation from his family. He managed to keep working on the novel through it all, and by the end of the month he had completed four more chapters, for a total of five. A sixth ('The Robinson Affair') was done by the second week in November, but the ending failed to please him. He was already worried that the project was starting to come apart. 'At present,' he wrote to Brod, 'the whole novel is in an uncertain state' (*Friends* 91–92).

The difficulties he was having with the novel stopped further work on that project for a while, but it failed to slow the pace of Kafka's creative effort. On November 17, 1912 he set to work on a new idea: 'a short story that occurred to me in bed in my misery, and now troubles me and demands to be written' (*Felice* 47). Many elements went into the new story, among them Kafka's memory of hearing his father compare Yitzhak Löwy to vermin; the feeling that he belonged in a zoo after his summer debacle with the girl in Weimar (*Friends* 83); his increasing anger at his family over the asbestos factory; an imagined tiff with Felice; and even a weird idea that had occurred to Raban, the hero of the abandoned 'Wedding Preparations':

As I lie in bed I assume the shape of a big beetle, [. . .] the form of a large beetle, yes. Then I would pretend it was a matter of hibernating, and I would press my little legs to my bulging belly. (*ComStor* 56)

The story of the man transformed into a monstrously huge bug occupied him for the next several weeks, taking up what time was left over from the demands of the office and his extensive correspondence with Felice.

He wrote to her constantly, often several times a day, and in those letters one can read not only the progress of his growing attachment to Felice but also the progress of his most famous story. When he was depressed in his missives, it was not only Franz who was depressed: 'my story's hero has also had a very bad time today, and yet it is only the last lap of his misfortune' (*Felice* 58). Just as the completion of the story was in sight, the firm sent him out of town on business. His regime of writing was very sensitive to interruption, and it took him a while after his return to regain confidence in the piece. On 1 December he proclaimed, 'at last I am getting a little excited about my little story; my pounding heart is longing to drive me further and further into it' (*Felice* 80); and six days later he said it was done. Of course, since he was Franz Kafka, he was not happy: 'today's ending does not please me at all, it really could have been better, there is no doubt about this' (*Felice* 91).

He tried to return to work on *The Missing Person*, perhaps encouraged by holding in his hands the first bound copies of the Rowohlt *Meditation* collection that arrived on December 12. The story of Gregor Samsa's transformation had been a detour from the novel, which was still very much on his mind. How much it still occupied him can be glimpsed in the manuscript of 'The Metamorphosis,' where his habituated pen started to write the hero's name as 'Karl' several times before the author corrected it. But Kafka could no longer muster the zeal for the novel that had thrust the narrative forward during the fall, and he was unable to complete another chapter. On January 26, 1913 he told Felice the novel was 'falling apart':

> though I write nothing that could be said to be completely dissociated from myself, it has recently become altogether too disconnected; wrong things appear and cannot be made to disappear; it will be in greater danger if I continue to work on it than if I drop it for the time being. (*Felice* 171–72)

This surrender marked the end of one of the most intense productive periods in Kafka's career. It was unquestionably the most important, as he knew at the time. He believed he had finally discovered the right way to produce fiction and considered that discovery—as have nearly all his readers after him—the crucial event that established him as a genuine artist. With 'The Judgment,' 'The Metamorphosis,' and 'The Stoker' (the opening chapter of *The Missing Person*, the only piece of the novel Kafka published), the characteristic fictional world of Franz Kafka was born.

6. FELICE, PART I (1913–15)

But that world immediately went dormant. Kafka was unable to make any progress on his fiction for months. All his energy for writing went into the office (where he was promoted to 'Vice Secretary'), his letters, and a few notebook entries. He dedicated all his emotional resources to his relationship with Felice and to the quandary into which that relationship forced him: to marry or to burn. The very urge to bond with her for the long term seemed to stiffen his resistance to the life of a family man. The equal power of the two forces pulling him apart is especially apparent in the letter of June 16, 1913, in which he asks Felice if she would consider marrying him. The proposal takes up only a few words of the very long letter, the bulk of which presents a very convincing case *against* the whole preposterous idea. He explains that he is sick; that he is subject to bad moods; that he cannot get along with people; that he has a bad memory; that he is irrational, inexperienced, and ignorant; that he has no skill at telling stories; and that taken all in all he is 'nothing, absolutely nothing' (*Felice* 270). Would she, in spite of all this, consent to become his wife?

No prosecuting attorney could have come up with a more damning indictment of the prospective bridegroom. It remains a wonder that Felice was willing to accept such a peculiar proposal. As soon as she did accept, however, Kafka began to get cold feet. He drew up in his notebook a 'summary of all the arguments for and against my marriage' in which there was one item in favor, six against (*Diaries* 225). Not surprisingly, he almost immediately contrived an excuse to put off any official engagement. The apartment he had selected as their new home would not become available until May 1914, so no wedding could take place for months.

The summer went by with the relationship continually on the edge of breaking apart. Felice declined Franz's invitation to visit Prague during her vacation. She went to the North Sea. Nor did he visit her in Berlin when his holiday came. He arranged instead to take a vacation by himself at the conclusion of a business trip to Vienna. He went on to Trieste and Venice, feeling terrible the whole time, and finally back to Riva on Lake Garda, where he had visited before with Max in 1909.

As had happened before on summer holidays—in Zuckmantel, Triesch, and Weimar—Kafka met a girl and fell in love. The scenario was by now familiar: the object of his affections was completely inappropriate, another teenager just like the crush of the previous year, and a Christian to boot. Even worse, this affair was also a betrayal, since he was allegedly in love with and informally engaged to marry Felice. But the Riva girl, about whom we know little except that she came from Switzerland,[43] hit him with the force of a steam locomotive. Years later Kafka remembered her as one of only two women he had ever been 'intimate with,' though exactly what that meant remains unclear. Intimacy did not necessarily imply sex for Kafka, who could declare with chilling sincerity: 'Coitus as punishment for the happiness of being together' (*Diaries* 228).

Whatever happened, Kafka acknowledged that he must have been 'utterly confused' to have become entangled in such an affair (*Diaries* 365). Confused or not, he was deeply affected. 'The stay in Riva was very important to me. [. . .] The sweetness and sorrow of love. To be smiled at by her in the boat. That was most beautiful of all' (*Diaries* 232; 234–35). The whole thing lasted only ten days, but its effects lingered on through the rest of the year. At the end of December he confessed his indiscretion to Felice. His letter both candidly set forth the Riva girl's profound impact and at the same time purported to find in this infidelity a benefit to his relationship with Felice: 'Paradoxical as it may seem, even this helped to make my feelings about you clearer to me. Besides, the Italian girl knew [. . .] my sole aim was to marry you' (*Felice* 335). And indeed at the beginning of January 1914 he not only wished Felice a happy New Year, he also renewed his proposal of marriage, insisting: 'And now decide, Felice!' (*Felice* 338).

Franz was asking Felice to make her decision in the face of exceedingly difficult circumstances, given his confession. But circumstances were about to become even more difficult, ironically as a result of a scheme Felice had designed to improve matters. She had asked Grete Bloch, a friend of hers, to act as intermediary and calm the rough waters that were threatening to swamp the Kafka-Bauer relationship. Grete, who worked in Vienna as well as Berlin, had easier access to

Prague than did Felice herself. In late October 1913 Felice sent her to visit Franz in hope of getting a clearer sense of where the 'engagement' stood. She did so, convincing Kafka to take a trip to Berlin in early November to speak with Felice directly. Unfortunately the trip was a fiasco, as he dutifully reported in a detailed letter to Grete.

Thus began a correspondence between Franz and Grete that went on for almost a year. The situation invited and indeed in some cases even required the sharing of confidences, leading perhaps inevitably to a certain intimacy. By early February 1914 it was becoming clear that Kafka was at least as interested in his connection with the intermediary as in his troubled engagement to the prospective bride. He wrote to Grete:

> I kept trying to get closer to you by breaking out of an impenetrable inhibition that simultaneously urged me forward and held me back, and despite all my nice self knowledge I blamed you for my failure. And yet this is just because you became acquainted with me through F. [. . .] But now it's very different: you are no longer a stranger to me, especially since the last letter [. . .]. And you should no longer add when speaking of yourself: 'the fact that you can't be interested in this.' (February 1, 1914, my trans.; cf. *Felice* 342–43)

Because Grete's letters to Kafka were not preserved, with one exception, it is difficult to assess Grete's role in this epistolary flirtation, but after several months she finally called a halt. In her single surviving letter to Franz (July 3, 1914), she professed to be taken aback by his interest: 'Could anything appall me more than your letter of yesterday [. . .]? Words, doctor, all but fail me' (*Felice* 430).

One might conclude that Grete had never been more than casually involved. But there is a twist to the story. Many years later Grete wrote a confessional letter to friend; and that letter perhaps unintentionally started a rumor that she had become pregnant by Kafka and had born him a son who died in childhood.[44] No one who has looked carefully into the matter finds the tale plausible, but it has at the very least kept alive the sense that Grete was far more deeply involved with Franz than her one extant letter to him would lead us to believe.

In the meantime, Felice had not responded to Kafka's New Year's command that she decide. She did not do so until late March, when quite suddenly she accepted his renewed proposal. No one knows for certain what brought Felice around, but her new decisiveness set the stage for a public engagement that was announced at a formal reception in Berlin on May 30, 1914. Everyone in both families seemed pleased, with one exception: Franz detested every moment. He felt that he was treated like a criminal. 'Had they set me down in a corner bound in real chains, placed policemen in front of me, and let me look on simply like that, it could not have been worse' (*Diaries* 275).

With an engagement begun so felicitously, what could possibly go wrong? No one looking at the matter in retrospect can feel the least surprised at the subsequent debacle. Grete, who was still the object of Kafka's warm attention, concluded at last that she ought to take action and warn her dear friend Felice that her fiancé was not the most enthusiastic of bridegrooms. She gathered up a carefully edited collection of letters she had received from Franz and showed them to Felice. On Kafka's next trip to Berlin in July he found himself confronted in his hotel room by an angry Felice, who had brought along for support her sister Erna and Grete Bloch. It remains unclear what Grete's role was, but Kafka thought she had somehow judged and condemned him. When the confrontation ended, so did the engagement. Elias Canetti was probably right in thinking that the outcome was 'just as he had wished.'[45] Kafka went swimming at a public pool the next day, then left Berlin and spent two weeks on holiday at the seashore.

As terrible as the ordeal in the hotel had been, it relieved Kafka of a huge burden. Once back from his vacation he experienced a new influx of artistic energy and began writing for the first time in a year and a half. Now that it was clear he was not going to marry, he could concentrate on stoking the creative fire. On July 29 he began a story about someone named Josef K., the 'son of a rich merchant' (*Diaries* 297). That idea went nowhere, but a new one with a hero of the same name occurred to him a couple of weeks later. And then he had an idea for something else, something about a man working for a railway in Russia. That, too, quickly ran out of steam, and he returned to Josef K. Within a matter of days he had written the first chapter of *The Trial* and proceeded (probably) directly to work on the last.[46] With the beginning and ending settled, he began filling in the middle.

Kafka's work was going well, but in August of 1914 the world in general was not going well at all, a contrast starkly illustrated by

Kafka's notebook entry for August 2: 'Germany has declared war on Russia—Swimming in the afternoon' (*Diaries* 301). The outbreak of the Great War affected everyone in Europe, but by no means equally. For Kafka, who was declared exempt from military service on account of his work with the insurance company, it turned out to have certain advantages. With the departure of his sister Elli's husband upon call-up of the reserves, Elli moved back in with her parents, and Franz took over her apartment. He still took his meals in the family home, but he at last had a place all to himself with privacy to work.

And work he did. His productivity in fall 1914 was astonishing. During a couple of weeks off from the office he progressed on *The Trial* and completed a new story, 'In the Penal Colony.' On top of that, he went back to *The Missing Person* with a new chapter about a 'back to nature' theater distantly reminiscent of his days at Jungborn. He got started on a couple of other ideas, too, one about a man who attempts to defend a village schoolmaster's pamphlet about a giant mole seen in the neighborhood, and another about an Assistant District Attorney who longs to become a Chief District Attorney or something even more exalted.

Even with all this achievement Kafka was often assailed by doubts. His creativity depended on very special circumstances and was easily disrupted:

> I feel all too keenly the limits of my abilities, which are doubtless rather narrow unless I am completely gripped by an idea [*ergriffen*]. And I believe that even in the grip of inspiration [*im Ergriffensein*] I am pulled inside these narrow limits, which I then no longer feel, of course, because I am being pulled. Nevertheless, inside these limits there is room to live, and therefore I'll probably exploit them to a contemptible extent [*bis zur Verächtlichkeit*]. (*Tag* 675–76; my trans.)

The word he uses for inspiration is 'Ergriffensein,' which implies being grasped by some powerful, not necessarily positive force. It is completely unpredictable, and it can go away as quickly as it comes.

In winter 1915 it went away. Even though he had made enormous progress on the middle sections of *The Trial*, he failed to finish it. He also gave up on 'The Village School Master,' the 'Assistant District Attorney,' the ending of *The Missing Person*, and the Russian railway story. The only thing he actually finished was 'In the Penal Colony.'

In February he started another new story, this one about an aging bachelor named Blumfeld who would like to have a pet; but once again the author was unable to finish. On February 15, 1915 he wrote in his notebook, 'Everything at a halt' (*Diaries* 331).

7. FELICE, PART II (1915–18)

Late in October 1914 Kafka had resumed his correspondence with Felice. The immediate occasion was a letter from Grete suggesting that renewed relations were possible. Kafka was, as always, ambivalent, but he sent Felice a long letter asserting that 'nothing whatever has changed between us in the past 3 months, either for the better, or for the worse' (*Felice* 436). The letter was voluminous, but there was nothing in it that suggested reconciliation was likely. Then on November 5, 1914 Felice's father died of a sudden heart attack. This sad event brought about renewed contacts between the Kafkas and the Bauers, and even though Franz remained on the sidelines, he was again thinking about how much he would 'like to try again to have F. back.' At the end of November he was resolute: 'I'll really try it, if the disgust I feel for myself doesn't prevent me' (*Diaries* 318; trans. modified).

After a few more letters, and perhaps prodded by his growing conviction that his creative fire was going out, Kafka agreed to meet Felice again. Making travel arrangements was difficult because of wartime restrictions, but they planned to meet on the weekend of January 23, 1915 in Bodenbach, on the border between Germany and Austrian Bohemia. Much might have happened at that rendezvous if Kafka had been inclined to let it happen. Felice apparently was so inclined. She went so far as to join him in his hotel room for a couple of hours, something a young lady did in those days only when she was willing to permit the ultimate intimacy. But matters never went so far. Instead, Kafka read to her a section from *The Trial* describing a man standing before a doorway meant only for him, a doorway he is invited to pass through, a doorway which he nonetheless declines to enter. Both of them understood the peculiar relevance of the story to their personal circumstance and joked about it with 'coarse remarks' (*Diaries* 329). Although he enjoyed the joke, Kafka refused to go through the door Felice had opened for him.

Kafka wrote little in 1915. He may have worked now and again on the Blumfeld story up until early April, when he could go no further, whether he thought it finished or not. From then until late fall 1916 he wrote no fiction. He wrote, of course; he wrote business documents and letters, and he wrote occasional diaristic entries in his notebook; but it was not the sort of writing he wanted to be doing. The notebook entries are a litany of self-accusations: 'A well gone dry' (*Diaries* 339); 'Completely idle' (*Diaries* 342); 'Am I broken? Am I in decline?' (*Diaries* 350); 'Days passed in futility, powers wasting away in waiting' (*Diaries* 352); and so on, week after week. There seemed to be no force within himself or available from outside that could break his paralysis.

He did have some literary success in the outside world. In fall 1915 'The Metamorphosis' appeared in print, and almost simultaneously the prominent—and independently wealthy—writer Carl Sternheim asked that his award money for the highly prestigious Fontane Prize be passed on 'to the young Prague writer Franz Kafka as a token of appreciation for the *Meditation*, "The Stoker," and "The Metamorphosis."'[47] Even this very public gesture of recognition failed to rouse Kafka out of his creative doldrums. He wanted to write, but somehow he could not. Even the notebook entries dried up from time to time: from May to September of 1915; and again from late December 1915 to late April of the following year.

His renewed relations with Felice churned on with little sign of progress. They got together in May of 1915, and again a month later, in a spirit of polite friendship but without any sign of resurgent affection. He was unhappy in mind and body, afflicted by insomnia and recurrent headaches, and would not have been good company for anyone. In spring 1916 he tried to get a period of leave without pay from the insurance firm, but instead his boss promised him a summer vacation—in spite of a wartime edict forbidding vacations for those deferred from military service.

After taking a business trip to Marienbad, a hot-springs resort near the Bavarian border, he decided that the spa there would be the perfect spot for his vacation. He told Felice about it, and she was waiting for him when he got there on July 3, 1916 (his 33 birthday). He was not pleased. After three days with her, he wrote in the notebook: 'Impossible to live with F.' (*Diaries* 364). But then, for reasons still unclear, their relationship suddenly warmed up again.

On July 10 the couple jointly sent a letter to Felice's mother in which Kafka addressed Frau Bauer as 'dear Mother' and told her that matters between him and her daughter had changed 'for the better' (*Felice* 473). In a letter to Brod of July 12–14, he explained that

> since it could not have gotten worse, it got better. [. . .] I was never afraid of anything as much as being alone with F. before the wedding. Now it's different and it's good. Our agreement is in brief: to get married shortly after the end of the war; to rent 2 or 3 rooms in a Berlin suburb, with each of us taking economic responsibilities for only for himself [. . .]. (July 12/14, 1916, my trans.; cf. *Friends* 117–18)

The assertion that 'being alone with F. before the wedding' no longer frightened him has suggested to some that Franz finally went through the erotic door that Felice had opened for him in Bodenbach.[48] We will probably never know, but Kafka's language seems to hint that he did.

The terms of the agreement outlined in the letter to Max may seem innocuous to a reader of the early twenty-first century, but in the early twentieth they represented a huge concession on Felice's part. They meant that her husband would not support her; that she would have to keep her job and probably give up the chance to have children; that she would have to forego the prestige of being married to a man with a respectable profession; that she would have to keep house herself in a tiny apartment; and that the couple would live in relative poverty. He had driven a hard bargain indeed.

In spite of Felice's evident willingness to do nearly anything to meet his needs, he nearly immediately started looking for a way out. Later that summer he even had fantasies of joining the army (*Diaries* 369). He did not share these reservations with Felice, for whom he maintained a polite and affectionate demeanor in his letters, and presumably in person as well. They had a few spats, bur for the most part they continued calmly down the path toward marriage.

In fall 1916 Kafka's writing career hit another low. He accepted an invitation to give a public reading at an art gallery in Munich, and chose to read from the as yet unpublished 'Penal Colony.' The audience was not pleased, the critics were not pleased, and Kafka himself was not pleased. When Felice asked about the reviews, he was unsparing of himself. The review from the *Münchner-Augsburger Zeitung*, he wrote, was

> somewhat kinder than the first, but since it is in complete agreement with the basic opinion of the other, its kinder tone merely

reinforces the actual grandiose failure of the evening. [. . .] In any case I have to admit that these opinions are justified, indeed almost true. (*Felice* 536)

But since things could not have become worse, they took a turn for the better. Thanks to his youngest sister Ottla, Kafka acquired a particularly good place to work. It was a tiny little house at 22 Alchemists Lane next to the Hradschin Castle wall. The doorway was so low that Kafka had to stoop to get in, and when Ottla first showed it to him he thought it was awful. Ottla, always a person of independent mind, found it charming and decided to rent it. Kafka did not know, but she intended to use it as a secret trysting place to meet with her gentile boyfriend, the man she would later marry. She fixed up the tiny interior (a mere eight by eight feet), and when her brother was unable to find a suitable place for himself, turned it over to him as his writer's refuge in the evenings. If Franz's nightly presence seriously complicated Ottla's amorous encounters, she never let on.

The little room turned out to be just what Franz needed. 'I am living in Ottla's house,' he told Felice. 'And better than at any time in the past two years' (*Felice* 537). After eating an evening meal provided by his ever-generous baby sister, he would write. At first he stayed only till 8 or 9 p.m., but after he got used to the place he was often there till midnight. A wartime coal shortage prevented the fire in the grate from getting very warm, but the fire in Kafka's creative center blazed as brightly as ever it had. New stories emerged in quick succession during the winter of 1916–17.

He was working with nearly the same ferocious consistency as in the fall of 1912 and the second half of 1914, but his progress did little to relieve his fundamental anxiety. He explained it to Felice:

My life goes on in a steady fashion within the confines of my innate and in a sense threefold misfortune. If I can't get anything done I'm unhappy; if I can there isn't enough time; and if I hope for the future then there's the immediate fear, or rather all kinds of fears, that I won't be able to work then either. A precisely calculated hell. But—and this is the main point—it's not without its good moments. (December 20, 1916, my trans.; cf. *Felice* 538)

If one can judge by the array of works he actually completed on Alchemists Lane, there must have been a greater than usual number of good moments.

In spring 1917 Ottla decided to try her hand at farming. Elli's husband owned a farm in the north Bohemian countryside, and Ottla went off to work there, giving up the little house next to the palace wall. Although Franz was forced to move, he was lucky enough to secure a place he had been hoping to get: a couple of large rooms with electric light, a pleasant view, and (best of all) quiet neighbors. It had no bathroom and was constantly chilly, but it was better than anything he had previously experienced. He even imagined that he and Felice might live there.

His pace of work slackened. He spent much of his free time studying Hebrew—not the biblical language he had struggled with for his bar mitzvah, but the spoken Hebrew favored by Zionists. But even though he was no longer burning quite so hot, he furthered his literary career by sending Kurt Wolff a collection of stories that had emerged from the creative spurt of the winter and spring. Wolff wrote back almost instantly that he wanted to publish them. The *Country Doctor* collection would not come out until 1919, after the disruptions of the war were past, but the project was all but settled in the summer of 1917.

Also all but settled was the matter of his future with Felice. In July she came to visit, and while she was in town the couple formally announced their engagement. They made the socially prescribed visits to family and friends and even had a formal portrait photograph taken for the occasion. Within a matter of a few weeks, however, something happened that made all these plans seem pointless: during the night of August 9, 1917 Kafka spat up massive amounts of blood.

At first the doctor Kafka consulted tried to wave the matter off as a minor case of bronchitis; then he admitted that it might be a bit more serious, 'a catarrh of the apex of the lung.'[49] Finally Max convinced him to see a specialist, who did not hesitate to diagnose tuberculosis and recommend treatment in a sanatorium. The patient accepted the diagnosis but rejected the prescribed cure. He applied for retirement from the insurance company and got instead a leave of absence for three months. On September 12, 1917 Franz left Prague to join Ottla on the farm in Zürau.

He believed that life away from Prague, away from the office, away from an unhealthy lifestyle, would work a cure better than any on offer from a sanatorium. And it might have worked. Many Europeans of the time recovered from tuberculosis infections and went on to live healthy lives. Kafka, however, did not really believe that any cure was likely. He confided in Felice:

> For secretly I don't believe this illness to be tuberculosis, at least not primarily tuberculosis, but rather a sign of my general bankruptcy. [. . .] And now I am going to tell you a secret [. . .]: I will never be well again. Simply because it is not the kind of tuberculosis that can be laid in a deckchair and nursed back to health, but a weapon that continues to be of supreme necessity as long as I remain alive. (*Felice* 545–46)

It was a terrible thing to say, in effect a confession that the disease was an integral part of who he was. As Brod quite perceptively commented, 'You are happy in your unhappiness' (*Felice* 546). Kafka complained about his friend's 'reproach' and told him he ought to adopt 'a different tone,' but he could not reject the assessment as inaccurate (*Friends* 154–55).

The disease was a useful tool, and Kafka intended to make use of it. 'You have a chance,' he wrote to himself in his notebook, 'as far as it is possible to make a new beginning. Don't throw it away' (*Diaries* 383). His first act of exploitation was obtaining extended leave from the office; his second and most dramatic was dissolving his engagement with Felice. She came to visit him at Christmastime in Prague and offered to stand by her commitment to him even in the face of his current adversity. He would not accept such a self-sacrificing offer. Instead, he took his weeping fiancée to the railway station and waved goodbye. They never saw each other again. Eighteen months later, she married someone else. When he heard about it, Kafka seemed pleased by the news.

He went back to the farm at Zürau, for the first time in many years freed from both the office and the pressures of his on-again-off-again relations with Felice. Thanks to the intercession of Ottla and his parents, the company had extended his leave—with full pay—through the winter. He therefore started the year 1918 in dramatically altered circumstances. With the grim assistance of a life-threatening illness, he had made the new beginning he had urged upon himself.

8. JULIE, MILENA, AND THE PROGRESS OF DISEASE (1918–21)

The sojourn on the farm was supposed to be a time of healing and relaxation, and indeed Kafka did not exert himself unduly. He helped on the farm a bit but prudently avoided taxing his afflicted lungs. He wrote very little, although he took his notebooks with him. He read quite a bit, especially Søren Kierkegaard. As with Goethe, Kleist, and Dickens, the principal spur to Kafka's interest was the biographical resonance he experienced. Kafka was—predictably—fascinated by the Danish writer's troubled engagement to Regine Olsen, which Kierkegaard broke off on the grounds that his character made him unsuitable for marriage.

The *Country Doctor* collection was in press in the winter of 1918. Kafka assumed it would be his last book, and perhaps prompted by the angel of death he asked that the publisher add a dedication to the author's father:

> Not that I could appease my father in this way; the roots of our antagonism are too deep, but I would at least have done something; if I haven't emigrated to Palestine, I will at any rate have traced the way there on the map. (*Friends* 201)

It would not be the last time he would trace the way to Palestine on the map without actually going there. But the intention was sincere. With the shadow of the disease constantly darkening his steps, he thought more and more earnestly about a return to Zion.

The return to the Holy Land was a distant dream; the return to Prague was an immediate reality. At the end of April he went back to his home city, to his job, and to his former residence in his parents' apartment. His rest cure apparently had been effective: he was feeling much better. He even seemed to be rid of the headaches that had plagued him for so long—long before there were any signs of TB. He had achieved a certain physical and spiritual serenity that helped him sail between the Scylla and Charybdis of the increasingly antagonistic Czech and German factions in the insurance company. He got along well with everyone, and they all liked him, even though the Germans thought of him as one of those Jews and the Czechs thought of him as one of those Germans.

He led a quiet life through the final summer of the war. He did not try to write fiction. He studied Hebrew, did a little gardening, went swimming, took walks, and appeared to have made a substantial recovery. There is reason to believe, in fact, that Kafka might have done as many others had and gone on to live a normal healthy life span. But on October 14, he caught the 'Spanish' flu in the great pandemic of 1918. Already run down by the TB, he nearly died within days.

But he did not succumb. It took three weeks, but he returned from the brink of death to resume his work at the insurance company on November 17. While he had been lying in bed, the company, along with the nation and much of the rest of the world, had changed dramatically. There was no more Austro-Hungarian Empire; there was the Republic of Czechoslovakia, with a president instead of a king. And at the office the Czechs had ousted the Germans from their positions of authority, including Kafka's immediate superiors. Kafka himself was an exception, perhaps as a defense against charges of a wholesale purge of the Teutonic element.

Kafka was paying very little attention to all this. Within a few days of his return to work he suffered a relapse. Medical advice called for another rest cure, and the new administration let him off for the rest of the fall. The farm at Zürau was no longer an option; it was being sold off; so he found another rural sanctuary in the little Bohemian town of Schelesen (Želizy). He stayed till Christmas, when his leave ran out. But it was clear to everyone that he was still in no condition to return to the office. Yet another release from work was granted, and eventually the firm extended that leave through the whole winter of 1919.

The little boardinghouse where Kafka stayed in Schelesen was populated entirely by people with symptoms of tuberculosis. One of the guests was a young lady of 29 years named Julie Wohryzek, the daughter of Jewish shoemaker from the suburbs of Prague who was also the sexton of the local synagogue. The two semi-invalids struck up a warm friendship, and although it might have been difficult for an outsider to understand the basis of their sympathy, Kafka's description of Julie in a letter to Brod contains details that suggest why the older Dr. K. found her attractive:

Not Jewish, and yet not not-Jewish, not German and yet not not-German, crazy about the movies, about operettas and comedies, wears face powder and veils, possesses an inexhaustible and nonstop store of the brashest Yiddish expressions, in general very ignorant, more cheerful than sad—that is about what she is like. (*Friends* 213)

Their friendship resumed after Kafka returned to Prague at the conclusion of his extended leave. During the spring and summer they spent a great deal of time together. He read to her a lot, and they discussed Zionism. Julie apparently had no expectation or wish for anything more serious, but in the middle of the summer Kafka suddenly decided they ought to get married.

Because Kafka's letters to Julie were lost, information about their relationship is sparse. Almost everything we know about it comes from the *Letter to His Father* and a long letter Kafka wrote to Julie's sister in November 1919, after the romance had cooled. His explanation for his push toward marriage, a push that Julie had not initiated or encouraged but did not resist once it commenced, was complicated and doubtless colored by a need to justify himself:

> I had no choice, for since my nature was striving toward marriage, I regarded the relatively peaceful happiness of the existing state as unjustified and thought that I might at least provide it with a subsequent justification by marriage or at least by an extreme, unsparing effort to arrive at marriage. (*Friends* 219)

Furthermore, he was sure that Julie, unlike Felice, would be such a perfect partner that the couple could have a genuine 'love-marriage'; and to top it all, the most convincing of all 'proof of the correctness of what I wanted to do' came in the form of his father's bitter opposition to his only son's alliance with the daughter of a lowly shammes. If father Hermann was against it—which he was, in the most extreme and obnoxious manner—then son Franz could only conclude he must be on the right track (*Friends* 218).

But he was not on the right track, as he quickly realized. After having lobbied for a short engagement and early wedding in October, he let circumstance intervene to bring the headlong rush into matrimony to an embarrassing halt. The apartment the couple had contracted to buy and live in as newlyweds was taken by a higher bidder just two days before the scheduled ceremony, and the wedding had to be put off. Kafka proposed that it be put off indefinitely, thinking Julie would 'be content with fidelity or love outside marriage' (*Friends* 220). Julie seems to have consented to this arrangement. They continued to see each other, still technically engaged, for several more months, but Franz evidently no longer believed there would ever be a wedding.

Kafka felt some combination of relief, frustration, and guilt over this debacle. Brod convinced him that he needed to get away, so he arranged for a two-week leave in November 1919. He and Max went back to Schelesen, where Franz sat down and wrote a kind of post-mortem on the failed engagement to Julie in the form of a long, essayistic *Letter to His Father*. Kafka claimed in the letter that he wanted to ease the tension between father and son that the engagement had brought to a crisis. It seems unlikely that such would have been the outcome if the document, which is unsparing of the feelings of both parties, had ever reached its intended recipient. But Franz never delivered it to Hermann, who remained unaware of its existence. Just as well, perhaps.

Kafka suffered from fevers from time to time, but he was strong enough to go back to work, which he did in late November. Although it is tempting to imagine Kafka as merely a minor functionary in the great insurance bureaucracy, the truth is quite different.[50] At the end of the year he was promoted to Institute Secretary, a position equivalent to that of a vice president in an early-twenty-first-century American firm. He was put in charge of one of the four departments of the company, a substantial increase in his responsibility, but compensated by relief from having to draft so many documents himself. Since the official language of the firm was now Czech, it was in fact better to leave that to others.

Kafka's Czech was good enough that he could appreciate the stylistic subtleties of others, but he was not capable of producing them himself. He was liable to make mistakes in grammar and spelling, and so he always got help when he needed to produce a document in truly fluent Czech. It was perfectly understandable, then, that he was pleased to grant permission to someone else to translate his fiction into Czech. In the fall of 1919 he had received a letter seeking such permission from a young woman in Vienna named Milena Jesenská (or Milena Jesenská-Polak, as she was sometimes known during her marriage to Ernst Polak).

Milena was looking for work as a freelance translator because her philandering husband Ernst gave her no money and expected her to support herself, but all Kafka knew was that someone thought highly enough of his work to believe it worth translating. He had actually met Milena briefly in Prague and knew (and liked) her husband, who socialized regularly with Brod and Werfel and thought of himself as a man of letters. It may have been Ernst who suggested that Milena read Kafka in the first place.

Over the winter Kafka heard nothing from Milena, but he had arranged for Kurt Wolff to send her copies of his published works. Wolff was moving ahead with the projects that had been delayed by the war: 'In the Penal Colony' came out in the spring, and *A Country Doctor* appeared in December 1919. The author went back to his notebooks and tried his hand at aphoristic writing, avoiding any commitment to large-scale projects. He kept calm, visited with Julie, and weathered the occasionally severe flare-ups of his illness. The doctor who consulted for the insurance company was concerned about further decline, and so he recommended that the Institute Secretary be put on leave for eight weeks. It took a while to make arrangements, but Kafka finally left Prague on April 2, 1920 for a rather posh resort hotel in Merano, Italy.

He wrote to Milena inquiring about the translations, and she wrote back immediately. Thus began an exchange of letters that in a remarkably short time metamorphosed into an epistolary romance, she writing in Czech, he in German. The rapidity with which their relationship heated up can be attributed in part to their shared experience of affliction and of illness (she also had symptoms of pulmonary disease), but most of all to Milena's remarkable intelligence and sensitivity. He could tell immediately, from the drafts of her translation of 'The Stoker' she sent him for comment, that she understood exactly what he was about. At the beginning of May, only a few weeks into their long-distance relationship, he told Brod in a letter:

> She is a living fire, of a kind I have never seen before, a fire that in spite of everything burns only for him [her husband]. Yet at the same time she is extremely tender, courageous, bright, and commits everything she has to her sacrifice, or to put it another way, perhaps, has gained everything by her sacrifice. Yet what kind of man must he be who could evoke that. (*Friends* 237)

Kafka expresses not so much jealously as awe at the hold Polak had over Milena, amazed that any man could command the affection and loyalty of such a dazzling woman. Beyond the amazement, though, is the clear sense that he found in her precisely what he had always hoped to make of himself: a living fire.

Kafka was still in Merano in June, thanks to an extension of his leave, and by that time his intimacy with Milena had advanced enough that he was addressing her by the familiar *Du* and asking that she reciprocate. In spite of the fact that they had not yet met in person (except fleetingly back in Prague, as strangers), they were already in love. She pressed him to return to Prague at the end of his vacation by way of Vienna so that they might have some time together. He resisted at first—he had already made a date to meet with Julie in Karlsbad—but ultimately he gave in. They spent four days together at the end of June and beginning of July 1920, and those four days turned out to be among the happiest days of Kafka's short life.

He could not stay longer. He had to get back to Prague, back to the office. Besides, there were substantial obstacles to their love: she had a husband, and he had a fiancée. At Milena's urging Kafka finally ended his engagement to Julie, although he did not stop seeing her. On her side, Milena was in no position to end her marriage with Ernst. It was not really a matter of deficient resources; it was primarily a matter of deficient will. Despite Polak's meanness, his lack of financial support, and his almost constant and very public affairs with other women, she still loved him. Kafka knew this, and he told her he knew it. 'Yes, you are right,' she wrote in reply, 'I do love him. But F[rank], I also love you' (*Milena* 84).

Kafka seems to have had some understanding of her attachment to Polak, but it could not help but be a source of tension. Milena wanted to live with Kafka, and she might have done so if she had been able to separate emotionally from Ernst. She had always been a flouter of convention ever since her school days. She had enraged and humiliated her Christian Czech Nationalist family by marring the Jewish Polak, and she would not have hesitated to take any other action she thought was right even if it meant scandal. In any case potential scandal was never the real barrier to a long-term relationship between Milena and Franz: it was her erotic attachment to Polak and his erotic attachment to his sickness unto death.

They met again later in the summer at Gmünd, an Austrian border town between Prague and Vienna, but they were unable to achieve again the happiness they shared in Vienna. She asked him if he had been faithful to her, to which he answered in the affirmative, though he chafed at the question. What could 'fidelity' mean in their relationship, when she was having regular sex with her husband? They did not meet like lovers; they confronted each other 'like strangers'

(*Milena* 166). Their correspondence continued, as did their friendship, but after Gmünd their romance simmered down. Kafka was certain she would never leave her husband and that their love had no future. He was half right. It was not until the summer of 1924, after she had written Kafka's obituary for a Czech newspaper, that Milena finally broke with Ernst.

In late summer, as both the weather and relations with Milena cooled down, Kafka tried to return to writing fiction. He had done almost nothing for two years, having convinced himself that his career as a writer was over. But he was still alive, still going to the office, and no longer obsessed with the possibility of a life with Milena. He came to the conclusion that he might as well resume his 'military service' of sleeping in the afternoon, taking an evening walk, then writing at night as long as his strength held out (*Milena* 169). He could not muster the energy for any big project, but various little ideas kept coming, and he kept writing them down.

Even this modest effort came to an end in December. His illness once again took precedence over everything else, and Kafka was placed on leave again. He left Prague for a cure in Matliary (now Matliare in Slovakia), where the high mountain air would supposedly help his ailing lungs. He would end up staying there for much of 1921.

9. RETIREMENT, DORA, AND THE FINAL ILLNESS (1921–24)

Kafka holed up in the little Matliary boarding house that passed for a sanatorium and went semi-dormant. He attempted no fiction, kept his letter-writing to a minimum, and even stopped doing much reading. He socialized a bit with the other patients, one of whom was a 21-year-old medical student from Budapest named Robert Klopstock. This remarkably warmhearted person attached himself to Kafka, who at least initially found the young man's admiration annoying. Franz could not understand Robert's almost instant devotion. He referred to him as 'the unfortunate medical student' and complained to his sister Ottla that he had never seen 'such a diabolical spectacle from close up. [. . .] In the Middle Ages he would have been regarded as possessed.'[51] In spite of this initial antipathy, the two developed a friendship that would mean much to Kafka later on.

All the quiet seemed to do some good. By August he was hiking in the mountains, and the medical authorities declared him sufficiently recovered to return home. He was back in the office on August 29, 1921, though each morning's effort left him so exhausted he had to go to bed immediately when the work day ended at 2 p.m. By mid-September the company physician was convinced another rest was needed, but Kafka continued with his office duties through September and October. During this time he received regular visits from Gustav Janouch, the aspiring young poet who would claim decades later to have kept an extensive record of everything Kafka said to him.[52]

Milena visited, too, causing both considerable stress and perhaps some bright moments. They were no longer lovers, but he still felt closer to her than to any other living person. In a remarkable demonstration of trust, he handed over to her a collection of his old quarto notebooks, the ones he referred to as his diaries. With this gift he communicated two things: his belief in her judgment, tact, and genuine affection; and his decision to commit himself not to her but to his erotic relationship with death. As Kafka had told Brod several months earlier, Milena's love had offered him 'the choice between life and death,' which for Franz Kafka was no choice at all (*Friends* 280).

He started making diary entries again in a new notebook on October 15, 1921, noting that it would be a 'different kind of diary' less concerned with keeping a memoir. He no longer felt the need to make notes of things to remember because he was himself 'a memory come alive' (*Diaries* 392). He spent a great deal of time lying in bed remembering things because he could not sleep at night. At the end of October he was once again placed on sick leave. This time he undertook a new health regimen at home under the care of his family physician. Unfortunately it was not effective, and Kafka's spirits weakened along with his lungs.

In the first weeks of January 1922 he slipped into a black depression. 'Everything seemed over with,' he wrote in his notebook, 'and even today there is no great improvement to be noticed' (*Diaries* 398). His doctor decided a radical change was needed. Since the doctor was planning to take his family on vacation to a resort in the mountains near the Polish boarder, he invited Kafka to come along. An extension of the patient's leave was quickly obtained, and at the end of January Kafka arrived in the snowy hills of Spindelmühle.[53] When he went to check in, he found that he had been listed in the reservation log as Josef K. 'Shall I enlighten them,' Kafka wondered to himself in his notebook, 'or shall I let them enlighten me?' (*Diaries* 407).

He decided to let himself be enlightened. In addition to sleigh riding, tobogganing, and skiing, he began writing again. Almost from the moment of his arrival he was immersed in his first major project in many years, and in fulfillment of the desk clerk's enlightening error he called the central character Josef K.[54] This new hero was a land surveyor trying to deal with the perplexing bureaucracy in charge of the local castle, its environs, and all the people living there. The snow-covered landscape of Spindelmühle shaped Kafka's conception of the novel's setting, a countryside fixed in seemingly perpetual winter.

He did not get far on the project before he had to leave the resort and return to Prague. But he was still on sick leave, and that respite from the office gave him the chance to make further progress on *The Castle*. He kept at it assiduously till his leave was up at the end of April, at which time he immediately took his annual five-week vacation. During May he was able not only to continue work on the novel but also to undertake—and bring to completion—a new story, 'A Hunger Artist,' about a man who makes his living by publicly starving himself.

In the meantime, Kafka had been promoted from Institute Secretary to Senior Secretary (February 14, 1922), in spite of the fact that since late 1917 he had been on leave far more often than he had been in the office. Perhaps Kafka's supervisors foresaw that their respected colleague would be unable to continue in service much longer and wanted him to retire under the best possible conditions. If so, they foresaw correctly. On June 7, 1922 Kafka formally requested to be classified as 'temporarily inactive,' with pension rights. Everyone understood the gravity of Kafka's condition, so there was no delay in approving his retirement from active service with an effective date of July 1 and with a pension sufficient to maintain bare subsistence. A week ahead of that date, Kafka was already on his way out of Prague. He would never again return to the office at the Workers' Accident Insurance Company.

Sister Ottla had rented a summer cottage in Planá in the Bohemian Forest, and Kafka went to join her there. She had a husband and a baby now, but everyone got along. Kafka was able to continue working on *The Castle* through much of the summer, but by the end of August he began losing control over the project. It met the fate of all his novels: he abandoned it, unfinished and perhaps unfinishable. He went back to Prague in September and moved back in with his parents, living the life of a poor sick relative. He was still able to do a bit of writing, but he attempted nothing on a large scale. He studied Hebrew and he dreamed once again of going to Palestine. He was very sick over the winter, with an intestinal infection adding further woes. Although he was somewhat better by spring of 1923, he was still too weak to do very much. In May he took a short train trip that went well enough for him to consider accepting his sister Elli's invitation to accompany her on her vacation at a beach resort on the Baltic coast of Germany.

In spite of the fact that Kafka was now a semi-invalid who spent his time on the beach at Müritz sitting immobile in a chair, he managed to do once more what he had done so often on his past summer holidays: meet a young woman and fall in love. The woman was Dora Diamant, 25 years old but passing for 19; short, dark-haired, an Eastern Jew from Poland who seemed to Kafka both exotic and reassuringly familiar. She was working as a volunteer at a Jewish children's holiday camp run by the Berlin Jewish People's Home, and one of the other volunteers had invited Dr. Kafka to stop by for the *Oneg Shabbat* celebration on Friday, July 13, 1923. Franz and Dora were apparently attracted to each other on first sight.

Kafka came to visit the camp everyday after that, and it was not long before the visits became an excuse to see Dora. 'Dora, especially, with whom I spend most of my time, is a wonderful person,' he wrote in early August (*Friends* 375). Although different in many ways, the two had enough in common to forge an immediate bond. On particularly powerful link in that bond was the shared dream of emigrating to Palestine. They probably started discussing the possibility of traveling together to the Holy Land on the beach at Müritz.[55] Perhaps they also discussed a more realistic but no less radical possibility: that they might live together in Berlin. A letter to Milena suggests as much: 'I started considering the possibility of moving to Berlin. At the time [in Müritz] this possibility was not much more real than the Palestine plan, but then it became so' (*Milena* 236). The reason that it became so was doubtless the new relationship with Dora.

Kafka left Müritz on August 6. Back in Prague, his symptoms worsened. His weight declined to 118 pounds, and his appearance so shocked his sister Ottla that she decided to intervene. She took him, along with her two children, to Schelesen. His health did not improve much, but he and Dora continued by way of letters (which have not survived) to plan for a life together in Berlin. By late September he had put on a few pounds and felt ready to attempt the unthinkable: to leave his parents' home and lead a life on his own in Berlin. On September 21 he returned to Prague from Schelesen, spent three days packing his things and taking leave of his relatives, and then left on the train for Berlin.

He moved into a little apartment in the suburban Steglitz section of Berlin, and sometime shortly thereafter Dora moved in with him. She had never lived with a man, and he had never lived with a woman who was not his sister, but they immediately adjusted to each other. The force of Dora's personality and the power of her love for her chosen partner swept away all impediments. Kafka showed no signs of the anxieties he had wrestled with in his previous relations with women. He took to being her housemate—and presumably her bedmate—with no fuss.

Of course there might have been much fuss if they had been forthright about their domestic arrangement. In the Berlin of the 1920s, unmarried people did live with each other from time to time, but it was still a very 'Bohemian' thing to do, certainly not something you discussed with your relatives and acquaintances. Franz, a genuine Bohemian with no desire to seem the other kind, kept quiet about it with all save a few trusted confidants like Max and Ottla. He did not have time or patience for all the questions and protests he would receive.

He did have time and patience for other things, however, among which were some that might come as a surprise to those who think of Kafka primarily as the author of 'The Metamorphosis' and 'In the Penal Colony.' One autumn afternoon when Franz and Dora were walking through a neighborhood park, they encountered a little girl in tears. When asked what was wrong, the child explained that she had lost her doll. On the spot, Kafka improvised a tale of consolation. He told the girl the doll was not lost but simply away on a trip. He knew this to be true, he said, because the doll had written him a letter. When asked to produce the letter, Dr. Kafka apologized, saying he'd left it at home by mistake and would bring it tomorrow. Dora later described how Franz went home and set to work immediately about composing the doll's letter 'with the same seriousness he displayed when composing one of his own works.'[56]

The next day he met the girl in the park. She was too young to read, so he read the letter to her. In it the doll said that she loved the girl but needed a change of scene. The doll wanted to live her own life, but she wouldn't forget her old friend. She promised to write every day. And for the next three weeks, Kafka produced a daily letter from the doll.

Of course the doll could not go on writing indefinitely, and the man who could not find a satisfactory conclusion for *The Castle* cast about for a way to end this small-scale epistolary novel. He came up with the idea of having the doll fall in love with a young man, get engaged, make wedding preparations in the country, and at last tell her friend in Berlin that as a married woman she could no longer write to those she had loved in former times. Apparently it worked. The little girl was happy for her doll's new happiness and no longer anguished over her loss. Kafka scholars continue to anguish over the loss of the doll's letters, however, because they have never been found. A series of prominent announcements in Berlin newspapers have never turned up the woman who once, as a little girl, met Franz Kafka in the park.[57]

Writing the doll's letters distracted Kafka from more distressing practical matters, for he had arrived in Berlin precisely at the onset of the worst inflation Germany (or any other country) had ever seen. Kafka's subsistence-level pension fell quickly below subsistence level. Dora had to come up with ingenious ways to make ends meet, as for instance by using candles or their kerosene lamp for cooking. Housing was a problem, too. They had to leave their first apartment because the landlady kept raising the rent. They found another in the same neighborhood, but later in the winter they had to move further away from the center of the city, again because of devastating rent increases.

In spite of all this, Kafka was writing again. He even contracted with a new publishing house (offering better terms than Wolff) to produce a collection of stories. Kafka got a welcome advance, and in return the publisher Die Schmiede obtained the rights to all his subsequent work. The firm would have reaped a bonanza if it had managed to survive the 1920s. Unfortunately it perished not long after Kafka himself. Only one of the stories he wrote in Berlin eventually appeared in the volume published by Die Schmiede ('A Little Woman'), but he wrote more, perhaps much more. The fragmentary novella 'The Burrow' comes from this period. The ending is missing, perhaps because Kafka never finished it, or perhaps because the final pages were destroyed with other papers that Kafka instructed Dora to burn. If Dora's later recollection about all the things she put in the fire was accurate, Kafka wrote much in Berlin that he consigned to the flames.

Over the winter of 1924, Kafka's health continued to decline, probably exacerbated by poor nutrition and lack of heat. Uncle Siegfried, the doctor from Triesch with whom Franz had stayed in happier times, came to visit and convinced his nephew that treatment in a medical facility was absolutely essential. In the middle of March Max came and took Franz back to Prague. Dora stayed in Berlin to await further developments. Back in his parents' home, he spent three weeks under the daily care of the medical student Robert Klopstock, the one who had befriended him in Matliary and whose instant devotion had puzzled Franz. Klopstock was now studying at the university in Prague, thanks in part to Kafka's help. Although he was extremely ill, Kafka managed to sit at his desk and produce one more story for the planned volume ('Josephine the Singer').

In early April arrangements were made at last for Kafka's treatment in an Austrian sanatorium in the Vienna Woods. Dora joined him shortly after his arrival, but the stay at the sanatorium was short. Kafka's infection had spread to his larynx, and he needed more specialized attention. He was therefore transferred to a laryngo-logical clinic associated with the University of Vienna. Dr. Hajek, the physician who ran the clinic seemed to know his business, but he was such an unpleasant person and the atmosphere of death in the TB ward was so frightening that Dora became alarmed. She worried that Franz was being crushed in spirit by the tyrannical doctor and all the patients dying around him, one after another. Her beloved Franz seemed to expect his turn to come soon, and he did not seem to mind.

Dora learned from Felix Weltsch, a friend of Kafka's who came to visit, about a small sanatorium run by a famous specialist where Franz could have a private room and pleasant surroundings. This seemed infinitely preferable to the mortuary atmosphere of the university clinic, in spite of the fact that the treatment provided by the insufferable Dr. Hajek appeared to be working. Dora visited the sanatorium in Kierling, approved, and convinced Kafka to make the move. Dr. Hajek objected, claiming (probably correctly) that his clinic offered far more advanced treatment and a better hope for a cure, but the patient overruled him. On April 19, Dora took Franz to Kierling, only half an hour outside Vienna. Shortly thereafter, Robert Klopstock joined them, breaking off his medical studies to devote himself entirely to Kafka's care.

Dora's assessment of Kafka's emotional condition proved accurate. Under the loving care of Robert and Dora, and in the pleasant springtime surroundings of the Kierling facility, Kafka's spirits improved greatly. In early May he was able to read the proofs for the story collection *A Hunger Artist* that was to be published by Die Schmiede. He appeared to be interested in living and at times believed he might do so. In that hope he asked Dora to marry him. He even sent a letter to her father asking for her hand. The father refused on the advice of the Gerer Rebbe, who had been informed that Kafka was not an observant Jew. But for all kinds of reasons it hardly mattered. In the spring of 1924 Franz and Dora considered themselves husband and wife, and that did matter.

The improvement in Kafka's emotional health did not slow the unrelenting decline in his physical condition. The lesions in his larynx soon made it impossible for him to talk, and he had to communicate by writing on slips of papers. That was bad enough, but as the pain from the lesions worsened more dire consequences ensued. When Franz tried to eat or drink his suffering became too excruciating to be endured. He simply could not take in enough nourishment and fluid to sustain his life.

Over the course of the last weeks in May and the first days of June, Franz Kafka starved to death.

At noon on June 3, 1924, it was over. Dora refused to leave the physical remains of her beloved until forcibly removed by Robert. They took the body back to Prague, where a funeral took place on June 11 in the Jewish cemetery at Strasnice on the edge of the city. Hermann and Julie Kafka had to watch as the casket containing their only son was lowered into the earth. One by one family members and friends dropped a handful of earth onto the coffin. Dora collapsed at the graveside, and no one could console her.

10. LITERARY LIFE POST MORTEM

In his last days with Dora, Kafka had made one last try to grasp hold of life. But during much of his illness he had harbored an attachment to death that perplexed, frustrated, and alarmed those who cared for him. As Milena wrote in her obituary, Franz had 'consciously nourished [his disease], and fostered it in his thoughts' (*Milena* 271). Such affection for the grave almost never does anyone any good, but in the case of Kafka one might have to admit an exception. If Kafka's publishing career had ended at his death, it is entirely likely that nobody outside a small circle of admirers would ever have heard of him.[58] But quite the opposite happened. Thanks to the efforts of that small circle, Brod foremost among them, Kafka had a post-humous success far beyond any dream of literary fame he might have had in life. The story of how he achieved the astounding life-after-death that turned him into a household word is an essential part of his biography.

Soon after Kafka's death Max Brod began going through the papers the deceased had left behind in his desk. Among them was a note addressed to 'Dearest Max' instructing him to burn 'everything I leave behind me [. . .] in the way of diaries, manuscripts, letters (my own and others'), sketches, and so on.'[59] Further searching disclosed another note, written at some earlier date, with a similar but somewhat less draconian instruction. He could spare certain previously published works ('The Judgment,' 'The Stoker,' 'The Metamorphosis,' 'In the Penal Colony,' the *Country Doctor* collection) and the as-yet-unpublished 'Hunger Artist,' but he was to burn everything else 'without exception.'[60] Such instructions put Max in a difficult moral position, since his heart's desire was to publish as much of Kafka's work as he could lay hands on. Such an aggressive strategy would not have represented any change from the situation during Kafka's life. Brod had regularly acted as Kafka's de facto agent, making the publication arrangements for nearly all Kafka's fiction that had appeared in print. In most cases he had to wheedle, cajole, and sometimes threaten before Franz would part with a man-uscript. But here was a most explicit statement of Kafka's wishes, and it absolutely forbade the action Brod wanted to take.

Brod had a spiritual sense of his duty to posterity. He firmly believed that Kafka would emerge as one of the great writers of all time, a prophet in whose work shone the Shekinah, the divine presence such as Moses saw in the burning bush.[61] For Brod, then, there was no real choice, especially since he never believed that his friend was as firm in his intention as the text of the notes might have suggested. If Kafka really wanted his papers destroyed, why did he entrust them to the one person in the world least likely to destroy them?[62]

And so Brod ignored Kafka's will and embarked almost immediately on his great publication scheme, starting with *The Trial*. The *Hunger Artist* collection was already on its way into print, with Kafka's final corrections completed just before his death. Brod convinced Die Schmiede, the publisher of that collection, to take on *The Trial* as well. In doing so, however, Brod had to let everyone believe that Kafka had left a manuscript complete enough to be presented as a novel. He carefully refrained from sharing with the world the extent of his own intervention. To be sure, Brod made clear from the outset that the manuscript was unfinished; what he failed to make clear was that the materials were not ordered in such a way as to form a narrative.

Franz Kafka never produced a novel called *The Trial*. The 'authentic' text that Kafka wrote is a disordered collection of episodes about a character named Josef K., often with no clear narrative relation among the pieces. The person who produced the novel we know as *The Trial* was Max Brod, even though Kafka wrote every word that was printed. It was Brod, not Kafka, who took the mass of material abandoned by its author and turned it into a book that people could read and understand as a coherent story—though one with a few inconsistencies and missing details here and there. We must admit as a fact of literary history that the world-famous novel about a man who woke up one morning to find himself under arrest was a collaborative effort between the living Max Brod and his dead friend.

Brod's version of Kafka's *Trial* appeared in 1925 with Die Schmiede. Although Die Schmiede collapsed shortly thereafter, Brod convinced Kurt Wolff to bring out *The Castle* in 1926 and *The Missing Person*, retitled by Brod as *Amerika*, in 1927. Sales were poor, but Franz Kafka was now established as a novelist. The fact that Kafka had never actually written anything that he would have been willing to call a novel seemed irrelevant. The critical reception of the books was good, and some interest was stirring abroad. In 1930 an English translation of *The Castle* by Willa and Edwin Muir appeared simultaneously in Britain and America.

When Brod published *The Castle* in 1926, Willa Muir made a remarkably prescient but still risky decision to include it among her translating enterprises. It is not known exactly what prompted her to select Kafka as one of the German authors she chose to translate.

It was certainly not his reputation. As her husband Edwin remarked in his introductory note to the 1930 edition, 'Franz Kafka's name [. . .] is almost unknown to English readers.'[63] But what prompted the larger project of making English versions of German literary works was almost certainly financial need. After the Muir's sojourn in Prague and other European cities in the early 1920s, family finances were tight, and the translations were a way to supplement the modest income Edwin was able to earn as a writer. The pair translated works of Gerhart Hauptmann, Hermann Broch, Heinrich Mann, and others. Although Edwin's name appeared after Willa's on the title page, Willa was the one who did the bulk of the labor. It was she who persuaded Martin Secker, the British publisher of Thomas Mann, to bring out the Muir version of Kafka's last novel.

The appearance of *The Castle* in London and New York bookshops in 1930 may have suggested to Alexandre Vialatte, who had become acquainted with Kafka's works during a stay in Germany in the 1920s, that a French translation of *The Trial* would be worth putting on the market. In 1933 his translation of *The Trial* came out with Gallimard in Paris, and five years later he followed up with a French *Castle*.

These foreign editions established Kafka's international reputation. In the 1930s it was easier to publish Kafka in translation than in German. After the rise of the Nazis in 1933 it became harder and harder for German publishers to bring out books by Jewish authors. But the indefatigable Brod continued his program of promoting Kafka's work in every way possible. He solicited the help of a small group of literary luminaries (including such internationally prominent writers as Heinrich and Thomas Mann, Hermann Hesse, André Gide, and Martin Buber) to urge the publication of Kafka's collected works. Eventually Brod made a connection with a publishing house newly founded in Berlin. The Jewish department-store owner Salman Schocken had established Schocken Verlag with the purpose of disseminating works of Jewish secular culture. Discussions with this small specialty house brought Max some hope.

Schocken had an exemption from the ban on Jewish authors predicated on the understanding that it would market its wares only to Jews. Brod understood that such a condition would be unenforceable and that Schocken's publications would surely reach many non-Jewish readers. He therefore offered Schocken the worldwide rights to Kafka's works if the house would agree to publish the 'complete works.' Brod planned for six volumes in all.

After some initial hesitation due to questions about marketability, Schocken agreed, and the three novels and a collection of stories and fragments from the notebooks appeared in 1934–35. Brod's edition of the diaries and letters followed, and even after the firm had to leave Berlin for Prague, Schocken continued to sell Kafka's works until Czech officials shut down the operation in 1939. Salman Schocken moved his publishing house again, first to Palestine and then to New York, where Schocken Books opened for business at the end of the war in 1945.

In the meantime the prominent people Brod had enlisted as his allies had not been idle. The Mann family made a huge contribution, as for example in an article Klaus Mann wrote in exile praising Kafka's works as 'the epoch's purest and most singular works of literature.'[64] When the Muirs followed up on the modest success of *The Castle* with an English translation of *The Trial* in 1937, Erika Mann must have suggested to her husband-of-convenience, the poet W. H. Auden, that he take a look. Auden was impressed. In 1941 he reviewed several translations of Kafka for *The New Republic* and delivered the dramatic proclamation that Kafka was 'the author who comes nearest to bearing the same kind of relation to our age as Dante, Shakespeare, and Goethe bore to theirs.'[65] Such a high-powered endorsement helped to thrust the relatively obscure Bohemian writer into the international literary limelight.

Thomas Mann himself contributed an appreciative preface to the 1941 American edition of *The Castle*. Mann had come across Kafka's writings in the summer of 1921, when a friend read some of it to him aloud at tea time. At first he did not seem very impressed: he noted in his diary that what he heard was 'remarkable enough. Otherwise rather boring.' But a few weeks later he procured for himself a printed copy (of which work we do not know) and decided that he was 'very interested' after all.[66] The 'Homage' to Kafka was probably written as a favor to Alfred Knopf, who was Mann's American publisher as well as Kafka's, but the little essay was carefully executed and sincere in its intention. In typical Mann fashion he praises Kafka by citing Kafka's admiration for Mann's story 'Tonio Kröger,' an admiration that was both genuine on Kafka's part and graciously appreciated on Mann's.

Even more influential than the great poet Auden and the mighty novelist Mann was the French intellectual Albert Camus. Vialatte's French translations of *The Castle* and 'The Metamorphosis' appeared in 1938, and this must have been the immediate stimulus for the essay on Kafka that Camus appended to his essay *The Myth of Sisyphus*, written in 1940–41 and published in 1942. 'Hope and the Absurd in the Work of Franz Kafka' is probably the single most important critical essay in the history of Kafka's reception, not primarily because it offers genuine insights into Kafka's writing (which it does), but because it made Kafka required reading for the literary avant-garde on both sides of the Atlantic.

The young Camus—he was in his late twenties when he wrote his Kafka essay—suffered from tuberculosis and considered himself unsuited to marriage, two characteristics that put him immediately in sympathy with his subject. The French-Algerian Camus evidently realized that the German-Bohemian Kafka inhabited the same marginal world he lived in, a world in which every man lives under the absurd but inviolable condition that he 'is condemned.'[67] The two novels that had been translated, *The Trial* and *The Castle*, seemed to Camus the central works of Kafka's career and comparable to the mighty tragedies of the ancient Greeks: 'Kafka expresses tragedy by the everyday and the absurd by the logical.'[68] Auden placed Kafka in the company of Dante, Shakespeare, and Goethe; Camus added Sophocles, Cervantes, Nietzsche, and Kierkegaard.

In postwar Europe and America, there was no more fashionable cultural heavyweight than Camus, and if he said Kafka was important, then one just had to get hold of Kafka. Among the literati of New York and Paris it became essential to know your way around *The Castle*. It was not pure literary bravado that prompted Anatole Broyard to give his memoir of postwar Greenwich Village the title *Kafka Was the Rage*. Broyard was citing the most salient characteristic of the intellectual climate of the late 1940s. As early as 1947 the term 'Kafka-esque' was appearing in highbrow American journalism,[69] and right on through the 1950s Kafka continued to be the rage. The people of New York, and soon the rest of the United States, wanted more and more Kafka. They wanted *The Trial*, *The Castle*, and 'The Metamorphosis.' They even wanted letters and diaries.

The little house of Schocken strove mightily to feed the growing appetite, and soon Kafka became the foundation of the company's business, as he remains to this day. Hannah Arendt, whom Salman Schocken engaged as one of the editors in his New York office, wrote to her boss in 1946: 'Though during his lifetime he could not make a decent living, he will now keep generations of intellectuals both gainfully employed and well-fed.'[70]

And indeed so it has been. Contrary to Werfel's prediction, Kafka managed to get a long way past Bodenbach, though he needed the services of both Max the editor and Charon the boatman to propel him on his way. Adolph Hitler helped, too, by making the self-righteous cruelty of 'In the Penal Colony' seem like an understated allegory of things to come. All in all, the reputation of Franz Kafka has soared very high with a little help from his friends.

What terms could possibly be adequate to characterize a biography that reaches its triumphant climax more than two decades after its subject's death?

Perhaps we would have to call it 'Kafkaesque.'

CHAPTER THREE

A SURVEY OF KAFKA'S LITERARY ESTATE

Kafka wrote a great deal but published very little.[1] After his death the unpublished manuscripts that managed to survive slowly found their way into print under the editorship of many different hands with many different agendas. Because of the circuitous route by which the bulk of Kafka's writing reached the public, what the reader gets when buying a book with Kafka's name on the cover is not necessarily pure and unvarnished Kafka. This is obviously and unavoidably the case for the reader who must rely on English translations, but it is true even for those who read German and therefore suppose they have access to the very thing Kafka wrote down. In most cases, what such readers get will have been considerably worked over by others. Sometimes these interventions are scrupulously announced and described by the editors; sometimes they are not.

Because of these complications, it is useful to make a survey of the writing Kafka actually left behind, keeping in mind that these literary remains do not comprise everything Kafka produced. Kafka seems to have periodically purged his desk of drafts that in retrospect displeased him, and there is no way to estimate how much he discarded. Furthermore, before he died he instructed Dora Diamant to burn many manuscripts in an effort to force a fresh start on what he hoped would be a new life as a writer; and after his death many letters and notebook materials in Dora's possession were seized by the Gestapo.[2] Just how much was lost in these two unfortunate incidents will probably never be known.[3] What survived, including works he published in his lifetime, can be divided into three principal categories:[4]

1. Documents Kafka composed as an insurance-company lawyer;
2. Personal letters;

3. The products of his intense, though sporadic, after-hours labor (what he called his 'nocturnal scribbling' [*nächtliches Gekritzel*]).[5] Most of it is fiction, but he tended to write his fiction in notebooks that also contain a kind of writing that resembles nothing so much as diary entries. The notebooks also include miscellaneous jottings, such as drafts of letters, and other material that defies generic categorization.

In addition to the notebooks are various bundles of paper and stray single sheets. Some of the bundles contain many pages, some only a few. Some are clearly related to other bundles, while others have no obvious connection to the rest. The material found in bundles and stray sheets is often very similar to what we find in the notebooks and 'diaries' and in some cases shows clear signs of having been ripped out of notebooks.

The materials in categories 1 and 2 are the least problematic because their generic status is clear and because we can readily understand the circumstances of their production. All of us have written letters, and nearly all of us have been obliged to write some reports or office memoranda in our work. Although some aspects of even these writings might provoke perplexity, we can deal with them adequately (for the purposes of this Guide) in the relatively brief overviews included in this chapter.

Category 3 is far more complex. It contains the diary/notebook material, which can and is examined as part of this survey; but it also contains all the fiction, and that of course requires separate treatment. The novels and stories will receive detailed discussion in subsequent chapters, even though in a certain very real sense they belong to the same characteristically Kafkan writing regime as the notebooks. The stories are what made Kafka a household word, and they are doubtless the reason you decided to consult a *Guide for the Perplexed*.

1. WORK-RELATED DOCUMENTS

The 'office writings' (*amtliche Schriften*) comprise 27 different items (as categorized by the editors of the Kritische Ausgabe) and cover nearly 700 printed pages of the Fischer critical edition. A substantial selection (18 items, some of them abbreviated) has now been translated into English and published by Princeton University Press under the editorship of Stanley Corngold and collaborators. It is testimony to the enormous power and prestige of Kafka's reputation that these business papers—until recently perused only by the most dedicated Kafka scholars—are now gaining a wider audience.[6] Those who understand Kafka principally as the poet of twentieth-century bureaucracy will naturally be drawn to these documents as sources of background illumination. Others may find them interesting simply because they open up another conduit into the life of one of the twentieth century's most seminal figures.

Most people will not find the office writings very good reading. As you might expect, they are technical reports produced for a very narrow audience and for very limited purposes. That is not to say that Kafka's skill as a writer does not occasionally shine through; it does. Kafka took his job at the insurance company seriously and he did it very well. He did not turn off his standards of excellence just because he was at the office. But this or that arresting passage will not, for most of us, repay the labor of slogging through the tedious mass of claims, arguments, statistics, and meticulously reported items of conflicting evidence. Of course, there will be some who happen to enjoy delving into the history of central European accident insurance law, and for them the documents Kafka worked on will have the added cachet of having been touched by celebrity.

Kafka considered himself a writer by calling, not a lawyer or an insurance-company executive. He was both of these, but not by choice. He would not have written these documents except that he had to in order to earn a living; and I suppose I might not have read them except that I had to in order to earn mine.

But he did write them. Much as he longed to free himself of the office, its daily pressures, and its often grindingly mundane concerns, his life and literary work owe something vitally important to those office hours he so much resented. The world of Kafka's fiction is in many ways the same world as the one he experienced in the office. Petty legal issues are everywhere; accidents overwhelm planning; mechanisms take on lives of their own, run awry, and destroy human bodies; evidence is never unambiguous; every assertion is met by a counter-assertion; and all sides have perfectly good reasons for their positions.

Kafka never escaped the insurance-company office, and neither did his fictional heroes. Just before Kafka retired from his insurance job he left Prague to visit a hotel in a snow-covered fairy-tale landscape. There he began writing a story in which a certain K. leaves his home for a foreign land, a snow-covered fairy-tale landscape with a castle in the middle. But K. finds himself effectively back in the office. Officials with ponderous titles and obscure responsibilities dominate everyone and everything. K.'s employment status is tenuous, and much of his time is spent in clarifying his position in an uncertain territory between the affairs of castle officialdom and the ordinary life of the village. *The Castle*, though unfinished, is Kafka's most sustained attempt to reconcile his life as a writer of fiction with his labor as an insurance bureaucrat.[7]

Since Kafka the writer could never fully disengage from the world of the insurance company, a glance at the business writings will help form a more accurate picture of Kafka's daily life and its relation to his nocturnal scribbling. One long-held stereotype of Kafka, for example, quickly withers: the office documents will not support the notion that the author of *The Trial* was a faceless minor drudge in a cubicle. He was in fact an important executive. The issues he was dealing with in the office were very technical, it is true, but they were significant and they touched many thousands of people.

Another stereotype may emerge not only unscathed but strengthened: Kafka certainly did live in a world of elaborate bureaucratic procedures that were enforced with punctual, almost mechanical rigor. Indeed, Kafka was himself one of the enforcers. Here is an example from a report he prepared on fixed-rate insurance premiums for farmers who use machinery (Document 3):

> Any farm owner who does not accept the fixed rate, in contrast, becomes subject to the provisions of § 21 of the Accident Insurance Law. According to this regulation, each farmer in this situation will have to calculate his own premiums; since the Institute will not, in such cases, be preparing the appropriate forms at all, the farm owners will have to procure these printed forms themselves and at their own expense. Timely submission of the completed forms will be strictly enforced, and proceedings [*Strafamtshandlung*, with emphasis added in the original document] according to § 52 of the law will be brought against anyone who fails to file by the deadline. (*Office* 75–76)

We think of Kafka perhaps more often as a victim of the bureaucratic machine, and at certain times and in certain circumstances he surely was. But in these documents we see a very different Kafka, not the victim whom the authorities might execute 'like a dog,' but one of the executing authorities. He is a powerful figure who can legitimately threaten to swing the sword of justice (that is, the *Strafamtshandlung* specified by § 52) against those who fail to conform to the provisions of § 21 of the Accident Insurance Law. I have no idea what sort of proceedings were authorized by § 52, but the term itself obviously implies that they aimed at *Strafe* (punishment). I cannot imagine they were pleasant.

This and other similar passages encourage us to posit a close relation between Kafka's life at the office and his life as a writer of fiction. Until recently, the community of Kafka's readers tended to pay too little heed to that relation. One wonders, however, if scholarship has not already reached the point of giving certain documents more attention than they merit. An example in point is a document rejecting the appeal by Norbert Hochsieder, the owner of a boarding house in Marienbad, of the classification of his hostelry as a 'motor-powered business.'[8] He had received this classification because his building was equipped with an elevator driven by an electric motor.

The most salient feature of the Hochsieder document for our purposes is that *there is no evidence Kafka wrote it*. Indeed, all the evidence supports the view that Kafka could not possibly have written it, because he was out of the office on vacation in the summer of 1912 when the document was produced. Neither the German nor the American editors dispute this fact, but both include the piece in a collection of Kafka's writings anyway on the ground that he must have been familiar with the contents.

One does not have to look far for the reasons driving this unusual editorial decision: the document deals with matters that come up later on in Kafka's fiction. The American edition puts the matter elegantly: 'Kafka's commentary on this case is not found in the official files but survives, in transfigured form, in a number of his fictions' (*Office* 194). Well and good, but by such a principle all sorts of material that turns up 'in transfigured form' in Kafka's stories could be included in anthologies of 'Kafka's' writings—the *Odyssey*, for example ('The Silence of the Sirens'); or *Don Quixote* ('The Truth About Sancho Panza'); or the various books of the Bible, including especially Genesis ('The City Coat of Arms'). Many, many works of our literary heritage could be seen retrospectively as torches that set Kafka's imagination alight. The complete anthology would take up many hundreds of volumes. It might be better to reserve space in volumes devoted to Kafka's works for works actually written by Kafka.

The Hochsieder document illustrates the point especially well, because one of the prominently cited reasons for its inclusion is the claim that it explains something about Kafka's story 'A Country Doctor' that can be explained in no other way.[9] One of the most striking passages in the story relates the doctor's surprise at finding a pair of horses in his pigsty:

> A man, huddling in the low shed, showed his open, blue-eyed face. 'Shall I harness up?' he asked, crawling out on all fours. I could think of nothing to say and merely bent down to see what else was in the sty. The maid stood next to me. 'You never know what things you have in your own house,' she said, and we both laughed. 'Hey there, Brother, hey there, Sister!' shouted the groom; and two horses, powerful animals with strong flanks, their legs tucked in beneath them, lowering their well-formed heads like camels, one after the other simply by the force of their twisting rumps pushed their way out of the low doorway, which they crammed full to bursting. But in a moment they rose up high on their long legs, their bodies thickly steaming. (*SelStor* 61)

Some scholars have wondered where Kafka came up with such a bizarre image as two horses wriggling out of a pigsty, and the editors of the office writings believe that the Hochsieder document supplies the answer. 'The horses point to the first paragraph of the Austrian accident-insurance law, which stipulates that the use of "engines [. . .] driven by elementary power or by animals" subjects a business to carrying accident insurance.' Both the editors of the Kritische Ausgabe and those of the Princeton edition cite the fact that, just as the horses give off steam in the story, so do those 'iron horses,' steam engines (*Office* 211–12).[10]

This is marginally plausible, perhaps, but hardly convincing. One cannot definitively exclude the possibility that Kafka's horses-in-a-pigsty could have emerged from the pages of the Hochsieder document, transformed from their original incarnation as motors in a boarding house. It seems far more likely, however, that they emerged from the pages of a famous story written by one of Kafka's favorite authors, Heinrich von Kleist, where they appeared as—well, as horses in a pigsty. In Kleist's 'Michael Kohlhaas' the hero has to give up two prized horses as bond securing his return to pay the toll required for a certain road. When he returns to claim his animals, he discovers that they have been quartered in a pigsty where they nearly starved to death. For Kafka, an avid reader of Kleist, the association of horses with pigsties would have been as natural as the association of horses with kingdoms for readers of Shakespeare's *Richard III*. There is no need to resort to an admittedly clever but nonetheless rather fanciful exegesis of an obscure insurance document.

Those in danger of falling into perplexity would therefore do well to approach the office writings with some diffidence. They can serve to enrich one's reading of the fiction, but only if taken in moderation and with a tiny grain of salt.

2. LETTERS

Kafka's letters hold a special fascination because they wear two faces. One face looks into the mirror of autobiography. It offers moments of startling insight and apparently unselfconscious personal revelation. The other gazes out into the misty land of fiction and offers elaborate rhetorical figures, psychological fantasies, and self-serving hype. Whichever face they offer, the letters are without question some of Kafka's most powerful literary constructions.

The letters currently available to the English-speaking reader are the following (dates refer to publication of the English editions):

- *Letters to Milena* (1953; revised edition including Milena's letters to Max Brod, 1990);
- *Letter to His Father* (1966);
- *Letters to Felice* (includes letters to Grete Bloch and a few letters from Kafka's relatives concerning Kafka's engagement to Felice, 1973);
- *Letters to Friends, Family, and Editors* (1977);
- *Letters to Ottla and the Family* (reprints some letters from the 1977 collection but adds others, 1982).

There is a complete German critical edition of the letters in progress as part of the Fischer Kritische Ausgabe, but so far it includes letters no later than 1917, seven years before Kafka's death. The volume for the years 1918 to 1920 has been announced and will probably be out by the time this Guide is in print.

The reader is well advised to regard these letters with the same caution Kafka himself applied to all epistolary activity. He wrote hundreds of letters and doubtless received just as many, but his unstinting dedication to the task was by no means an unconditional endorsement of its value. That he had the gravest doubts about the practice of letter-writing is evident from a letter to Milena of March 1922:

> Actually I don't have to apologize for my not having written, after all, you know how much I hate letters. All my misfortune in life [. . .] derives, one might say, from letters or from the possibility of writing letters. People have hardly ever deceived me, but letters always have, and as a matter of fact not those of other people, but my own. In my case this is a particular misfortune of which I do not want to discuss further, but it is nevertheless also a general one. (*Milena* 223)

One of the reasons for Kafka's negative view must surely have been the unhappy outcome of his relationship with Felice Bauer. Their relationship was rarely physical and personal but primarily intellectual and epistolary. Back in the early days of their romance, Kafka apparently believed strongly in the possibility of establishing and maintaining intimacy through letters. He told her in a letter sent in November of 1912 that he treated one of her letters 'like some living thing,' as if it carried with it a genuine piece of her organic substance. 'Dearest,' he writes, 'have you noticed how astonishingly of one mind we are in our letters? If there is a question in one, the following morning brings the answer' (*Felice* 65). Earlier that same month he proposed that the intimacy of letter-writing is similar to the intimacy of using *Du* in German, a sign of emotional and spiritual constancy:

> But the *Du* stands firm; it stays here like your letter and doesn't move when I kiss it over and over again. But what a word that is! Nothing unites two people so completely, especially if, like you and me, all they have is words. (*Felice* 38)

But of course there is potentially a lot of room for trouble in a relationship between two people who have nothing but words, especially if those words are inscribed on paper and delivered back and forth by post between Berlin and Prague. Although Kafka always searched for signs of life in the written words of Felice's letters, he was regularly disappointed. Even the mode of inscription could provoke his dissatisfaction:

> Dearest, many thanks for the letter and its welcome amount of detail. There is indeed something disappointing about typescript; one is tempted to turn over the cold page to see if there isn't something living on the other side, nevertheless it has great advantages. Besides, it almost seems as though you feel more at home with the typewriter. (*Felice* 494)

Kafka's concern about something 'cold' in the letter seems at first to be confined to the typescript: like many people, he apparently considered handwriting more personal. A second look suggests something else. By adding the remark about how at home Felice feels with the typewriter, he hints at a metonymic relation between the lady and her preferred writing implement: the coolness he detects in the mechanical typescript might represent Felice's attempt to stay cool. And in August 1916, when the letter in question was written, that supposition might have been correct. The couple was just in the process of resuming relations two years after the breakup of their engagement. Felice needed to be careful.

No matter how much Kafka wanted to establish epistolary intimacy, it nearly always eluded him. And no wonder: such intimacy as letters can provide is always tempered by the reality of physical distance. It did not take very long for Kafka to realize that his letters to Felice enact 'a futile striving for an impossibility—i.e., your presence' (*Felice* 114). He recognizes in his own letters the severe limitations the epistolary relationship places upon him: 'But what am I capable of, anyhow? Kissing, yes, kissing from afar!' (*Felice* 184). He asks himself 'why I, who force myself upon you with letters, refrain from doing so in person' (*Felice* 188). He comes to realize that 'all these letters,' even the ones he praises for their apparent intimacy, 'can't create a presence, only a mixture of presence and absence that becomes unbearable' (*Felice* 73).

What makes matters worse is that the same Kafka who characterizes this form of intimacy as 'unbearable' is the Kafka who can tolerate no other kind. He says as much to Felice in a letter from early 1913:

> And with what hand, in what dream, did you write down that I have won you completely? Dearest, you believe that for a brief moment, from far away. To win you from close up, and for the long term, requires other forces than the muscles that drive my pen forward. Don't you believe it yourself when you think about it? It seems to me sometimes that this intercourse [*Verkehr*] by letter, beyond which I long almost constantly for reality [*Wirklichkeit*], is the only kind of intercourse [*Verkehr*] that corresponds to my wretchedness (wretchedness that of course [*natürlich*] I don't always feel as wretchedness), and that overstepping this limit imposed on me would lead us both to disaster. (February 17–18, 1913, my trans.; cf. *Felice* 197)

The published English translation glosses over a crucial point by translating the word 'Verkehr,' which means 'traffic' or 'intercourse,' as 'communication.' The translation is not wrong, it is simply misleading—apparently the result of a wish to spare the English reader's delicate feelings. But Kafka did not spare Felice: he put the matter candidly before her by confessing that epistolary eroticism was the kind that suited him best. He doesn't mince words: he has an almost constant longing for actuality (*Wirklichkeit*), that is, for genuine intercourse; but that longing is resisted by the belief that physical intimacy is not appropriate for his state of misery.

It is also worth noticing that Kafka cloaks in parentheses an important confession: he does not always experience 'wretchedness' negatively. He even slips in that little word 'natürlich' ('naturally,' 'of course'), as if to suggest that experiencing misery as something other than misery is only to be expected. He gets away with it because he is Franz Kafka, and Felice (along with the rest of us) is quite ready to accept this sort of outrageous assertion from him. We all assent to the claim that a person like Kafka would 'of course' sometimes fail to feel misery as misery. But in accepting that claim, we have to accept also that Kafka in fact prefers intercourse by letter and that he feels a certain comfort with the very mixture of intimacy and distance that he denounces as 'unbearable.'

Kafka clarified somewhat his notion of epistolary intercourse in the letter to Milena already partially quoted above.

> The easy possibility of writing letters—from a purely theoretical point of view—must have brought wrack and ruin to the souls of the world. Writing letters is actually an intercourse [*Verkehr*] with ghosts and by no means just with the ghost of the addressee but also with one's own ghost, which secretly evolves inside the letter one is writing or even in a whole series of letters where one letter corroborates [*erhärtet*] another and can refer to it as a witness. (*Milena* 223)

Kafka resurrects his comparison of letter writing to sexual intercourse nearly a decade after introducing it in his correspondence with Felice, but now in an even more distressing image. No longer is the letter intercourse, even if of an unsatisfactory sort, between two people; now it is intercourse between a person and spectral creatures inhabiting the spaces between the letter's lines. The letter's actual recipient does not participate at all. The letters collude in facilitating this ghastly copulation by acting as witnesses that establish a firm reality for the letter-writer's ghost. Kafka's word 'erhärtet' conveys much more strongly than the English 'corroborates' a sense of making something hard and solid out of these insubstantial spirits.

The ghosts seem stronger and more likely to thrive than the persons from whom they supposedly derive:

> How did anyone ever get the idea that people can traffic with each other [*miteinander verkehren*] by letter! One can think about a distant person and one can hold on to a nearby person; everything else exceeds human power. Writing letters, on the other hand, means baring oneself in front of the ghosts, who are greedily waiting for that to happen. Written kisses never reach their destination, but instead get drunk up by the ghosts along the way. By means of this ample nourishment they multiply so astonishingly [*unerhört*]. (Late March 1922, my trans.; cf. *Milena* 223)

Kafka hammers home the sexual image by, first of all, depicting the letter-writer as 'baring himself' (*sich entblössen*) in front of the specters, then presenting the ghosts as 'drinking up' and nourishing themselves on the written kisses. Finally, as the capping figure of sexuality, Kafka mentions the 'astonishing' (*unerhört*) success with which the ghosts reproduce. The ghosts get all the benefits of epistolary intercourse; the correspondents get none.

In spite of such vividly formulated reservations about letters, we have to take with a large grain of salt Kafka's complaints about them and about relationships that consist of nothing but words. When Kafka outwardly complains about having nothing but words, he is also inwardly rejoicing. The manipulation of words in letters permitted him various liberties that he could never have taken in person and fostered precisely the kind of spectral intimacy that, even if it was sometimes troubling, was also sometimes exhilarating.

A case in point is one of the early letters to Milena, at a stage in their relationship when he still addressed her with the formal and distant second person *Sie* (rather than the *Du* he told Felice was the marker of a firm bond): 'Look [*Sehen Sie*], Milena, I'm lying on the chaise in the morning, nude, half in the sun, half in the shade, after an almost sleepless night' (June 3, 1920, my trans.; cf. *Milena* 29). This is quite a piece of impertinence to serve up before someone you address with polite reserve. What makes it marginally acceptable is the fact that the writer's nakedness is clothed in epistolary distance. When Kafka dares to open a letter to a distant acquaintance with a command that she 'look' at his naked body he is taking full advantage of the ghostliness of letter-writing. He gets away with it precisely because it is the literary ghost of his naked body, not its corporeal substance, which confronts the letter's recipient. There could be no more dramatic example of the possibilities of rhetorical intimacy, and there is not the slightest doubt about what the writer is up to. We don't ordinarily think of Franz Kafka as a flirt, but this passage demonstrates beyond all doubt that he could flirt outrageously and unblushingly when it suited him.

The same ghostly naked body appears again in the letters to Milena, but in different circumstances and therefore in a very different form:

And now please, Milena, don't torture yourself any more, and I never understood physics (or at most just the thing about the pillar of fire, that's physics, isn't it?) and I don't understand the 'scales of the world' either and they certainly understand me no better (what could such monstrous scales make of my 55 kilograms in the nude [*55 kg Nacktgewicht*], they wouldn't even notice and doubtless wouldn't budge), and I am here the way I was in Vienna, and your hand is in mine as long as you leave it there. (July 29, 1920, my trans.; cf. *Milena* 118–19)

Kafka's body now enters the scene in a context that emphasizes both its pure corporeality and its insignificance. The two are connected. As a mere body, Kafka's 55 kilos (120 pounds—not much for a six-foot-tall man) can have little impact on the physical universe. The question the letter proposes, though, is what emotional impact that bare body will have on Milena. The biblical allusion to the pillar of fire that led the wandering children of Israel through the wilderness serves as a reminder that what is at stake here is not really the physical impact of things; it is their spiritual import.

The open question about the spiritual value of physical bodies is apparently answered, at least in part, by Kafka's reassuring insistence at the end of the letter that he is still holding Milena's hand—in spirit. Spiritual hand-holding (like epistolary kissing) is a ghostly business, mediated once again by untrustworthy letters. In spite of the cozy sentiments, Kafka and Milena are emphatically *not* together. In such circumstances it is perhaps not surprising that Kafka finds it necessary to erase himself from the closing signature. He writes first 'Franz' but immediately crosses it out; then he tries 'F' but crosses that out, too. 'Yours' meets the same erasure. Finally he offers his correspondent 'nothing more, silence, deep forest.' Not only is the slight 55-kilo body gone; so too is any physical sign of that body. Even the bare letter F is ceremoniously withdrawn. Kafka wants to give her some aspect of himself, but every time he does he turns around and takes it back—over and over again. Upon witnessing such repeated gestures of self-removal, Milena could hardly have felt much reassurance in the offer of Kafka's ghostly hand.

Letters enact a complicated dance between partners who are there and yet not there, together and yet apart. Kafka would like some aspect of himself to be present in the letters he writes to Milena, but his constant fear is that there is so little of Franz to be found there that honesty compels him to withhold even the letters of his name. But the opposite can also happen. Sometimes the letters of a name can invoke the spectral presence of a person the writer would prefer to exclude—Milena's husband, for example:

> What I said about your 'speech' was serious [*ernst*] (Ernst keeps
> barging into this letter. Perhaps I'm doing him a horrible injustice—
> I can't think about it—but the feeling is equally strong that I'm
> more and more tightly bound to him, I almost might have said: in
> life and death. If only I could speak with him! But I'm afraid of
> him; he's very much my superior. You know, Milena, when you
> went to him you took a big step down from your own level, but if
> you come to me you will be dropping into the depths. Do you
> know that? No, that wasn't my 'loftiness' in that letter but yours)—I
> was talking about your 'speech,' you meant it seriously [*ernst*], too
> [. . .]. (June, 1920, my trans.; cf. *Milena* 46)

Ernst, the German word for 'earnest' or 'serious,' is also the German
version of the name we write in English as Ernest, and in this case it
is a particularly resonant name. Milena's husband was named Ernst,
and his spectral appearance in this series of love letters is obviously
unwelcome. Although Kafka expresses the rhetorical wish to speak
with Ernst, the very next sentence makes clear that he very earnestly
hopes for the opposite. Ernst's paronomastic appearance in a letter
is a bit daunting; his corporeal presence face to face with the man
aspiring to be his wife's lover would be downright terrifying. And yet,
no matter how serious the writer is about keeping apart from Ernst,
the two remain locked in an intimate union. Kafka feels 'bound
tightly' to Milena's husband, and no wonder: the more he insists he is
serious, the more 'Ernst' he becomes.

Kafka sometimes hated and sometimes loved this interplay of
presence and absence in the letters of words and the words of letters,
but he never failed to exploit it. He found a constant source of fascination and perplexity in the complex relation between a signifier,
whether written or spoken, and the entity for which it supposedly
stands. We saw how he tried to remove his own name from a letter
and how he found Ernst's name horning in on another. In yet another
he pondered the difficulties of trying to match up the woman he
knew as 'Milena' with the sound of her name:

> Today something which may explain a few things, Milena (what a
> rich, heavy name, almost too full to lift and which I didn't like very

much at first; it seemed to me a Greek or Roman gone astray in Bohemia, violated by Czech; the accent has been betrayed and yet the name is marvelous, in color and form: a woman to be carried in one's arms out of the world, out of the fire—I don't know which— and she presses herself into your arms willingly and full of trust, except the strong accent on the 'i' is bad, doesn't the name jump right back away from you? Or might that just be a leap for joy, which you yourself perform with your burden?) (*Milena* 44–45)

Because 'Milena' has the accent on the first syllable—a pronunciation that stumbles awkwardly over German lips, which would prefer to say Mi-LAY-nah—Kafka seems profoundly uncertain as to whether the name fits or fails to fit the character of the woman. Do these three syllables jump away, or do they leap for joy? Do they help you carry the lady off, or do they render her somehow too 'heavy' to lift? Kafka isn't sure, and therefore neither are we.

What is sure is that the three syllables Mi-le-na take on a life of their own. They go their own way, possibly aiding or possibly impeding the progress of the person to whom they are allegedly attached. Perhaps they are congruent with her personality, perhaps they are not, but in neither case are they controlled in any decisive way by her will. In this respect her name behaves in the same impertinent, distressing manner as the name of her husband. His shows up when it shouldn't and gets in the way of the lovers' intimacy; hers bounces in an alarming fashion that makes her lover ill at ease.

Discourse like this meditation on Milena's name leads one to wonder whether people are in charge of words, or words are in charge of people. If we seek a clear decision on this issue in Kafka's writing, we seek in vain. The ghostly intercourse mediated by letters engenders wave after wave of indecision, and Kafka rode those waves with the skill of a pipeline surfer. He may or may not have felt comfortable or safe in the curl, but he lived much of his life there.

Here is another example of a linguistic crux upon which Kafka deftly balanced his 55 kilos. Kafka and Milena had been having a minor disagreement about their differing tastes in furniture, and Kafka offered his tongue-in-cheek commentary:

Yes, the wardrobe [*Schrank*]. It will probably be the object of our first and last fight. I'll say: 'We're throwing it out.' You'll say: 'It's staying.' I'll say: 'Choose between it and me.' You'll say: 'Just

a second. Frank[11] and *Schrank*, they rhyme. I'll take the *Schrank*.'
'Fine,' I'll say and slowly walk down the stairs (which?) and—if
I still haven't found the Danube Canal, I'll be living happily
ever after. And incidentally I'm all in favor of the wardrobe.
(*Milena* 112)

Kafka plays an elaborate game with various signifiers that stand for
Franz. With the help of Milena's version of his own name, he sets up
a situation in which there is little or nothing to choose between the
person and the wardrobe. After all, their signifiers are rhyme words
that differ by only a single phoneme. That similarity allows the
anticipated discussion about keeping or discarding the Schrank to
slide over into a debate about whether Milena should continue
her relationship with Franz or dump him. That was not a topic that
had been on the table, as far as we can tell, but it was evidently on
Kafka's mind all the same. Anxieties about rejection were always
on his mind.

But there is another game going on besides this word play that
equates Frank with Schrank. The conversation Kafka reports is not
one that has actually taken place: it is rather a proleptic fiction.
Skilled rhetoricians since antiquity have used prolepsis—that is, the
technique of anticipating what an opponent will say, saying it for
him, and then countering it in advance—to take the teeth out of an
argument that might do the speaker harm. Such seems to be Kafka's
strategy here. He stages a lovers' quarrel, lets himself lose, and finally
tries to drum up some sympathy by suggesting that he would be so
downcast at his defeat that he might throw himself into the Danube
Canal. The goal of the elaborate rhetorical charade would be to ward
off any future tussles over the sensitive issue of the Schrank by
suggesting a potentially lethal outcome. 'Don't even *think* about
arguing in favor of the wardrobe,' he seems to tell Milena. 'I might
end up dead, or at least wishing I were dead.'

But of course it's all a joke. Kafka underlines that fact by adding
a capper, as any good comic writer would do. In this case, the irony
of the fictional quarrel doubles back on itself when Frank, presumably the wardrobe's life-and-death opponent, declares himself on
the side of the Schrank. It's a good joke, and part of what makes it
so is our recognition that there is a genuine logic to Kafka's paradoxical declaration of support for his rival. Just as Franz had to ally
himself with Milena's husband on the linguistic grounds that both

were 'Ernst,' so too must he see himself as bound together with an object bearing a title that contains most of the sounds of his own (assumed) name.

Both the 'Frank' and the 'Schrank' of this letter are linguistic ghosts. They are fictional straw men that Kafka erects in his effort to ward off any possible future rejection by Milena. In spite of their spectral status, or perhaps because of it, they are endlessly useful for symbolically manipulating the world. With their help, Kafka can enter into intimate intercourse with women whom he mostly keeps at a great physical distance. Symbolic objects are wonderful in this respect, much better than living persons, as Kafka once pointed out to Felice:

> Sometimes my need for you gets to be too much. The case [with Felice's picture in it] is torn open, and in a friendly and nice way you show yourself instantly to my insatiable gaze. [. . .] And the fact that this little photograph is so inexhaustible actually produces as much pleasure as pain. It doesn't pass away, it doesn't disintegrate like a living thing, but instead it remains preserved forever, a lasting comfort, it won't pierce me through and through, but it won't leave me, either. (December 27–28, 1912, my trans.; cf. *Felice* 127)

As in the letter about the Schrank, the underlying issue in this panegyric on the photograph is the possibility of rejection. The enormous virtue of the picture is that it 'won't leave me,' not by walking away, not by pushing away, and not even by fading away in decay. Kafka's attitude toward the photo is the precise opposite of his reaction to Felice's typescript: the photographic representation improves upon the living person, whereas the typescript represents a step down from living warmth into objectified, mechanized coldness.

Kafka's effusive praise for the picture derives from his frequent preference for exploitable, durable signs over the demanding, ephemeral things they stand for. Signs are 'inexhaustible'; they do not 'disintegrate'; they remain 'a permanent comfort'; and they never say good-bye. But they have a further advantage: unlike living lovers, you can put them aside and ignore them when you have other matters to attend to, even if those other matters require your attention for months at a time. Signs let you manipulate them as you will.

This manipulability is much on display in one of the most interesting of all of Kafka's letters, the justly famous *Letter to His Father*. This bravura rhetorical performance ends with a dramatic prolepsis in which Kafka puts into his father's mouth all sorts of quite plausible objections to his son's behavior. The fictional father accuses his son of being thoroughly self-serving. He complains that the letter has been no more than an elaborate act of self-justification on the part of the son, who tries to portray himself as guiltless. But the father argues that the son is in fact a bloodsucking vermin (*Ungeziefer*), unfit for life.[12]

> Why should it bother you that you are unfit for life, since I have the responsibility for it, while you calmly stretch out and let yourself be hauled through life, physically and mentally, by me. For example, when you recently wanted to marry, you wanted— and this you do, after all, admit in this letter—at the same time not to marry, but in order not to have to exert yourself you wanted me to help you with the not marrying, by forbidding this marriage because of the 'disgrace' this union would bring on my name. I did not dream of it. (*Father* 123)

Indeed, Kafka's father did not forbid his son's marriage to Julie Wohryzek, but the paternal voice of the letter complains that his forbearance did him no good. The son blamed him anyway, and indeed an earlier part of the letter presents the son's explanation of why he felt his father had in effect prevented the marriage to Julie, in spite of having never explicitly vetoed it. The father sums it up in a fine peroration:

> Basically, however, in this as in everything else you have only proved to me that all my reproaches were justified, and that one especially justified charge was still missing: namely, the charge of insincerity, obsequiousness, and parasitism [*Schmarotzertum*]. If I am not very much mistaken, you are preying on me [*schmarotzest Du an mir*] even with this letter itself. (*Father* 125)

Kafka has given his father some very powerful ammunition in this prolepsis, and the reader wonders what counterarguments a debater could muster against such a massive attack. Kafka's strategy, however, is not that of the debater. He never joins the battle on his father's grounds. Instead, he pulls a white rabbit out of his fiction-writer's hat: 'My answer to this is that, after all, this whole rejoinder—which can partly also be turned against you—does not come from you, but from me' (*Father* 125). The son wins the rhetorical battle with his father by making him into a fictional creature born of the son's imagination. Not only that, the son becomes the victor by creating the father's most cutting criticisms. 'Not even your mistrust of others is as great as my self-mistrust' (*Father* 125), he says, all the more convincingly for having taken on himself total responsibility for documenting his many shortcomings.

Kafka easily assumes rhetorical ownership of not only his own but of others' flaws as well. He takes up any failings that might have been found in Milena's Schrank, loads them onto his own back, and heads off in the general direction of the Danube Canal. If he finds letters deceptive, he refrains from blaming others but points to himself as the source of epistolary deception. This willingness, even eagerness, to become the bearer of the sins of the world is evident in another letter to Milena. In this one, he confesses his love for a sentimental story by a fellow Austrian, Franz Grillparzer:

> What you say about 'The Poor Fiddler' is entirely correct. If I said it didn't mean anything to me I was only being cautious, since I didn't know how you would like it, also because I'm ashamed of the story, as though I had written it myself and the beginning is indeed wrong and it does have a number of defects, ridiculous moments, dilettantish features, and deadly affectations (which are especially noticeable when read aloud, I could show you where) and particularly this way of practicing music is a lamentably ridiculous invention; it is enough to make the girl (and the whole word, too, myself included) so extremely angry that she hurls everything in her shop at the story, until it is torn to pieces by its own elements, a fate it richly deserves. (*Milena* 81–82)

Kafka's strategy in dealing with Grillparzer's story is similar to the strategy in the letter to his father: he tears the victim apart with skill and apparent relish, even though the victim is none other than himself. In this case the victim appears in the guise of another writer, but the distinction between Kafka and Grillparzer disappears under the force of Kafka's emotional identification with his predecessor.

It is particularly telling, and entirely typical, that Kafka's negative judgment of Grillparzer's prose (and his own) undergoes a metamorphosis into something positive. The long list of criticisms (the story is 'wrong,' 'ridiculous,' 'dilettantish,' and so on) comes to a head with the assertion that the narrative is so bad that it essentially tears itself apart. But the next sentence paradoxically swerves in the opposite direction:

> Of course there is no more beautiful fate for a story than to disappear, and in this way. Even the narrator, that droll psychologist, will agree to this completely, since he himself is probably the real poor fiddler, playing this story as unmusically as possible, exaggeratedly thanked by the tears from your eyes. (*Milena* 82)

In identifying a mode of writing that succeeds by undermining itself, by botching its own performance, and by teetering always on the verge of disappearance, Kafka is proposing a radical literary aesthetic. He is praising—and criticizing—a certain droll psychologist who deliberately writes self-destructive fictions and self-effacing letters that elicit Milena's tears.

The psychologist's name, of course, is Franz.

3. 'DIARIES' AND NOTEBOOKS

The designation 'diaries' has to be put in quotation marks because Kafka's practice did not always allow clear boundaries between one sort of writing and another. He left behind a great deal of material in his literary estate that looks like diaries, and nearly all of it is of considerable interest to those of us who want to understand Kafka. But how much of it should be segregated out into a special category labeled 'diaries' remains an open question. One might think the matter could be settled simply, but this overview will try to explain why it cannot. Here is another case in which the reader's perplexity is likely to remain a chronic condition.

Diaries can ordinarily be distinguished from other texts by their form and their purpose. In form, they are usually dated, and entries present the personal observations of the author. In purpose, they are not—at least initially—intended for public view but instead are primarily or exclusively meant for the author's private use. Thomas Mann's diaries, for example—to cite someone close to Kafka in time, space, and native language—are easy to tell apart from his other writings. Mann himself made certain that no doubts could arise. He wrote his diaries in physically distinct volumes and even went so far as to segregate his diary writing temporally: he composed his novels in the morning, his diaries at night.

In the case of Kafka, the situation is far less clear-cut. Obliged to spend his mornings earning a living at the Workers' Accident Insurance Company, Kafka could write only at night, frequently very late. Even if he had wanted to, he could never afford himself the luxury of rigorously separating one sort of writing from another. And all the evidence suggests he was reluctant to harness his muse in this way. He preferred simply to write, often with no particular plan in mind. He seems to have tried at least for a time to keep a diary separate from everything else in special notebooks, but this intention never really came to fruition. When he was ready to write, he generally used the materials he had at hand.

Max Brod selected a number of entries he found among the materials Kafka left behind at his death, particularly material found in the quarto notebooks, and published them as 'diaries.' They first appeared in 1948 and 1949 in a two-volume English translation (*The Diaries of Franz Kafka: 1910–1913* and *The Diaries of Franz Kafka: 1914–1923*) and only later (1951) in the original German (*Franz Kafka: Tagebücher 1910–1923*). It was Brod's edition that promulgated the notion that Kafka kept what most people would think of as a diary.

But Kafka's notebooks contain all kinds of things, including sketches, letters, entire stories, and sometimes dated, diary-like entries that seem to offer the author's personal observations or accounts of experiences from his daily life. Brod picked out from this undifferentiated mass those notebooks that in his opinion most corresponded to the generic concept of 'diaries.' To him, the quarto notebooks looked more like diaries than the octavo notebooks. To another eye, all the notebooks look very similar. One could argue that, in setting one set of notebooks apart from the others, Brod created a distinction without a difference.

Later editors followed Brod's lead. In the important Kritische Ausgabe one can find a volume titled *Tagebücher* ('Diaries'). The editors are quite aware, however, that the title does not exactly fit the contents. In the editorial preface they offer an interesting clarification: 'By "diaries" we mean the twelve quarto volumes found in

Kafka's *Nachlass* [papers left behind after his death] which he used—at least for a certain period of time—for diaristic entries.' The editors also claim 'that Kafka considered these twelve volumes, which form a group unified by content and format, to be his real diary.' Perhaps he did, at least in the sense that he used the term 'Tagebücher' to refer to them; but if Kafka really intended to keep a regular diary, then we have to concede that he never followed through. The editors of the *Tagebücher* therefore offer an essential hedge: 'certain notebooks possess the character of a diary only from time to time.'[13]

In many respects the volumes published by Brod and his successors do indeed look like diaries. But one cannot fail to notice that they also contain other kinds of things. There are also drafts of letters, descriptions of dreams, a few fragmentary autobiographical notes and sketches, and even portions of novels or entire novellas. The complete text of 'The Judgment' appears there in an entry from late in September of 1912. It would be fair to say that these 'diaries' are Kafka's literary workshop, a workshop that includes a number of other diary-like notebooks hardly distinguishable in content from those which Brod and others presented to us as diaries. Kafka's octavo notebooks contain the same mixture as the so-called diaries, though with fewer explicitly dated entries.

Since Kafka never maintained a firm distinction between diary-writing and fiction-writing, he did not hesitate to take pieces out of the diary—pieces that seem in context to be very personal meditations on his own situation—and publish them out of context as works of fiction.[14] On the other hand, he fictionalized some of the allegedly 'honest' diary entries. On the occasion of turning over to Brod the journal he kept on his trip to Weimar in 1912, he wrote:

> Here is my diary. As you'll see, I faked it up a little because it wasn't intended just for me, I can't help it, at any rate this sort of faking isn't intentional but rather comes from my inmost nature and I really ought to respect what I see down there. (July 9, 1912, my trans.; cf. *Friends* 78)

In the light of this confession one has to wonder just how much of this unintended dissimulation suffuses the rest of the diary material. After all, if his faking really came from his 'inmost nature' it could hardly be turned on and off at will.

Perhaps we should consider the possibility that *everything* found in such notebooks and scattered papers could quite legitimately be considered diaries, if we use the term in the same broad sense implied by the editors of the Kritische Ausgabe. Perhaps, contrary to all appearances, he followed up on the intention he voiced in late 1910 not to give up his diary ever again.[15] Indeed, in a certain sense the diary was his characteristic genre. The possible objection that the novel-manuscripts and other bundles of papers in the Nachlass constitute a separate category must confront the fact that these drafts have the same tentative and fragmentary character as the diaries. Kafka never managed to complete any of them. Instead, he treated them exactly as he treated his notebooks, taking certain passages out and publishing them as independent narratives. 'The Stoker' and 'Before the Law' are fragments taken out of *The Missing Person* (*Amerika*) and *The Trial*, just as 'The Judgment' and others among his most famous stories are passages ripped out of the 'diaries.' In all these notebooks and all this notebook-like material, Kafka created warehouses of writing. When the opportunity arose he ransacked their disorderly but richly stocked shelves for publishable fiction.

Kafka seemed to prosper best as an author when he scribbled in these diary-like notebooks. This sense of comfort is evident in the notebook entry that follows directly upon the conclusion of 'The Judgment' (September 23, 1912):

> I wrote this story 'The Judgment' in a single sitting from 10 PM to 6 AM during the night of the 22nd to the 23rd. I'd been sitting so long I could scarcely drag my stiffened legs out from under the desk. The terrible effort and joy as the story developed before me, as I skimmed across the waters. Often during the night I carried my whole weight on my back. How everything can be said, how a great fire is prepared for everything, even the strangest notions, a fire in which everything is consumed and resurrected. [. . .] One can write only this way, only with this kind of coherence, with this kind of complete opening up of body and soul. (*Tag* 460–61; my trans.)

Kafka speaks explicitly of his physical discomfort, but only in contrast to his spiritual joy. His stiffened legs testify to the utter dedication of his 'body and soul' to the task, a task which could be completed in a single sitting and a single notebook passage precisely because it fits so easily into the diary context. Not only does the cited entry refer back to the story that precedes it, the story itself seems to refer back to the immediately preceding diary entry: 'Sept. 20. Letters to Löwy and Fräulein Taussig yesterday, to Fräulein B[auer] and Max today' (*Diaries* 212; trans. modified).

Löwy and Fräulein B reemerge as characters in 'The Judgment' in only slightly metamorphosed condition. Löwy, the leader of the Yiddish theater troupe that had excited Kafka's interest during the foregoing year, was apparently traveling at the time somewhere in the east, and Felice Bauer was the young lady in Berlin to whom Kafka would later become engaged. 'The Judgment' begins by asserting that its hero Georg Bendemann was just completing a letter to his friend in Russia to announce his engagement to a certain Miss F. B. The connection between the story and the diary entry is evident, a connection that disappears as soon as the story is removed (as Kafka himself removed it) from its local context. We can see exactly the same process of deliberate decontextualization in the case of 'The Stoker' and 'Before the Law.'

A transition from notebook entries, or similarly inchoate 'scribbling' (*Gekritzel*), to publishable fiction marks much of Kafka's literary activity. Roland Reuss speaks of a movement between draft ('Entwurf,' a German term that means not only 'draft' but also 'outline, sketch, plan, blueprint') and printable text, where in most cases the draft stage predominates.[16] Reuss's work as an editor of the Stroemfeld/ Roter Stern critical editions has provided ample evidence for this view. All of Kafka's work retains at least a whiff of its 'draft' character even when finalized. Indeed, everything in Kafka's life, including Kafka's life as an author, has this work-in-progress character. Each of his three plans for marriage (two with Felice Bauer and one with Julie Wohryzek) seems less the establishment of a relationship than an 'Entwurf' toward such a relationship. None of them led to a firm commitment. So it was with his writing. Kafka instructed Dora to burn substantial amounts of manuscript material in Berlin shortly before his death and requested Max Brod to burn more, thus as it were crossing out the great bulk of his effort as a writer and stamping its status permanently as draft.

This fundamental congruence between life and literary production leads us perhaps in a direction other than the one we might expect. Certainly Kafka regularly incorporated personal experience into his fiction, but it by no means follows that Kafka's fictions should be read as autobiographical ciphers to be decoded with the help of historical records. The relation between life and work is much more intimate and more complicated. Perhaps the best way to describe it is to use a German term normally associated with the technical terminology of literary analysis: *erlebte Rede*. German scholars use this expression (which literally means 'experienced discourse') to refer to what the French call 'le style indirect libre,' the free indirect style, the merger of the first-person point of view of a principal character into the third-person voice of a narrator.

But Kafka's 'erlebte Rede' is more than just a version of Flaubert's free indirect style familiar to readers of both *Madame Bovary* and *The Trial*. In Kafka's writing, the connection between experience and discourse (*Erlebnis* and *Rede*) is so complete that it both includes and surpasses the concept of 'autobiographical fiction' (*Erlebnisdichtung*). While it is quite true, as we have seen, that Kafka's fictions do indeed frequently derive from his interpersonal experiences, the most important experiences for Kafka were often not so much the events of his life as the language in which those events were cast. For Kafka, language itself is a crucial part of experience, and the experience of language plays a fundamental role in nearly all his writing. The diaristic notebooks, wherein we find so much of his significant literary work, are the place where we regularly find discourse that is itself the result of an experience of discourse, an *erlebte Rede*.

Perhaps this notion can be clarified best by means of examples. Here is a relatively early diary entry (January 19, 1911) that reminisces about Kafka's awkward beginnings as a novelist:

> I once intended to write a novel in which two brothers got into a fight. One emigrated to America and the other was imprisoned in Europe. I started to write down just a few lines here and there, because the effort wore me out immediately. One Sunday afternoon when we were visiting the grandparents, I wrote a bit [. . .]. It is possible that I was just showing off and [. . .] wanted to induce someone to pick up what I was working on, look it over, and admire me [. . .]. An uncle who liked to make jokes finally came by and grabbed the page that I was holding rather laxly, took a quick look, gave it back again without even a chuckle, and said to the others who were carefully following what he was doing: 'The usual junk.' To me he said nothing. I just sat there and went back to bending over my now useless page, but in actual fact I was driven

out of society with a shove; the uncle's verdict echoed in my mind with almost literal significance; and I obtained—even among close relatives—a glimpse into the cold empty space of our world, a space that I would have to warm with a fire I that I would first have to seek out. (*Tag* 146–47; my trans.)

Here Kafka depicts two closely related events, one in the realm of human relations and the other in the realm of rhetoric. On the level of human relations, the text presents a painful experience that awakens a terrible sense of loneliness even within the intimate circle of the family. The young Kafka feels his isolation as banishment, feels himself ejected 'with a shove,' that is, with something like physical force. This violent expression serves as a metaphor for the uncle's emotional rejection, but the uncle—apparently Richard Löwy—has committed a different sort of dismissive act: he has pronounced his opinion, his judgment about the value of his nephew's writing. In Kafka's mind this judgment (*Urteil*) becomes a verdict 'with almost literal significance.' The uncle's casual and superficial evaluation, 'the usual junk,' strikes the nephew with the force of a judicial condemnation.

One of the most significant features of this reminiscence is how the rhetorical expression merges with the experience of personal suffering. The feeling of being shoved out into the cold world by no means lessens over the years, as the diary entry testifies. Indeed, the sense of loneliness described here becomes a permanent feature of Kafka's fictional world, as powerful in 'Josephine the Singer' at the end of his career as it is in 'The Judgment' as its inception. It is worth noting, however, that this sense of painful ejection arises out of the experience of language itself, out of the possibility that one kind of 'Urteil,' an opinion, can be metamorphosed into another, a verdict of banishment. Neither meaning has priority over the other.

Arguably the sense of pain must have been the origin of the linguistic expression, but the more important point is that the particular form taken by this pain was decisively determined by the resources of the German language. Certainly Kafka could have felt the sting of his uncle's rejection independent of its expression; but it would have been a different kind of pain if Kafka had experienced it in a different linguistic shape.

It is hardly surprising that a young man would experience such a rejection personally, but this rejection had serious long-term effects.

It became a permanent feature of Kafka's experience of the world, not least because Kafka was unable to separate himself from his work. The experience inscribed in the diary came into being only because self and work, person and language, were inseparably fused together in the mind of the writer. This inseparability in turn shaped the form of the notebook report. Because Kafka felt so at one with his language he could easily transform one kind of 'Urteil,' a simple opinion, into another, a lethal verdict.

The close connection between the rhetorical form of expression and the structure of the self became even clearer as his 'junk' developed. In spite of his uncle's dismissal, he never gave up on the plan to write a novel set in America. He made a substantial draft in spring and summer of 1912, which he subsequently destroyed. But then, during the extraordinarily productive fall of 1912, just a few days after finishing 'The Judgment,' he returned to the abandoned work with renewed vigor, although with some changes in the plot. The two fighting brothers are gone, replaced by a single hero (Karl Rossmann) who departs for America. There Karl becomes *The Missing Person* referred to in Kafka's original title. Max Brod, who understood the importance of titles in marketing books, published the unfinished manuscript as *Amerika*, and it is by that title that most people know the book today.

Where Karl Rossmann was exiled is important precisely because exile is *The Missing Person*'s central theme. America was a land from which immigrants rarely returned, and that is why Karl's family sends him there. The family sees him as a threat to their future prosperity, and they get rid of him. Thus the metaphorical 'shove' that the young writer felt during his first attempt at an America novel becomes the basic plot mechanism of the subsequent version. The pain experienced by the author those years ago becomes the starting point for his new story and is incorporated into it. But there is an interesting twist. The hero of the new novel finds himself banished because his family refuses to support the child he engendered out of wedlock. There is an obvious similarity between the family's rejection of Karl's offspring and the uncle's rejection of Kafka's literary effort. Underlining this relation is the fact that Karl's child in the novel has the same name, Jakob, as Karl's American uncle. And this uncle Jakob commits another act of banishment later in the story, dismissing Karl from the protection of the New York branch of his family: 'after the incident today I am absolutely obliged to send you away' (*Missing* 81). Uncle

Jakob in effect retroactively endorses the banishment that sent Karl to America in the first place.

There is an evident symmetry between the insupportable, illegitimate text that prompts Uncle Richard's condemnation and the insupportable, illegitimate child that prompts Karl's family to ship him off to America. Symmetries of this sort weave a thick texture of connections between human experience and rhetorical form. Kafka's works in general are marked by this same texture, which becomes yet thicker and more complex in 'The Judgment,' written at the same time and under the same pressure of concerns that operate in *The Missing Person*.

In this case the rhetorical transformation of an opinion into a condemnatory verdict that we see first in the diary entry from 1911 becomes the mechanism driving a critical turn of the plot. As Stanley Corngold has pointed out, Georg Bendemann approaches his father with a request for one sort of 'Urteil,' his opinion, but obtains instead a very different kind of 'Urteil,' a verdict condemning him to death.[17] Exactly as Kafka solicited his uncle's opinion by his ostentatious act of writing, so does Georg solicit an opinion from his father about his writing. In this case the written material in question is the letter in which he informs his friend in Russia about his engagement to a certain Frieda Brandenfeld. The father's 'Urteil' consists of a series of surprising responses. He puts his son's entire writing project into question, including its purpose (the friend already knows about the engagement), its veracity (he calls Georg's letters 'false letters'), and even the existence of its recipient ('Do you really have this friend in St. Petersburg?' [*SelStor* 7]). That these various objections at least partially contradict each other does not reduce in the least their devastating effect on Georg, who might have been looking for recognition and even approbation for his writing but obtains instead an utterly horrifying condemnation.

But it is not only Georg who understands this set of opinions as a verdict of banishment; the father does so as well, as he makes clear when he says, 'I now sentence [*verurteile*] you to death by drowning' (*SelStor* 12). What initially felt like banishment out of the family or out of human society now comes across as banishment out of the realm of the living. In this respect 'The Judgment' is obviously different from the notebook entry of 1911. It is far more extreme. The two nonetheless share a significant feature: both have as their mainspring a rhetorical moment that is suffused with personal pain.

We might engage in our own radical act of editing and propose that all three, the diary entry, the passage from the novel, and the story, belong to the same unfinished text with the same implicit title: 'Der Verurteilte,' (that is, 'the one who has been judged and condemned'). In all three cases a living person experiences and extends the resources of his living language, especially the polysemy of certain key terms. Kafka thus poses the problem of biography, the problem of the relation between life (*bios*) and writing (*graphein*), in its most radical form. He will not allow us to prefer the personal over the linguistic aspect of his work, or vice versa. Each is always conditioned by the other.

Even when he inscribed his personal experience in diary entries ostensibly meant only for his own private use, he wrote in the same rhetorical, multivalent manner we recognize from his fiction. It is fair to say that it was natural for Kafka to write this way, that it was part of the structure of who he was. He lived rhetorically. We find everywhere in his writing linguistic expressions that are inseparable from his experience. As an example one need only consider the rhetorical multiplicity of the travel diary Kafka kept during the summer before he met Felice Bauer and wrote 'The Judgment.' During his vacation in July of 1912 he visited two interesting locations, Weimar and Jungborn. The first had been a tourist mecca for many years, thanks to its central importance for German classical literature; the other, nowhere near as well known, was a rather trendy mountain resort specializing in natural healing, nudism, and what we might today call a macrobiotic diet.

The combination of these two very different destinations may seem peculiar, with the dignified grandeur of Goethe's residence and heritage on the one hand and the occasionally outrageous behavior of the nudists on the other. But for Kafka both places seemed to have equal value as receptacles of the great cultural traditions in which he saw himself implicated. Weimar may have had a house where Goethe lived, a house therefore named the 'Goethe House,' but Jungborn had a house named 'Ruth' in which Kafka lived for several days. The Goethe House appears in the diary principally as a rendezvous point where Kafka could meet a young lady who caught his fancy. On the other hand the nudist resort figures as the scene of religious and philosophical discussions. Each place functions as the center of a movement that takes Kafka simultaneously in two opposite directions.

Kafka's description of his stay at Jungborn displays this double movement with particular clarity. The diary entry from July 8, his first complete day at the resort, is characterized by remarkable honesty and surprising complexity.

> My house is named 'Ruth.' Very practical set up. Four dormers, four windows, one door. Rather quiet. They're playing soccer, but only at some distance, the birds sing lustily, a few naked people are lying quietly in front of my door. Everyone, right down to me [*alles, bis auf mich*], without bathing suits. Lovely freedom. In the park, the reading room, and so on, you get to see pretty, plump little feet. (*Tag* 1040; my trans.)

Although the passage seems perfectly straightforward and devoid of artifice, closer inspection shows how carefully Kafka seeks to hide what his language purports to disclose. He reports for instance that his house is 'rather quiet,' but the sentence that follows not only fails to substantiate the claim, it contradicts it outright. Is the quiet disturbed by the soccer game taking place 'only at some distance?' Is it compromised or enhanced by the lusty singing of the birds? Is the writer's repose reflected in the naked people lying 'quietly' in front of his door, or is it instead shattered by their presence? When we take a second look, we realize that 'rather quiet' (*ziemlich still*) might mean 'quiet with some slight exception' or 'not really as quiet as one might wish.' This textual ambivalence doubtless reflects the concrete situation of the writer: he did not know himself, and perhaps did not wish to know, whether Jungborn was stimulating or calming, or whether he wanted to be stimulated or hoped to be calmed.

The self presented in the diary entry does not know and cannot say. The Kafka of the inscribed page cannot even say whether he is naked or wearing a bathing suit. The German phrase 'alles, bis auf mich' (which I have translated as 'everyone, right down to me') could mean 'everyone except me' or 'everyone including me.' The words 'bis auf' often appear in expressions like 'alle starben, bis auf drei' ('all died except three') but also can be used in just the opposite sense, as in 'alle starben bis auf den letzten Mann' ('they all died down to the last man'). In this case the reader is likely to opt for the former reading, not least because subsequent revelations in the diary authorize this choice. Nonetheless there remains an ambiguity that one cannot ignore.

Did Kafka wear his bathing suit or not? It must have been a question of some moment to the writer, because he did all he could to obfuscate the issue and leave the reader in perplexity. When he confesses (in parentheses) in the entry from July 9, 'I'm called the man in the swimming trunks' (*Diaries* 478) one might suppose the matter settled. One is perhaps surprised to learn that Kafka went to a nudist resort and then insisted on wearing a bathing suit, but on the other hand it seems to fit the personality of the man and express appropriately the embarrassment he so modestly encases in parentheses. On July 15, however, he reports that he 'posed for Dr. Sch.' and then goes on to note 'the large part the naked body plays in the total impression an individual gives' (*Diaries* 481). One is led to the conclusion that Kafka was posing nude for Dr. Sch., about whom he had written a few days before in another rhetorically knotty passage: 'With Dr. Sch. (43 years old [Kafka was 29]) in the meadow in the evening. Taking walks, stretching, rubbing, pummeling and scratching. Stark naked. Shameless' (*Tag* 1045; my trans.). On the basis of the text it is impossible to say whether it was Dr. Sch. or Kafka or both who were indulging in this 'shameless' nudity. On July 16 Kafka is prepared to make more or less a clean breast of it: speaking of a conversation he had with another guest of the resort, Guido von Gillshausen, he writes, 'start sweating (we're naked) and speak too softly' (*Tag* 1048; my trans.). Once again Kafka uses parentheses to enclose the embarrassing confession in at least the semblance of decency.

There is little point in asking whether Kafka was or was not naked at this or that moment in his stay. It makes more sense simply to acknowledge that the Kafka represented in the travel diaries was always both naked and clothed at the same time. This rhetorical Kafka existed in an indeterminate condition rather like that of Schrödinger's famous thought-experiment cat, about which one could not say for certain whether it was alive or dead. Since the condition of the cat depended on a quantum state that stabilized only upon observation (collapse of the wavefunction), Schrödinger argued—ironically, to be sure—that the cat had to be understood as *both* alive and dead as long as the observation remained unmade. The physics of the real world may not in fact sanction the existence of cats that are both alive and dead at the same time, but the resources of rhetoric can do so easily. The Kafka who was subject to the physics of the real world knew whether he was clothed or naked, but this knowledge did not penetrate into his discourse.

With rhetoric it is possible to solve the problem of going in opposite directions at once. We can get a good sense of the sort of psychic division that afflicted Kafka during his 'quiet' holiday from a dream he described in a journal entry from July 15, the same day he posed for Dr. Sch.:

A dream: The nudists destroy one another in a brawl. After the company, divided into two groups, has joked around for a while, one person emerges from one of the groups and calls out to the others: 'Lustron and Kastron!' The others: 'What? Lustron and Kastron?' The first one: 'Of course.' The brawl starts. (*Tag* 1047; my trans.)

Lustron and Kastron are nonsense words, but they are not entirely devoid of meaning. They appear to be deformations of the ordinary German words 'Lust' (fun, desire) and 'kastrieren' (castrate), but prettified with the pseudo-Greek termination *–on*. 'Lustron' suggests both enjoyment (perhaps looking back to the fun the nudists were having together) and desire, including sexual lust. 'Kastron,' on the other hand, points to a violent denial of sexuality. Kafka's dream expresses the emotional ambivalence he feels when caught between a powerful wish to participate in the 'stretching, rubbing, pummeling and scratching' of the naked body and an equally powerful wish to denounce such doings as 'shameless.' This conflict is complicated by another: the urge to proclaim 'Lustron and Kastron!' encounters an incredulous response ('What? Lustron and Kastron?'). It seems that these two things, Lustron and Kastron, whatever they are, cannot be united. Kafka could not himself decide whether he was visiting the Jungborn resort out of pure, moral motives (and Kafka did indeed harbor a certain puritan longing for physical and ethical cleanliness) or out of 'shameless' sensual desires. Thanks to the rhetorical deployment of this indecision in his journal, Kafka succeeds in maintaining both Lustron and Kastron without instigating a psychic brawl inside himself that would destroy the recreational value of his vacation. It is the rhetoric of the diary—dramatized in the dream—that allows him to acknowledge, without tearing himself apart, both the necessity and the impossibility of Lustron and Kastron.

Thus the boundary between experience and its linguistic representation disappears. We may doubt that it ever existed for Kafka. He even experienced his stay in Jungborn as residing in a book. The little cabin he inhabited bore the name of a book: Ruth. He mentions the Book of Ruth at the beginning of the entry for July 15. If he had the intention of reading this portion of the bible, it must have been at the instigation of the name of his house. The tale of the Moabite woman who, residing among a strange people (Ruth 2. 11), came to feel at home among them has a clear resonance with Kafka's situation among the nudists. Kafka must have realized that his Jungborn journal was a personal, perhaps slightly racy, modern version of the Book of Ruth. His book could unify in its linguistic form the conflicts inherent in his experience by both exposing and covering the nakedness of the author's body.

Kafka's sojourn in a house with the name of a book, where he lived both in a cabin and in the pages of a book he was working on—the scene of the most important aspect of his existence, as far as he was concerned—can serve as the paradigm for Kafka's life as a writer. He lived in a world of 'erlebte Rede' where it was by no means easy to distinguish between the experience of life and the experience of language. Little wonder, then, that the diary-notebook became Kafka's preferred medium of expression. Since Kafka's life experience was dominated by the experience of language, it is entirely understandable that his life found its most suitable home in the experiential discourse of the diary.

We can find this same mixture of life and writing in Kafka's other diary-like notebooks, in particular the octavo notebooks. Here we find the same combination of fiction and truth that characterizes the material that Brod published as diaries and journals. More than that, he even theorizes his illness as the transformation of discourse into experience:

> If I should die or become totally disabled in the near future [. . .] it would be legitimate to say that I tore myself apart. If my father used to offer up wild but empty threats like 'I'll tear you apart [*ich zereiße dich*] like a fish'—though really he never laid a finger on me—then the threat is being carried out quite apart from him. The world—F. is its representative—and my ego [*mein Ich*] are tearing apart my body in an irresolvable conflict. (*8vo* 61; trans. modified)

Kafka proposes that one of the most important events of his life should be understood as the realization of his father's violent metaphor. The father's language has now somehow divorced itself from its progenitor and started acting independently, without paying the slightest heed to the intentions of the speaker. Even the word 'ich' (I) moves away from its pronominal function and no longer refers to the father (who first uttered it in his threat) and turns into a noun, the 'ego' or 'self' of the son. At the time of the son's illness, the father's remembered phrase 'I'll tear you apart' comes far closer to the truth than it ever did when initially uttered, since in fact the father never laid violent hands upon the son. Once the word 'ich' becomes the sign of the son's self, however, the threat comes true. The 'ich' colludes in a violent process that Kafka experiences as his body being torn apart.

Kafka's experience of his father's discourse impacted his life as well as his writing. His consciousness was so completely informed by language that he perceived the world and himself primarily through linguistic figures. He even regarded himself as a linguistic entity— not only in the sense that he described himself as consisting entirely of literature,[18] but also and more fundamentally in that a noun masquerading as his own surname (*kavka* is the Czech word for 'raven' or 'jackdaw') enormously influenced his self-perception:

> You raven, I said, you old bird of ill omen, what are you doing constantly in my way? Wherever I go, there you are, sitting and preening your few feathers. Nuisance!
>
> Yes, he said, and paced back and forth in front of me with his head lowered like a teacher giving a lecture, that's right; it's almost uncomfortable even for me. (*8vo* 62; trans. modified)

The bird addressed in these lines is a reified form of the author's name, translated from Czech into German. The morpheme 'Rabe' (raven) is introduced twice: first by itself and then in the compound form 'Unglücksrabe' (translated as 'bird of ill omen'). The compound suggests both that the raven is itself unlucky and that it brings bad luck to others. The word 'Unglücksrabe' serves as a rhetorical hinge. On the one hand the expression conjures up an ancient tradition that associates ravens with death and disaster; on the other it points to the writer's personal situation of ill fortune.

Even when one acknowledges that the raven represents the authorial self, there remains a question as to why the bird is 'constantly in my way.' The next sentence offers an answer by suggesting that the raven may in fact be more than the writer's shadow or alter ego. The bird does not simply appear; it sits and preens its 'few feathers.' This may seem like a perfectly reasonable elaboration of the text's central figure, since of course real birds do preen their feathers. But the German expression 'sträubst die paar Federn' suggests more. The fact that there are only a few feathers suggests that the bird is not in the best of health—another reason why it might be right to call him an 'Unglücksrabe.' In addition, the words 'sträuben' and 'Feder' belong to a conventional expression that will lurk somewhere in the conscious-ness of every German reader: 'Die Feder sträubt sich,' that is, 'the pen hesitates.' The raven possesses feathers that also could be pens, and pens ought to facilitate writing. A literary creature like this old bird has every right, perhaps, to preen such feathers. In this case, however, the pens in question might instead balk at the task of writing. Neither the reader nor the writer can be sure which way the text is leading. Whichever it is—whatever activity is indicated by 'sträuben'—it is uncongenial to the writer, who labels it as a 'nuisance.'

The raven demonstrates his connection to the writer and agrees with his opinion by admitting that what is a 'nuisance' for the writer is also 'uncomfortable' for the bird himself. He does so not simply by affirming the writer's view but by appearing in the character of a rhetorician, a 'teacher giving a lecture.' Thus outfitted with pen and lecture, the bird cuts quite the rhetorical figure. In its pacing back and forth it even enacts the paranomastic meaning of its name: there is an old German verb 'rabantern,' rarely used any more, which means to move about in an agitated manner.

In this passage we can see how clearly Kafka recognizes the rhe-torical nature of his own activity when he identifies himself with the rhetorical 'Rabe.' The possibility of transforming 'Kafka' into 'Rabe' is also the possibility of wielding pens and holding lectures; it is the possibility of creating texts. Kafka recognizes also that his rhetorical nature is essential to his literary activity—that it always in some sense lies 'in his way.' One simply cannot do without the old bird, whose presence is always half nuisance, half essential stimulus: without the rhetorical raven there can be neither author nor work.

Bird, bird, bird—bird is the word. The bird-word stands there, preening its disreputable feathers, the subject matter and central problem of Kafka's notebooks. It is the word that made his life and his writing possible and impossible; and it is the word that never fails to fascinate the twenty-first-century reader whom this 'erlebte Rede' almost certainly never expected to reach.

CHAPTER FOUR

THE STORIES AND FRAGMENTS

This chapter introduces important selected works of Kafka's shorter fiction, the form in which he particularly excelled. One essential criterion of selection has been the availability of texts in English translation. I have therefore focused on works published in two widely available collections: the Schocken edition by Nahum N. Glatzer (*ComStor*) and the Norton edition by Stanley Corngold (*SelStor*). I prefer the Corngold translations and cite them whenever possible. The selection includes stories Kafka published in his lifetime and some extracted from his papers after his death.

Kafka's mature writing career was characterized by spurts of intensely productive creativity followed by slack times when he wrote little or no fiction. This chapter is organized around those creative spurts, the first of which took place in the fall and early winter of 1912–13. (The work earlier than this—a few fragments and the *Meditation* collection—are treated in section 1.1.) The second major creative period spanned the six months just after Kafka broke his first engagement to Felice Bauer in the summer of 1914, when he wrote *The Trial* and 'In the Penal Colony'; and the third lasted through much of 1917, though it was most intense during winter and spring when Franz wrote in his sister Ottla's little house in Alchemists Lane (the *Country Doctor* stories).

In late 1920 after his love affair with Milena Jesenská had simmered down, he attempted to return to the regimen of writing at night that had been successful for him in the past. Although he wrote a great deal, none of it satisfied him. He did not see fit to publish a single line from this fourth productive period. The fifth and final creative period encompassed two spurts between the winter of 1922 and his death in June 1924. This was the period of *The Castle* and the stories published in the *Hunger Artist* collection.

In each section that follows, the 'status' line explains the state of the text at the time of Kafka's death. The dates in parentheses are those of composition, not first publication. Works are presented in chronological order, according to our best estimate of the date of composition. In general I have followed the dating proposed by the editors of the Kritische Ausgabe. The discussions assume that users of this Guide have already read the works in question and are familiar with the story lines.

1. EARLY FICTION

1.1. 'Description of a Struggle'

In many respects the 'Description' displays in paradigmatic form the difficulties that confront the English-speaking reader of Kafka's works. The translations that are widely available are based on a German text that Max Brod created by editing together portions of two different manuscripts. The narrative that Brod constructed is therefore not anything one could properly call a 'story by Franz Kafka.' Only those able to read German have access to the texts as Kafka wrote them.

The first version (A) was probably initially conceived in the summer and fall of 1904, abandoned for a while, and then developed further in 1907. Brod used Version A as the main basis for his publication, and although he modified it with sections from Version B, the main outline of the earlier text is still visible. Readers of this compilation (*ComStor* 9–51) can therefore discern the plot outline of Version A, with its Chinese-box structure of changes in narrative perspective. The progression moves from the first-person narrator who initiates the story to the character known only as 'the fat man' (*ComStor* 29), then to 'the supplicant' (*ComStor* 36), then back to the fat man (*ComStor* 44) and finally returns to the first-person narrator at the end (*ComStor* 46).

The violence suggested by the word 'struggle' (*Kampf*) in the title takes physical form at several points in the A-Version narrative, particularly at its conclusion: the narrator's acquaintance suddenly pulls out a knife and stabs himself in the arm. Although the story begins in a conventionally realistic manner, it moves early on into a dream world where the landscape can change at a whim and where characters split apart and then merge again. None of the major figures has a name, and at times they speak and act in ways that suggest they are all parts of the same personality. The plot hardly exists except as a loosely connected series of strange, sometimes whimsical vignettes.

Kafka decided in spring 1909 that the project needed revision, an effort that lasted into the spring of 1910 and, in a few fits and starts, beyond. In this new draft (Version B) the fat man disappears completely, as do the many shifts in narrative perspective that characterize Version A. One first-person narrator relates the entire tale. The conversation with the supplicant remains, but now it is a dialogue between the supplicant and the narrator; and it is preceded by a new section, a dream in which the narrator relives his childhood in a country village. This dream passage was later published, almost word for word, as the story 'Children on a Country Road' in the *Meditation* volume (see 1.3 below). The B Version then returns to further conversations between the narrator and the supplicant, much of which is revised material from Version A, and concludes—or rather breaks off—with the narrator and supplicant going to a social gathering where the narrator is expected. Kafka kept trying to bring the project forward with occasional additional fragments written in his notebook, but even these came to an end in the summer of 1911.

Since Kafka never completed either version, it is not possible to interpret either one (never mind Brod's compilation) as a coherent whole. What we can say with confidence is that Kafka was experimenting with the idea of writing fiction, not so much in that he was trying his hand at fiction as a neophyte, but rather in that he was writing about writing. The concept of *Beschreibung* (description) cited in the title, a word which literally means 'writing something down,' names the topic that Kafka wanted to explore. The story is about the power of language to create a situation and then to alter it at will, sometimes arbitrarily, in any direction whatever. All the weirdness of the plot is a direct consequence of the author's exploring the boundless potential of making things up and writing them down.[1]

Kafka relished the strange ideas to which his imagination could give shape through writing, but he was also aware of the potential dangers of giving those ideas free rein. One of his most famous notebook entries spells it out:

> The tremendous [*ungeheure*] world I have in my head. But how to free myself and free it without being torn to pieces. And a thousand times rather be torn to pieces than retain it in me or bury it. That, indeed, is why I am here, that is quite clear to me. (*Diaries* 222)

The word translated here as 'tremendous' can also mean 'monstrous.' It is the same adjective Kafka uses to describe the monstrous verminous creature into which Gregor Samsa is transformed in 'The Metamorphosis.' What we find in the 'Description' is one of Kafka's earliest attempts to set that monstrous world free, an attempt in which the persona of the narrator is indeed torn to pieces. The world in Kafka's head already displayed in this early draft shows clear signs of the agonizing self-dismemberment that necessarily accompanied its liberation.

1.2. 'Wedding Preparations in the Country' (Max Brod's title)

Status: Opening chapters of an unfinished novel in several drafts (1906–07, 1909).

In the wake of his affair with an older woman during the summers of 1905 and 1906, Kafka began work on a novel about a man engaged to marry an older woman. He completed a draft of the first chapter and read it to Brod sometime prior to July 20, 1907, then went right to work on the next chapter. The surviving ms. of this second chapter breaks off in mid sentence at the bottom of a completed page, suggesting there were more pages that have not survived. These two (or one-and-a-fraction) chapters constitute Version A of the project (*ComStor* 52–71). He handed over the incomplete text of Version A to Brod, with pages missing, in early July of 1909. There are two additional drafts of the opening pages of the first chapter, both probably written in the summer of 1909. The first new draft (Version B) appears as the 'Second Manuscript' in some English editions (*ComStor* 71–76), and it is not only incomplete but also full of gaps. Version C never got very far (about three pages) and requires no further discussion here.

The hero of 'Wedding Preparations,' Eduard Raban, is the first of Kafka's many bachelor figures. Like them, he fears the loss of his bachelorhood, and like many of them—including in particular Georg Bendemann, Gregor Samsa, and Josef K.—Raban bears a name that is a slightly altered version of Kafka's own. The German word *Rabe* is a direct translation of the Czech *kavka* (crow), and the similarity of Rabe and Raban is obvious.

The shifts of narrative perspective we encounter in Version A of 'Description' also occur in this story, but they are less jarring. There is a noticeable but not especially intrusive movement back and forth between first-person and third-person narration. The third-person perspective actually coincides almost completely with the consciousness of the hero. Kafka appears to have been adapting to his own needs the 'free indirect style' of Flaubert, in which the third-person narrative frequently takes up the viewpoint of a particular character.

Like the 'Description' fragment, 'Wedding Preparations' plays with various issues of self-fragmentation that can confront a writer struggling to maintain his integrity and yet liberate the 'tremendous world' inside his head.[2] When one writes about one's self, one cannot fail to notice that the self-who-writes must exist as a separate agent from the self-who-is-written-about. When Kafka's hero Raban muses on this problem, he is horrified:

> "Well," he thought, "if I could tell her the whole story she would cease to be astonished. One works so feverishly at the office that afterwards one is too tired even to enjoy one's holidays properly. [. . .] And so long as you say 'one' instead of 'I,' there's nothing in it and one can easily tell the story; but as soon as you admit to yourself that it is you yourself, you feel as though transfixed and are horrified." (*ComStor* 53)

Raban proposes that what enables autobiographical storytelling is precisely the possibility of turning part of the self into a third person, a 'one' (*man* in German). The moment that such a self-alienation breaks down, when the narrating self realizes that it is also the narrated self ('you' in both cases), then anxiety wells up and stops the process.

A similar moment of self-alienation sets up what is for most readers the most striking scene in the whole fragment, anticipating the opening pages of 'The Metamorphosis.' Raban fantasizes about how he might avoid the trouble of meeting his prospective in-laws and making plans for the wedding: 'I don't even need to go to the country myself, it isn't necessary. I'll send my clothed body' (*ComStor* 55). While the clothed body is on its mission, the self can remain snug at home in bed:

> As I lie in bed I assume the shape of a big beetle, a stag beetle or a cockchafer, I think. [. . .] The form of a large beetle, yes. Then I would pretend it was a matter of hibernating, and I would press my little legs to my bulging belly. And I would whisper a few words, instructions to my sad body, which stands close beside me, bent. (*ComStor* 56)

Raban presents this as a happy fantasy of resolving his ambivalence, but the anxieties of the earlier passage remain in the background: if you were to 'admit to yourself that it is you yourself' who exists both as a sad body in clothes and as a big naked beetle, horror would quickly set in.

A few years later Kafka would see much greater narrative potential in the large beetle, but in 1909 he was not ready to see it. He abandoned the novel, handed the draft over to his friend Max, and dismissed it as 'my curse' (*Friends* 56).

1.3. The Meditation Stories

Status: Collection of 18 short prose pieces published by Kafka (1904[?]–12).

The parts of this collection came into being over the course of nearly a decade. When Kafka sent one of the first bound copies of *Meditation* to Felice Bauer on December 11, 1912, he enclosed a note in which he commented on the long history of its inception: 'I wonder if you notice how the various pieces differ in age. One of them for example is certainly 8 to 10 years old' (*Felice* 100). If Kafka's memory was correct, the genesis of the oldest of these texts might be as early as 1902–04. Since some of the material was lifted from Version A of the 'Description' draft, which was probably begun no later than 1904, a few of the pieces must have been at least that old. Others, however, were finished at the last minute, just before Kafka sent the manuscript off to Rowohlt on August 14, 1912. In many cases there is no evidence at all concerning the exact date of composition because the manuscripts were lost.

The volume Kafka gave to Felice represented the last of several stages in the publication of this material. In 1908 he had published eight of the pieces in the journal *Hyperion*, and in 1910 he published five more in the Prague daily paper *Bohemia*. Only a small part of the book, then, actually presented stories that were new to the public, and little of it was new to Kafka. Some pieces were taken from the 'Description' drafts: 'Children on a Country Road' (Version B), 'Excursion into the Mountains' (Version B), 'Clothes' (Version A), 'The Trees' (Version A). An incomplete draft of 'Unhappiness' appears in the notebook; it seems to have been written in several stages between November 1909 and March 1911. Other pieces Kafka took from the notebooks in slightly revised form are 'Bachelor's Ill Luck,' 'The Sudden Walk,' and 'Resolutions' (*Diaries* 117, 165, 178).

If there is any single compositional principle that unites this collection, it is the principle of taking things out of context. Kafka had a practical reason: he had promised to offer material for publication when he had nothing but fragments to offer. But he also had a more interesting artistic motivation: he was experimenting with decontextualization as a literary tool. Like the German Romantics before him, he understood that a piece of discourse with no context to guide its interpretation can take on an aura of unplumbed latent significance. A good example is the tiny piece 'The Trees' that Kafka took from the mouth of the fat man in section *iii d* of 'Description of a Struggle' (Version A). Kafka first wrote it as the second paragraph in the following extract:

> We build useless war machines, towers, walls, curtains of silk, and we could marvel at all this a great deal if we had the time. We tremble in the balance, we don't fall, we flutter, even though we may be uglier than bats. And on a beautiful day hardly anyone can prevent us from saying; 'Oh God, today is a beautiful day,' for we are already established on this earth and live by virtue of an agreement.
>
> We are like tree trunks in the snow, as a matter of fact. In appearance they lie flat on the ground, and a little push should be enough to move them along. But no, it can't be done, for they are firmly bound to the earth. But see, even that is merely appearance. (*ComStor* 45; trans. modified)

In its original context, the 'tree trunks' passage is one in a series of loosely associated observations on the state of the world that follow one upon the other almost like non-sequiturs. Because it resides in a whole set of offbeat remarks on all sorts of topics, the paragraph serves mainly to establish the bizarre character of the fat man and the dream-like quality of the narration.

When Kafka removed the paragraph from its place in the story to make it an independent text, he also made some small but important changes:

> For we are like tree trunks in the snow. In appearance they lie flat on the ground, and a little push should be enough to move them along. No, it can't be done, for they are firmly bound to the earth. But see [*aber sieh*], even that is only appearance. (my trans.; cf. *ComStor* 382)

The alteration of the first sentence serves to heighten what Kafka recognized as a slightly biblical quality of the rhetoric. The last sentence in particular reminds the reader of the passage in Ecclesiastes (1.14) where the preacher concludes, 'And behold [*und siehe*], all is vanity and vexation of spirit.'

With no explicit contextual clues to rely on, the reader must produce an imagined context. The hint of biblical rhetoric shows the way, suggesting that the passage is some kind of deep meditation on the mysteries of the human condition. Now, instead of serving to characterize a bizarre personality in a bizarre situation, the little text seems like a piece of scriptural 'wisdom literature' offering profound truths and requiring our most reverent attention. That is exactly the outcome Kafka was seeking. It would not be the last time he used such a strategy to achieve a similar effect.

2. 1912–13: THE BREAKTHROUGH PERIOD

2.1. 'The Judgment'

Status: Short story published by Kafka (September 1912).

Kafka wrote this alarming tale in his notebook in a single sitting during the night of September 22–23, 1912. (For more on its place in the notebook, see the discussion in Chapter 3, section 3.) He thought at the time—and history has proved him right—that this act of composition was the decisive turning point in his career as an artist. With this story, Franz became the Kafka we know. He also became the Kafka that Franz would henceforth strive to be, for good or for ill. He always hoped to achieve again the perfect textual coherence he thought he had attained during that sublime night when the words flowed in a single uninterrupted surge from mind to paper. It turned out nearly always to be an unrealizable goal.

In a notebook entry from February 11, 1913, he wrote down his own reactions to the story as he read over the proofs. Although he claimed that he as author was the only person possessing 'the hand that can reach to the body [of the story] itself' (*Diaries* 214), these reactions do not represent a definitive interpretation. They are useful, however, as a guide to some of the issues Kafka believed (in retrospect) were particularly important.

Kafka asserted that the key figure in the story was the absent friend in Russia, who serves as 'the link between father and son, [. . .] their strongest common bond' (*Diaries* 214). The father then exploits this bond, Kafka says, to strengthen his position against Georg, who is left defenseless against the father's sentence of death. Kafka also noted the connections between himself and the story's protagonist: 'Georg has the same number of letters as Franz. [. . .] But Bende has exactly the same number of letters as Kafka, and the vowel *e* occurs in the same places as does the vowel *a* in Kafka' (*Diaries* 215). In the same vein he commented on the similarities between the names of Frieda Brandenfeld, the fiancée in the story, and Felice Bauer, the woman he had just started wooing.

The points Kafka makes are good ones, but they only begin to hint at the complexity of this dreamlike story, as Kafka no doubt would have agreed. He observed that 'the story came out of me like a real birth' (*Diaries* 214), and like a thing truly born it developed immediately a life of its own beyond the control of its parent. That is as Kafka would have wished, because his goal as a writer was always to set his writing loose from conscious control. The best stories, in his opinion, were those that emerged directly from the depths of the author's psyche with only the most minimal authorial oversight. Kafka called this mode of writing 'being in the grip' (*im Ergiffensein*), and it was not unlike the classical conception of inspiration by the muse. But Kafka did not suppose he was in the clutches of a supernatural power; he was held in thrall by the tremendous/monstrous world inside his own head.

Writing this way meant working without a net. He made no notes, outlines, or preliminary sketches, and when he started on a story he had only an initial idea or image to guide him; he ordinarily had no notion of where it was going or how it would end.[3] In fact, the great majority of his fictions do not end. They just stop where the author lost contact with whatever had held him 'in the grip.' That, as Kafka knew well, was the huge price he had to pay for composing in this manner. He wrote stories the way salmon produce offspring: a colossal number of eggs yields a far smaller number of fry and ultimately only a handful of mature adults.

Another consequence of this compositional principle was that Kafka avoided revision. After his unsatisfactory experience with revising the 'Description' and 'Wedding Preparations' drafts, he gave up almost entirely on the idea of reworking an unsatisfactory text into something better. Nearly all the changes he made in his manuscripts were done on the spot, in the moment of composition. If he thought the narrative had started going off in a bad direction, he crossed out his work back to the point where he imagined the detour had begun and then started constructing a new road.

In Kafka's estimation 'The Judgment' was the perfect embodiment of his compositional ideal. Pursuing the narrative in a single stint from beginning to end, with no interruptions and no hindrance to the gush of ideas from deep inside the psyche to the ink flowing onto the page, was in his view 'the only way to write' (my trans.; cf. *Diaries* 213).

2.2. 'The Stoker'

Status: Novel chapter published as a separate 'fragment' by Kafka (September–October 1912).

Because this text is also the first chapter of the novel *The Missing Person*, I will comment on it in that context (see Chapter 5, section 1). We need to keep in mind, however, that Kafka himself took it out of context. Although he explicitly acknowledged its fragmentary nature, he still felt the piece could stand on its own. Indeed he thought it was the only portion of the novel ms. worthy of publication.

2.3. 'The Metamorphosis'

Status: Short story published by Kafka (November–December 1912).

This most famous of all Kafka's fictions was written over a period of several weeks between November 17 and December 7, 1912. The progress of the composition can be followed quite closely in the copious letters Franz wrote to Felice during these early days of their relationship. To have completed such a powerful work in a mere three weeks might have been a cause for celebration for most writers, but not for Kafka. He thought it had taken too long. The need to ration his time carefully because of obligations at the office meant that he could not gallop through this story the way he had through 'The Judgment.' He told Felice that

> my story, alas, has already been harmed enough through my method of working. This kind of story should be written with no more than one interruption, in two 10-hour sessions; then it would have its natural spontaneous flow, as it had in my head last Sunday [November 17]. But I haven't got twice 10 hours at my disposal. (*Felice* 64)

He gave his story the title 'Die Verwandlung.' Although it will always be known to English-speaking readers as 'The Metamorphosis,' a more accurate translation would be 'The Transformation.' The allusions the English title makes both to Ovid's *Metamorphoses* and to the process of maturation in certain insects are appropriate, but they were not foremost in Kafka's imagination. The original title suggests something miraculous and radical, as when a magician changes a white scarf into a white rabbit. It can also suggest a religious conversion, a chemical transmutation, a theatrical change of scenery, and a theological transubstantiation. The entomological metamorphosis is there, too, but it must compete for attention with all those others.

Another unfortunate consequence of using the term 'metamorphosis' for the title is that the word's association with the insect world leads readers to the erroneous conclusion that the story is primarily or exclusively about Gregor's transformation into a large bug. Such is not the case. An attentive reader will notice right away that the action of Kafka's story actually has almost nothing to do with the process of Gregor's bodily alteration from human to insect, which is already complete before the story begins. It has everything to do with the consequences of that transformation, the most significant of which is yet another transformation: the radical and miraculous change in Gregor's family, especially his sister Grete.

The plot of the tale follows a classical crossing or 'chiastic' pattern, in which the fortunes of one character or set of characters improve while the fortunes of others decline. In this case it is Gregor who declines and his parents and sister who improve, and because of that improvement the story does not (indeed cannot) conclude with Gregor's death. It is critical that we see the family, now freed of the verminous burden that had held it back, beginning to blossom like the spring weather. They declare their independence by firing the maid and dismissing the roomers. They eagerly look forward to a day when Grete will establish further independence by finding herself 'a good husband' (*Meta* 42). The last image the story offers is of blooming youth: 'their daughter got up first and stretched her young body' (*Meta* 42).

A chiastic crossing also takes place within Gregor, for as his physical condition deteriorates, his spiritual condition actually improves. As his verminous insect body becomes ever more burdensome and vile, his human consciousness actually becomes more sensitive and charitable. The climactic turning point occurs when Grete plays the violin, thereby unintentionally luring Gregor out of hiding in his room. 'Was he an animal that music could move him so?' (*Meta* 36). Yes and no. Gregor's body is more inhuman than ever, but his human spirit has become more humane. Gregor has overcome its self-centeredness and is now primarily focused on his family and its welfare.

His appearance precipitates a crisis. The roomers catch sight of him and in their horror immediately give notice that they wish to vacate the premises. In response Grete finally comes to the conclusion that this monster (who perhaps once was Gregor but is no longer) 'has to go' (*Meta* 38). Gregor hears her and returns to his room. 'He thought back on his family with deep emotion and love. His conviction that he would have to disappear was, if possible, even firmer than his sister's' (*Meta* 39). He dies within hours, and the cleaning woman reports to her employers: 'you don't have to worry about getting rid of the stuff next door. It's already been taken care of' (*Meta* 42).

The Samsas do not wish to hear about the remains. They belong to the past, and the Samsas are no longer interested in the past. They have far too much to look forward to in the future.

3. 1914–15: THE TIME OF THE TRIAL

3.1. 'In the Penal Colony'

Status: Novella published by Kafka (October 1914).

In the summer and fall of 1914, after the collapse of his first engagement to Felice, Kafka experienced a new burst of creative energy. He had started work on a new novel, *The Trial*, which he hoped to advance during a vacation from October 5 to 18. Some time during those two weeks he also wrote 'In the Penal Colony.' The story was first presented in a reading Kafka held at an art galley in Munich in November 1916, an occasion which the author experienced as a disaster. It seemed as if the story might need revision, although as a matter of principle Kafka resisted making changes after the heat of inspiration had cooled down. In connection with a later plan for publication, Kafka experimented in his notebooks with some alterations of the ending (*Diaries* 376–82), but they did not satisfy him, and in any case that particular publication plan fell through.[4] Still, he seems to have believed that there was a fatal flaw in the story: 'Two or three of the final pages are botched, and their presence points to some deeper flaw; there is a worm somewhere which hollows out the story, dense as it is' (*Friends* 136).

When Kurt Wolff finally reached a firm decision in 1918 to bring out the story, Kafka asked that he be given a chance to look over the typescript once more before typesetting. At that time he 'cut out a small section' (*Friends* 208), but despite his dissatisfaction with the concluding pages he apparently made no other changes. In this respect he was true to his post-'Judgment' principle of avoiding revisions. No manuscript version has survived, but the text published by Wolff in early 1919 probably reproduces (with some deletions) the ms. he produced during the two-week vacation in October 1914.

In its bizarre fashion 'In the Penal Colony' mirrors the basic plot of 'The Judgment': one man seeks from another his judgment (*Urteil*) about the propriety of a certain course of action and receives a condemnatory verdict (*Urteil*) that leads to the seeker's death. The course of action in question in the penal colony is the execution of condemned prisoners by means of a mechanism that uses multiple needles to inscribe on the victim's body the commandment the prisoner has been accused of breaking. The seeker is the penal-colony officer in charge of executions, and he seeks judgment about the propriety of such executions from a foreign traveler who is visiting the facility. Just as 'The Judgment' consists primarily of a conversation between the father and the son about the advisability of the son's sending a letter to a friend announcing his recent engagement, so the 'Penal Colony' consists primarily of a conversation between the officer and the traveler about the appropriateness of executions carried out by the inscription machine.

The officer wishes to convince the traveler that the procedure is just, that it delivers not merely painful punishment to the condemned prisoner but also profound understanding (*SelStor* 44). The officer's elaborate explanation of the construction, operation, and history of the machine is the centerpiece in his effort to win the traveler's support. The traveler's announcement that the officer has failed in this effort strikes the officer with the force of a death sentence, and for that reason he straps himself to the machine and sets it in deadly motion.

The fact that the machine writes on the body of its victim might suggest that its principal role is to write, but there is more to it. The machine does indeed write, but its ultimate goal is to facilitate reading.[5] After six hours of being written upon, the officer explains, the victim begins to feel the significance of the text:

> Understanding dawns even on the dumbest. [. . .] Nothing more actually happens, the man merely begins to decipher the script, he purses his lips as if he were listening hard. You've seen that it is not easy to decipher the script with your eyes, but our man deciphers it with his wounds. (*SelStor* 44–45)

That violent wounds are necessary to facilitate reading is a self-evident tenet of the officer's system of belief.

Kafka himself shared such a belief—or at least he had done so earlier in his life. As a young man of 20 years he wrote a remarkable letter to his school friend Oskar Pollak about the proper goal of reading. 'I think we ought to read only the kind of books that wound and stab us,' he said (*Friends* 16). Pollak had apparently expressed a preference for books that made him happy. But such books, Franz replied,

> are the ones we could write ourselves if we had to. But we need the books that affect us like unhappiness, that hurt us deeply, like the death of someone we loved more than ourselves, like being pushed out into the woods far away from people, like a suicide, a book must be the axe for the frozen sea within us. That's what I believe. (January 27, 1904, my trans.; cf. *Friends* 16)

Wounding, stabbing, hacking with an axe—such were the figures Kafka thought appropriate for *good* reading in 1904. The execution machine of 1914 recapitulates this idea in one of the most memorable and horrifying images the writer ever devised.

As the plot of the 'Penal Colony' makes clear, the Kafka of 1914 had somewhat reworked the idea about reading by means of wounding, stabbing, and hacking that had first occurred to the Kafka of 1904. He was now less interested in the image of the text as a weapon inflicting wounds than he was in the wound as an organ of perception. In this later incarnation it is not the text itself but the reading apparatus that opens up the wounds through which understanding may enter the reader. The text, the Old Commandant's 'scripture,' exists quite apart from the mechanism and does no stabbing on its own. But the traveler in the story has no interest in such distinctions and has little patience for the theory that authorizes them. It is the officer alone who defends the procedure of opening up the frozen sea inside various condemned prisoners.

The level of the officer's commitment becomes clear when the visitor expresses his firm disapproval, thereby in effect accusing the officer of not being just. In the world of the penal colony 'guilt is always beyond all doubt' (*SelStor* 40), and therefore the traveler's accusation is in itself a verdict of guilt. The officer acts with perfect logic by releasing the condemned prisoner, upon whose body was to be inscribed the injunction 'Honor thy superiors' (*Selstor* 39), and instead placing himself on the bed of the machine, to have embossed on his own skin the words 'Be just' (*SelStor* 54).

As long as the prisoners obey their superiors, and as long as their superiors are always just, the system will work flawlessly. But the traveler has proposed that the superiors are not just. In doing so he has condemned not only the officer and the deceased former commandant but the entire governance system of the colony, including the machine. If indeed guilt is always beyond all doubt, then the machine must execute not only the officer but itself as well.

To do both at once proves difficult for the machine. The execution turns out not to be the long and complex process of gradual enlightenment the officer had described; it is instead relatively rapid, messy, and unproductive of the 'promised deliverance' (*SelStor* 58). And no wonder. As it was killing the officer, the machine 'was obviously falling apart' (*SelStor* 57). At the story's end the officer is dead, the machine is a dismembered wreck, and the traveler yearns to escape from the reading/writing system in which texts really do 'wound and stab us.'

There is no assurance that escape is possible, even if the visitor can leave the colony. Before he departs, the traveler visits a teahouse in which he discovers the grave of the old commandant. On the marker is inscribed the following message: 'A prophecy exists that after a certain number of years the commandant will rise again and lead his followers from this house to reconquer the colony. Have faith and wait!' (*SelStor* 59).

This is the most alarming of all the inscriptions in this colony ruled by inscriptions. Sooner or later the regime of stabbing and wounding will rise again. It's just a matter of time.

3.2. 'The Village Schoolmaster' and 'Blumfeld, an Elderly Bachelor'

Status: Unfinished stories (December–February[?] 1914–15).

On December 19, 1914 Kafka wrote in his notebook that he had begun work on a story called 'The Village Schoolmaster.' From the outset he had his doubts about the project, but he consoled himself with the hope that it could end up better than it looked at the start:

> Beginning of every story ridiculous at first. It seems hopeless that this still incomplete and utterly vulnerable organism will be able to hold its own against the self-sufficient organization of the world [. . .]. But to think so is to forget that the story, if it is justified, carries its complete organization within itself, even if it hasn't yet fully developed; therefore [. . .] one never knows whether the despair one feels is justified or unjustified. (*Tag* 711; my trans.)

In this case, Kafka's anxiety was quite justified. Two-and-a-half weeks later (January 6, 1915) he admitted failure: 'For the time being abandoned "Village Schoolmaster"' (*Diaries* 325). The abandonment turned out to be not just for the time being but forever. If the narrative did indeed harbor 'its complete organization' somewhere within, Kafka never found it.

It would be vain to believe that we will be able to find what Kafka could not, but we can at least discern the main issues he wanted to examine in this unfinished effort. First and foremost, this was to be a story about people dealing with a story—and not just any story, but an especially incredible tale about a creature that reason and experience indicate could not exist: a giant mole. The very thought of such a monstrous animal is so disgusting that it turns the stomach of the story's narrator (*ComStor* 168), and in that respect the mole reminds us of the 'monstrous vermin' Gregor, who turned the stomach even of his loving sister.

The narrator is a businessman who takes an interest in the matter when he learns that an account of the sighting of the giant mole written by a local village teacher has been scorned by the academic authorities. Most of the fragment concerns the complicated relationship between the village schoolmaster, author of a pamphlet on the giant mole, and the businessman, author of another pamphlet on the same topic written out of a desire to vindicate the teacher. Unfortunately the teacher discerns in this second pamphlet an attempt to undermine his credibility, and the two pamphlet-writers find themselves enemies instead of allies.

The focus of the story moves rapidly away from the issue of the mole's existence and fastens instead on the relationship between the two authors. It is not difficult to discern lurking in the background the conflict that arose between the two letter-writers, Franz Kafka and Grete Bloch, over Kafka's engagement to Felice. They had begun as allies but developed into adversaries—or at least so it must have looked to Franz when confronted in the Berlin hotel by a prosecutorial Felice with Grete as her assistant. Such an observation should not lead to the conclusion that the story is 'about' Grete's relations with Franz; but it does indicate the emotional context in which the narrative arose. Kafka's personal life always decisively affected the direction of his fictions.

The businessman who began his intervention with such benevolent intentions discovers that his pamphlet has failed. The teacher reads in it evidence of ill will and duplicity; the businessman defends himself; and the two pamphleteers begin to exchange reproaches. The word 'Vorwurf' (reproach) occurs over and over again in the fragment, probably even more often than the similar-sounding 'Maulwurf' (mole). When the two words appear in the same sentence, the effect is striking: 'the man's reproaches [*Vorwürfe*] were really due to the fact that he clung to his mole [*Maulwurf*], so to speak, with both hands' (*ComStor* 173). Kafka's 'Maulwurf' story was thus more of a 'Vorwurf' story, and as such it had no clear line of development. The trading of reproaches propelled the narrative forward for a while, but eventually the author could not sustain it. He attributed his lack of progress to not having extended periods of time for writing: 'If I can't pursue the stories through the nights, they break apart and disappear' (*Diaries* 324–25). Whatever the reason, he moved on to something else.

Among the things he moved on to was his reunion with Felice in Bodenbach. Upon his return he started a new project that he initially thought of as his 'dog story.' He never gave it a title. The 'Blumfeld' title under which the fragment usually appears in publication is its incipit, that is, its opening words. In a notebook entry for 9 February 1915 he mentions briefly having worked on the dog story and then goes on at some length about his dissatisfaction with its beginning. He calls it 'ugly [. . .] wicked, pedantic, mechanical, a fish barely breathing on a sandbank' (*Diaries* 330). Kafka was always highly self-critical, but this assessment seems unusually harsh. It was perhaps a self-fulfilling prophecy, for indeed the dogfish died on the sandbank, although we do not know exactly when.

Because Kafka never completed the narrative, we cannot say for certain where he might have taken it. Its basic idea, however, is clear: the old bachelor Blumfeld is looking for companionship. The question is: what sort of companions would be suitable? As the story develops, the idea of 'companions' goes through several transformations. At first they are to be a dog and—unfortunately—the dog's inevitable companions, fleas; so he decides against dogs, but shortly thereafter he discovers in his room a pair of miraculous but annoying bouncing celluloid balls imbued with consciousness. He has no idea where they came from or what to do with them. They are some kind of infestation, like fleas. If he had a dog, perhaps the animal would destroy them, but he has no dog, and so the bouncing balls continue to plague him, making their constant racket. They are companions, to be sure, but bad ones.

The next morning before he leaves for the linen factory where he is employed, he tries to give the balls away to some children. Unhappily he cannot be sure he has succeeded, because 'he has no desire to be present at the liberation of the balls' (*ComStor* 197). We soon discover that the situation at the linen factory is much the same as at home. He is plagued by a pair of assistants who 'give Blumfeld a great deal of trouble' (*ComStor* 197). Indeed these two assistants act like human transformations of the annoying celluloid balls. The rest of the fragment is taken up with an account of the bachelor's frustrating interactions with the assistants. Having companions, Blumfeld might conclude, is perhaps not worth the trouble.

In light of Kafka's renewed contact with Felice, we can readily understand that such concerns about companionship would have dominated the author's thoughts. Which would be worse, lonely bachelorhood, or a less lonely life constantly disturbed by dogs/fleas/balls/children/assistants—and, most disturbing of all, a wife?

4. 1917: TALES FROM ALCHEMISTS LANE

The third of Kafka's intensely productive periods began when Ottla gave him access in December 1916 to the little house she had rented on Alchemists Lane next to the Hradschin Castle wall. Perhaps another spur to his activity was the terrible reception accorded his public reading of 'In the Penal Colony' on November 10 in Munich. For whatever reason, Kafka began to feel himself 'in the grip' of his creative fire before the year was out. The fire continued to burn hot right on through the winter of 1917 and into the spring.

4.1. The Country Doctor Stories

Status: Collection of 14 'little stories' [*kleine Erzählungen*] published by Kafka (1916[?]–17).

The principal product of the winter spurt of 1917 was a collection of short pieces Kafka published with Wolff in 1919 as *A Country Doctor*. As early as sometime in February he was already thinking of such a collection and had written down a list of possible titles, including 7 of the 14 that would eventually make up the volume. At the end of March he made a new list, adding a few more titles. In April he wrote to Martin Buber that he was planning to put together certain of these stories in 'a book, collectively titled *Responsibility*' (*Friends* 132). The title would change completely, but the contents were already nearly set by the time in spring when Kafka had to leave the little house on Alchemists Lane and find other quarters. Over the summer the author and his publisher came to an understanding about the title and contents, and with one exception (the removal of 'The Bucket Rider') the volume would eventually appear in the form agreed upon then. As the book went to press Kafka added a dedication to his father.

It is not possible in this brief Guide to discuss each of the 14 stories in *A Country Doctor*. Two of them, 'Before the Law' and 'An Imperial Message,' were originally parts of longer narratives (*The Trial* and

'Building the Great Wall of China') and therefore will be treated later in the discussions of those larger texts. Because of its use of the name Josef K., some scholars believe that Kafka might have written 'A Dream' in 1914 and intended it too to be part of *The Trial*; others suspect it was written later, perhaps in 1916, as an independent fiction. No manuscript survives, and it may never be possible to establish a firm date of composition. In any case, it seems perfectly reasonable to understand the sketch as Josef K.'s premonition of his demise at the end of the unfinished *Trial*.

4.1.1. 'A Country Doctor' (Winter 1916[?]–17)
The story that gave its name to the volume as a whole must have struck its author as particularly successful. No manuscript has survived, and there is no direct testimony in the notebooks or letters relating to its composition, so we can only guess about Kafka's level of satisfaction. It is nonetheless safe to assume that completing 'A Country Doctor' represented one of the 'good moments' Franz mentioned to Felice in a letter written around the same time as the story (*Felice* 538). And certainly he would not have named his book after a piece that displeased him.

In many ways this tale is Kafka at his best, writing 'in the grip' of an inspiration from deep within. The narrative is such a direct recreation of the world in the writer's head that much of it reads like a dream transcript. In fact, Kafka may have been trying deliberately to present a tale of repressed and displaced erotic wishes in a manner that would respond to Freud's theory of dreams. He had 'thoughts about Freud, of course' when composing 'The Judgment' (*Diaries* 213), and it seems altogether likely that similar thoughts accompanied this work as well. In any case Kafka's dream-concept led him in a direction almost diametrically opposed to Freud's. The author of *The Interpretation of Dreams* had proposed that the task of the dream was to make unacceptable libidinous wishes unrecognizable to consciousness, whereas Kafka's dream narrative does just the opposite. It makes such wishes distressingly explicit.

Although at first the surface narrative presents the country doctor's central concern as his professional relations with his patients, not far into the story it becomes clear that his thoughts and actions are dominated by worries about personal relations with the serving girl Rosa. The doctor is not aware of his worries until, as he departs in his carriage on an urgent house call, he realizes that the stable groom is about to ravish Rosa. The opening of the story demonstrates that the doctor is unaware of many powerful forces within his own household, including especially the horses the groom brings out of the pigsty—the very horses that carry the doctor's carriage with miraculous swiftness away from the vulnerable Rosa and toward the wounded patient waiting for him in bed.

With the logic of dream, however, the wounded patient and the vulnerable Rosa merge, since the gash in the patient's hip is introduced in such a way as to make it a stand-in for the girl and the center of attention. No translation can duplicate the effect Kafka achieves when he describes the wound. The sentence that begins in English 'Many shades of pink' (*SelStor* 63) opens in Kafka's German with a word that is indistinguishable, especially when capitalized, from the servant's name: 'Rosa, in vielen Schattierungen.' Kafka's intended audience could hardly fail to make the connection. The patient may be male, but the dream-structure of the narrative treats him figuratively as female.

Other sexual elements emerge in the interaction between the doctor and his 'Rosa' patient. The wound is the site of fertility, though of a sort that turns the stomach: it is full of worms 'thick and as long as my little finger' (*SelStor* 63). Along with its color, the fact that it is found 'near the hip' and is 'the size of a palmprint' gives it the character of a female sex organ (*SelStor* 63). Furthermore, the family treats the doctor as if he were the bridegroom in some pagan rite of marriage. They and other villagers undress him, sing a song over him, and put him into bed next to the patient, making sure he is on the side next to the wound. The words of the song suggest that if the bridegroom does not serve well as a physician he may serve instead as a human sacrifice (*SelStor* 64).

As often happens in dreams, the built-up erotic tension leads to no moment of merger and release. The doctor, understandably alarmed by the threatening song of the villagers, jumps out the window into his carriage in an attempt to escape. Unfortunately for the doctor, the horses that had formally moved with the speed of thought have lost their vigor: 'as slowly as old men we rode through the snowy waste' (*SelStor* 65). The story ends with the old physician apparently condemned to wander forever naked through the frozen landscape of his own dream.

4.1.2. 'Jackals and Arabs' (January–February 1917)

Many of Kafka's stories are about animals, and the reason once again emerges from the writer's personal life. A man named 'Kafka,' especially one competent in Czech, could hardly fail to feel a certain kinship with the animal kingdom. The significance of the Czech word *kavka* was hammered home nearly every day of Kafka's life, since his father used a drawing of a crow as his business logo. For Hermann the significance of his surname merely provided a convenient way to advertise his shop; for Franz, however, it seemed like destiny. The crow is a verminous creature, a carrion eater proclaimed unclean by the Torah. No *kavka* could ever make himself thoroughly pure.

A key issue in 'Jackals and Arabs' is how carrion eaters might achieve purity. The jackal spokesman declares the prime drive of his species: 'Purity, nothing but purity, is what we want' (*SelStor* 71). Kafka undoubtedly sympathized with the jackal. He too sought purity, and he too was a kind of jackal, not only because he bore the surname of a carrion eater but also because on his mother's side he was a Löwy. The name 'Löwy' was also sometimes spelled 'Löwe,' which is the German word for 'lion.' The German word for jackal, 'Schakal,' is nearly identical to the Hebrew word used in the Bible to mean 'lion.' A carrion-eating jackal is therefore a multilingual figure that neatly represents a Jew who is both a *Löwe* and a *kavka* at once. Such a figure reminds us of the predatory nomads of 'A Page from an Old Document,' whose language sounds like the 'screech of jackdaws' and whose horses, like themselves, are voracious carnivores (*SelStor* 66–67).

The story explores the paradox of an unclean beast whose life is dominated by a quest for cleanliness. There is an additional, subsidiary paradox: what would be disgusting to human beings—decaying flesh—is irresistibly alluring to the jackals; it is living flesh that disgusts them. The Arabs in particular seem foul beyond endurance: 'Filth is their white; filth is their black; their beard is a horror; [. . .] and when they lift their arm, all hell breaks loose in their armpits' (*Selstor* 71). Such a nauseated reaction to the living human body was hardly alien to Kafka, who had a nearly fanatical devotion to personal cleanliness and found sexual contact sometimes too repulsive to bear. It was this same Kafka, however, who now and then purchased the services of prostitutes. No wonder he empathized with jackals. He could understand all too well beings who sought 'purity, nothing but purity' but could not resist gorging themselves on the carcass of a dead camel.

4.1.3. 'A Report to an Academy' (March–April 1917)

Here is another animal story and another story of transformation. It inverts the plot of 'The Metamorphosis' in that its protagonist is changed from animal to human rather than from human to animal. As the ape's report makes clear, it's a bad bargain either way.

Kafka plays on a widespread popular misconception of Darwin's theory of evolution: the notion that man descended from apes. Kafka's fictional ape tells the gentlemen of the Academy that their own 'apedom [. . .] cannot be more remote from you than mine is from me' (*SelStor* 77) and thereby compresses the period of this 'descent' from animal to human to a few years. In the course of his report the ape puts considerable emphasis on the costs inherent in the transformation; what we thought was a genealogical descent turns out to be in many ways a moral descent from a life of genuine freedom to a human life of obligations and constraints. The descent from ape to man thus recapitulates the fall from Eden.

The 'Report' underscores the negative aspects of becoming human by presenting spitting, smoking, and drinking as the key events in the ape's conversion. The apprentice Homo sapiens finds it easy to master the first two skills, but the third is a huge obstacle: 'It was the brandy bottle that gave me the greatest trouble' (*SelStor* 81). Darwin had commented on the fact that certain monkeys 'have a strong taste for tea, coffee, and spirituous liquors,' concluding that monkeys and men must have similar nervous systems and indeed must share an overall 'similarity of the tissues and blood.'[6] Kafka, however, assumed just the opposite: that the ape's distaste for alcohol represented the enormous gap between himself and humanity. To bridge the alcohol gap would therefore bridge all other gaps as well. And indeed so it turns out in the 'Report.' The moment he can drink the brandy bottle dry is the exact moment the ape becomes fully human. At that instant he 'broke out in human speech,' fully aware that in doing so he had 'leaped into the human community' (*SelStor* 82).

It is a great achievement, for at a stroke this jungle ape has reached 'the average cultural level of a European' (*SelStor* 83). But the story in fact puts the value of such an achievement seriously into question. What has the animal actually gained? Human freedom? The ape mocks such a notion, saying that 'human beings all too often deceive themselves about freedom' (*SelStor* 79). As an ape he knew freedom; what he gained by becoming human was only 'a way out' of his imprisonment (*SelStor* 80). He is careful to explain that he uses the term 'way out' [*Ausweg*] in 'the most common and also the fullest sense' (*SelStor* 79). Since the German word means 'expedient, shift, dodge' as well as a physical exit, there is no mistake about what we are being told. Being human is no great thing; it is merely a dodge used by animals to avoid being locked up in zoos.

4.1.4. 'The New Lawyer' (1917)

Kafka chose 'The New Lawyer' to stand at the head of his *Country Doctor* collection, which indicates his sense of its importance. Like the academic 'Report' that concludes the book, this little sketch involves the not-altogether-happy transformation of an animal into a human being. In this case the reader gets no information about how the transformation took place; all we know is that the creature who once was Alexander of Macedon's battle charger is now an attorney successfully practicing law in the local courts.

As with the ape, so with the transformed horse—we are confronted with the thorny problem of what it means to be free. When he was a battle steed Bucephalus was able to do the impossible: under Alexander's direction he reached the gates of India. 'Even in those days India's gates were beyond reach,' but the horse and the conqueror reached then anyway (*SelStor* 60). Now the onetime horse's options are limited, and he has to use more indirect and cerebral methods to reach what is unreachable. 'Perhaps, therefore, it is really best, as Bucephalus has done, to immerse oneself in law books' (*SelStor* 60). After all, reading the Law is what Kafka's Löwy ancestors did, and what countless generations of Jews have done, in hopes of reaching something that cannot be attained in any other way.

4.2. 'The Bucket Rider'

Status: Short prose piece published by Kafka (1917).

For unknown reasons Kafka decided to remove 'The Bucket Rider' from the *Country Doctor* collection at the last moment—the book was already in proof—and publish it separately elsewhere. The story clearly derives from Kafka's experience of wartime coal shortages in Prague. The central image that drives the little sketch is spelled out in the narrator's call to the coal dealer: 'My bucket is so light that I can ride on it' (*ComStor* 413). The way Kafka uses this image illustrates one of his favorite modes of invention. He builds a fantastic story by acting out the implications of figurative language. In this case the figure is a hyperbole, a dramatic exaggeration. 'My bucket is so light that . . .' sets up a familiar hyperbolic formula that we are familiar with in jokes and insults: 'Your momma's so fat . . .' There are dozens if not hundreds of ways to complete the formula, each more outrageous than the last.

Kafka's hyperbole makes an analogously outrageous claim. An empty bucket is lighter than a full one, so perhaps a very empty bucket would become so light that it would float up in the air. At first riding around on a floating bucket sounds like fun, but when it becomes clear that the coal dealer, and especially the coal dealer's wife, has no intention of donating free coal, the bucket becomes dangerously light. The breeze from the woman's flapping apron is enough to send it flying ever higher. 'And with that I ascend into the regions of the ice mountains and am lost forever' (*ComStor* 414).

4.3. Sketches from 1917

Status: Unpublished drafts found in the Octavo Notebooks (1917).

Much of what Kafka wrote during his evenings in Alchemists Lane went into a set of octavo notebooks that he used in much the same manner as his quarto-format 'diary'; he put into these pages whatever occurred to him that seemed worth recording. A few pieces of it struck him as worthy of publication, and those he placed in the *Country Doctor* collection or in various periodicals. But by far the bulk of the material he left as fragments, expecting that they would someday be destroyed. Fortunately the notebooks were for the most part preserved, and in them we find some very interesting pieces of fiction that Kafka abandoned.

The very first entry in one of the notebooks Kafka used in the winter of 1917 (Notebook B) is a little sketch that Brod extracted after Kafka's death and published under the title 'The Bridge.' Like 'The Metamorphosis' and so many other Kafka stories, this draft presents a situation in which the central character is in two conditions at once. As Gregor is both human and inhuman, so is the narrator of the 'Bridge' sketch both animate and inanimate, both a person and a bridge, perhaps also both male and female (the German word for bridge, *Brücke*, is feminine). It is an inherently unstable situation, since human beings are creatures who experience pain, curiosity, and from time to time the urge to turn around. Bridges, on the other hand, no matter how much pain they may feel and no matter how curious they become, cannot turn around. To do so would violate the nature of bridge existence: 'no bridge, once erected, can stop being a bridge' (*SelStor* 108). But this bridge does turn around, and in that instant its bridge nature gives way to its mortal, fallen human nature. 'I had not yet turned around when I was already falling; I fell, and in a moment I was torn apart' (*SelStor* 109).

Directly following the fall of the bridge in Notebook B is some disjointed material about a character called 'the hunter Gracchus.' The stories published by Schocken as 'The Hunter Gracchus' and 'The Hunter Gracchus: A Fragment' (*ComStor* 226–34) are in fact both fragments, the first of which was edited together out of several entries in Notebook B, with the order somewhat rearranged at the end. Corngold gives a more accurate rendition of the Notebook B material as 'The Hunter Gracchus [Two Fragments]' (*SelStor* 109–13). The so-called 'Fragment' in the Schocken text comes from Notebook D.

It is difficult, given the state of the manuscript, to see a coherent narrative in these entries, though Brod tried to make one out of what he found in Notebook B. It is highly suggestive that the action is set in Riva, the site of one of Kafka's most intense summer romances. While he was engaged in his romantic interlude with the 'Swiss girl' in 1913, he was also engaged to marry Felice. Kafka's Riva holiday therefore placed him in the odd position of living in two engagements at once, as fiancé of one woman and lover of another. Gracchus (a Roman name akin to the Latin word meaning 'jackdaw') experiences a more dramatic version of this double existence in that he is alive and dead at the same time. That Kafka believed something similarly dramatic about his own situation cannot be doubted, and the connection to the central theme of the 'Bridge' sketch is evident.

In Notebook C Kafka drafted a lengthy but still fragmentary sketch under the title 'Building the Great Wall of China' (*SelStor* 113–24). Presented as a memoir by a Chinese historian, the narrative begins as an inquiry into the reasons why the wall was built in disconnected pieces to be joined together later. Before long, however, the inquiry turns into a meditation on the nature of China, its complexity, its system of imperial administration, and especially its vastness. The narrator chooses to illustrate these matters by means of a parable, and it was this parable that Kafka extracted from the sketch and published in the *Country Doctor* collection as 'An Imperial Message.'

The parable, as its author recognized, is not only the heart of the matter he was trying to deal with in the sketch but also a poignant case study in the nature of human hope. Kafka's tale of the emperor's dying message to one of the least among his subjects, a message that has to traverse the endless spaces of the empire, and therefore a message that its recipient can only dream of ever actually obtaining, both deepens and sharpens an observation Kafka once made to Brod. Max asked Franz if he thought God allowed humanity any hope, and Franz replied, 'Plenty of hope—for God—no end of hope—only none for us.'[7]

A couple of entries from Notebook G are worth special attention. These were written later in 1917, probably in the fall, and therefore after Kafka learned of his tuberculosis. Kafka's thoughts during this period turned often to the book of Genesis and now and then to classical mythology. He was apparently trying to reconnect with his heritage, both Jewish and classical, as he faced his own mortality. He was also looking at various ways of dealing with hopeless situations. His little sketches about the heroes Odysseus and Prometheus address ways of meeting a fate that cannot be avoided.

The piece published as 'The Silence of the Sirens' (*SelStor* 127–28) is introduced as 'proof that inadequate, even childish stratagems can also serve as a means of rescue.' The 'Prometheus' fragment (*SelStor* 129) deals with 'attempts to explain the inexplicable.' In both cases the classical heroes must deal with hopeless situations, although with dramatically different results. Odysseus escapes destruction by the Sirens, not by the means described in Homer, but by ignoring their seductive silence. Prometheus, condemned by the gods to be chained forever to a rock, does not escape; instead he becomes one with the rock and endures until everyone, including the gods, becomes tired of the whole business and forgets about it. All that remains is an inexplicable legend about the inexplicable mass of rock into which Prometheus has merged. The question remains open as to whether Prometheus has been obliterated or has survived in an altered state.

5. 1920: A SHEAF OF EXPERIMENTS

Kafka's resolution in August 1920 to resume his 'military service' of sleeping in the afternoons and writing at night bore some interesting results. Unfortunately none of them met the author's standard of success, and he left them abandoned in a sheaf of 51 loose leaves that was found after his death (the so-called '1920 Sheaf'). A number of passages from this experimental miscellany were published posthumously as individual pieces under titles mostly supplied by Brod; and they have subsequently become part of the Kafka canon.

Status: All of the texts treated in this section were unpublished at the time of Kafka's death.

5.1. 'On the Question of the Laws' (Kafka's title; August 1920) and 'The Conscription of Troops' (Brod's title; August 1920)

Many of the same concerns found in the 'Great Wall of China' material from 1917 recur in some of the entries in the papers from 1920, especially the two closely related pieces 'On the Question' and 'Conscription.' Indeed, this pair of texts seems to belong to the same fictional universe, perhaps Chinese, in which the state is ruled by distant and inscrutable powers whose will must be divined by acts of imagination. The first of the pair shows this kinship most clearly, since the problem of the laws is congruent with the problem of the message in the 'Imperial Message.' Just as it is certain that the emperor has sent a personal message to you, an insignificant subject in a distant and unimportant part of the empire, so too is it certain that the common citizens of the land are ruled by laws. The problem of these laws is that the common citizens do not know what they are. Perhaps the whims of the nobility are the only law.

Such a governance system hearkens back even further than the 'China' material of 1917 to the world of the 1914 'Penal Colony.' The colony is ruled by only two injunctions ('Be just' for the nobility and 'Honor thy superiors' for everyone else), and it appears that the community in 'On the Question of the Laws' operates under a similar system. The people must honor the nobility as the embodiment of the (unknown) law and hope the nobles are just. 'The only visible, indubitable law that is imposed on us is the nobility' (*SelStor* 130). A revolution overthrowing the nobility, easy in theory, is impossible in practice because the will of the nobility is the only mechanism guaranteeing social order. That is why the apparently successful overthrow of the old commandant's system in the penal colony was only a temporary discontinuity. In the analogous world of the problematic laws, there is no need to have faith and wait; the old system is still completely in charge, with all its sharp edges. The inhabitants may not be wounded and stabbed by needles, but they 'live on this knife's edge' (*SelStor* 130).

5.2. 'Poseidon' (Brod's title; September 1920)

One might well regard Kafka's 'Poseidon' draft as another look at the problem of inscrutable governance, but this time from the point of view of one of the ruling powers. Poseidon's task is to oversee (*übersehen*) the oceans, but as a result of his huge administrative burden he is obliged to overlook (also *übersehen*) and essentially ignore the vast tracts of his realm. Kafka's Poseidon is blood brother to Gilbert's Sir Joseph Porter in *Pinafore*: he sticks close to his desk and never goes to sea. Kafka was surely as aware as Gilbert of the comic implications, but he kept a straight face. Unlike the ruler of the Queen's Navy, the god of the sea aspires to become more closely acquainted with the world's waters. He just lacks the time at present—and for the foreseeable future.

The paradox of enormous power is that it imposes equally enormous constraints on the rulers, who then lose contact with that over which they rule. As Kafka suggested to Brod, there is perhaps more hope for gods than for us, but the case as presented in this story is a slim one: 'he was waiting until the end of the world [. . .] when, just before the end and after going over the final reckoning, he could still make a quick little tour' (*SelStor* 131).

5.3. 'The City Coat of Arms' (Brod's title; September 1920)

In the 'Great Wall of China' draft of 1917, there is a passage in which the historian-narrator comments on a theory that the Wall's ultimate purpose would be to serve as 'a solid foundation for a new Tower of Babel' (*SelStor* 116). Kafka returned again and again to the book of Genesis, especially to the passages on the Garden of Eden and the Tower of Babel, and he followed up on the hint he dropped in the 'Great Wall' about a reinterpretation of the Tower story in this sketch from 1920. The premise of both pieces is the same: 'it was not for the generally stated reasons that construction of the Tower of Babel failed to accomplish its goal' (*SelStor* 116).

The generally stated reason, of course, is the Genesis account of the confusion of tongues. Kafka's account proposes that the Tower failed because the builders never actually got around to working on the Tower. There was always a good reason to delay, not least because a belief in progress assured that 'the next generation with their perfected knowledge will [. . .] tear down what has been built so as to begin anew' (*ComStor* 433). So instead of building the Tower, the builders work on building a city to house the builders. It does not take long before the enterprise seems so pointless that the builders long for the destruction of their own city.

Exactly this sort of endless preparatory labor with little or nothing to show for it was Kafka's regular experience as a writer, especially in 1920. The whole '1920 Sheaf' is like a city built as the support structure for a work that was not only never accomplished but never even properly begun. There were many moments in the years of his illness that Kafka, too, longed for the destruction of both his city and its builder.

5.4. 'The Vulture' and 'A Little Fable' (Brod's titles; September–October 1920)

There are two intriguing little animal stories among the papers in the 1920 Sheaf. 'The Vulture' (*ComStor* 442–43) is remarkable in that the vulture's victim, the narrator, appears to be rescued from being eaten alive, not by the passerby who offers to get a gun to shoot the bird, but by the vulture's suicide. Even more remarkable, the bird destroys itself by hurling itself through the victim's mouth into the depths of his body, where it drowns in his blood. The long-suffering narrator feels immediate relief from the vulture's attacks, but his rescue comes at the cost of having the vulture reside inside him.

We recall what Kafka told Felice about his tuberculosis, that it was 'a weapon that continues to be of supreme necessity as long as I remain alive' (*Felice* 546). The disease was tearing him apart, and yet he felt it was an essential part of who he was. And so it turns out in this story. Vultures are unclean carrion-eaters just like jackdaws; nasty as they may be, they are of one blood with those named *kavka*.

The little fable about a philosophical mouse appears in the '1920 Sheaf' in two nearly identical passages, one right after the other. Brod selected the second version for publication under the title 'A Little Fable' (*ComStor* 445). Brod's title was appropriate in that the piece deliberately mimics the style of the Aesopian animal fable popularized in seventeenth-century France by La Fontaine. Talking animals with human concerns and human consciousness encourage the reader to see in the story an illustration of some important moral or philosophical principle. But Kafka's piece sets up such an expectation only to pull the rug out from under it: the figures that look initially like spokesmen for principles may be such, but only in the most unexpected, ironic, and disquieting fashion. At the level of the direct narration they act like an ordinary cat and mouse, brutal predator and slaughtered prey. The story's double irony thus acts out the vengeance of the literal upon the figurative, and vice versa.

5.5. 'The Top' (Brod's title; December 1920)

Another confrontation between the literal and the figurative occurs in the passage Brod extracted and called 'The Top' (*ComStor* 444). Here the potential for philosophical significance is embedded in the narrative, since the central character in the little story is a philosopher. Like any philosopher, this one wants to grasp (*begreifen*) the essence of things; but in the case of the spinning top, he finds that the act of physically gripping (*begreifen*) the object to examine it causes it to stop spinning and therefore to lose the very property the philosopher wanted to investigate. In other words, a literal grasping makes figurative grasping impossible. In a second rhetorical flip, the meaning of the word 'whip' (*Peitsche*) switches from its figurative use, referring to the device that sets the top in motion, to a literal lash that drives the philosopher away.

Physicists of Kafka's time who were trying to understand the spin of subatomic particles might have felt much like this fictional researcher. In many circumstances it is impossible to observe a phenomenon without altering it in some fundamental way. Kafka was no physicist and disclaimed any knowledge of science, but he had an intuitive grasp of the uncertainty principle.

6. 1922–24: LAST STORIES

In the winter of 1922, a few months before he officially retired from the insurance company, Kafka began another intensive program of writing fiction. The first fruits of this new harvest were several chapters of *The Castle*, but in the spring he took time out from the novel for some stories ('First Distress,' 'Hunger Artist'). He continued work on the novel and a few other projects through the summer

('Researches of a Dog'), but after August he was unable to make further progress on *The Castle*. In the late fall his literary activity slowed ('A Comment,' 'On Parables'), and by the end of the year it was at a temporary halt. Severe illness kept him from working for much of 1923. He was able to resume productive activity again in the fall and winter after he moved to Berlin with Dora ('The Burrow,' 'A Little Woman') and managed to complete one last story ('Josefine the Singer') before the final stages of tuberculosis ended Kafka's nocturnal scribbling forever.

6.1. 'First Distress' and 'A Hunger Artist'

Status: Stories published in the *Hunger Artist* collection (Spring 1922).

As his health deteriorated and his career as an artist drew to a close, Kafka wrote several stories about the place of artists in the world and the function of art. He was particularly intrigued by artist figures with a stubbornly uncompromising commitment to their chosen profession.

The trapeze artist of 'First Distress' is so devoted to his highflying way of life that any departure from it is painful. His unwillingness to compromise is such that he travels up in the luggage rack when he is obliged to take a train to his next performance. Even the limitation of performing on a single trapeze is unacceptable, and he tells his manager he must have a second. What the manager understands, and what worries him about the future, is that the demands of such an absolute commitment are potentially endless. Providing a second trapeze is easy; but what will happen when two are not enough, or when the bar seems no longer high enough? This performer's first distress will not be his last.

The hunger artist (or 'starvation artist' in Corngold's translation) displays a similarly uncompromising attitude toward his 'art' of fasting. Just as the trapeze performer would prefer never to descend from his trapeze, so would the hunger artist prefer to go on fasting forever. There are some interesting differences, however. The first is that the art of starvation, unlike acrobatics, is a display of inaction; its fulfillment is a non-performance. Starvation can potentially go on for weeks and months; it seems to go on forever at the conclusion of Kafka's story. The fasting artist dies, 'but his shattered gaze retained the firm, if no longer proud, conviction that he was still starving' (*SelStor* 94). The second major difference is that everyone agrees that performing on the high trapeze 'is one of the most difficult of those [arts] attainable by human beings' (*SelStor* 84). Starvation, on the other hand, seems more like an affliction than an art.

It is the hunger artist himself who casts the most serious doubt on the status of his chosen profession. Although he seems utterly convinced of the greatness and necessity of his art, he does not attempt to defend it. 'Try to explain the art of starving to someone! Those who have no feel for it can never be made to understand' (*SelStor* 93). Indeed he does not try to explain it or make others understand; on the contrary, when he is close to death he confesses to his supervisor that, although he wanted admiration for his fasting, he did not deserve any. He had no choice but to starve, he says, 'because I could not find the food I liked' (*SelStor* 94). Is it an art to do something supremely well if you do it, not by choice, but by necessity?

Even though the hunger artist believes it is not, Kafka's narrative does not compel the reader to agree. In fact, if offers evidence to the contrary. After the artist's death they clean out his cage and put in a wild animal. The powerful young panther is irresistible to the public: 'the joy of life sprang from its maw in such a blaze of fire that it was not easy for the spectators to withstand it' (*SelStor* 94). This creature has no choice but to be what it is, and yet people admire it enormously. Perhaps the artist too deserved admiration for being what he had to be. The story leaves the issue open.

6.2. 'Researches of a Dog' (Brod's Title)

Status: Unfinished story (Summer–Fall 1922).

In the closing lines of *The Trial*, as a knife is being twisted in his heart, Josef K. complains that he is ending his life 'like a dog' (*Trial* 231). The canine analogy was more than a spur-of-the-moment rhetorical flourish; it arose from Kafka's deep sense of kinship with animals, though it was not a kinship in which the author took pride.[8] On the contrary, as is clear from the last sentence of *The Trial*, he felt a strong element of shame in acknowledging it.

It is no surprise, then, that the canine investigator in 'Researches' is not a wholly admirable figure. He is a dogged researcher, one has to admit, and the ultimate truth he seeks is linked to a desire for freedom. But he seems limited in his canine perspective to matters of a distinctly doggish sort: Where does food come from? The fact that, from his limited perspective, nourishment seems to come from some transcendent beyond cannot quite transform the dog's researches into a spiritual quest, because we human readers know all the answers and know that they are all quite mundane. The entire narrative is suffused with irony precisely because we in the audience have the solutions to the riddles that perplex the narrator in his utter ignorance of human beings. But this irony is not the wrenching dramatic irony of Sophocles' *Oedipus* or the gentle romantic irony of Goethe's *Wilhelm Meister*; it is a comic, or perhaps even a burlesque form of irony. The knowledge we readers have that is hidden from the central character is not terrible in its implications, nor is it philosophically complex. It is merely better than that of a dog who does not have access to the human world.

It is perhaps not surprising that Kafka gave up on this text even after he had produced many pages. It is difficult to imagine how he could have made his premise pay off in an interesting way. The plot choices were limited: the dog could fail in his quest, or he could succeed either by finding the right answers or by constructing wrong ones. Kafka appears to have avoided making such a choice by letting his dog scientist renew his investigations over and over again on different objects. That narrative strategy is inherently inconclusive, and therefore the author never concludes.

6.3. 'A Comment' and 'On Parables'

Status: Fragments from the notebooks (November–December 1922).

At the other end of the spectrum from the rambling and interminable 'Researches' are two very short texts that pack an enormous punch. 'A Comment' (which Brod published under the title 'Give it Up!') is quintessential Kafka at the top of his form. The tiny tale turns the world inside out in the compass of a few sentences, taking the narrator in the blink of an eye from the petty concerns of trying to find his way to the railroad station to vast metaphysical questions about how to live his life. The device that makes the story work is a rhetorical turn whereby the policeman responds to a simple request for directions as if he were being asked for philosophical enlightenment.[9] The story conjures up that sense of cosmic despair people often feel when simple little things go unexpectedly wrong. In Kafka's fictional world, however, such despair is not only justified, it is certified as valid by the authorities.

'On Parables' (*SelStor* 161–62) illustrates the difficulties of Kafka's very own readers. It dramatizes the situation of those trying to find meaning in texts that seem to mean something other, and much more significant, than what they say. The word translated as 'parable' is 'Gleichnis,' and in German the term covers a rather large semantic field. It includes 'parable' but also 'image, simile, comparison.' The heavenly chorus at the end of Goethe's *Faust*, recapitulating Plato, proclaims that everything transitory is only a 'Gleichnis,' that is, a simulacrum of something else. But of what?

Kafka's little fragment asks just that question; then it proposes an answer that is not only frustratingly parabolic but also so paradoxical as to defy logical analysis. The conclusion that 'in the parable you lost' suggests that there is always a catch in parables. Even when you win 'in reality,' you lose in the parable, because in parable it is impossible to win. Once you are inside a parabolic universe, the only way out is to deny the parable's premise—as Alice does in Wonderland, for example, when she saves herself from the Queen of Hearts by declaring, 'You're nothing but a pack of cards!' Alice wins in reality: she brings her trial to an immediate halt and reestablishes her place in the real world. But in parable she has lost, because she has lost the parable. Wonderland has collapsed into a deck of cards.

6.4. 'The Burrow' (Brod's title)

Status: Unfinished story (November–December 1923).

Kafka's tale of the fearful burrowing animal reflects the concerns of a maker of things who finds himself in mortal danger. The title ('Der Bau') was Brod's, but the key term 'Bau' (translated as 'burrow') was Kafka's. It appears again and again as the term used by the digging creature to describe his home. Unfortunately, the English word 'burrow' cannot reproduce the larger implications of Kafka's 'Bau,' a term that refers to anything constructed on, in, or above the earth. The verb 'bauen' means 'to dig,' to be sure, but also in general 'to construct' or 'to develop.' Someone who digs in the earth to plant crops is a 'Bauer' (farmer), a word that obviously had special relevance to Kafka as his former fiancée's surname. An author who constructs fictions also engages in the activity of 'bauen.'

The first half of the story deals with the construction of the burrow and its properties, focusing particularly on the pride of the builder in his security measures against outside threats. The second half focuses on threats. As he continues to expand and improve his structure, the burrower lives in constant and growing fear of something out there, something perhaps already encircling his burrow, some 'large animal' (*SelStor* 185) that could destroy him. The crucial question becomes how the burrower should deal with this real or imagined enemy. Then the text breaks off abruptly.

There is not enough evidence to permit a reasonable guess as to how Kafka might have developed the story further. It is possible he wrote a conclusion that no longer exists. Brod asserted that in a final section, now lost, the burrower confronted the invading 'large animal,' fought with it, and was killed. Valuable as Brod's testimony often is, this particular claim has met with considerable skepticism.[10] Since 'The Burrow' is a first-person narrative, Kafka would have been obliged to let his protagonist narrate his own death, a difficult feat. We should note, however, that the first-person narrator of 'The Bridge' does exactly this.

More troubling evidence against Brod's claim is this: Kafka was careful to plant the suggestion that the 'large animal' is a figment of the burrower's anxious imagination. Could Kafka's story really have ended with its hero killed by an imaginary entity? Although such an outcome defies reason, it cannot be excluded out of hand in Kafka's world, where stranger things have happened and where the figurative might well wreak vengeance on the literal. We should also note that Heinrich von Kleist, one of Kafka's favorite authors, concludes one of his plays by having his heroine kill herself with an imaginary dagger.

Kafka could have done just as Brod said. We will never know.

6.5. 'A Little Woman'

Status: Story published in the *Hunger Artist* collection (December 1923–January 1924).

According to Dora Diamant, this little story presents a portrait of the landlady who owned the apartment in Berlin-Steglitz where Franz and Dora lived in the fall of 1923.[11] The landlady became suspicious of her foreign tenants and eventually drove them out with staggering rent increases. Kafka's character, to whom 'every scrap of my life would certainly be an offense' (*ComStor* 317), displays an attitude that seems entirely congruent with the existential disapproval displayed by the Berlin landlady. This is one of the few pieces in the Kafka canon that can be read as a straightforward realistic sketch, and perhaps that is the most appropriate way to read it.

6.6. 'Josefine, the Singer or The Mouse Folk'

Status: Story published in the *Hunger Artist* collection (March–April 1924).

Kafka wrote 'Josefine' only a dozen weeks before he died, probably in the knowledge it would be his final artistic testament. It brings together many features of earlier stories. The central character is a verminous animal like Gregor Samsa; she is an uncompromising artist like the trapeze acrobat and the hunger artist; she bears the feminine version of the name borne by the hero who dies like a dog at the end of The Trial; she disappears never to be heard from again like the hero of *The Missing Person*; and like the officer in the penal colony, she departs from the scene toward a purported 'Erlösing' ('deliverance, redemption') that appears highly dubious.

The first-person narrator, a mouse researcher, reminds us of investigating narrators in earlier works: the researching dog, the Chinese historian of the Great Wall, the scholar/businessman interested in the giant mole, the philosopher trying to grasp the top, and the civilized ape who reports to an academy. Like those others, the curious mouse discovers that the evidence relevant to his inquiry is fragmentary and often contradictory. It is not even certain that Josefine's singing really constitutes music; and if it does, it is not clear what significance such music has for the community. 'Is it even song, then? Isn't it perhaps just squeaking?' (*SelStor* 95).

The word translated here as 'squeaking' is 'Pfeifen,' and like 'Bau' it presents a major problem to the translator. Some translations use 'piping,' but that choice fails to address the difficulty. When used in connection with mice, 'Pfeifen' does indeed mean 'squeaking,' but when used with human beings it means 'whistling.' Whistling is particularly relevant because human whistling stands precisely in a twilight zone between actual music and the meaningless discharge of nervous energy. Some few people can whistle as melodiously as a symphonic instrument; most just blow air. Is Josefine's 'Pfeifen' also a whistling in this human sense, and if so, which kind is it? The narrator is not sure.

What is sure is that this whistling/squeaking has an enormous impact on the mouse folk. When she performs, 'something of her squeaking—this cannot be denied—inevitably forces its way to us. [. . . It] comes almost as a message from the people to the individual' (*SelStor* 100). Because her art, whatever it is, has this effect of binding the community together, Josefine can claim to be doing a public service. She presses this claim by asking for special privileges, including 'to be excused from all work in consideration of her song' (*SelStor* 104). Josefine's creator could hardly have sympathized more with her request; he had sought just such an exemption for himself, and thanks to his illness had actually obtained it; but the mouse folk are not so generous with their singer. They listen to her arguments and calmly reject them all.

Josefine brings it on herself, perhaps, because she scorns the community whose special treatment she has solicited. 'I don't give a squeak for your protection' she says, employing a German locution (*Ich pfeife auf . . .*) that turns the word describing her art into a vulgar insult (*SelStor* 99). It implies that her singing to the people is always also a rather nasty, low-class rebuke (*pfeifen auf das Volk*). The uncompromising artist thus puts herself in the untenable position of demanding respect from those to whom she gives none. It is little wonder that her claim for exemption from labor is met with rejection that is 'sometimes so harsh that even Josefine staggers' (*SelStor* 104).

The artist believes she has one invincible weapon in pressing her claim: she can withhold her art by vanishing from the scene. But the mice quickly discover that the song's absence is indistinguishable from its presence. No one denies the power of her art; but by her absence Josefine merely demonstrates how unnecessary the singer is for the song to have its effect. 'Was her actual squeaking notably louder and livelier than the memory of it will be? Even during her lifetime was it ever more than a mere memory?' (*SelStor* 107–08).

Perhaps not. And perhaps literature is no different from singing in this respect. Josefine's creator called himself 'a memory come alive' (*Diaries* 392), and no doubt he expected to share the fate he assigned to his diva heroine: to achieve 'the heightened redemption [*Erlösung*] of being forgotten, like all her brethren' (*SelStor* 108). His expectation was not fulfilled. In the reception the world gave Franz Kafka after his death, 'no sign of the promised deliverance [*Erlösung*] could be detected' (*SelStor* 58). His brethren never quite managed to forget him.

CHAPTER FIVE

THE NOVELS

Any discussion of Kafka's novels requires a disclaimer. Although Kafka made several attempts, he never produced a novel-length manuscript with a complete narrative structure. None of his novel-drafts has a firm story line with a clear beginning, middle, and end. Although all three have excellent beginnings, only one (*The Trial*) has a clear end, and unfortunately the one with the unmistakable end has no secure middle. Kafka considered all of them failures, and although he never destroyed them himself he asked others to do so. Only Max Brod's fierce resistance prevented his friend's request from being carried out.

Kafka's dissatisfaction with his novelistic efforts was not total, however. He published the opening chapter of the America novel as an independent story, and he ripped a section out of the 'Cathedral' chapter of *The Trial* for inclusion in the *Country Doctor* collection ('Before the Law'). He never published anything from *The Castle*, but that does not necessarily mean that he wished to discard all of it. He spared this and the other two unfinished manuscripts from the flames to which he consigned many of his other rejected writings, and it is therefore likely that he hoped to return to them at a later time. He gave two of them (*The Missing Person* and *The Castle*) to Milena Jesenská for safekeeping and kept one with his other papers. Given new energy, new inspiration, and sufficient life span, Kafka might have completed one or more of the manuscripts and rescinded his directive for their cremation.

In spite of their fragmentary character, these texts—especially *The Trial* and *The Castle*—have had an enormous impact on readers all over the world. No matter how great their cultural value, however, it would be a mistake to dismiss their author's self-critical judgments as mere symptoms of psychopathology. Kafka had an excellent sense of what was most interesting in his own work, and we must therefore respect his impulse to reject all of *The Missing Person* save its opening chapter, all of *The Trial* save the priest's 'Before the Law' parable, and all of *The Castle* without exception. These were defensible, even if alarmingly radical, literary evaluations, and no discussion of the viability of these novels can fail to take them into account.

1. THE MISSING PERSON (AMERIKA)

In a letter of November 11, 1912 Kafka explained to Felice that henceforth he was going to write her only short letters in order to devote as much time as possible to his current project:

> The story I am writing, which I must admit is heading off into endlessness, is called, to give you a tentative sense of it, 'The Missing Person,' and takes place entirely in the United States of America. So far 5 chapters are completed, the 6th almost. [. . .] After 15 years of despairing effort (except for rare moments), this is the first major work in which, for the past 6 weeks, I have felt confidence. It must be completed, as I feel sure you will agree [. . .] (my trans.; cf. *Felice* 35–36)

One of the most telling features of this letter is Kafka's ambivalence about the future of the novel. On the one hand he was determined to finish it, but on the other he was fearful that it was 'heading off into endlessness.' His determination was great, but his fears were justified. For a long time he continued to hope he might devise an ending that would accommodate the story's endlessness. He completed the sixth chapter (not quite finished when he wrote the letter), drafted a seventh (called 'A Refuge' by Brod but left untitled by Kafka), and started on an eighth. By late January 1913, however, he began to feel he was losing control of the story, so he decided to put it aside for a while.

In early March he decided on a whim to read through the incomplete manuscript. He explained to Felice that he was deeply shaken by the experience and

> came to the irrefutable conclusion that of the entire book only the first chapter stems from an inner truth, while all the rest, with

the exception, of course, of some isolated short and even longer passages, was written as it were from recollections of deep but totally absent feelings, and consequently has to be rejected [. . .]. (*Felice* 218)

He acted on this assessment by offering the first chapter to Kurt Wolff for publication as an independent piece, and indeed later that year 'The Stoker' appeared in Wolff's series 'Der jüngste Tag' with the subtitle 'A Fragment' (May 1913).

Despite the fact that the piece was meant to be the beginning of a longer narrative, it works rather well on its own. The interaction between Karl and the stoker is a little drama complete in itself and does not require the rest of the novel for support. The critical reception to 'The Stoker' was very positive, and Kafka could have let the matter rest there, feeling justified in his decision to reject the rest of the book. But he did not let it rest, and because he did not we have to suspect that the author's condemnation of the later chapters was not as wholehearted as the letter to Felice makes it seem.

In the productive period that began in the summer of 1914 after the dissolution of his first engagement to Felice, Kafka returned to the project and tried to advance the story a bit. He added a couple of paragraphs to the chapter he had been working on in 1913 when he put the manuscript aside, but he apparently could not work his way back into that material. He began another episode in the Brunelda saga, but that too never caught fire, and he abandoned it after a few pages.

In the fall, during a two-week break from the office when he was working on *The Trial* and 'In the Penal Colony,' he hit upon a completely new plot twist for the America novel. Karl was to get a new job with a colossal and mysterious enterprise called the 'Theater of Oklahama.' He made good progress: he got his hero through the chaotic and daunting hiring process and onto the train that was to take the new members of the troupe to Oklahama. But then, for reasons unknown, his inspiration gave out, this time for good. He put the manuscript aside and never took it up again.

When Brod edited the fragments together for publication, he decided the Oklahama material should stand as the eighth and final chapter. Correcting what he assumed was a mistake, he altered 'Oklahama' to 'Oklahoma' and called this concluding section 'The Nature Theater of Oklahoma.' There were several other cases where

Kafka's fictional America diverged from actuality, as in the opening paragraph where the Statue of Liberty appears brandishing a sword instead of a torch. But even early reviewers realized that such divergences were appropriate,[1] so Brod wisely left those other 'mistakes' uncorrected.

Kafka had placed no title at the head of the manuscript, but Max recalled that Franz had often spoken about his 'America novel,' so he decided to release the book under the title *Amerika*. It was a very smart marketing decision, as history proved, though a misstep in the eyes of scholarship. The novel became known to the world in the form Brod gave it upon its first publication in 1927, and this remained the canonical version until the appearance of the Kritische Ausgabe in 1983.[2]

Even those who agree with Kafka's verdict that the text fails as a coherent novel must concede that its somewhat incoherent fragments reward attention. 'The Stoker' is indeed, as Kafka judged, a self-sufficient vignette. It offers a nuanced depiction of the confrontation between an innocent zeal for justice and the everyday world where good and evil are difficult to disentangle. Although it is not exactly a work of pure realism, it never steps over the edge into fantasy in the manner of 'The Judgment,' 'The Metamorphosis,' and other familiar titles among Kafka's mature fictions. It is in fact rather more closely bound to the everyday world than later portions of *The Missing Person* itself, such as the intentionally bizarre Oklahama section.

Like Kafka's other novel drafts, *The Missing Person* dramatizes the problem of the individual thrust into a situation where he feels radically out of place. For Karl, uprooted from his homeland in consequence of a sexual misdemeanor, the entire continent of America is an alien landscape where he does not belong. The plot consists of Karl's attempts to make a place for himself in this land of exile, attempts which regularly miscarry. He seems condemned to suffer repeated expulsions from every potential home until—perhaps—he finds permanent acceptance in the paradisiacal Theater of Oklahama.

The narrative—as far as it goes—takes Karl further and further away from the European origin to which he remains at least initially connected. New York may be on another continent, but it is directly linked with home both by the ships that cross the Atlantic and by the family ties embodied in the uncle who rescues him from the ship, offering him what seems at first like a cozy refuge in the new land.

But Uncle Jakob has another, less propitious connection to the European relatives: he, too, is ready to thrust Karl away on the slightest excuse. Just as the innocent boy failed to realize that his dalliance with the maidservant would bring about his exile, so too did the slightly older Karl fail to imagine that disobeying his uncle by spending the night with a friend would have a similar outcome.

This pattern of apparent rescue followed by humiliating rejection continues to push Karl further toward the margins of society and of civilization, but perhaps also toward greater freedom. The moral ambiguity of Karl's situation appears perhaps most clearly in the scene in sixth chapter ('The Robinson Affair') where Karl is fired from his post as elevator boy in the Hotel Occidental. The matter of Karl's dismissal (*Entlassung*) appears in one sense to be a clear case of another misfortune brought on by another minor lapse—in this instance Karl's leaving his post to look after the drunken Robinson. But a scene that follows his official firing puts this evaluation into question. The headwaiter has instructed Karl to get out of the hotel within 15 seconds, but when he tries to do so, Karl finds his way blocked. It takes him longer than a quarter of a minute to get his things together and reach the door, by which time the head porter stops him in annoyance.

'You call that a quarter of a minute' [. . .] he said, and led him into the large porter's lodge. [. . . Karl] tried to push aside the head porter and get away. 'No, no, it's this way,' said the head porter, and spun Karl around. 'But I've been let go [*entlassen*],' said Karl, meaning that he no longer had to take orders from anybody at the hotel. 'Well, you've not been let go [*entlassen*] as long as I'm still holding you,' said the head porter, which was certainly true too. (*Missing* 172; trans. modified)

The play on the expression 'let go' is more than a passing joke. It points to a genuine uncertainty in the nature of Karl's position as a missing person in America. His continually repeated experience of *Entlassung*, which he feels as dismissal and banishment, could also be understood as something positive. To be 'let go' by the head waiter meant dismissal, but to be 'let go' by the head porter would mean release from physical capture. This suggests in turn that Karl's service as a lift boy in the hotel might also have been a form of capture from which he has now secured release.

KAFKA: A GUIDE FOR THE PERPLEXED

The theme of release from bondage was probably part of Kafka's original conception of his novel. *The Missing Person* bears a number of similarities to the Joseph story in Genesis, which serves as the biblical explanation for how the children of Israel came into the land where they would eventually be reduced to bondage. The Joseph story is itself a tale of a missing person who progresses from one form of servitude to another, though in each case he manages to improve his situation. That Kafka intended readers to make the connection is suggested by his naming an important location in the novel 'Ramses,' thus aligning his mythical America with the biblical land of exile. Kafka underscores the theme of exile by giving his fictional statue of Liberty a sword instead of a torch. She is still the goddess of freedom (*Freiheitsgöttin*), but at the same time she is the angel with the flaming sword guarding the gates of a lost Eden to which one may never return.

The wavering valorization between a negative exile and a positive sense of freedom is captured exactly in the pun on being 'let go' in the Robinson chapter. Karl's experience in the hotel has many positive aspects, including particularly his relationship with Therese, the head cook's secretary. But much of what he learns about Therese's history suggests that America is as much a land of exploitation as of opportunity, and his dismissal underscores the precarious position of lowly employees. Kafka apparently wished to explore that notion further, for the seventh (untitled) chapter places the boy in a position of menial servitude in the apartment occupied by Robinson, Delamarche, and the grotesquely corpulent singer Brunelda. If Kafka planned to let his hero join the Oklahama Theater (as seems likely), he must have envisioned some additional scene in which Karl is dismissed/released (*entlassen*) from his abject bondage in the apartment. Such a scene, had it been written, would surely have foregrounded the positive aspects being 'let go' from a condition of slavery.

Even the possibility of a new life with the Oklahama Theater cannot dispel the threat—or at least the fear—of further enslavement. When Karl is asked for his identity by the theater officials hiring him, he decides against giving his real name. But he finds he cannot make up a false name on short notice:

> And so, unable to come up with a name on the spot, he simply gave them the nickname from his last few positions: 'Negro.' 'Negro?' the manager asked, turning his head and grimacing, as if

Karl had attained the height of implausibility. The clerk too
scrutinized Karl for a moment, but then repeated, 'Negro,' and
wrote down the name. 'But you didn't write down Negro,' the
manager snapped. 'Yes, Negro,' the clerk said calmly, waving his
hand as though the manager should see to the rest. Overcoming his
reluctance, the manager rose and said: 'So the Theater of Oklahama
has—' But he got no further, for unable to quell his scruples, he sat
down and said: 'His name isn't Negro.' (*Missing* 278)

The incident leaves the matter of Karl's identity and his potential
status unresolved. He is subsequently introduced as 'Negro' to other
theater personnel, but the manager has acknowledged that the name
is false. Perhaps the name's unhappy implications will be proven
false as well. Perhaps his employment with the Oklahama Theater
will be different from 'his last few positions.' Perhaps he will find
some degree of genuine freedom and not just the 'way out' taken by
the academic ape. Or perhaps he will descend even deeper into a
degradation so terrible that he cannot escape alive.

Both possibilities are allowed by the unfinished draft Kafka left
behind, and there is evidence in support of both. Brod made a claim
for a positive outcome:

In enigmatic language Kafka used to hint smilingly, that within
this 'almost limitless' theatre his young hero was going to find
again a profession, a stand-by, his freedom, even his old home and
his parents, as if by some celestial witchery.[3]

Brod's account would sound very convincing were it not for an entry
in Kafka's notebook from September 30, 1915: 'Rossmann and K.,
the innocent and the guilty, both finally executed [*strafweise umge-
bracht*] without distinction, the innocent one with a gentler hand,
more shoved aside than struck down' (*Tag* 757; my trans.).[4] These
lines were written months after the draft of the Oklahama chapter,
at which time Kafka evidently still envisioned a bad outcome for
Mr. Negro's engagement with the theater troupe. Maybe he considered happier alternatives at other times, but the evidence does not
offer much comfort to those who prefer to think so.

One has to suppose that Karl's story would have ended in a manner
typical of Kafka's other stories, with the hero's downfall unredeemed
by 'celestial witchery.' Perhaps he would have been spared the shame

of dying like a dog, but an execution that pushes one aside is still an execution. Karl and K., the innocent and the guilty, would have come to a similar end.

2. THE TRIAL

In the wake of the dissolution of his first engagement to Felice in summer 1914, Kafka found the time and energy once again to work on his fiction. On August 15 he wrote in his notebook:

> I have been writing for a few days, may it go on. Today I am not so completely protected and holed up in my work as I was two years ago, still I have the sense that my regular, empty, lunatic bachelor's life has some justification. I can carry on a conversation with myself again and don't stare so much into complete emptiness. This is the only way there could be any improvement for me. (*Tag* 548–49; my trans.)

The principal reason for this glimmer of optimism was the new project he had just started (probably about August 11), a story about the arrest and trial of a man named Josef K.

Kafka experimented in *The Trial* with what was for him an uncharacteristic method of writing. Perhaps out of a concern that he might once again, as in *The Missing Person*, begin a novel he could not end, he appears to have written the opening and closing sections in close succession. Once the beginning and ending were set, he could fill in the central episodes as they occurred to him. As far as one can tell, he did so in helter-skelter fashion, without regard to the eventual placement of these episodes in an overall narrative structure. Perhaps he worked on several different episodes at once. In any case, he worked diligently and productively on the story from the middle of August until early October 1914, during which time he produced about three quarters of the surviving manuscript.

From October 1914 to late January of the following year his progress was sporadic and punctuated by periods of inactivity. Entries in the notebooks paint the picture:

> 21 October. Almost no work for four days [. . .]. 25 October. Work almost at a complete standstill. [. . .] 1 November. Yesterday, after a long time, made good progress, today again almost nothing [. . .].

25 November. Empty despair [. . .]. 30 November. I can't write any further. [. . .] 8 December. Yesterday for the first time in quite a while an indisputable capability of doing good work. And still wrote nothing more than the first page of the 'mother' chapter [. . .]. 14 December. Miserable creeping progress [. . .]. 15 December. No work at all. (*Tag* 681–709; my trans.)

On January 20, 1915 he announced dramatically: 'The end of writing.' Of course it was not the end of all his writing, but it did seem to mark a temporary end of work on *The Trial*. For all the finality of his declaration in the notebook, he must not have considered the project completely abandoned: some time later—we do not know when—he took the trouble of tearing leaves out of various notebooks and arranging them in the collection of 16 sheaves Brod found in 1924.

These sheaves did not constitute a novel any more than a pile of lumber constitutes a house. They were clearly parts of a structure, but by no means all the parts, and maybe some of the parts on hand didn't really belong. The most crucial missing part was the plan, so it was impossible to say what sort of structure the parts were supposed to make. None of this daunted Max Brod, who believed so strongly in his friend's genius that he was sure all such impediments could be overcome.

The 16 sheaves of loose leaves ranged from a maximum of 29 leaves ('Lawyer/Manufacturer/Painter') to a minimum of a single sheet ('To Elsa'). Each sheaf save one had a cover sheet on which Kafka had written indications of the contents (for example, 'The Flogger' or 'End'). Brod interpreted these indications as chapter titles ('the chapter headings are his work'), but Kafka may not have had any intention beyond reminding himself about the subject-matter of each sheaf. In any case Brod was not as scrupulous with the 'chapter headings' as he claimed: the title of the first chapter in Brod's edition was his, not Kafka's.[5]

One of the first things Brod did was to separated the sheaves into two categories, one of which he called 'chapters' and the other 'unfinished chapters.' He refers in his 'Postscript' to the first edition to 'the completed chapters' as if this were a self-evident category. In fact there is no reason to suppose that Kafka considered any of the sheaves to represent 'chapters' or that any of them had been 'completed.' Brod decided that certain materials represented chapters while others remained fragments. Examination of the manuscript shows that Brod followed no clear principle in making the division. At the end of the one of the sheaves he published as a completed chapter ('Block, the Merchant/Dismissal of the Lawyer'), Brod wrote, 'This chapter is incomplete.' Later on he crossed out his perfectly sound observation, probably because he did not want to relegate the contents of this sizable sheaf to the scrap heap of 'unfinished' chapters. After completing his highly subjective analysis, he had ten 'chapters' and six 'unfinished chapters.' In the initial publication of *The Trial* in 1925, only the ten 'chapters' appeared. In later editions he included the 'unfinished chapters' as an appendix.

Brod asserted that 'the completed chapters taken in conjunction with the final chapter which rounds them off, reveal both the meaning and the form with the most convincing clarity.'[6] This may be true now, but it was not true when Brod first saw the manuscript. The form in which the novel exists today is Brod's construction, not Kafka's. After having made his initial division into chapters and fragments, he arranged the sheaves he had dubbed chapters into an order that seemed to him to produce a coherent story. In two cases, he could be absolutely certain he was right: the sheaf marked 'End' had to be the conclusion, and the one beginning 'Someone must have slandered Josef K.' had to be the beginning. Everything else, however, had to be ordered according to Brod's—not Kafka's—sense of narrative progression and coherence. This was not a willful or self-indulgent act on Max's part, and he carried it out with intelligence; but it was entirely his. He felt he had not only the right but the obligation to do it because only thus could he make a publishable text out of the jumble of materials Kafka left behind.

Brod's construction has now become canonical: even the Kritische Ausgabe continues to follow it, with just a few relatively minor alterations. Only Reuss's facsimile text reveals the true state of Kafka's draft, and that version is unreadable as a novel. The unavoidable fact of literary history is that, if we wish to have a legible novel called '*The Trial* by Franz Kafka,' we have no choice but to accept Brod's editorial intervention, or something very similar. For good or for ill, the Kafka-Brod collaboration is the only game in town.

We readers are confronted with the issue of how to play that game with the odd hand we are dealt. It would seem far more presumptuous for us than it was for Kafka's friend and literary executor to make a coherent arrangement of materials that its author left in a fundamentally incoherent state. It is perhaps better to admit, first, that at least some perplexity is warranted when confronting *The Trial*; and, second, that a basic uncertainty of narrative structure inherent in the manuscript cannot be ameliorated by scholarship. That said, however, we must also recognize that the Kafka-Brod *Trial* stands as one of the most important literary monuments of the twentieth century and demands attention as a unified work—even if its unity is to a large extent an artifact of editorial intervention and interpretive skill.

Although we will never be able to state with any assurance what the correct story is, we can confidently identify a few issues that were foremost in the mind of the author when he was working on the book. The first of these was already mentioned in connection with *The Missing Person*: each of the novel drafts is centrally concerned with characters who must try to find their bearings in difficult, not to say outlandish situations. Josef K.'s situation is perhaps the most outlandish of all, because he is never certain what relation he has to the legal institution that has apparently taken him into custody.

I use the word 'apparently' advisedly. Kafka carefully sets up the opening scene in such a way as to leave in doubt the status of K.'s arrest. K. is told that he has been taken into custody, but no one actually arrests him. When K. makes a move to leave his room where two strangers are detaining him, he is told, 'You can't leave, you're being held,' to which K. replies, 'So it appears' (*Trial* 5). Indeed, so it appears, but appearances can be deceiving. Later on in the same scene K. is told that he is free to go to work. The inspector explains, 'you're under arrest, certainly but that's not meant to keep you from carrying on your profession. Nor are you to be hindered in the course of your ordinary life' (*Trial* 17). K. comments that being under arrest might not be so bad, and the inspector does not disagree.

So who has arrested K., of what crime does he stand accused, and what does it mean to be held in such loose custody? What, in other words, is the relation of such an ambiguously accused defendant to the institution of the Law (*Gesetz*)? The various episodes that Kafka worked on for the center of his novel pursue these questions without offering any definitive explanations. An apparent explanation, in the form of a parable, appears in the sheaf Kafka labeled 'In the Cathedral,' and it was this parable that Kafka selected as the single portion of the manuscript worthy of publication. It seems reasonable to follow the lead of the author, who saw in this passage the vital heart of his project, and look there for guidance in our perplexity.

Reasonable or not, our hope for guidance is largely disappointed. The problem of course is that this parable, like all parables, requires the reader to unlock a treasure chest to which the key is missing. One is invited to see in the parable something immensely valuable and relevant to one's own situation, but one must find one's own means to open up the story's profound lesson. How should we do so? How should Josef K.? Is K. another version of the man from the country who comes to seek admittance to the Law? Perhaps, but we cannot fail to recall that it was the Law's agents who appeared in K.'s bedroom one morning to inform him of his arrest. K. did not seek the Law until the Law had summoned him. The figure of the doorkeeper in the story is powerfully and frustratingly ambiguous, since he both keeps the entrance always ready for use by the man from the country, and by him alone, but also forbids the man's entry. We can never know what would have happened if the man had forced his way past the doorkeeper and into the 'radiance that streams forth inextinguishably from the door of the Law' (*Trial* 216).

Nothing illustrates better the difficulty of using a parable in a concrete situation than the original context of 'Before the Law' in the 'Cathedral' section of the novel. Nearly every line of text following the priest's recitation of the parable is devoted to an attempt by K. to work out, with the priest's help, an interpretation of the story that would help him understand his situation with respect to the court. But for all the effort he puts into his exegesis he fails to come to any helpful conclusion. In his view the discouraging lesson of the story is that 'lies are made into a universal system' (*Trial* 223).The moment K. gives firm voice to his opinion, however, the narrator steps in to report that K. might indeed have spoken 'with finality, but it was not his final judgment. He was too tired to take in all of the consequences of the story' (*Trial* 223).

The parable of the Law could not save K., nor could it save Kafka's novel from 'heading off into endlessness' just as *The Missing Person* had done. The salvation of the project, at least as far as its author was concerned, was to resort again to the tactic he had used successfully in the past: decontextualization. He published the priest's fable as an independent piece, taking Josef K. out of the picture entirely and thus relieving K. of the need to interpret it. It became our duty, not that of Kafka or his characters, to follow the little narrative 'into unaccustomed areas of thought' and to decide whether or not 'the simple tale had become shapeless' (*Trial* 223). Kafka appears to have foreseen correctly that the fable would fascinate readers on its own, as much or even more than the larger story in which it was originally embedded.

3. THE CASTLE

It was on a winter rest cure in the mountain resort of Spindelmühle that Kafka hit upon the idea of a novel about a land surveyor seeking permission to reside in the precincts governed by the Castle of Count Westwest. The snowy hills, the sleighs, the horses, and other paraphernalia of the resort all made their way into the setting of the story. He began work at the end of January 1922 and kept at it through the winter and into the spring after his return to Prague. Upon his permanent retirement from the insurance company on July 1, he took up residence at his sister's rented summer cottage in Planá, where he continued with the project through much of the summer.

At some point in August, however, his creative fire died out. On September 11 he wrote to Max:

> I have been back here for about a week, and have not spent the week very happily (for I will evidently have to drop the Castle story forever, cannot pick it up again [. . .] even though the part written in Planá is not quite as bad as the part you know). (*Friends* 357)

He had begun the work, as he regularly did, with no plan in mind beyond the opening pages. He appears to have kept track of his progress by means of a running list of chapter headings to which he usually added a new entry every time he completed a section. It is from this list that editors derived the chapter titles given in the Kritische Ausgabe and translations based upon it. He made one false start on the project, which he rejected after only a few pages. The second attempt pleased him better, and he was able to proceed in fairly regular increments up to the point where he gave up on the story for good. The only significant revision he made in this second version was to change the first-person narration of the opening paragraphs (e.g. 'It was late evening when I arrived') to the third-person, 'free indirect style' that he would employ throughout the remainder of the manuscript ('It was late evening when K. arrived' [*Castle* 1]).[7]

As usual, personal matters played a role in lighting Kafka's creative fire. The fictional triangle involving K., Frieda, and Klamm may well have been based on the comparable real-life relationship involving Kafka, Milena Jesenská, and Ernst Polak. Brod believed as much, and he found much in the novel to substantiate his belief.[8] Among the narrative details supporting such a hypothesis is the name of the inn where the Castle officials stay when they have business in the village. Kafka called it the Herrenhof, which was the name of Polak's favorite café in Vienna. But Frieda and Klamm and the Herrenhof are only some of the elements in a much larger story, and biographical information is of limited help in determining the significance of that more complex structure.

The fictional structure we find in this great fragment, as in the other novel drafts, draws us into a world that is both strange and familiar. Its strangeness is the result not of an outrageous premise such as we find in 'The New Advocate' or 'Jackals and Arabs' but rather of incongruities among a multitude of realistic details. There is nothing strange about a situation in which man with a wife and children must leave them in order to seek employment in a distant place. Such things happen all the time. Nor is there anything strange about a man courting a barmaid and planning to marry her. But the two elements taken together do indeed seem rather odd when we note that those two men are the same person.

This may not seem like the mind-bending oddness we experience when reading the opening of 'The Metamorphosis,' but in its details *The Castle* frequently operates in the same metamorphic manner as Kafka's more startling fictions. In the third chapter, for example, Frieda becomes annoyed with Klamm's servants, who have been dancing with Olga and making a racket with 'their hungrily rattling shouts.' She tells K. that their beastly behavior is typical: 'they always burst in, like cows into a shed' (*Castle* 39).

The instant she says this, her metaphorical language starts to take over the narrative:

'But now they're really going to be put in the shed, where they belong. [. . .] I'll have to drive them out myself.' Taking a whip from the corner, she leaped toward the dancers [. . .]. 'In the name of Klamm,' she cried, 'into the shed, all of you into the shed,' they

now saw that this was serious, and in a fear that K. found incom-
prehensible [. . .] all of them disappeared with Frieda, who
was evidently driving them across the courtyard into the shed.
(*Castle* 39–40)

Frieda treats the creatures she had introduced as figurative cattle as
if they were real cattle, and the figurative stalls actually become real
stalls. The presentation is quite realistic, in its way, but it develops in
exactly the same way that Gregor Samsa develops from a person into
a gigantic insect. The story's action comes into being by performing
the literal signification of figurative language.

Knowing how individual incidents were generated is useful, but it
does not tell us much about the novel's overall conception. Acknowledging that it is risky to make sweeping claims about a work that is
both complicated and incomplete, one may nonetheless safely propose that the fundamental idea behind *The Castle* is a variation on
the same theme we find in the two earlier novels. The central character finds himself in a peculiar circumstance not entirely of his own
making and must somehow find a way to make an accommodation
with the strange world into which he has been dropped, as if from a
passing spaceship.

The difference between the land surveyor's situation and that of
Josef K. and Karl Rossmann is that *The Castle*'s protagonist seems
to have sought out the bizarre situation that baffles him. The reader
never learns exactly why the land surveyor left his native land to come
to work for the Castle, and it appears that K. is not sure himself.
Indeed his motives for seeking acceptance into service and permission for permanent residence are never made clear anywhere in the
story. But having arrived in the village for whatever reason, K. must
try to find a place for himself. In a very real sense this K. faces a legal
problem akin to that of the K. in *The Trial*. In both cases the protagonists exist in a condition of legal limbo from which they spend much
of their time trying to escape. For Josef K. in *The Trial*, the issue has
to do with his status as a defendant before the mysterious court; for
Land Surveyor K. the question has to do with 'admission' (*Aufnahme*)
to residence in the village as well as to official Castle service.

The uncertainty of K.'s position arises from an ambiguity in the
document he receives from Klamm attesting to his acceptance: 'Dear
Sir! As you know, you have been accepted into the Count's service'
(*Castle* 22). K. himself is quick to note that the letter does not itself

admit him, as would have been the case if it had said, 'The Count hereby accepts you into his service.' It merely asserts that an act of admission has taken place previously. It may be a small detail, but K. seizes upon it as a source of concern:

> Indeed, the letter made no secret of the fact that if it came to a struggle, K. was the one who had been reckless enough to start, this was delicately put and could only have been noticed by a troubled conscience—troubled, not bad—namely, the three words 'as you know,' concerning his being accepted into the Count's service. K. had announced his presence and ever since then he had known, as the letter put it, that he was accepted. (*Castle* 24–25)

The letter suggests, in other words, that K. has in effect admitted himself and that the Castle bureaucracy has merely taken note of that fact.

But self-admission is not the same as official acceptance, and that discrepancy leaves K. in an uncertain status with respect to both the Castle officials and the village society. Every reader comes away with a strong sense of K.'s insecurity, but not every reader agrees on what Kafka meant to express by its depiction. Max Brod thought that the land surveyor's plight was an analog of European Jewry: 'It is the special feeling of a Jew who would like to take root in foreign surroundings [. . .] but who does not succeed in thus assimilating himself.'[9] Albert Camus, who agreed with Brod's conception of Kafka as a religious allegorist, argued for a more general interpretation. He saw K. not as a Jew seeking assimilation but as a believer seeking grace:

> That stranger who asks the Castle to adopt him is at the end of his voyage a little more exiled because this time he is unfaithful to himself, forsaking morality, logic, and intellectual truths in order to try to enter, endowed solely with his mad hope, the desert of divine grace.[10]

Subsequent generations of literary critics have been reluctant to find religious implications of any kind in the story, and scholars of the late twentieth and early twenty-first centuries have preferred to see the text as a self-referential parable about the alluring but inconclusive quest for definitive meaning.

The story itself illustrates the process of such an inconclusive quest. K.'s effort to make contact with the Castle is structured by a series of metonymic substitutions whereby the seeker is obliged to accept in place of the true object of his quest one stand-in after another. Thus, in the first instance, K. accepts Klamm as the representative of the Castle authorities and concentrates his efforts on getting access to this high official. When he is thwarted, he pursues Frieda, Klamm's village girlfriend, as the best means to get close to Klamm. After Frieda leaves K. for one of his assistants, he transfers his efforts to Pepi, who actually serves as Frieda's stand-in as a barmaid at the Herrenhof.

These are just a few of many displacements that characterize K.'s approach to the Castle, but they indicate the overall nature of a pattern that leads the seeker in a spiraling trajectory away from, not closer to, the actual goal of his quest—however the reader may interpret that goal. From time to time, K. does manage to come into contact with people who are direct extensions of the Castle, such as the officials Momus and Bürgel, but in every case he fails to exploit the opportunity offered to him. At the point where the narrative breaks off, K. hardly seems any closer to his goal than he was when he first set foot on the bridge leading into the village.

Anyone who reads Kafka's fiction seeking enlightenment is likely to have a similar experience. None of these stories will help those who come to them looking for the right way to find acceptance, the Law, the truth, or even the railroad station:

> 'You want me to tell you the way' 'Yes,' I said, 'since I can't find it myself.' 'Forget about it! Forget about it!' he said, and with a broad swing of his body he turned away, like people who want to be alone with their laugher. (*SelStor* 161)

But of course we will not, indeed we cannot 'forget about it.' As vividly as Kafka's stories depict the overwhelming difficulty of finding the way, they are equally powerful in their insistence that we must try every means possible to make our own way. Those who fail, like the man who stands before the law, are precisely those who 'forget about it.' One might succeed, as Kafka's Odysseus does in 'The Silence of the Sirens,' by sufficiently persistent use of utterly inadequate means.

The truth is out there, just as in 'An Imperial Message' the Emperor's message is out there, somewhere. We may not ever get the Emperor's message, but there can be no doubt that it's on its way. If the only way to get its content is to dream it up, then we should by all means dream. Myths help us dream such dreams— even and perhaps especially those myths of helplessness and bafflement that emerged from Franz Kafka's nocturnal scribbling.

NOTES

1. WHY YOU MIGHT BE PERPLEXED

1. Patrick A. Kellner, reviewing Kakfa's *Complete Stories*, http://www.amazon.com/Complete-Stories-Franz-Kafka/product-reviews/0805210555/
2. Broyard 31.
3. Adorno 246.
4. For more on Auden's reaction, see Chapter 2, section 10.
5. *Gesammelte Werke* VI, 164, quoted in Schlant 88.
6. Adorno 246.
7. Cf. Politzer 190.
8. My trans. Cf. *Der Proceß*, *Apparatband* 174, in the Kritische Ausgabe.
9. This is why scholars find the deletions so helpful. They give information about Kafka's intentions that the revised text withholds.
10. My trans. Cf. *Der Proceß*, *Apparatband* 181.
11. My trans. Cf. *Der Proceß*, *Apparatband* 322.
12. My trans. Cf. *Der Proceß*, *Apparatband* 230.

2. A SHORT LIFE OF FRANZ K.

1. As Ritchie Robertson points out, with some understatement, 'it was difficult for Jews to scale the heights of Prague society' (Robertson 3).
2. Kafka did *not* speak a special dialect of Prague German inhabiting 'linguistic Third World zones,' as is proposed by Deleuze and Guattari (27). For an excellent discussion of the distortions wrought by Deleuze and Guattari, see Corngold *Traces* 142–57.
3. Cf. Kafka's 'Introductory talk on the Yiddish language' (1912).
4. The name *Löwy* is a common one among Jews all over the world, often seen in the related forms *Loewy*, *Loewe*, *Levi*, *Levy*, etc.
5. For a copy of the invitation, see Wagenbach *Pictures* 37.
6. 'Gymnasium' in German refers to secondary schools, not to buildings devoted to athletics. The term deliberately conjures up the image of ancient Greek boys engaged in strenuous exercise.
7. See for example *Milena* 245.
8. Wagenbach claims that 'the "spirit of antiquity" remained alien [to Kafka]; very rarely does even the name of an ancient author appear in his diaries or letters' (*Kafka* 23).

9. Janouch (1903–68) was an aspiring author and the son of one of Kafka's colleagues in the insurance firm. He published a book allegedly based on the copious notes he took of all his conversations with Kafka. Brod accepted Janouch's accounts as genuine, but others have suspected them to be largely fiction. See Goldstücker, 'Kafkas Eckermann?' for a skeptical assessment.

10. Janouch 115.

11. See Wagenbach *Kafka* 35.

12. Pollak (1883–1915) planned to become an art historian. He enlisted in the Austrian army when hostilities broke out between Austria and Italy and was almost immediately killed in action.

13. Some have detected homoerotic elements in this relationship, though most scholars are skeptical. See the entry on 'Homosexuality' in the *Franz Kafka Encyclopedia*.

14. Pawel (90) calls the *Kunstwart* 'pretentious' and claims it had 'distinctly noxious side-effects' on Kafka, but he concludes that in the end its influence 'was overwhelmingly positive.'

15. Brod *Kafka* 43.

16. Brod *Kafka* 43–44.

17. See the 'Further Reading' section of the entry on 'Nietzsche' in the *Franz Kafka Encyclopedia*.

18. Brod *Kafka* 58.

19. The evidence is not conclusive. See for example Reuss's discussion ('Zur kritischen Edition von "Beschreibung eines Kampfes" und "Gegen zwölf Uhr [. . .]," *Franz Kafka: Beschreibung eines Kampfes, Gegen zwölf Uhr [. . .], Franz Kafka-Heft 2*, 5).

20. Brod thought he might have found a postcard signed by Kafka's Zuckmantel lover. He read the nearly illegible signature as 'Ritschi Grader.'

21. Jews had little hope of obtaining government jobs without some personal connection. See Hayman 64.

22. This is the supposition made by the editors of the Kritische Ausgabe (*Nachgelassene Schriften I, Apparatband*, 49.)

23. Alfred Löwy was director of a Spanish railway. For details on his interesting life, see Northey 31–39.

24. Siegfried was a half-brother of Julie (Löwy) Kafka.

25. The English edition dates one of the letters 'probably early 1908' that the Kritische Ausgabe places in late October, 1907.

26. In a letter to Felice about the book publication of the same material, he claimed that one of the pieces was 'certainly 8 to 10 years old' (*Felice* 100).

27. Willy Haas, 'Um 1910 in Prag,' *Forum IV* (1957): 42. Quoted in Hayman 66.

28. These were 'Conversation with the Supplicant' and 'Conversation with the Drunk,' both of which had been written earlier, the first probably in 1904 and the second in 1907.

29. 'The Aeroplanes at Brescia,' *Bohemia*, September 29, 1909. The text is available in English in *Colony* 297–309.

30. One other short piece of fiction from this period, the 'Reflections for Gentlemen-Jockeys,' was published in *Bohemia* in spring 1910, along with some of the 'Meditation' material.
31. The first dated entry in the notebook is from May 18, 1910, but a few at the very beginning could go back as far as spring 1909. See *Tagebücher, Apparatband* 86–89.
32. This passage was likely written late in 1909. See *Tagebücher, Apparatband* 88.
33. See for example a diary entry from March 1912: 'Today burned many old, disgusting papers' (*Diaries* 193).
34. Brod believed that passages were autobiographical. See his footnote, *Diaries* 493, where he refers to 'Kafka's critique of his education.'
35. Brod *Kafka* 104.
36. Brod *Kafka* 67.
37. 'The First Long Train Journey' was published in the *Herderblätter* in 1912. The translated text can be found in *Colony* 279–96.
38. The surname was similar to that of Kafka's mother's family, but there was no blood relation. The actor normally spelled it 'Levi.'
39. Anderson *Reading Kafka* 266.
40. Kafka and Löwy reunited briefly in Budapest in the summer of 1917. See Pawel 357.
41. See *Diaries* 37.
42. For more on Jungborn, see Stach 86–93.
43. Kafka refers to her in his notebook as 'W.' or 'G. W.' Some claim her name was Gerti Wasner; see for example Murray 186–87 and *Briefe 1913–1914*, 518.
44. Pawel says 'she specifically asserted that she had a boy, fathered by Kafka' (305), but this overstates the case. In a letter of April 21, 1940 she says that the boy's father was 'a man who had meant very much to me; he died in 1924, and his greatness is hailed to this day' (Stach 434). She does not mention Kafka's name, and she says the boy's father died 'in his homeland,' which was not true of Kafka. Brod, however, accepted the supposition that she was speaking of Kafka, and his acceptance gave credence to the story. Grete did indeed have a son who died in childhood, but no evidence exists to support the claim of Kafka's paternity.
45. Cf. Canetti 58–59.
46. The evidence is not decisive, but it is likely that Kafka went directly from the beginning of the story to the end. For the evidence in favor, see Malcolm Pasley's account in *Der Proceß, Apparatband* (111) in the Kritische Ausgabe. For the argument against, see Reuss's objections to Pasley in 'Franz Kafka-Hefte 1' of *Der Process* (6–8) in the Historisch-Kritische Ausgabe.
47. See Pawel 342.
48. Pawel assumes 'physical intimacy' (345).
49. Letters to Ottla 19.
50. Brod took so seriously all the negative things Kafka said about his job, both in person and in his notebooks, that he unintentionally left the

impression that Kafka was an insignificant minor bureaucrat. Cf. Brod *Kafka* 98.

51. *Letters to Ottla* 66–67.
52. See Janouch 196–97.
53. In 1923 the name was officially changed to 'Spindlermühle.'
54. Kafka started to write the novel in the first person, but he soon replaced every 'I' with a 'K.' That this K. might also be a Josef is a possible but by no means necessary conclusion that can be drawn from hints in the text.
55. Diamant 14. Kathi Diamant, the author of the most complete biography of Dora, coincidentally shares Dora's surname.
56. Diamant 51.
57. For a more complete version of the doll story, see Diamant 51–52.
58. The critical reception to Kafka's work in his lifetime was not extensive. The collection put together by Jürgen Born (*Franz Kafka: Kritik*) finds only 41 reviews of his publications, plus a few notices of public readings and other scattered items—not much, especially when one considers that six of the reviews were written by Kafkas friends Max Brod, Otto Pick, and Felix Weltsch.
59. Brod 'Postscript' 328.
60. Brod 'Postscript' 328–29.
61. See Diamant 128.
62. Cf. Brod 'Postscript' 330.
63. 'Publisher's Note,' *The Castle* (New York: Modern Library, 1969), v.
64. Arthur H. Samuelson, 'Publisher's Note' (*Trial* x).
65. 'The Wandering Jew,' *The New Republic*, February 14, 1941, 185–86; quoted in Flores and Swander 1.
66. Mann's diary entries of August 1 and September 22, 1921 (my trans.).
67. Camus 126.
68. Camus 127.
69. The earliest use cited by the OED comes from *The New Yorker* of January 4, 1947.
70. Quoted in Samuelson, 'Publisher's Note' (*Trial* xii).

3. A SURVEY OF KAFKA'S LITERARY ESTATE

1. Everything Kafka published in his lifetime totals about 112,000 words. As a basis for comparison, this brief Guide is about 70,000.
2. See Diamant 84–85 and 183–84.
3. The papers confiscated by the Nazis could still exist, stored in some forgotten file cabinet.
4. This taxonomy intentionally diverges from that adopted by the editors of Kafka's works.
5. Cf. an early letter to Felice: 'at 10:30 (but often not till 11:30) I sit down to write, and I go on, depending on my strength, inclination, and luck, until 1, 2, 3 o'clock, once even till 6 in the morning' (*Felice* 22).

6. The Princeton edition received prominent notice in the *London Review of Books* ('Double Thought,' November 20, 2008), which indicates the expectation of a wide readership.

7. See Stanley Corngold, 'Kafka and the Ministry of Writing' (*Office* 3).

8. Listed as Document 10 in the *Office Writings* (*Office* 194–207) and #24 in the Kritische Ausgabe of the *Amtliche Schriften* (721–41).

9. Cf. the Princeton edition: 'The most fantastic return of Hochsieder's *Betriebsverdrängung* is to be found in Kafka's dream story, "A Country Doctor"' (*Office* 211).

10. Cf. Amtliche Schriften 970.

11. Kafka signed a few of his early letters to Milena as 'Franz K.' Because Kafka's 'K' looked like it could be lower case, Milena misinterpreted the signature as 'Frank.' Kafka embraced this misreading as a marker of his intimacy with Milena.

12. 'Ungeziefer' appears in the opening sentence of 'The Metamorphosis' (*Meta* 3).

13. Franz Kakfa, *Tagebücher: Apparatband* 7.

14. For example 'Bachelor's Ill Luck' and 'Großer Lärm' ('A Lot of Noise').

15. 'I won't give up the diary again. I must hold on here, it is the only place I can' (*Diaries* 29).

16. Reuss most recently put forward this idea at the international conference *Kafka At 125*, held in April, 2009, in Durham and Chapel Hill, NC.

17. Corngold, 'Kafka's "The Judgment"' 15–21.

18. 'I have no literary interests, but am made of literature, I am nothing else and can be nothing else' (*Felice* 304).

4. THE STORIES AND FRAGMENTS

1. See Koelb *Rhetoric* 182–95.

2. See Bernheimer 'Splitting of the "I".'

3. One possible exception is *The Trial*. See Chapter 5, section 2.

4. See *Drucke zu Lebzeiten, Apparatband* 273, in the Kritische Ausgabe.

5. For more see Koelb *Rhetoric* 66–108.

6. Quoted in Koelb *Rhetoric* 155–56.

7. Brod *Kafka* 75.

8. For another perspective on 'Researches' see Kuzniar 20–24.

9. Cf. Koelb *Rhetoric* 7–9.

10. See the 'Further Reading' section of the *Kafka Encyclopedia* article on 'Der Bau' for some of the scholarship on this controversy.

11. Diamant 59–60.

5. THE NOVELS

1. See for example Camill Hoffmann's review reprinted in Born *Kritik* 47–48.

2. The Harman translation cited in this Guide was based on the Kritische Ausgabe. The Muir translation follows Brod.

3. 'Afterword,' *Amerika* (New York: Schocken, 1962), 299.
4. The English translation published in the Schocken edition (*Diaries* 343–44) has 'the guilty one with a gentler hand'—just the opposite of what Kafka actually said.
5. See Brod 'Postscript' 334–35. Pasley posits that Brod's chapter title came from a cover sheet that has since been lost (*Proceß*, *Apparatband* 124, n. 1), but Reuss doubts the hypothesis (see *Proceß*, *Franz Kafka-Hefte 1*, 14).
6. Brod 'Postscript' 334.
7. For the significance of this change, see Cohn's 'K. enters *The Castle*.'
8. See Brod *Kafka* 219–20.
9. Brod *Kafka* 187.
10. Camus 133.

BIBLIOGRAPHY AND SUGGESTED FURTHER READING

The standard bibliographical reference work is Maria Luise Caputo-Mayr and Julius M. Herz, *Franz Kafka: An International Bibliography of Primary and Secondary Literature* (Munich: K. G. Saur, 2000). What follows is a small selection of those works the author has found particularly useful, with emphasis on titles available in English. Those who wish to delve more deeply into Kafka scholarship on a particular topic will find relevant specialized works among these titles.

1. WORKS BY KAFKA

1.1. In English Translation

Amerika: The Missing Person. Trans. and with a preface by Mark Harman. New York: Schocken, 2008.

The Blue Octavo Notebooks. Ed. Max Brod. Trans. Ernst Kaiser and Eithne Wilkins. Cambridge: Exact Change, 1991.

The Castle. Trans. and with a preface by Mark Harman. New York: Schocken, 1998.

The Complete Stories. Ed. Nahum N. Glatzer. New York: Schocken, 1995.

Diaries 1910–1923. Ed. Max Brod. Trans. Joseph Kresh and Martin Greenberg, with the cooperation of Hanna Arendt. New York: Schocken, 1976.

The Great Wall of China: Stories and Reflections. Trans. Willa and Edwin Muir. New York: Schocken, 1970.

'An introductory talk on the Yiddish language.' In Anderson, 263–66.

Kafka's Selected Stories. Trans. and ed. Stanley Corngold. New York: W. W. Norton, 2007.

Letter to His Father/Brief an den Vater. Trans. Ernst Kaiser and Eithne Wilkins. New York: Schocken, 1966.

Letters to Felice. Ed. Erich Heller and Jürgen Born. Trans. James Stern and Elizabeth Duckworth. New York: Schocken, 1973.

Letters to Friends, Family, and Editors. Trans. Richard and Clara Winston. New York: Schocken, 1977.

Letters to Milena. Trans. and with an introduction by Philip Boehm. New York: Schocken, 1990.

Letters to Ottla and the Family. Ed. N. N. Glatzer. Trans. Richard and Clara Winston. New York: Schocken, 1982.
The Metamorphosis. Trans. and ed. Stanley Corngold. New York: W. W. Norton, 1996.
The Office Writings. Ed. Stanley Corngold, Jack Greenberg, and Benno Wagner. Trans. Eric Patton with Ruth Hein. Princeton: Princeton UP, 2009.
Parables and Pardoxes. New York: Schocken, 1961.
The Penal Colony: Stories and Short Pieces. Trans. Willa and Edwin Muir. New York: Schocken, 1961.
The Trial. Trans. and with a preface by Breon Mitchell. New York: Schocken, 1998.

1.2. In German

At the time of this Guide's publication, both of the following important editorial projects were still incomplete and in progress.

Born, Jürgen, Gerhard Neumann, Malcom Pasley, and Jost Schillemeit, eds. *Franz Kafka: Schriften, Tagebücher, Briefe. Kritische Ausgabe.* Frankfurt: Fischer, 1982–.

In this edition, the following titles have appeared so far: *Amtliche Schriften*; *Briefe 1900–1912*; *Briefe 1913–1914*; *Briefe 1914–1917*; [the fourth volume of the five-volume set of letters, *Briefe 1918–1920*, is currently in press]; *Drucke zu Lebzeiten*; *Nachgelassene Schriften und Fragmente I*; *Nachgelassene Schriften und Fragmente II*; *Der Proceß*; *Das Schloß*; *Tagebücher*; *Der Verschollene*.

Reuss, Roland and Peter Staengle, eds. *Franz Kafka: Historisch-Kritische Ausgabe sämmtlicher Handschriften, Drucke, und Typoskripte.* Frankfurt: Stroemfeld/Roter Stern, 1995–.

In this edition, the following titles have appeared so far: *Beschreibung eines Kampfes/Gegen zwölf Uhr [. . .]*; *Drei Briefe an Milena Jesenská; Einleitung*; *Oxforder Quartheft 17/Die Verwandlung; Oxforder Quarthefte 1 & 2*; *Oxforder Oktavhefte 1 & 2*; *Oxforder Oktavhefte 3 & 4*; [*Oxforder Oktavhefte 5 & 6* are currently in press]; *Der Proceß*.

2. BIOGRAPHICAL STUDIES AND MATERIALS (IN ENGLISH)

Adler, Jeremy. *Franz Kafka.* New York: Overlook, 2004.
Brod, Max. *Franz Kafka: A Biography.* Trans. G. Humphreys Roberts and Richard Winston. New York: Schocken, 1963.
Diamant, Kathi. *Kafka's Last Love: The Mystery of Dora Diamant.* New York: Basic, 2003.

Glatzer, Nahum N. *The Loves of Franz Kafka.* New York: Schocken, 1986.

Hayman, Ronald. *Kafka: A Biography.* New York: Oxford UP, 1982.

Hockaday, Mary. *Kafka, Love and Courage: The Life of Milena Jesenská.* New York: Overlook, 1999.

Janouch, Gustav. *Conversations with Kafka.* 2nd ed. Trans. Goronwy Rees. New York: New Directions, 1968.

Murray, Nicholas. *Kafka.* New Haven: Yale UP, 2004.

Northey, Antony. *Kafka's Relatives: Their Lives and His Writing.* New Haven: Yale UP, 1991.

Pawel, Ernst. *The Nightmare of Reason: A Life of Franz Kafka.* New York: Farrar Straus Giroux, 1984.

Stach, Reiner. *Kafka: The Decisive Years.* Trans. Shelley Frisch. Orlando: Harcourt, 2005.

Unseld, Joachim. *Kafka: A Writer's Life.* Trans. Paul F. Dvorak. Riverside: Ariadne, 1997.

Urzidil, Johannes. *There Goes Kafka.* Trans. Harold Besilius. Detroit: Wayne State UP, 1968.

Wagenbach, Klaus. *Franz Kafka: Pictures of a Life.* New York: Pantheon, 1984.

---. *Kafka.* Trans. Ewald Osers. Cambridge, MA: Harvard UP, 2003.

Zischler, Hanns. *Kafka Goes to the Movies.* Trans. Susan H. Gillespie. Chicago: U of Chicago P, 2002.

3. SCHOLARSHIP AND COMMENTARIES

3.1. In English

Adorno, Theodor W. *Prisms.* Trans. Samuel and Shierry Weber. Cambridge, MA: MIT Press, 1982.

Alter, Robert. *Necessary Angels: Tradition and Modernity in Kafka, Benjamin and Scholem.* Cambridge, MA: Harvard UP, 1991.

Anders, Günther. *Franz Kafka.* Trans. A. Steer and A. K. Thorlby. London: Bowes & Bowes, 1960.

Anderson, Mark M. *Kafka's Clothes: Ornament and Aestheticism in the Habsburg Fin de Siècle.* Oxford: Clarendon, 1992.

---. ed. *Reading Kafka: Prague, Politics, and the Fin de Siècle.* New York: Schocken, 1989.

Bauer, John and Isidor Pollak. *Kafka and Prague.* Trans. P. S. Falla. New York: Praeger, 1971.

Beck, Evelyn Torton. *Kafka and the Yiddish Theater: Its Impact on His Work.* Madison: U of Wisconsin P, 1971.

Bernheimer, Charles. *Flaubert and Kafka: Studies in Psychopoetic Structure.* New Haven: Yale UP, 1982.

---. 'The splitting of the "I" and the dilemma of narration: Kafka's Hochzeitsvorbereitungen auf dem Lande.' In Struc and Yardley, 7–23.

Boa, Elizabeth. *Kafka: Gender, Class, and Race in the Letters and Fictions.* Oxford: Clarendon, 1996.

BIBLIOGRAPHY AND SUGGESTED FURTHER READING

Bridgwater, Patrick. *Kafka and Nietzsche*. Bonn: Bouvier, 1974.
Brod, Max. 'Postscript to the first edition.' In Kafka, *The Trial*, trans. Willa and Edwin Muir. New York: Modern Library, 1964. 326–35.
Broyard, Anatole. *Kafka Was the Rage: A Greenwich Village Memoir*. New York: Carol Southern Books, 1993.
Camus, Albert. 'Hope and the absurd in the work of Franz Kafka.' *The Myth of Sisyphus and Other Essays*. Trans. Justin O'Brien. New York: Vintage, 1991. 124–38.
Canetti, Elias. *Kafka's Other Trial: The Letters to Felice*. Trans. Christopher Middleton. New York: Schocken, 1974.
Cohn, Dorrit. 'K. enters *The Castle*: On the change of person in Kafka's manuscript.' *Euphorion* 62 (1968): 28–45.
---. *Transparent Minds: Narrative Modes for Presenting Consciousness in Fiction*. Princeton: Princeton UP, 1978.
Corngold, Stanley. *The Commentator's Despair: The Interpretation of Kafka's 'Metamorphosis.'* Port Washington: Kennikat, 1973.
---. *Franz Kafka: The Necessity of Form*. Ithaca, NY: Cornell UP, 1988.
---. 'Kafka's "The Judgment" and modern rhetorical theory.' *Newsletter of the Kafka Society of America* 7 (June 1983): 15–21.
---. *Lambent Traces: Franz Kafka*. Princeton: Princeton UP, 2004.
Deleuze, Gilles and Félix Guattari. *Kafka: Toward a Minor Literature*. Trans. Dana Polen. Minneapolis: U of Minnesota P, 1986.
Derrida, Jacques. 'Devant la loi.' In Udoff, 128–49.
Dodd, W. J., *Kafka and Dostoyevsky: The Shaping of Influence*. London: Palgrave Macmillan, 1992.
Emrich, Wilhelm. *Franz Kafka: A Critical Study of His Writings*. New York: Ungar, 1968.
Flores, Angel, ed. *The Kafka Debate: New Perspectives for Our Time*. New York: Gordian, 1977.
Flores, Angel and Homer Swander, eds. *Franz Kafka Today*. Madison: U of Wisconsin P, 1964.
Gilman, Sander L. *Franz Kafka: The Jewish Patient*. New York: Routledge, 1995.
Goebel, Rolf J. *Constructing China: Kafka's Orientalist Discourse*. Columbia: Camden House, 1997.
Grandin, John M. *Kafka's Prussian Advocate: A Study of the Influence of Heinrich von Kleist on Franz Kafka*. Columbia: Camden House, 1987.
Gray, Richard T., ed. *Approaches to Teaching Kafka's Short Fiction*. New York: MLA, 1995.
---. *Constructive Destruction: Kafka's Aphorisms*. Tübingen: Niemeyer, 1987.
Gray, Richard T., Ruth V. Gross, Rolf J. Goebel, and Clayton Koelb. *A Franz Kafka Encyclopedia*. Westport: Greenwood, 2005.
Gray, Ronald. *Franz Kafka*. Cambridge: Cambridge UP, 1973.
Gross, Ruth V., trans. and ed. *Critical Essays on Franz Kafka*. Boston: Hall, 1990.
---. 'Fallen bridge, fallen woman, fallen text.' *Literary Review* 26 (1981): 577–87.

---. 'Kafka's short fiction.' In Preece, 80–94.

---. 'Of mice and women.' In Struc and Yardley, 117–40.

---. 'Rich text/poor text: A Kafkan confusion.' *PMLA* 95 (1980): 168–82.

Grötzinger, Karl Erich. *Kafka and Kabbalah*. Trans. Susan Hecker Ray. New York: Continuum, 1994.

Harman, Mark. 'Irony, ambivalence, and belief in Kleist and Kafka.' *Journal of the Kafka Society of America* 8 (1984): 3–13.

Heidsieck, Arnold. *The Intellectual Contexts of Kafka's Fictions: Philosophy, Law, Religion*. Columbia: Camden House, 1994.

Heinemann, Richard. 'Kafka's oath of service: "Der Bau" and the dialectic of the bureaucratic mind.' *PMLA* 111 (1996): 256–70.

Heller, Peter. 'On not understanding Kafka.' In Flores, *The Kafka Debate*, 24–42.

Hoesterey, Ingeborg. 'The intertextual loop: Kafka, Robbe-Grillet, Kafka.' In Udoff, 58–75.

Koelb, Clayton. 'Critical editions: Will the real Franz Kafka please stand up?' In Rolleston, *Companion*, 27–31.

---. 'Kafka imagines his readers: The rhetoric of "Josefine die Sängerin" and "Der Bau."' In Rolleston, *Companion*, 347–59.

---. *Kafka's Rhetoric: The Passion of Reading*. Ithaca: Cornell UP, 1989.

Kuzniar, Alice. *Melancholia's Dog: Reflections on Our Animal Kinship*. Chicago: U of Chicago P, 2006.

Martens, Lorna. 'Art, freedom, and deception in Kafka's "Ein Bericht für eine Akademie."' *Deutsche Vierteljahresschrift für Literaturwissenschaft und Geistesgeschichte* 61 (1987): 720–32.

Mitchell, Breon. 'Kafka and the hunger artists.' In Udoff, 236–55.

Nägele, Rainer. 'Kafka and the interpretive desire.' In Udoff, 16–29.

Pascal, Roy. *Kafka's Narrators: A Study of His Stories and Sketches*. Cambridge: Cambridge UP, 1982.

Politzer, Heinz. *Franz Kafka: Parable and Paradox*. Ithaca: Cornell UP, 1962.

Preece, Julian, ed. *The Cambridge Companion to Kafka*. Cambridge: Cambridge, UP, 2001.

Robert, Marthe. *As Lonely As Franz Kafka*. Trans. Ralph Manheim. New York: Harcourt, 1982.

Robertson, Ritchie. *Kafka: Judaism, Politics, and Literature*. Oxford: Clarendon P, 1985.

Rolleston, James, ed. *A Companion to the Works of Franz Kafka*. Rochester: Camden House, 2002.

---. *Kafka's Narrative Theater*. University Park: Pennsylvania State UP, 1974.

Schlant, Ernestine. *Hermann Broch*. Chicago: U of Chicago P, 1986.

Sokel, Walter. *Franz Kafka*. New York: Columbia UP, 1966.

---. *The Myth of Power and the Self: Essays on Franz Kafka*. Detroit: Wayne State UP, 2002.

Spector, Scott. *Prague Territories: National Conflict and Cultural Innovation in Franz Kafka's Fin de Siècle*. Berkeley: U of California P, 2000.

Spilka, Mark. *Dickens and Kafka: A Mutual Interpretation*. Bloomington: Indiana UP, 1963.

Struc, Roman and J. C. Yardley, *Franz Kafka (1883–1924): His Craft and Thought*. Waterloo: Wilfrid Laurier UP, 1986.
Sussman, Henry. *Franz Kafka: Geometrician of Metaphor*. Madison: Coda, 1979.
Udoff, Alan, ed. *Kafka and the Contemporary Critical Performance*. Bloomington: Indiana UP, 1987.
Zilcosky, John. *Kafka's Travels: Exoticism, Colonialism, and the Traffic of Writing*. New York: Palgrave Macmillan, 2003.

3.2. In German

Anders, Günther. *Kafka—Pro und Contra*. Munich: C. H. Beck, 1951.
Beicken, Peter. *Franz Kafka: Eine kritische Einführung in die Forschung*. Frankfurt: Athenäum, 1974.
---. *Franz Kafka, Der Proceß: Interpretation*. Munich: Oldenbourg, 1995.
Binder, Hartmut. *Kafka-Handbuch*. 2 vols. Stuttgart: Kröner, 1979.
---. *Kafka: Der Schaffensprozeß*. Frankfurt: Suhrkamp, 1983.
---. *Kafka Kommentar zu den Romanen, Rezensionen, Aphorismen, und zum Brief an den Vater*. Munich: Winkler, 1976.
---. *Kafka Kommentar zu sämtlichen Erzählungen*. Munich: Winkler, 1975.
---. *Motiv und Gestaltung bei Franz Kafka*. Bonn: Bouvier, 1966.
Born, Jürgen, ed. *Franz Kafka: Kritik und Rezeption zu seinen Lebzeiten 1912–1924*. Frankfurt: Fischer, 1979.
---. *Kafkas Bibliothek: Ein beschreibendes Verzeichnis*. Frankfurt: Fischer, 1990.
Caputo-Mayr, and Maria Luise, ed. *Franz Kafka: Eine Aufsatzsammlung nach einem Symposium in Philadelphia*. Berlin: Agora, 1978.
David, Claude, ed. *Franz Kafka: Themen und Probleme*. Göttingen: Vandenhoeck & Ruprecht, 1980.
Goldstücker, Eduard. 'Kafkas Eckermann? Zu Gustav Janouchs "Gespräche mit Kafka."' In David, 238–55.
Jagow, Bettina von and Oliver Jahraus, eds. *Kafka-Handbuch*. Göttingen: Vandenhoeck & Ruprecht, 2008.
Karst, Roman. 'Kafka und die Metapher.' *Literatur und Kritik* 179–180 (1983), 472–80.
Kittler, Wolf. 'Brief oder Blick: Die Schreibsituation der frühen Texte von Franz Kafka.' In Kurz, 40–67.
Koch, Hans-Gerd, ed. *'Als Kafka mir entgegen kam . . .': Erinnergungen an Franz Kafka*. Berlin: Wagenbach, 1995.
Kurz, Gerhard, ed. *Der junge Kafka*. Frankfurt: Suhrkamp, 1984.
Menczel-Ben-Tovim, Puah. 'Ich war Kafkas Hebäischlehrerin.' In Koch, 165–67.
Nagel, Bert. *Kafka und die Weltliteratur: Zusammenhänge und Wechselwirkungen*. Munich: Winkler, 1983.
Nekula, Marek. 'Franz Kafkas Deutsch.' *Linguistik Online* 13, 1/03. http://www.linguistik-online.de/13_01/nekula.html

Neumann, Gerhard. *Franz Kafka, 'Das Urteil': Text, Materialen, Dokumente.* Munich: Hanser, 1981.

Nikolai, Ralf R. 'Wahrheit und Lüge bei Kafka und Nietzsche.' *Literaturwissenschaftliches Jahrbuch im Auftrage der Görres Gesellschaft* 22 (1981): 255–71.

Pasley, Malcom. 'Der Schreibakt und das Geschriebene: Zur Frage der Entstehung von Kafkas Texten.' In David, 9–25.

Reed, T. J. 'Kafka und Schopenhauer: Philosophisches Denken und dichterisches Bild.' *Euphorion* 59 (1965): 160–72.

Ries, Wiebrecht. 'Kafka und Nietzsche.' *Nietzsche-Studien* 2 (1973): 258–75.

Robertson, Ritchie. 'Der Künstler und das Volk: Kafkas *Ein Hungerkünstler: Vier Geschichten.' Text und Kritik: Sonderband Franz Kafka.* Ed. Heinz Ludwig Arnold. Munich: Text & Kritik, 1994, 180–91.

Ryan, Judith. 'Die zwei Fassungen der "Beschreibung eines Kampfes": Zur Entwicklung von Kafkas Erzähltechnik.' *Jahrbuch der deutschen Schiller-Gesellschaft* 14 (1970): 546–72.

Schillemeit, Jost. 'Kafkas *Beschreibung eines Kampfes*: Ein Beitrag zum Textverständnis und Geschichte in Kafkas Schreiben.' In Kurz, 102–123.

Sebald, W. G. 'Thanatos: Zur Motivstruktur in Kafkas *Schloß.' Literatur und Kritik* 66–67 (1972): 399–11.

Sokel, Walter. 'Zur Sprachauffassung und Poetik Franz Kafkas.' In David, 26–47.

Wagenbach, Klaus. *Franz Kafka: Eine Biographie seiner Jugend.* Bern: Francke, 1958.

INDEX